Teaching
William Morris

Teaching William Morris

Edited by Jason D. Martinek
and Elizabeth Carolyn Miller

FAIRLEIGH DICKINSON UNIVERSITY PRESS
Vancouver • Madison • Teaneck • Wroxton

Published by Fairleigh Dickinson University Press
Copublished by The Rowman & Littlefield Publishing Group, Inc.
4501 Forbes Boulevard, Suite 200, Lanham, Maryland 20706
www.rowman.com

6 Tinworth Street, London SE11 5AL, United Kingdom

Copyright © 2019 by The Rowman & Littlefield Publishing Group, Inc.

All rights reserved. No part of this book may be reproduced in any form or by any electronic or mechanical means, including information storage and retrieval systems, without written permission from the publisher, except by a reviewer who may quote passages in a review.

Fairleigh Dickinson University Press gratefully acknowledges the support received for scholarly publishing from the Friends of FDU Press.

British Library Cataloguing in Publication Information Available

Library of Congress Cataloging-in-Publication Data Available

ISBN 978-1-68393-073-0 (cloth : alk. paper)
ISBN 978-1-68393-074-7 (electronic)

∞™ The paper used in this publication meets the minimum requirements of American National Standard for Information Sciences—Permanence of Paper for Printed Library Materials, ANSI/NISO Z39.48-1992.

Contents

Acknowledgments   ix

Introduction: Teaching William Morris: "The Earthly Paradox"   1
Jason D. Martinek and Elizabeth Carolyn Miller

PART I: PASTS AND PRESENTS

1. Teaching Morris in Chicago, c. 1900   11
   Elizabeth Helsinger

2. Naturalizing the Dignity of Labor: The Hull-House Labor Museum and William Morris's Influence on the American Settlement House Movement   25
   Elizabeth Grennan Browning

3. Time Travelling with William Morris   41
   John Plotz

4. "Work and Fun" and "Education at Its Finest": Teaching Morris at Kelmscott House   49
   Helen Elletson

5. The Medievalism of William Morris: Teaching through Tolkien   65
   KellyAnn Fitzpatrick

PART II: POLITICAL CONTEXTS

6   A Dream of William Cobbett? Teaching Morris's *John Ball* in an Interdisciplinary Course on Victorian Radicalism   79
Linda K. Hughes and William M. Meier

7   "Vive La Commune!" The Imaginary of the Paris Commune and the Arts and Crafts Movement   99
Morna O'Neill

8   "Living in Heaven": Hope and Change in *News from Nowhere*   115
David Latham

PART III: LITERATURE

9   Morris Matters: Teaching *News from Nowhere* in a Seminar on Victorian Materialities   133
Susan David Bernstein

10   Teaching *News from Nowhere* in a Course on "The Simple Life"   149
Michael Robertson

11   Teaching Morris the Utopian   161
Deanna K. Kreisel

12   Teaching *Guenevere* through Word and Image   175
Pamela Bracken

13   Morris and the Literary Canon   187
Michelle Weinroth

PART IV: ART AND DESIGN

14   Morris for Art Historians   207
Imogen Hart

15   "William Morris, designer": Morris and the History of Design as Social Engagement   219
James Housefield

16   William Morris and the Intersection of the Histories of Art and Design   235
Julie Codell

PART V: DIGITAL HUMANITIES

17 Morris for Many Audiences: Teaching with the William Morris Archive 251
    Florence Boos

18 William Morris on Social Media: A Personal Experience, 2007–2017 265
    Tony Pinkney

19 Digital Design with William Morris 275
    Amanda Golden

Index 283

About the Contributors 303

Acknowledgments

William Morris scholars are some of the most generous, welcoming scholars in the world, in our experience, and we would like to thank all those who have held the doors open for us in a spirit of fellowship—Florence Boos, Elizabeth Helsinger, Clive Wilmer, and others who have given generously of their time and expertise. We owe a special note of thanks to ATMA, who offered kind permission to put an image of the Wood Street Morris mural on the cover.

Jason D. Martinek would like to thank Jack Walsdorf and Jane Carlin for their early support of the William Morris Society in the United States's Teaching Morris initiative. He also needs to thank his co-editor for saying yes to taking on this project. We did it! Harry Keyishian, former director of Fairleigh Dickinson University Press, was enthusiastic about the project from the start. His support, along with Jonathan Rose's, was pivotal to bringing this volume to fruition. And thanks to James Gifford's continued support for the project after he became director. He gives a special note of thanks to Zach Nycum who was there every step of the way. Finally, he thanks Jacqueline Ellis, Rosemary Fox Thurston, Elizabeth Hickey, and Anyce Martinek for their love and support.

Elizabeth Carolyn Miller would like to offer special thanks to John Plotz, Susan Bernstein, Mark Allison, Deanna K. Kreisel, Benjamin Morgan, Morna O'Neill, John Kucich, Margaret Linley, Marcus Waithe, and co-editor Jason Martinek for all the friendly, helpful conversations about Morris over the years. Thanks, too, to Martin Stott for extending an invitation to speak at Kelmscott House in 2017—life achievement unlocked!—and to Owen Holland for his excellent work with the *Journal of William Morris Studies*. She also wishes to thank the students with whom she has studied Morris over the years, especially two PhD students who became Morris scholars themselves, Tobias Wilson-Bates and Michael Martel, and an exceptional undergraduate named Hannah Cadigan-Carranza whose independent research project on Morris during fall 2018 was a welcome inspiration. Finally, thanks to Matthew Stratton and Ambrose and Giacomo Stratton-Miller, for everything.

The editors wish to dedicate this book to the memory of Jack Walsdorf, in fellowship. All royalties will be donated in his memory to the William Morris Society in the United States.

Introduction

Teaching William Morris: "The Earthly Paradox"

Jason D. Martinek and Elizabeth Carolyn Miller

Our introduction's subtitle is from a caption for an 1885 political cartoon. The cartoon appeared after William Morris was arrested for allegedly assaulting a police officer, a charge he denied.[1] Morris ultimately received leniency from the court and the cartoon shows a police officer shining Morris's shoes, suggesting that Morris was let off due to his social position and highlighting the rift between Morris's wealth and status and his radical working-class politics. Morris's career was indeed marked by paradox, as this cartoon attests, but only insofar as we assume the impracticability of traveling the distance he sought to travel—the distance from his own lofty social position to that of the working classes. Morris traveled this distance in many different ways, not least of which was by teaching. He spent countless nights on the road, speaking to working-class audiences about social conditions under capitalism, endeavoring to educate the masses toward socialism. But Morris could also be skeptical of the pedagogical mode—he described his own childhood school as a mere "boy-farm," and joked, "if my parents had been poorer and had had more character they would have probably committed the fatal mistake of trying to educate me"—and he was often a harsh judge of his own capacities as a teacher.[2] Describing an outdoor meeting at Ryton Willows, near Newcastle, for example, Morris describes a "fair meeting there of most attentive persons, though I guess I tried their patience as I got 'lectury' and being excited went on and on till I had gone on too long." Most teachers can probably relate to Morris's fear of having lost his audience in his enthusiasm for his subject, but in the end, Morris says, the meeting "was successful and the audience stayed till it was nearly dark."[3]

Our work as teachers in the modern classroom may little resemble Morris's "lectury" outdoor address on the banks of the Tyne, but the social conditions against which he railed have little changed since the 1880s. Just as economists have come to draw connections between the reconcentration of capital today with the concentration of capital in the Gilded Age (or Belle Epoche, to use Thomas Piketty's phrase), we think that Morris's response to the greed and ugliness of the Victorian Era is as relevant today as ever, and that it does us well to revisit Morris's social ideal, resting, as it did, on the pillars of personal liberty, democracy, fellowship, environmental stewardship, and equality for all. He represents a tonic to the political conditions of Trumpism and neoliberalism, and we believe he should be an integral part of the twenty-first-century classroom.

But how do you teach someone like William Morris who made significant contributions to several different fields of study? Do you teach him as a writer, an artist, a designer, or a political activist? Do you lop off the part that fits your course best and leave the rest of the corpus to rot? The amputative approach has long been the prevailing one, and unsurprisingly so. Higher education in the twentieth century emphasized specialization over generalization, and Morris, who does not fit neatly into any disciplinary category, poses a challenge to the disciplinary needs of instructors, making it difficult, nigh impossible, for them to present Morris in all of his multivarious complexity.

How can teachers succeed in capturing Morris's multi-dimensionality within the exigencies of the modern educational system? This is a question that engages, in different ways, all the contributions in this volume. Although an entire term could easily be spent on Morris, historically there have been very few opportunities for students to immerse themselves so completely in his oeuvre. Shakespeare, yes; Morris, no.[4] Even at the graduate level, Morris tends to be part of a larger thematic course (e.g., Victorian literature) rather than the focal point. Given Morris's expansive career and wide-ranging contributions, it has been nearly impossible to do him justice, which is a problem given that his work—in all its dimensions—seems to hang curiously together. It is difficult to grasp the significance of his literary works without reading them in relation to his politics, difficult to understand his politics without conceptualizing them in relation to his theories of craft, difficult to envision his aesthetic theories without reading his poetry, and so on. There is a reason why the major biographies of Morris are so long; Morris was never idle and mastered a whole array of arts and crafts.[5] Just as his patterns for Morris & Co. are suggestive of endlessness, of borderless botanical growth with the seeming capacity to entwine its way around everything, so too every aspect of Morris's multi-faceted career seems to connect with every other aspect.

Jorge Luis Borges was another writer who knew something about seemingly endless, labyrinthine patterns and the sublimity of interconnection, and he was also a teacher who lectured on Morris. His lectures for a course on English literature that he taught at the University of Buenos Aires in 1966 provide insight not only into his own debt to Morris, but also into mid-twentieth-century approaches to teaching this Victorian polymath. Of the twenty-five lectures in the course, three were devoted to Morris, demonstrating that Borges viewed Morris as an important and pivotal figure. Borges described that pivotal role rather narrowly, focusing on how Morris brought a Germanic inflection to English literature; he delved most deeply into Morris's *The Earthly Paradise* and Icelandic sagas, and he marveled at Morris's cleverness with language. Wistfully perhaps, Borges ended his lectures on Morris with reflections on why twentieth-century students seemed to lack a greater appreciation for Morris's literary contributions: "Morris's work garnered what the French call a *succès d'estime*"—work that is critically acclaimed but never catches on with the public. Borges's thoughts on Morris's failings as a writer are also illuminating here: "The defect Morris suffered from is slowness; the descriptions of battles, the death of the dragon, they are a bit languid. After the death of Brynhild, the poem [*Sigurd the Volsung*] falls off."[6] One wonders if Borges had taught Morris's poetry in the context of Morris's political beliefs or artistic pursuits if this "slowness" might have taken on another register in his classroom. But the story his lectures tell of Morris remains, nevertheless, an illustrative one when considering the challenges Morris poses in the classroom.

G.D.H. Cole, the first Chichele Professor of Social and Political Theory at Oxford University, was another intellectual luminary who taught Morris in the mid-twentieth century, and like Borges, he tended to reduce Morris's legacy to a part of the whole. Whereas Borges focused on Morris's Germanic influence, Cole was drawn most to Morris's artist-craftsman ideal. His three-part Morris lectures are from about 1950 and were prepared as a filmstrip for Common Ground—an attempt to reach a wide audience, perhaps not unlike Morris's outdoor lecture on the banks of the Tyne. Cole's lectures, in contrast to Borges's, offer a wider introduction to Morris's various pursuits, but they do not provide the connective tissue to show the interrelation of these numerous parts of Morris's career. Cole loosely built his lecture around Morris's ideal of craft labor: "The gist of William Morris's theory was that, to the fullest practicable extent, everything that men made ought to be 'a joy to the makers and to the user.'"[7] Cole was so enamored with this turn-of-phrase that he repeated it at the conclusion of his lecture. In his elaboration of Morris's theory of art, he highlighted Morris's material contributions and his emphasis on the pleasure of the producer as well as the consumer, yet he meditated little on how this theory shaped Morris's writings. As with Borges, Cole rued that Morris's popularity had waned—"At present, both as writer and as a designer, Morris is rather out of fashion"—but he looked forward to the day that Morris, or at least a part of Morris, would come back in vogue.[8] Cole, who was a leading voice of the Guild Socialism movement of the 1920s, never entirely left that vision for the world behind, even as the movement itself crumbled. His teaching notes present a highly romanticized version of Morris, and it is clear that he saw the waning of Morris's ideas as a lost opportunity for the remaking of British society along more egalitarian lines.

Borges and Cole both provide clues into how Morris was taught in the twentieth century, but neither manage to capture—or even try to capture—Morris's incredible range. We think the best way to find models for how to approach Morris more holistically is to look at how he is taught today. In the twenty-first century, disciplinary silos are beginning to come down and interdisciplinary programs and integrative learning experiences are replacing them. But long before the word "interdisciplinary" entered the lexicon of higher education, Morris embodied that ideal. Thus, as you prepare your syllabi for next term, we hope you will draw inspiration from these essays about teaching Morris and that they will help you imagine how to bring greater interdisciplinary consideration to his life and works. Whether you only have fifteen minutes to talk about Morris, or an entire semester, and whether you are teaching college students or preschoolers, we hope you will find the following essays, representing a range of perspectives from a variety of scholars and teachers, to be useful, and perhaps even beautiful, as we ourselves have found them to be.[9]

The essays in this volume are divided into five sections, broadly representative of five different avenues of approaching Morris's life and work: "Pasts and Presents," "Political Contexts," "Literature," "Art and Design," and "Digital Humanities." As with Morris's own career, however, threads of interconnection pass between and among them, linking the essays together across the sections as well as within them. But since all interdisciplinarity begins in disciplinarity, we have attempted to group the essays according to the authors' primary areas of intervention.

The essays in the opening section, "Pasts and Presents," all, in different ways, wrestle with the question of Morris's legacy, relevance, and afterlife. Some examine the surprising histories of Morris's reception in various pedagogical endeavors of the past, while others seek to bring Morris into the present. Elizabeth Helsinger's "Teaching Morris in Chicago, c. 1900" sifts through the archives of the University of Chicago to show Morris's central place in the English curriculum there at the turn of the century, and the ways that his work, perhaps surprisingly, encouraged pedagogical innovation. If this essay makes you wonder how the other half of Chicago learned about

William Morris, we find out in the next essay, Elizabeth Grennan Browning's "Naturalizing the Dignity of Labor: The Hull-House Labor Museum and William Morris's Influence on the American Settlement House Movement," which narrates how Jane Addams and Ellen Gates Starr sought to provide aesthetic and craft education to urban tenement dwellers in late-nineteenth-century Chicago. Next John Plotz's "Time Travelling with William Morris" teleports us to the present, describing Plotz's endeavor to write a young adult novel about Morris, *Time and the Tapestry* (2014), as a way of making Morris's ideas alive for a new generation of readers. In "'Work and Fun' and 'Education at its Finest:' Teaching Morris at Kelmscott House," Helen Elletson describes the pedagogical initiatives undertaken by the Kelmscott House Museum in Hammersmith, and their innovative means of reaching students of all ages, but especially those in the middle grades. Finally, in "The Medievalism of William Morris: Teaching through Tolkien," KellyAnn Fitzpatrick brings the past and the present together to describe how the fantasy novels of J. R. R. Tolkien—as well as the films and video games they've inspired—can prove an avenue toward teaching Morris in the undergraduate classroom.

The "Political Contexts" section offers various themes and topics by which Morris's social and political views might be introduced in the context of the history, literature, or art history classroom. In "A Dream of William Cobbett? Teaching Morris's *John Ball* in an Interdisciplinary Course on Victorian Radicalism," Linda K. Hughes and William M. Meier describe an interdisciplinary course, open to graduate and undergraduate students, that focused on Victorian political radicalism as a historical and literary field of study, including Morris's *A Dream of John Ball* and other works from his socialist newspaper *The Commonweal*. In "'Vive La Commune!' The Imaginary of the Paris Commune and the Arts and Crafts Movement," Morna O'Neill reads Morris and his circle against the backdrop of the Paris Commune of 1871 and its continuing influence on British radicalism, offering ways of integrating the British response to the Commune into the art history classroom and other areas of study that touch on Morris. In "'Living in Heaven': Hope and Change in *News from Nowhere*," David Latham discusses strategies for bringing "the flight of dreams" into the classroom—that is, for teaching Morris to a pessimistic generation of students who may see little possibility for improving the world in the way that Morris hoped to do.

The essays gathered in the "Literature" section offer a range of approaches, including critical methods, themes, and genres through which to teach Morris's literary work; specific examples of how to teach specific texts by Morris; and explorations of Morris's place in the literary canon. Susan David Bernstein in "Morris Matters: *News from Nowhere* in a Seminar on Victorian Materialities," describes teaching Morris's utopian masterpiece in the context of an

English graduate seminar on objects, thing theory, and the new materialisms, and includes examples from graduate student projects on objects from *News from Nowhere*, such as red bricks and the Maple-Durham lock. In "Teaching *News from Nowhere* in a Course on 'The Simple Life,'" Michael Robertson describes his experiences teaching Morris together with Thoreau's *Walden*, the recent documentary *The Queen of Versailles*, and other works that consider materialism and overconsumption and how one might resist these bedevilments of modern life. Deanna K. Kreisel's "Teaching Morris the Utopian" describes teaching *News from Nowhere* in a class on utopian and dystopian literature, and offers a number of suggestions for theories, supplementary texts, and angles of approach that work with and against students' longstanding complaint that utopian novels generally, and *News from Nowhere* specifically, are "boring." Turning from Morris's prose to his poetry, Pamela Bracken's "Teaching *Guenevere* through Word and Image" offers a detailed, play-by-play account of how one might approach "The Defence of Guenevere" in the classroom by analyzing it in close comparison with Morris's work in art and design. Finally, Michelle Weinroth investigates Morris's liminal place in English literary history in "Morris and the Literary Canon," and traces his critical neglect to nineteenth-century debates about style and translation, debates in which Morris participated by way of his own translation work.

The essays in "Art and Design" together conceive of Morris's places within the fields of art history and design as they exist today. Imogen Hart, in "Morris for Art Historians," describes the challenges Morris poses to the traditional art history curriculum, and shows how introducing his work to students can usefully undermine their assumptions about the nature of art. In "William Morris, designer," James Housefield traces a utopian impulse through the history of design, beginning with Morris and extending to activist craft collectives and theories of human-centered design today, and establishes Morris's continuing relevance for theorists and practitioners of socially-conscious design. Julie Codell, in "William Morris and the Intersection of the Histories of Art and Design," looks at the histories of art and of design as fields of study and practice, and examines how Morris carried out a "transaction of values" between the two that is only now being incorporated into art history and design as disciplines.

In the final section of the book, "Digital Humanities," three Morris scholars describe their work to extend the teaching of Morris into the digital sphere. Florence Boos, in "Morris for Many Audiences: Teaching with the William Morris Archive," offers several means by which teachers can incorporate the online William Morris Archive—edited by Boos, and itself a pedagogical endeavor of global scope—into the undergraduate and graduate curriculum as a means of teaching digital humanities (DH) methodologies. In "William

Morris on Social Media: A Personal Experience, 2007–2017," Tony Pinkney recounts a decade of experiments in using new digital platforms such as blogs, YouTube films, and Twitter to engage the public in learning more about Morris and his ideas. And bringing us back to design, this time in the digital sphere, Amanda Golden's "Digital Design with William Morris" describes a digital design course on art and technology where students design e-book versions of Oscar Wilde's *The Picture of Dorian Gray* in conjunction with Morris's ideals of book design.

A theme that runs across many of these essays is that Morris is difficult to teach. As Borges would attest, Morris was never the easiest sell in the classroom, but he may be particularly challenging for students today. His conscious rejection of accepted forms (social forms, aesthetic forms, political forms) only gets more confounding and more in need of explanation as the years go on. Clearly, for all teachers of Morris, a good class on Morris is a hard-won class, one that will require imagination and preparation. And yet we continue to teach Morris because he offers a perspective unavailable elsewhere in nineteenth-century literature and art, and because his ideas and creations continue to sustain us today. Above all, we continue to teach Morris because we feel our students need him. By teaching Morris we hope to equip our students with the capacity to imagine and dream a better world even while recognizing the injustices of this one. The "earthly paradox" of our subtitle is, in this sense, emphatically not a reference to Morris's own contradictory social position, but to the paradoxical condition of possibility within a fallen world that Morris helps us to see. Morris was uniquely gifted with the capacity to hold together seemingly incompatible visions of condemnation and imagination, and it is this capacity for critical hope that we go to him for again and again.

NOTES

1. For more on the circumstances surrounding his arrest, see E. P. Thompson, *William Morris: Romantic to Revolutionary* (New York: Pantheon, 1955), 395–99.
2. *Collected Letters of William Morris*. Vol. 2, Part B, ed. Norman Kelvin. (Princeton: Princeton University Press, 2014), 546.
3. *William Morris's Socialist Diary*. 2nd ed., ed. Florence Boos. (Nottingham: Five Leaves, 2018), 109.
4. Yale University professor Edward S. Cooke Jr.'s course "William Morris: The Theory and Practice of Craft" represents the rare exception. See "British Studies 497c: William Morris: The Theory and Practice of Craft," https://britishart.yale.edu/sites/default/files/files/William%20Morris_The%20Theory%20and%20Practice%20of%20Craft%20_497c%20syllabus.pdf.

5. If you're looking for a short biography that packs a lot of punch we recommend Peter Stansky, *William Morris* (Oxford, 1984). Morris gets the full treatment in two standard biographies: E. P. Thompson's *William Morris: Romantic to Revolutionary* and Fiona MacCarthy's *William Morris: A Man for Our Time* (New York: Knopf, 1995).

6. Jorge Luis Borges, *Professor Borges: A Course on English Literature*, ed. Martin Arias and Martin Hadid, trans. Katherine Silver. (New York: New Directions, 2013), 237.

7. G. D. H. Cole, *Life of William Morris.* (London: Common Ground, c.1950), 8, 11.

8. Ibid.

9. But we need to provide a word of caution, tongue-in-cheek though it may be: as Elizabeth Helsinger shows in her essay, taking a Morrisian approach to Morris can be risky, for it contributed to Oscar Lovell Triggs's dismissal from the University of Chicago in 1904.

BIBLIOGRAPHY

Borges, Jorge Luis. *Professor Borges: A Course on English Literature*. Edited by Martin Arias and Martin Hadid. Translated by Katherine Silver. New York: New Directions, 2013.

Cole, G. D. H. *Life of William Morris.* London: Common Ground, c.1950.

MacCarthy, Fiona. *William Morris: A Man for Our Time*. New York: Knopf, 1995.

Morris, William. *The Collected Letters of William Morris*. Edited by Norman Kelvin. Princeton: Princeton University Press, 2014.

———. *William Morris's Socialist Diary*. 2nd ed. Edited by Florence Boos. Nottingham: Five Leaves 2018.

Thompson, E. P. *William Morris: Romantic to Revolutionary*. New York: Pantheon, 1955.

Stansky, Peter. *William Morris*. New York: Oxford University Press, 1984.

Part I

PASTS AND PRESENTS

Chapter One

Teaching Morris in Chicago, c. 1900

Elizabeth Helsinger

Four years before Morris's death, a new university opened in a city of big business and immigrant labor—a place and time breeding powerful and sometimes conflicting political and aesthetic desires. This was the city Carl Sandburg was to hail as "Hog Butcher for the World," but it was also the city where a newly appointed professor and an enthusiastic young instructor brought the study of William Morris to the University of Chicago. The contrasting careers of these two early teachers of Morris offer an unusual window on a place and time as frame for new pedagogies and ideas. This essay will focus on the now forgotten career of that young instructor, Oscar Lovell Triggs (1865–1930), but I begin with a brief look at his contemporary at Chicago, Professor Richard Green Moulton (1849–1924).

Moulton, one of a distinguished English family of Wesleyan ministers, educators, and jurists, found a second home teaching not only university students but Chicago's adults, hungry for self-improvement. An early advocate for literary criticism that was neither philological nor biographical but focused on comparative critical analysis of texts, he was also a strong believer in the university extension movement (lecture courses by university professors offered to the general public). Moulton taught in the extension divisions of Cambridge University, the University of London, and, from its opening in 1892 until his retirement in 1919, the University of Chicago.[1] He gave regular academic courses while lecturing at the University's many extension centers—in churches and synagogues, libraries, the YMCA, Hull House, the Joliet Steel Works Club, the Owen Scientific Institute, and the People's Institute. From 1893–1894, for example, he offered three series of six lectures each at different centers on "The Literary Study of the Bible," "Shakespeare's Tempest," and "Stories as a Mode of Thinking"; attendance at his public lectures ranged from 165 to 500.² As an outgrowth of his extension teaching, Moulton published well-received books for the general reading public on the Bible as literature; classical drama; epic; Shakespeare; Milton; and William Morris's epic retelling of the Völsunga Saga, *Sigurd the Volsung*. In 1902 he was made professor of literary theory and interpretation and head of the Department of General Literature.

Moulton was clearly a valued member of the new university's experiments in intellectual leadership and community service. As a popular lecturer and dedicated teacher, Moulton was always careful to keep his audience's experience in mind. In his publications, as in his teaching, he was an early advocate of world literature, he taught that it should be approached through the angle of vision provided by the reader's chosen country and its language, which in his own case, and, he assumed, in the case of his American audiences, would be English.³ Moulton turned to Morris as a subject of his extension teaching in 1904, publishing in the same year a small book intended as a supplement and study guide to his lectures. Morris mattered to Moulton as an epic poet who brought the stories of the Icelandic Völsunga Saga into modern English in his *Sigurd the Volsung* (1876). "Morris," he wrote,

> belongs to the inmost circle of the world's poets. . . Just as Milton constitutes a translating medium through which biblical thought and poetry has become a part of English literature, so that the English world (without knowing it) draws its conception of biblical cosmogony from the *Paradise Lost* rather than from the Bible, so Morris makes a similar translating medium for the wonderful poetry of the Norse sages, hitherto so little known. As *Sigurd* becomes more and more extensively read, it may be expected that Norse thought and imagination, like biblical, will be naturalized in the mind of the English-speaking peoples.⁴

Moulton's small book is full of acute readings and both structural and figural analysis, informed by his comparative work on classical, medieval, and Renaissance epic. It still has much to offer Morris scholars.

Oscar Lovell Triggs, in his brief but all too well publicized career at the same university, was an instructor in the English department; like Moulton, he also lectured in the extension division. The son of a minister from a small town in Illinois, Triggs received his BA and MA in English from the University of Minnesota (1889, 1893) and his PhD from Chicago (1895). While on a two-year fellowship at Berlin and Oxford (1890–1892), before coming to Chicago, Triggs sought out Morris at home in London and traveled down to the Morris & Co. workshops at Merton Abbey. In a glowing article published in the American magazine *Poet Lore,* he described his impressions of Morris at Merton Abbey:

> In the designing-room is Mr. Morris himself. . . . Morris is dressed as usual in a plain suit of blue serge and flannel. He is short of stature, but robust, and full of the most restless energy. The features of his face are large and rugged, but full-blooded, luminous, and well modeled. A kindly poet's expression is given by the eye, and the mouth beneath the gray beard. His head is covered with curly gray hair, which he brushes back over his forehead with his hand, as he leans to his work. One feels in the presence of a vital personality who is in love with labor and all the life of the world.[5]

But Morris was not only the energetic craftsman poet in love with life and labor, he was also deeply troubled by the conditions of modern work. "The social burden of the times has been laid upon the poet's mind and heart," Triggs continues,

> before him perpetually is the city of London, huge and unsightly. He hears the murmur and moan from the hard-used race of men. From his home by the river he sees the workings of a selfish commercialism which has taken monetary profit and loss, and not the human kind, as its basis for calculation. With a heart laden with anger, he enters a protest against "man's inhumanity to man." With a heart laden with love he preaches the doctrines of brotherhood,—even if needs be by revolution. . . . The democratization of art is the social aim of William Morris.[6]

"As a prophet of the new industrialism," Triggs told his American readers, "William Morris is one of the most significant men of this century."[7]

In 1893 Triggs arrived at the University of Chicago for his PhD. Its brand new, neo-Gothic campus faced the shining white city of the Columbian World Exhibition just across the street. There he wrote a second article for *Poet Lore* on Whitman, implicitly contrasting the English scene with the American.

> No one can stand to-day at the centre of the World's Fair grounds without being impressed by the strange beauty of the scene: the city so white and wonderful, the lake gleaming beneath the high summer's sun and gently pulsing from afar, the water-birds wheeling above, and the people streaming and endless, thronging street and shore with youthful ardor; all the world is here,—the careless, the curious, the thoughtful; the faces of a few are seen to glow with a newly awakened hope. On many a day before I have watched from this spot the building of the city, and while walls and arch and dome were rising to complete the plan of a perfect deed, I have asked from one and another the meaning of it all, and have received a variable answer. Not until the city was completed did one, who seemed more thoughtful than the rest, say to me as we stood admiring the classic outlines of the noble Art Gallery,—and somewhat sadly did he speak,— "This city is not for us, but for the future. I understand it as a type appearing ere the times are ready, and I look to see it vanish soon as being but a momentary

embodiment of an ideal purpose. But while it hovers here upon the shore I take it as a sign to men of the beauty and the romance, the ideality and the reality, of our life here and now."[8]

Whitman embodied for Triggs an optimistic faith in democratic America and its industry, whose future he saw imaged in the shining city of the Columbian Exhibition. Morris mattered not only as a poet-leader of a nineteenth-century renaissance of beauty but as an apostle of labor and a socialist.[9]

While Triggs was no doubt expected to teach medieval English when he was appointed as an instructor at Chicago, since he was editing John Lydgate's 1498 *The Assembly of the Gods* as his dissertation, he was much more interested in teaching the forward-looking authors of his own century: Shelley, Browning, and Morris; Emerson, Poe, and Whitman.[10] And he could be impassioned and eloquent about the works he loved. Urging a new approach to art and literature for an age of democracy, he rejected both an older reliance on taste and a more recent interest in scientific methods: "The end of [art's] work is not 'good taste,' not knowledge, but life and character," he taught.[11] "Art is the expression of man's entire being . . . A perfect response to literature requires the activity in the reader of those faculties of being to which the author has made his appeal."[12]

Like Moulton, Triggs published books and articles, most aimed at a general reader. Triggs, however, tried to do justice to Morris in all his multiple activities: as poet, artist, and socialist. His interest in Morris did not stop at the lecture room door: Triggs embraced the larger city and its opportunities for social and educational reform, armed with a strange synthesis of Morris, Whitman, Leo Tolstoy, and John Dewey. He was a founding member of the Arts and Crafts Society of Chicago (1897, based at Hull House, where Jane Addams served the immigrant labor community and Ellen Gates Starr taught handicraft skills) and of the Industrial Art League (1899; it coordinated arts and crafts workshops in the city and started training workshops for immigrants to make furniture and other objects for sale). He was also a founder and later president of the William Morris Society (1903–1905). He published a well-regarded study of the Arts and Crafts movement in 1902 as well as articles on Morris in *Poet Lore* (1893), Gustav Stickley's *The Craftsman* (1902), and *To-Morrow: A Magazine for Rational Thinkers/A Monthly Handbook of the Changing Order* (1905), which he briefly edited. He helped a Chicago millionaire plan a utopian community for bettering the lives of immigrant laborers, whose centerpiece Triggs hoped would be a People's Industrial Arts College for training not only the head but the hands. In 1904, the University declined to renew his contract. Triggs never held another university position, disappearing almost entirely from history.

Moulton and Triggs were not unknown to one another. Though Moulton was nearly twenty years older, they began teaching at the University at almost the same time, one a professor and published author (*Shakespeare as a Dramatic Artist,* 1885; *The Ancient Classical Drama,* 1890), the other still a graduate student but already the author of *Browning and Whitman: A Study in Democracy* (1893). Both became charter members of the William Morris Society; Triggs was its first secretary, its most active lecturer, and later its president. The Society's *Bulletin* for early 1904 announces lecture series on Morris by both men.[13] At least on the subject of Morris, each recognized the usefulness of the other's work: Moulton's booklet on Morris as poet recommends Triggs's *Chapters in the History of the Arts and Crafts Movement* (1902); Triggs's 1905 article on Morris the craftsman socialist for *To-Morrow* cites Moulton's praise of Morris as "our English Homer."[14]

Like Moulton, Triggs was an extremely popular teacher. One student, writing many years later, recalled of his course in American literature (which disposed of all the "so-called standard writers" in one lecture to spend the rest of the time on the poetry of Emerson, Poe, and Whitman) that "Mr. Triggs' enthusiasm and love for these writers opened before us a world of new thoughts and new meanings and made our native literature something far more electric than a catalog of authors."[15] Others who attended Triggs's lectures on Morris found their later lives shaped by his teaching. One was Lilian Steichen, sister of Edward Steichen the photographer, who listened to Triggs on Morris, became a socialist, and married a young poet and fellow socialist, Carl Sandburg, who worked with Triggs on *To-Morrow*. Another was Susan Glaspell, a playwright inspired by Triggs's call for a new approach to literature, who with her husband George Cram Cook went on to found the Provincetown Players, producing the work of Djuna Barnes, Theodore Dreiser, and Eugene O'Neill.[16] Yet another was Murray Schloss, a former student who served as managing editor under Triggs on *To-Morrow,* ran for Congress on the Socialist ticket in New Jersey, and after some years as a social worker in Los Angeles, assembled 2500 acres to found a utopian community called "Heart of the Hills" (the land now belongs to San Diego State University, where it is a conservation refuge).[17] Both Triggs's wives first fell in love with him as their teacher. Laura McAdoo, daughter of a professor at the University of Tennessee, heard Triggs lecture in Nashville, came to Chicago and took classes from him, and married him in 1899; she became active as a lecturer and journalist promoting democracy, arts and crafts, and women's higher education. (They were divorced in 1907.)[18] Ada Beall Cox, also Triggs's student, was inspired to a career of social work and teaching; when he left Chicago, she followed him to California and became his second wife.[19]

Given his interest in the energies and ideas of the present day, the temptation to provocation sometimes proved too much for Triggs, and copy-hungry reporters soon began to attend his lectures as well. They delighted to report, in large headlines, that Triggs referred to many hymns as little better than doggerel and spoke of Henry Wadsworth Longfellow's poetry as overrated. But worst of all, according to the papers, Triggs suggested that Rockefeller was as great in his way as Shakespeare and Milton. How, the papers asked, could someone who denigrated Longfellow, Shakespeare, and Milton be allowed to teach at the University of Chicago? As the student newspaper put it, "Dr. Triggs is not a man/To cut up many capers;/ But if he even bats his eye,/It gets into the papers." [20] Fame, alas, came in the guise of notoriety. Triggs became an object of mockery. Whether it was for this reason, or because Triggs's socialist views irritated the University's businessman trustees, or because Whitman's ideas of free love were thought to have influenced Triggs's actions (as the papers suggested when Triggs's wife filed for divorce in 1904), that year was Triggs's last at the University.

Triggs was an idealist and an enthusiast, and not always very wise. He urged his students—and his public audiences—to seize the opportunity to realize a different future, reorganizing labor, education, art, and even the state along lines he believed Morris had suggested. He continued to be heavily involved in the Morris-inspired Arts and Crafts movement, lecturing widely outside Chicago as well. Yet at the urging of Chicago friends and colleagues Frank Lloyd Wright (whose influential 1901 lecture at the Arts and Crafts Society of Chicago had urged art to adapt to the new age of the machine), the philosopher-educator John Dewey (founder of the University's Laboratory Schools, where manual training, including the use of machines, was part of the curriculum), and Thorstein Veblen (whose 1902 essay "Arts and Crafts," published in the *Journal of Political Economy,* acknowledged the necessity of the machine), Triggs too came to embrace machines for American industry even as he continued to promote Morris's craft-based ideals for art and labor.

Triggs proposed a "co-operative individualism," a workshop-based system of fellowship through labor as a renovating model for American society, though he never fully faced the contradictions between a Morrisian socialism and the new industrialism he urged.[21] "I see only one remedy for the class system of modern society—that is, to reconstruct the institutions that embody the social spirit," he wrote in 1902.[22] His workshops would replicate the model developed through the Industrial Art League. Worker-owned machine workshops would serve as a basis for education (learning by making), and—he hoped—with the freedom of laborers from the factory system, art would flourish. There, he wrote, the hopes of Carlyle, Ruskin, Whitman, and Morris (and of Tolstoy and Dewey) might be fulfilled in democratic America. In a series of articles in Gustav Stickley's *The Craftsman,* Triggs asked

> Is it not possible to create new institutions—institutions that will not be masks and lies, but represent what we really think and hope to be? One such institution I propose—the institution of the workshop; a workshop of a new type, such as may be properly the unit of organization in the industrial commonwealth we are forming. The workshop I have in mind will embody to the full the high ideals of labor, conceived by such writers as Ruskin, and current in the world now for nearly a century. It will be a genuine manufactory where materials shall be shaped into the things we use. It will be a "studio," where work shall be creative and not devoid of a sense of beauty. It will be a school where the doing of things shall be educative, since work will there be conducted to the ends of expression, as art is at its best and as life is at its freest. In a sense, it will be a state, since it will be a community of self-governing individuals. In a sense, too, it will be a church, since it will be established upon the basis of co-operation and comradeship.[23]

Invoking Morris ("where work shall be creative and not devoid of a sense of beauty"), Dewey ("a school where the doing of things shall be educative"), Tolstoy ("a state, since it will be a community of self-governing individuals"), and Whitman ("a church, since it will be established upon the basis of . . . comradeship"), Triggs returned to Morris as "the type–erect and forceful" of the new workman, "who actually realizes the ideal of the nobility of labor that Carlyle pronounced to be possible."[24]

Triggs not only taught, lectured, and wrote, he also turned to those who might help him fund his vision of democracy remade: wealthy American businessmen. In doing so he was following the example set by his own University. The University of Chicago owed its then unique form to its first president, William Rainey Harper (a private, co-educational college with a graduate research and teaching institution formed along German lines, to which were attached a laboratory school for primary and secondary teaching, an extension division for reaching the broader community, and a university press for publishing the results of both research and practice). But it owed its existence to a very wealthy businessman indeed, John D. Rockefeller. Harper's gamble—that he could convince money and power to give him the university he wanted—paid off. Triggs, unfortunately, lacked Harper's academic prominence, persuasive skills, and powerful friends. He had not even the security of a tenured position. It was perhaps inevitable that he should find that millionaire businessmen had their own ideas.

Figure 1.1. Cartoon (before 1904) of President Harper's search for "All-Round Talkers" and "Novelties for the Midway" (as it supposedly competes with President Teddy Roosevelt's speech-making) that includes (on right hand scroll tumbling from Harper's Hat) one labeled "Programme: Triggs."
Reproduced courtesy of Special Collections Research Center, University of Chicago Library.

Triggs's first opportunity to realize his workshop-based system on a larger scale came through one of the early supporters of the Industrial Art League, Marguerite Warren Springer. Born Maggie Maginness, a daughter of Irish immigrants, she married Warren Springer, an eccentric real estate and manufacturing millionaire.[25] Warren Springer was also excited by Triggs's reforming energies. Known to operate at the boundaries of the law (he was a slum landlord), he reserved for his retirement a pet project for which, in 1902, he approached Triggs. Together they planned an Industrial Arts College that would use the workshop system as part of the self-sufficient community Springer wanted to found.[26] The problem, for Triggs, was that Springer's intention was to locate his community well outside the city, as a primarily agricultural enterprise—thus solving the problem of immigrant labor by removing it to a safe distance. Perhaps this is why, despite Springer's desire that Triggs take charge and lead the proposed community, Triggs declined to do so. (When Springer died in 1912, Marguerite announced that she would recall Triggs, by this time living in California, to ask him to realize her late husband's wishes. Triggs did not return.)

Triggs's second opportunity came in the shape of another successful entrepreneur of somewhat suspect dealings (in bicycles and Mexican commercial banking) with his own eccentric enthusiasms, Parker H. Sercombe.[27] When Triggs's first wife left him and the University did not renew his contract, Sercombe offered Triggs refuge–an office and a home—in his Herbert Spencer-Walt Whitman Center, where a philosophy of individual self-cultivation and free love was preached. Triggs accepted—Whitman was, after all, the other of his great heroes. Moreover, Sercombe agreed to finance a new journal, *To-Morrow,* which Triggs would edit. The journal started publication in January, 1905. Newly energized, Triggs embarked on lectures and books to promote the new order he envisioned. He also traveled to New York and signed the organizational call for a Collegiate Socialist Society, together with Charlotte Perkins Gilman, Jack London, Clarence S. Darrow, and Upton Sinclair. Triggs's writing, editorial skills, and both socialist and Arts and Crafts connections allowed the journal to attract many contributors who would go on to become well known. The journal promoted Sercombe's Spencer-Whitman Center, but also the ideas of William Morris–the Arts and Crafts movement and socialism—as well as Triggs's plans for a People's Industrial College. But as his divorce trial approached, Triggs's association with Sercombe proved a liability for both men. Five months after *To-Morrow* began publishing, Triggs left the journal. Subsequent issues of *To-Morrow* rarely missed a chance to sneer at Triggs and his pretensions. Though he started his own magazine, it did not long survive.

Triggs's last book, *The Changing Order* (1905), was reprinted several times in the next decade. It did not save its author's career. Publicity surrounding his divorce trial, not concluded until 1907, only compounded earlier ridicule.[28] For this teacher of Morris, reduced by the press to a figure of fun, Chicago no longer held out promises of a new order. Retreating to farm in California, Triggs disappears from history; he died in Manitoba, in 1930.

Looking back from the perspective of 2018 to 1900, it is striking that these early teachers of Morris in the United States were both, in different ways, educational pioneers. We may not usually think of Morris as a spur to radical pedagogic innovation. Yet these two teachers' immersion in Morris's varied works helped both to extend their educational ambitions. Their appointments at a new university in a brash and growing city offered the opportunities. Both broke with reigning pedagogical approaches to literature: in Moulton's case, embracing close comparative analysis of texts that should be taught to everyone; in Triggs's, modeling a passionate sympathy that opened students to new writers and their words. The university extension movement in which both Moulton and Triggs participated led in each case to further engagements with the surrounding city. Both joined the William Morris Society and gave talks at the Jane Addams Settlement house. Triggs went further, throwing himself wholeheartedly, if not very wisely, into the tasks of promoting and organizing an American, workshop-based education under the aegis of socialism. The visions of American possibility evoked by the World's Columbian Exhibition in this young teacher of William Morris would remain, as his friends had warned him, visions yet to be fulfilled.

NOTES

1. See Richard Green Moulton, "University Extension and the University of the Future," in *Education, History, and Politics* 3–4, *The Johns Hopkins University Studies in Historical and Political Science* 9 (1891), 1–14.

2. *Quarterly Calendar, University of Chicago* 2.3 (1893): front cover.

3. See Moulton, *World Literature and Its Place in General Culture* (London: Macmillan, 1911), and Sarah Lawall, "Richard Moulton and the 'Perspective Attitude' in World Literature," in *Routledge Companion to World Literature,* eds. Theo D'haen, David Damrosch, and Djelal Kadir (London: Routledge, 2012), ch. 6, Credo.

4. See Moulton, *The Poetry and Fiction of William Morris* (Chicago: University of Chicago Press, 1904), 4. https://babel.hathitrust.org/cgi/pt?id=chi.43619134;view=1up;seq=71.

5. Oscar Lovell Triggs, "The Socialistic Thread in the Life and Works of William Morris," *Poet Lore* 5 (1893): 116–17.

6. Ibid., 217.

7. Ibid., 218.

8. Triggs, "Walt Whitman," *Poet Lore* 5 (1893): 292.

9. See also the student notes for Triggs's Spring 1894 course, "Nineteenth Century Literary Movements," Edward Kirby Putnam papers, Box 1, Folder 2, University of Chicago Special Collections.

10. For Triggs's course offerings, see the *Annual Register of The University of Chicago* for the years 1893–1906. Triggs's edition of Lydgate's *Assembly of the Gods* was published by the University of Chicago in 1895, in conjunction with the Early English Text Society, where it was also issued as Ex. Ser., lxix, 1896; it remains the standard edition of this work.

11. Triggs, "On the Study and Teaching of Literature" (Address delivered before the English Conference at The University, July 21, 1896), *University Record* 1 (September 11, 1896): 346.

12. Ibid., 345.

13. *Bulletin of the William Morris Society* February (1904). http://www.morris society.org/publications/newsletter.html. See also Florence S. Boos, "The First Morris Society: Chicago, 1903–1905," *Journal of the William Morris Society* (Winter 2014), 35–48, and Elizabeth Helsinger, "'A Vestibule of Song': Morris and Burne-Jones in Chicago," *Journal of the William Morris Society* (Winter 2014), 49–69.

14. Moulton, *William Morris,* 5; Triggs, "William Morris," *To-Morrow* 1 (March 1905): 19–20; citing Moulton, *Morris,* 2.

15. Bennett Epstein, "College without Cheers," *The University of Chicago Magazine* 37 (1945): 9.

16. See Linda Ben-Zvi, *Susan Glaspell: Her Life and Times* (New York: Oxford University Press, 2005), 54.

17. See Claudia J. Keenan, "Introducing Murray Schloss," Wednesday, May 4, 2016 on *Through the Hourglass. Evoking American History: New Stories about Other Times,* http://www.throughthehourglass.com/.

18. Ibid., Wednesday, March 2 and Thursday, March 10, 2016 "Edmond, Oscar, Laura." Laura filed for divorce in 1904, took their young son, and left for France, where she remarried, had a passionate affair with Anatole France, and when he ended it, took her own life. See also Elizabeth Watkins Jorgensen and Henry Irvin Jorgensen, *Thorstein Veblen: Victorian Firebrand* (Armonk, NY: M.E. Sharpe, 1999), 80–83. Veblen and Triggs were friends, though Veblen was skeptical of arts and crafts. Veblen's estranged wife accused him of an affair with Laura, which Veblen denied.

19. Keenan, "Edmond, Oscar, Laura," *Through the Hourglass.* See also *San Francisco Call,* vol. 103, no. 133, April 11, 1908, "Triggs of Free Love Fame Is Again Married." https://cdnc.ucr.edu/cgi-bin/cdnc?a=d&d=SFC19080411.2.9.

20. "Praise for the Profs No. 5," *Daily Maroon,* November 21, 1902. Triggs sued one especially egregious New York paper for libel, but lost on appeal. For some of the offending sarcasms, see Edwin A. Bedell, *Reports of Cases Decided in the Court of Appeals for the State of New York,* vol. 179 (Albany: J.B. Lyon, 1905), 144–55; see also "Significance of Professor Triggs's Dismissal," *The Literary Digest* 28 (March 12, 1904): 365–66.

21. Triggs, *Chapters in the History of the Arts and Crafts Movement* (Chicago: Bohemia Guild of the Industrial Art League, 1902), 189. On Triggs's limitations as social theorist, see T. J. Jackson Lears, *No Place of Grace: Antimodernism and the Transformation of American Culture* (Chicago: University of Chicago Press, 1981), 67–92.

22. Triggs, "The Workshop and School," *The Craftsman* 3.1 (October 1902): 21.

23. Ibid., 25–26.

24. Ibid.

25. Triggs dedicated his 1902 book on Morris and Arts and Crafts to her, though Chicago society regarded her as a nouveau riche publicity seeker. See *Chicago Tribune,* March 16, 1902, 60. http://archives.chicagotribune.com/1902/03/16/page/60/.

26. See *Chicago Tribune,* February 14, 1912, 1, http://archives.chicagotribune.com/1912/02/14/page/1.

27. On Sercombe, see Keenan, "The Uncompromising Parker Sercombe," *Through the Hourglass,* Wednesday, April 6, 2017, http://www.throughthehourglass.com/.

28. Reporters were quick to seize on the fact that free love was certainly espoused by Sercombe. A witness at the trial accused Triggs directly of improper relations with a woman who distributed hygienic devices (birth control) while living at the Spencer-Whitman Center.

BIBLIOGRAPHY

Ben-Zvi, Linda. *Susan Glaspell: Her Life and Times*. New York: Oxford University Press, 2005.

Boos, Florence S. "The First Morris Society: Chicago, 1903–1905." *Journal of the William Morris Society* 21 (2014): 35–48.

Epstein, Bennett. "College without Cheers," *The University of Chicago Magazine* 37 (1945): 9.

Helsinger, Elizabeth. "'A Vestibule of Song': Morris and Burne-Jones in Chicago." *Journal of the William Morris Society* 21 (2014): 49–69.

Hewitt, Mark A. *Gustave Stickley's Craftsman Farms: The Quest for an Arts and Crafts Utopia*. Syracuse University Press, 2001.

Jorgensen, Elizabeth Watkins and Henry Irvin Jorgensen. *Thorstein Veblen: Victorian Firebrand*. Armonk, NY: M.E. Sharpe, 1999.

Kahler, Bruce. "Arts and Life: The Arts and Crafts Movement in Chicago, 1897–1910." PhD dissertation, Purdue University, 1986.

Keenan, Claudia J. "Through the Hourglass. Evoking American History: New Stories about Other Times." http://www.throughthehourglass.com/.

Lawall, Sarah. "Richard Moulton and the 'Perspective Attitude' in World Literature," *Routledge Companion to World Literature*, edited by Theo D'haen, David Damrosch, and Djelal Kadir, ch. 6. London: Routledge, 2012. Accessed online through Credo, University of Chicago, July 2, 2017.

Lears, T.J. Jackson. *No Place of Grace: Antimodernism and the Transformation of American Culture*. Chicago: University of Chicago Press, 1981.

Moulton, Richard Green. "University Extension and the University of the Future." Education, History, and Politics 3–4. *The Johns Hopkins University Studies in Historical and Political Science* 9 (1891): 1–14.

———. *The Poetry and Fiction of William Morris*. Chicago: University of Chicago Press, 1904. https://babel.hathitrust.org/cgi/pt?id=chi.43619134;view=1up;seq=7l.

———. *World Literature and Its Place in General Culture*. New York: Macmillan, 1921.

Sandburg, Margaret. *The Poet and the Dream Girl: The Love Letters of Lilian Steichen and Carl Sandburg*. Urbana: University of Illinois Press, 1987.

Triggs, Oscar Lovell. "On the Study and Teaching of Literature." University of Chicago Record 1.23 (September 4, 1896):337–39 and 1.24 (September 11, 1896): 345–46.

———. "Nineteenth-Century Literary Movements." Student notes for Spring 1894 course, University of Chicago Special Collections, Edward Kirby Putnam papers, Box 1, Folder 2.

———. "The Socialistic Thread in the Life and Works of William Morris," *Poet Lore* 5, 1893: 113–22, 210–18.

———. Some Chapters in the History of Arts and Crafts. Chicago: The Bohemia Guild of the Industrial Art League, 1902.

———. "The Workshop and School," "The New Industrialism," "A School of Industrial Art," *The Craftsman* 3, 1902–1903: 20–32, 93–106, 215–24.

———. "Walt Whitman," *Poet Lore* 5, 1893: 289–305.

———. "William Morris," *To-Morrow: A Magazine for Rational Thinkers/A Monthly Handbook of the Changing Order*, 1905: 19–20.

Wright, Frank Lloyd. "The Art and Craft of the Machine." *Brush and Pencil* 8.2 (May 1901): 77–1, 83–85, 87–90.

Chapter Two

Naturalizing the Dignity of Labor

The Hull-House Labor Museum and William Morris's Influence on the American Settlement House Movement

Elizabeth Grennan Browning

In 1892, seven-year-old Polish immigrant Hilda Satt was distraught on her first morning in Chicago's southwest side, where she failed to find even a hint of nature in what appeared to be a vast, filthy cityscape. She could not help but reminisce about her view of the Vistula River from her home in Poland. Understanding his daughter's shock at being uprooted, Louis Satt assured Hilda that Chicago had such a massive lake that the Vistula would seem but "a dishpan full of water." Yet consumed with the difficulties of helping to support her family, it was not until 1900—eight years later—that she made what was merely a two-mile trip from her home in Chicago's Nineteenth Ward to see Lake Michigan. Fired from her knitting factory job after she had attended a union meeting, Satt sought out the lake's tranquil waters in a moment of desperation. Her long-awaited first glimpse was revelatory. She claimed that the lake's natural beauty inspired her to "rebel against a life that offered only food and warmth and shelter."[1] Like other immigrants who faced the difficult process of creating a new home, the Satts used the natural landscape to establish a sense of place to which they could anchor their identities.[2] Despite the lake's pollution along the Chicago shoreline, its immensity gave it the veneer of pure nature by pointing toward the pristine shores of the city's hinterlands. Although Satt did not have convenient access to this remaining vestige of untrammeled nature in the city, she soon discovered that just three blocks away from her home, along Halsted Street's cramped stretch of tenements, was a reform community that tried to reenergize the immigrant masses in the same way that Satt's glimpse of Lake Michigan had proved revitalizing. Hull-House—America's most prominent social settlement, co-founded by Jane Addams and Ellen Gates Starr in 1889—attempted to fill the moral and aesthetic void left by city dwellers' alienation from nature.

Inspired by William Morris and John Ruskin, originators of the Arts and Crafts movement, Addams and Starr sought to reinvigorate industrial workers' lives with meaning. It was a visit to the first university settlement house—Toynbee Hall, founded in 1884 by Samuel and Henrietta Barnett in East London's slums—that galvanized Addams to establish one of America's first settlements.[3] The settlement house movement's mission was to bridge the divide between the rich and poor, with upper- and middle-class volunteers living in the settlement house and serving the needs of the neighborhood's working class and impoverished communities. Settlements provided basic services, such as health clinics, kindergartens, and English classes, as well as cultural programming, including concerts, social clubs, and lectures on literature, history, and art.

Drawing on environmental and cultural history, this essay examines how the teachings of William Morris and John Ruskin inspired Hull-House reformers to reenvision labor and nature in order to diagnose and treat the social ills of the modern city. During the Progressive Era, Hull-House residents brought nature to urban tenement dwellers in multiple ways—from literature and art classes that incorporated traditional concepts of wild and pastoral environments, to youth summer camps in the countryside. But the initiative that most vividly addressed industrial workers' alienation from the natural world was the Hull-House Labor Museum. Created by Addams in 1900, the Arts-and-Crafts-inspired museum projected a nostalgic and romantic understanding of the relationship between workers of the past and untamed nature. Intended as a kind of occupational therapy for immigrant industrial workers, the museum's exhibits highlighted traditional and non-industrialized labor skills. The aim was to induce in workers a moral renewal and a return to nature through studying didactic exhibits that revealed workers' continued ties with nature beyond the city's borders.

Immigration, industrialization, and urbanization made turn-of-the-century Chicago into a sociological-environmental laboratory, where new combinations of people and nature provided fertile ground for Hull-House residents to rethink the links between human health and nature. Acting as a kind of cultural missionary servicing the immigrant population on the urban frontier, Hull-House residents advocated social justice reforms that reimagined the urban environment in response to debates over the workplace and its hazards.[4] While Chicago's industrial capitalists relied on the city's surrounding hinterlands for resources like lumber, metal, meat, and grain, marginalized workers responsible for transforming these natural materials into commodities were exposed to unprecedented, often crippling, and even lethal environmental health risks.[5] In unregulated workplaces, workers created a newly hazardous kind of nature. Upon entering commodity chains of production, materials that had originally represented healthful hinterland nature became threats to workers' health. For example, in copper foundries, workers' transformation of mined copper ore, originally from Lake Superior's picturesque shores, produced a fine dust that irritated their eyes and respiratory systems. So too did industrial Chicago's high-density cityscape—a byproduct of the capitalist-industrial system—create environmental health risks, as microbes and toxins transgressed geographical borders between disadvantaged tenements and wealthy neighborhoods, commercial borders between producer and consumer, and gendered borders between domestic and public spaces. Hull-House residents aspired to separate workers and the larger public from environmental hazards, and inscribe healthy boundaries between humans and "nature" in the city.[6]

Like other progressive reformers influenced by romanticism, Jane Addams expressed concern about the moral and aesthetic void created by the lack of nature in urban residents' daily lives. Trapped within a polluted city environment, tenement residents had seemingly become resigned to their plight due to their lack of the spiritually revitalizing influence of ideal nature. To address this deficiency during Hull-House's early years, Addams drew on all she knew as a young university graduate and refined world-traveler.[7] She believed that the best way to uplift the urban poor was through high-culture romantic representations of nature, largely in the form of literature courses and fine art exhibitions. Yet Addams later concluded that high art alone was not a practical medium of reform because the desperately poor had no direct use for it in their daily lives. She found the Arts and Crafts movement's aesthetic more effective for her audience. To understand the Labor Museum, however, it is important first to trace its roots in Hull-House's early fine arts focus. While the museum's material representations of nature contrasted with the fine arts program's abstraction, they both adhered to the progressive wilderness narrative of nature existing solely beyond the borders of the city. Hull-House's transition from high-culture romanticism to an Arts and Crafts aesthetics was largely due to Addams's and her colleagues' evolving reform strategy as the settlement residents became more attuned to the quotidian realities of their working class and poor neighbors' lives.[8]

Although the high-culture romanticism from Hull-House's early years ultimately gave way to the Arts-and-Crafts aesthetic, it provided an important foundation for the settlement's work. Hull-House co-founder and arts-programming leader Ellen Gates Starr drew her inspiration for Hull-House arts-appreciation from Ruskin and Morris. From their teachings, Starr learned that ethics, aesthetics, and environment were never separate. In his essay "The Nature of Gothic" (1853), Ruskin posited that authentic art required the inspiration of a beautiful environment.[9] Morris built upon

Ruskin's critique of capitalism's degradation of nature, but secularized it and directed moral aesthetics toward socialist ends.[10] Starr embraced the main tenet shared by Ruskin and Morris: that only free labor existing in a naturally beautiful environment could produce true art. Starr wrote, "Into the prison-houses of earth, its sweat-shops and underground lodging-houses, art cannot follow.... If in all the environment of a man's life, there is nothing which can inspire a true work of art, there is nothing to inspire a true love of it, could it be produced."[11] For Starr, the physical environment was crucial to facilitating the most advanced form of civilization. This pinnacle of cultural evolution only became manifest through a society's capacity to capture nature's magnificence in fine art. Morris had hoped to foster public demand for fine craftsmanship, even within a capitalist society, with his famous golden rule: "Have nothing in your houses that you do not know to be useful, or believe to be beautiful."[12]

If Hull-House itself had been consciously designed so that each fixture and decoration would refine the cultural tastes of immigrant visitors, the Butler Art Gallery, established at Hull-House in 1891, represented this aesthetic-instructive purpose writ large. Starr and Addams sought to inspire an appreciation for the beauty of fine art so as to "improve" what they believed to be a coarse and uneducated immigrant population.[13] Besides its Art Institute-worthy exhibitions, the gallery offered a library of framed reproductions available for home display. This program mirrored Starr's Chicago Public School Art Society, which she founded in 1894 to loan artwork for classroom display. Concerned about tenement children's lack of "daily association with nature and beautiful buildings," Starr's school initiative recognized fine artwork as not replacing such experiences, but rather "creating an image of them in the mind."[14]

While this fine arts curriculum dominated the early years of Hull-House programming, Addams and Starr later discovered that the Arts and Crafts aesthetic proved more powerful for their working-class communities.[15] Addams noted the dehumanizing effects of the machine on the industrial worker: "What happens to a man when he finds himself detached from his country experiences and permanently settled in a modern city? In the country he tilled his fields, harvested his crops and fed his children with the proceeds, a perfectly simple and direct process between cause and effect, between the discharge of energy and its reward."[16] Addams argued that the factory system prevented workers from maintaining control over the fruits of their own labor. Thus, in order for workers to reclaim their dignity, it was necessary to redefine work in terms of the moral authority of the craftsperson over the capitalist factory owner. Addams viewed Morris's and Ruskin's work as integral to the settlement's project: "Ruskin has said that labor without art brutalizes.

The man who labors without knowing why he does it, without any refreshment or solace from his labor, grows more or less dehumanized."[17]

At the vanguard of this effort to promote the dignity of labor in the city was the Chicago Society of Arts and Crafts, founded at Hull-House by Frank Lloyd Wright and other artists and reformers in 1897. The Society identified "the craftsman ideal" as its inspiration for the morally regenerative force that reunited art, labor, and nature. The Society asserted its mission as cultivating "a just sense of beauty" and directing laborers toward instilling in produced goods "the highest beauty through a vital harmony with the conditions of production."[18] Such harmony stemmed from challenging the factory system's segmentation and regimentation of labor by granting workers complete control over the production process. Society members believed that laborers would only achieve personal fulfillment by learning about commodities' origins, thus maintaining some connection with nature beyond the confines of the city. Chicago offers a unique view on how the American manifestation of the Arts and Crafts movement sharply diverged from the anti-technology foundations of Morris and Ruskin. Many Chicago Arts and Crafts advocates embraced the machine in the creation of art that the working classes could afford. Hull-House sat at the crossroads of this issue by serving as a platform for the leading artists, labor advocates, and sociologists of the day. In first delivering his influential, pro-technology paper "The Art and Craft of the Machine" at Hull-House in 1901, Frank Lloyd Wright affirmed the settlement house's pivotal role in this cultural debate. In his address, Wright directly stated his view of Morris's legacy: "That [Morris] miscalculated the machine does not matter. He did sublime work for it when he pleaded so well for the process of elimination its abuse had made necessary; when he fought the innate vulgarity of theocratic impulse in art as opposed to democratic; and when he preached the gospel of simplicity."[19] In Wright's telling, if Morris had been against the machine, his plea for simplicity was a nod in its favor. Wright believed that the machine could nurture creativity among artists by liberating them from the drudgery of labor and by facilitating novel artistic production beyond the reproduction of past designs.

Opened in the Butler Building in November 1900, the Labor Museum built upon Hull-House's efforts to create meaningful arts programming for the working classes by engaging issues closely related to laborers' daily lives.[20] The museum erased divisions between high and low art and recognized immigrant laborers' cultural authority regarding their own ethnic labor traditions.[21] In this way, the museum imbued nature with nostalgic associations of pre-industrial Arcadian simplicity. Its four original departments—metal, wood, grain, and textile—comprised an international collection of labor tools and materials, as well as pedagogical charts, maps, and exhibits. A workshop for artisan production throughout the week, the museum was at its busiest on Saturday evenings when it hosted live demonstrations by immigrant performers in traditional costumes.

The museum's interconnected founding principles, as articulated by Jane Addams, were threefold: first, bridging the widening generational gap between older immigrants and their more culturally assimilated children and grandchildren; second, alleviating immigrant factory workers' social isolation by making them aware of their connections with other ethnicities through a broad historical context of their work; and third, providing occupational therapy to older immigrants by offering them the opportunity to reconnect with their cultural traditions and remember the landscapes of their homelands. Addams first imagined the museum one spring afternoon when she walked past an Italian woman spinning thread with a "simple stick spindle." Describing the woman as looking quite homesick, Addams claimed that "it seemed so difficult to come into genuine relations with the Italian women and . . . they themselves so often lost their hold upon their Americanized children."[22] Addams argued that misunderstandings between immigrants and their children, as well as between immigrants and their American neighbors, arose because individuals did not have "the power to see life as a whole."[23] Addams invoked pragmatist philosophy to explain her museum's pedagogy and reveal people's interconnections through industrial history. Pragmatists like John Dewey claimed that the philosophical "truth" of an idea was best determined by testing it in the real world. Addams believed that teaching young workers about industrial history would foster a new appreciation for their work, and stronger intergenerational ties.[24]

Most visitors to the Labor Museum were well-versed in the labor movement's agenda, but labor activism was only a subtle undertone in the museum's mission. Residents Florence Kelley, Sophonisba Breckinridge, Ellen Gates Starr, and Alzina Stevens were among those active in labor unions, including the Knights of Labor and the Women's Trade Union League. However, Jane Addams walked a fine line between her elite philanthropic supporters and the Nineteenth Ward's working classes and poor. Addams recalled that prior to the most famous American labor conflict in the late nineteenth century, the Pullman Strike of 1894, Hull-House was known as "a kindly philanthropic undertaking," but after the strike the settlement came under attack for its pro-labor sympathies and "lost many friends."[25] One resident claimed that after the strike upper-class people denigrated Addams as a "traitor to her class."[26] At the same time, workers and labor activists were frustrated that Addams did not speak more emphatically on behalf of their cause. Addams did her best to remain unencumbered by alliances to both labor and capital. Her position was decidedly apolitical, and this was on account of her deeper philosophical beliefs. In deliberating the significance of the strike, Addams moved away from her previous perspective of moral absolutism—the notion that a single, moral path existed. Instead, she pursued the idea of a moral democracy grounded in empathy and a sense of "universal kinship." Addams was optimistic that "no factory child in Chicago can be overworked and underpaid without a protest from all good citizens, capitalist and proletarian."[27] She did not directly call for a betterment of workers' conditions, but rather advocated a greater sympathy among the social classes.[28] At the same time, she invoked the teachings of Ruskin and Morris to advocate for child labor legislation, claiming that protecting youth from labor exploitation was a matter of "industrial efficiency" that would advance the "power of contemporary industrialism." Americans were obliged to safeguard children from industrial labor and secure their education, Addams asserted, "not only that they may secure the training and fibre which will later make that participation [in industrial capitalism] effective, but that their minds may finally take possession of the machines which they will guide and feed."[29]

Figure 2.1. "Jane Addams, sitting next to a spinning wheel and loom, at an exhibition in Chicago," 1927, DN-0084134, Chicago Daily News negatives collection.
Reproduced courtesy of the Chicago History Museum.

Taking precedence in the museum's design was the Arts and Crafts focus on recovering labor's connections with nature. In her memoir, textile worker Hilda Satt claimed, "The [textile exhibit] case on wool fairly made my eyes pop out of my head. I had seen sheep many times, but it never occurred to me that wool came from sheep."[30] Having emigrated from rural Poland to urban Chicago as a young girl, Satt retained some memory of the countryside, but she had largely forgotten the natural origins of commodities that she both produced and consumed on a daily basis. Noting her surprise in discovering that cotton grew out of the ground, she stated, "I had never thought just how the cotton cloth that I worked with every day was made. . . . First, here was the plant; then the various steps of getting the plant ready for spinning into thread."[31] In describing the silk exhibit's inclusion of silkworm cocoons, Hilda enjoyed the opportunity to study the natural sources of textiles associated with other cultures.

Indeed, the museum curators intended this dual local and cosmopolitan focus. They encouraged workers to anchor their identities to both Chicago's tangible immediacy and ancient civilizations' distant landscapes. Addams described the museum's mission as presenting "human progress as developed [through] the laborer's efforts," and she connected the exhibits "as closely as possible with the growth and history of Chicago."[32] Addams traced the sources of Chicago's industries to its hinterlands, associating metals with Lake Superior's copper, wood with Wisconsin's and Michigan's lumber, and grain with Illinois's and Indiana's wheat and corn. Expanding workers' geographical consciousness beyond the Midwest, Addams outlined the long evolution of industry to imply its importance to civilization's development, and thus to inspire workers to recognize their civic importance.

The textile exhibit highlighted the evolutionary tone underlying the museum's anthropological focus. An implicit prejudicial message undergirded many of the exhibits: if some nations continued with "primitive" forms of manufacturing, they had clearly fallen off the inexorable march toward progress, with the modern factory tools in America representing the teleological endpoint of such advancement. In weaving, displays included five "processes from the earliest Indian method to the power loom . . . [powered] by electric dynamo."[33] Addams explained the evolutionary advancement of the craft as imbricated in the museum design: "Even the casual visitor was able to see that there is no break in the orderly evolution from the spinning of the Navajo woman with her one disc stick, trailing on the ground like a top, to the most complicated machine. . . . [H]istory looked at from the industrial standpoint at once becomes cosmopolitan, and the differences of race and nationality inevitably fall away."[34] Intending to encourage social cohesion by revealing different ethnicities' shared industrial histories, Addams in fact situated them along a hierarchical spectrum from primitive to advanced. Like other progressive social theorists, Addams embraced stage theory as a way to overcome racial tensions. Popular among American intellectuals after the Civil War, social evolution theories became a tool for affirming the capacity of all people to adapt to modern society.[35] However, in retrospect, Addams's use of stage theory in the Labor Museum exhibits reflected the space's underlying project of inculcating visitors with the idea of Anglo-American racial supremacy.

This evolutionary perspective appeared throughout the larger museum design as each department occupied a separate room that flowed according to the perceived historical sequence of industry, from primitive basics to civilized refinery. First came grains, then textiles, wood and metals, and finally, Ellen Gates Starr's bookbindery. Printing and bookbinding occupied the terminal point of the museum since the curators recognized that "the need of books came into man's life later than the necessity for means of feeding, clothing and housing himself."[36] The evolutionary aesthetic similarly drove the individual departments to their contemporary manifestations. For example, the grains exhibit led to the public kitchen where cooking classes highlighted new experimental dietary practices. The department of wood ended in the Hull-House Guild room where skilled artisans marketed their carpentry and woodcarving.

In addition to ordering ethnic artisans and the museum's space according to a cultural-evolutionary logic, the museum conveyed the course of industrial evolution through photographs, charts, maps, models, and artifacts. These explanatory devices underscored connections among labor practices, environmental conditions, and anthropological studies. A society's labor practices clearly shaped the lived environment, according to these exhibits, but the physical environment was an equally key determinant of culture. In 1902 the museum expanded its anthropological narrative of industrial history by adding much of the Field Columbian Museum's textile department. As Addams incorporated artifacts of indigenous craftsmanship from around the world, she reflected her adherence to the pragmatic philosophical tradition by inviting viewers to study and participate in this foreign artistry as a way to bridge cultural divides.[37] Addams invited visitors to compare the Field Museum textiles' artisanship with samples of modern cloth donated by a department store, and challenged Hull-House visitors to instill in "the machine product more of the beauty of the hand work which was of necessity limited in quantity."[38] Tension between respect for "primitive," nature-conscious labor forms and the advancements of modernized technology made for a complicated museum aesthetic for both the museum's visitors and curators. At the same time that Addams valorized primitive labor practices' closeness to nature, she was cautious not to reject the utility of mechanized industry in freeing people for more leisure and education. Although Addams avoided alienating her wealthy benefactors, the pro-labor sentiment held by many Hull-House residents was subtly woven into the Labor Museum's mission.

Further complexities in the Labor Museum's aesthetics emerged when settlement house residents attempted to make sense of the space's political undertones with respect to the settlement movement's cultural assimilation imperatives. In the confines of the museum, residents possessed the power to define Americanness. Museum curator Mary Hill, for example, approached Hilda Satt after she perused the exhibition to inquire whether she would "like to learn to weave something that was typically American."[39] Satt proceeded to follow Hill's instruction on the intricacies of Navajo weaving. That American Indian craftsmanship represented authentic American art to the Hull-House residents revealed the residents' nostalgic association of Indians with the "strenuous life" of the frontier and an idealization of wilderness. However, the residents viewed the true American ideal as the midpoint between this vital wildness on the one hand, and refined culture on the other. Too much wildness made for a barbarian society, and too much civilization led to the weakening of the human race. In working with immigrant populations, settlement residents endeavored to "better" them (although residents did not usually expound upon their racial assumptions outlined here), and the benchmark for socioeconomic and cultural improvement was "Americanization," a process that aspired to the backgrounds of the residents themselves: old-stock Anglo-American, the very definition of "whiteness" at the turn of the century.[40] Part of what residents hoped immigrants would achieve in assimilating to American culture was absorbing and experiencing a kind of nostalgia that celebrated the hardy resourcefulness of American settlers, and the civilizing forces of democratic institutions. But this was a two-way process. Anglo-American civilization was not the only desired assimilation target for Hull-House residents. They also prioritized revitalizing what they saw as America's declining white race by infusing it with the "barbarian virtues" of indigenous and immigrant peoples.

The museum's foundational mission centered on uplifting the marginalized worker who lacked access to nature, which Addams considered the ultimate repository for American democratic principles and morals. A common refrain among American reformers in the late nineteenth century was anxiety over the declared closing of the frontier in 1890 by the U.S. Census Bureau. To many Americans, the end of the frontier signaled a loss of America's democratic and racial proving ground. Historian Frederick Jackson Turner famously argued that the unique spirit of American democracy and individual hardiness was constantly born anew on the frontier, where Americans waged a conquest against "savage" people and landscapes to transform the land into agricultural abundance and civil democratic society. Without this challenge of "taming the wilderness," Americans would lose their core democratic values, according to Turner.[41] Addams reflected the popular concern over the "closing of the frontier" in the Labor Museum through her attempt to keep the frontier alive by reminding workers of their continued interaction with the natural material of the frontier.

By drawing on the Arts and Crafts movement to instill in workers an appreciation of their own labor as the creative engine of civilization, Addams sought to consolidate their identities as valued citizens and encourage them to take their rightful place in civic affairs. "A man often cannot understand the machine with which he works," Addams argued, "because there is no soil out of which such an understanding may grow, and the natural connection of the workshop with culture is entirely lost for him."[42] Workers failed to understand their importance to American society because they had no way to connect their daily lives with the larger national narrative of virtuous citizenship. More than anything, the Labor Museum reflected Addams's desire to use ideas of social evolution to spur laborers to assimilate to cultural norms of Anglo-American whiteness, and to appreciate their centrality in a properly functioning modern American democracy and industrial economy.

NOTES

1. Hilda Satt Polacheck, *I Came a Stranger: The Story of a Hull-House Girl*, ed. Dena J. Polacheck Epstein (Urbana: University of Illinois Press, 1989), 29, 60.

2. Many immigrants noted landscape features that reminded them of their homeland. See Colin Fisher, *Urban Green: Nature, Recreation, and the Working Class in Industrial Chicago* (Chapel Hill: University of North Carolina Press, 2015), 147.

3. Allen F. Davis, *Spearheads for Reform: The Social Settlements and the Progressive Movement* (New York: Oxford University Press, 1957), 5–7, 23, 47.

4. Environmental historians have looked to labor history and the history of capitalism as an important lens through which to examine the intermingling of humans and nonhuman nature. See Thomas G. Andrews, *Killing for Coal: America's Deadliest Labor War* (Cambridge: Harvard University Press, 2008); Richard White, *The Organic Machine: The Remaking of the Columbia River* (New York: Hill and Wang, 1995); Richard White, "Work and Nature," in *Uncommon Ground: Rethinking the Human Place in Nature*, ed. William Cronon (New York: W.W. Norton, 1995), 171–85.

5. For Chicago's relationship between its urban market and hinterland natural systems in the nineteenth century, see William Cronon, *Nature's Metropolis: Chicago and the Great West* (New York: W.W. Norton, 1991).

6. Environmental historians and scholars of the environmental humanities have long critiqued the idea of nature as monolithic, recognizing that humans are part of nature (see William Cronon, "The Trouble with Wilderness; or, Getting Back to the

Wrong Nature," in *Uncommon Ground: Rethinking the Human Place in Nature*, ed. William Cronon (New York: W.W. Norton, 1995), 69–90. Jane Addams and her contemporaries would have been hard-pressed to identify traditional forms of "nature" within the city, outside of urban parks and playgrounds. Even though Hull-House residents did not recognize it at the time, the messier definition of "nature"—that is, one encompassing toxins and microbes that we recognize today—was a key focus of their reform efforts. See Alice Hamilton, *Exploring the Dangerous Trades: The Autobiography of Alice Hamilton, M.D.* (Boston: Little, Brown and Company, 1943).

7. For differences between the settlement house movement and the charity organization movement, see Davis, *Spearheads for Reform*; Helen Lefkowitz Horowitz, *Culture and the City: Cultural Philanthropy in Chicago from the 1880s to 1917* (Chicago: University of Chicago Press, 1989); Kathleen D. McCarthy, *Noblesse Oblige: Charity & Cultural Philanthropy in Chicago, 1849–1929* (Chicago: University of Chicago Press, 1982); Judith Ann Trolander, *Professionalism and Social Change from the Settlement House Movement to Neighborhood Centers, 1886 to the Present* (New York: Columbia University Press, 1987).

8. "Arts and Crafts and the Settlement," *Chautauqua Assembly Herald* 27 (July 9 1902): 2–3; Jane Addams, "To Aid Craftsmen," *Los Angeles Times* (August 15, 1902), 11.

9. Eileen Boris, *Art and Labor: Ruskin, Morris, and the Craftsman Ideal in America* (Philadelphia: Temple University Press, 1986), 4.

10. E. P. Thompson, *William Morris: Romantic to Revolutionary* (New York: Pantheon, 1977).

11. Ellen Gates Starr, "Art and Labor," in *Hull-House Maps and Papers: A Presentation of Nationalities and Wages in a Congested District of Chicago, Together with Comments and Essays on Problems Growing Out of the Social Conditions*, ed. Jane Addams (1895; repr., Urbana: University of Illinois Press, 2007), 135.

12. William Morris, "The Beauty of Life," in *Hopes & Fears for Art. Five Lectures by William Morris* (London: Longmans, Green, and Co., 1911), 108.

13. Shannon Jackson, *Lines of Activity: Performance, Historiography, Hull-House Domesticity* (Ann Arbor: University of Michigan Press, 2000), 99.

14. Ellen Gates Starr, Hull-House circular describing art loan program, October 29, 1892, University of Illinois at Chicago Hull-House Collection (hereafter UIC HHC), Folder 507.

15. For the Arts & Crafts Movement in Chicago, see Judith A. Barter, ed., *Apostles of Beauty: Arts and Crafts from Britain to Chicago* (Chicago and New Haven: Art Institute of Chicago and Yale University, 2009); Bruce Robert Kahler, "Art and Life: The Arts and Crafts Movement in Chicago, 1897–1910" (PhD diss., Purdue University, 1986).

16. Jane Addams, "Public Recreation and Social Morality," *Charities and the Commons* 18 (August 3, 1907): 492–93.

17. "Arts and Crafts and the Settlement," 2.

18. Hull-House Bulletin, December 1, 1897, 9, UIC HHC, Folder 427.

19. An address by Frank Lloyd Wright to the Chicago Arts and Crafts Society, at Hull-House, March 6, 1901. See Frank Lloyd Wright, "The Art and Craft of the Machine," *Brush and Pencil* 8, no. 2 (May 1901): 77.

20. Davis, *Spearheads for Reform*, 43, 47–48.

21. For visual and material culture studies' relevance to this analysis, see Patricia Johnston, *Seeing High and Low: Representing Social Conflict in American Visual Culture* (Berkeley: University of California Press, 2006); Jackson Lears, *No Place of Grace: Antimodernism and the Transformation of American Culture, 1880–1920* (Chicago: University of Chicago Press, 1994); Lawrence W. Levine, *Highbrow/Lowbrow: The Emergence of Cultural Hierarchy in America* (Cambridge: Harvard University Press, 1988).

22. Jane Addams, "Immigrants and Their Children," in *Twenty Years at Hull-House* (1910; Reprint, New York: Signet, 1961), 156.

23. Jane Addams, "Some Early Undertakings at Hull-House," in *Twenty Years at Hull-House* (1910; Reprint, New York: Signet, 1961). See also Jane Addams, "Hull House and its Neighbors," *Charities and the Commons* (May 7, 1904), 450–51.

24. Jane Addams, "The Hull-House Labor Museum," in *The Child in the City: A Series of Papers Presented at the Conferences Held During the Chicago Child Welfare Exhibit* (Chicago: Chicago School of Civics and Philanthropy, Department of Social Investigation, 1912), 410–14; Jane Addams, "The Humanizing Tendency of Industrial Education," *The Chautauquan*, 39 (May 1904): 266–72. See also Christopher Lasch, *The Social Thought of Jane Addams* (Indianapolis, IN: Bobbs-Merrill, 1965), 184. For Chicago pragmatism, see Andrew Feffer, *The Chicago Pragmatists and American Progressivism* (Ithaca: Cornell University Press, 1993).

25. Addams, "Some Early Undertakings at Hull-House," 151. Led by Eugene Debs and the American Railway Union, the Pullman Strike was a nationwide railroad strike that began when industrialist George Pullman lowered the wages of his workers without reducing rents in his company town of Pullman on Chicago's South Side. The strike turned violent after the federal government issued an injunction to end the boycott, and then sent the Army to get the trains running again.

26. Alice Hamilton, "Jane Addams: Gentle Rebel," *Political Affairs*, March 1960, 34.

27. Addams, "The Settlement as a Factor in the Labor Movement," in *Hull-House Maps and Papers*, 147.

28. See Louise W. Knight, *Citizen: Jane Addams and the Struggle for Democracy* (Chicago: University of Chicago Press, 2005), 319.

29. Jane Addams, "Child Labor Legislation: A Requisite for Industrial Efficiency," American Academy of Political and Social Science *Annals*, 25 (May 1905), 543.

30. Polacheck, *I Came a Stranger*, 64.

31. Polacheck, *I Came a Stranger*, 65.

32. Jane Addams, "Social Education of the Industrial Democracy: Settlement Problems in Educational Work with Adults. Labor Museum at Hull House," *The Commons* 47 (June 30, 1900): 3.

33. Hull-House Bulletin Mid-Winter 1903–1904, Vol. 6, No. 1, UIC HHC, Folder 425.

34. "First Report of a Labor Museum at Hull House" in Hull-House Bulletin Vol. 5, No. 1 addendum, 1900–1901, 7, UIC HHC, Folder 515.

35. For example, U.S. Bureau of Ethnology director John Wesley Powell relied on the social evolutionary approach. See Louis S. Warren, *God's Red Son: The Ghost*

Dance Religion and the Making of Modern America (New York: Basic Books, 2017), 325–33.

36. Hull-House Bulletin Semi-Annual 1902, Vol. 5, Nos. 1, 12, UIC HHC, Folder 430.

37. See Charlene Haddock Seigfried, "Cultural Contradictions: Jane Addams's Struggles with the Life of Art and the Art of Life," in Maurice Hamington, ed., *Feminist Interpretations of Jane Addams* (University Park: Pennsylvania State University Press, 2010): 55–80.

38. Hull-House Bulletin Mid-Winter 1903–1904, Vol. 6, No. 1, UIC HHC, Folder 425.

39. Polacheck, *I Came a Stranger*, 64.

40. Jane Addams, "Americanization," *Papers and Proceedings of the Fourteenth Annual Meeting of the American Sociological Society* 14 (1920): 210.

41. Frederick Jackson Turner, "The Significance of the Frontier in American History," *Annual Report of the American Historical Association for the Year 1893* (Washington, DC: Government Printing Office, 1894), 197–228.

42. "First Report of a Labor Museum at Hull House," Folder 515.

BIBLIOGRAPHY

Addams, Jane. "Americanization." *Papers and Proceedings of the Fourteenth Annual Meeting of the American Sociological Society held at Chicago December 29–31, 1919*, Vol. 14, 1920. Chicago: University of Chicago Press, reprint 1971.

———. "Child Labor Legislation: A Requisite for Industrial Efficiency." In American Academy of Political and Social Science *Annals*, 25 (May 1905): 542–550.

———. "Hull House and Its Neighbors." *Charities and the Commons* (May 7, 1904): 450–51.

———. "The Hull-House Labor Museum." In *The Child in the City: A Series of Papers Presented at the Conferences Held during the Chicago Child Welfare Exhibit*, edited by Sophonisba P. Breckinridge, 410–414. Chicago: Chicago School of Civics and Philanthropy, Department of Social Investigation, 1912.

———. "The Humanizing Tendency of Industrial Education." *The Chautauquan* 39 (May 1904): 266–72.

———. "Public Recreation and Social Morality," *Charities and the Commons* 18 (August 3, 1907): 492–494.

———. "The Settlement as a Factor in the Labor Movement." In Jane Addams and Residents of Hull-House. *Hull-House Maps and Papers: A Presentation of Nationalities and Wages in a Congested District of Chicago, Together with Comments and Essays on Problems Growing Out of the Social Conditions*, 138–150. 1895. Reprint, Urbana: University of Illinois Press, 2007.

———. "Social Education of the Industrial Democracy: Settlement Problems in Educational Work with Adults. Labor Museum at Hull House." *The Commons* 47 (June 30, 1900): 1–6.

———. "To Aid Craftsmen." *Los Angeles Times.* August 15, 1902, 11.

———. *Twenty Years at Hull-House*. 1910. Reprint, New York: Signet, 1961.

Andrews, Thomas G. *Killing for Coal: America's Deadliest Labor War*. Cambridge: Harvard University Press, 2008.

"Arts and Crafts and the Settlement." *Chautauqua Assembly Herald* 27 (July 9 1902): 2–3.

Barter, Judith A., ed. *Apostles of Beauty: Arts and Crafts from Britain to Chicago*. Chicago and New Haven: Art Institute of Chicago and Yale University, 2009.

Boris, Eileen. *Art and Labor: Ruskin, Morris, and the Craftsman Ideal in America*. Philadelphia: Temple University Press, 1986.

Cronon, William. *Nature's Metropolis: Chicago and the Great West*. New York: W.W. Norton, 1991.

———. "The Trouble with Wilderness; or, Getting Back to the Wrong Nature." In *Uncommon Ground: Rethinking the Human Place in Nature*, edited by William Cronon, 69–90. New York: W.W. Norton, 1996.

Davis, Allen F. *Spearheads for Reform: The Social Settlements & the Progressive Movement, 1890–1914*. New York: Oxford University Press, 1967.

Feffer, Andrew. *The Chicago Pragmatists and American Progressivism*. Ithaca: Cornell University Press, 1993.

"First Report of a Labor Museum at Hull House" in Hull-House Bulletin Vol. 5, No. 1 addendum, 1900–1901, 7, University of Illinois at Chicago Hull-House Collection, Folder 515.

Fisher, Colin. *Urban Green: Nature, Recreation, and the Working Class in Industrial Chicago*. Chapel Hill: University of North Carolina Press, 2015.

Hamilton, Alice. *Exploring the Dangerous Trades: The Autobiography of Alice Hamilton, M.D.* Boston: Little, Brown and Company, 1943.

———. "Jane Addams: Gentle Rebel." *Political Affairs*, March 1960: 33–35.

Horowitz, Helen Lefkowitz. *Culture and the City: Cultural Philanthropy in Chicago from the 1880s to 1917*. Chicago: University of Chicago Press, 1989.

Hull-House Bulletin, December 1, 1897, Vol. 9, University of Illinois at Chicago Hull-House Collection, Folder 427.

Hull-House Bulletin Semi-Annual 1902, Vol. 5, Nos. 1, 12, University of Illinois at Chicago Hull-House Collection, Folder 430.

Hull-House Bulletin Mid-Winter 1903–1904, Vol. 6, No. 1, University of Illinois at Chicago Hull-House Collection, Folder 425.

Jackson, Shannon Patricia. *Lines of Activity: Performance, Historiography, Hull-House Domesticity*. Ann Arbor: University of Michigan Press, 2000.

Johnston, Patricia, ed. *Seeing High and Low: Representing Social Conflict in American Visual Culture*. Berkeley: University of California Press, 2006.

Kahler, Bruce Robert. "Art and Life: The Arts and Crafts Movement in Chicago, 1897–1910." PhD dissertation, Purdue University, 1986.

Knight, Louise W. *Citizen: Jane Addams and the Struggle for Democracy*. Chicago: University of Chicago Press, 2005.

Lasch, Christopher. *The Social Thought of Jane Addams*. Indianapolis, IN: Bobbs-Merrill Company, 1965.

Lears, Jackson. *No Place of Grace: Antimodernism and the Transformation of American Culture, 1880–1920*. Chicago: University of Chicago Press, 1994.

Levine, Lawrence W. *Highbrow/Lowbrow: The Emergence of Cultural Hierarchy in America*. Cambridge: Harvard University Press, 1988.

McCarthy, Kathleen D. *Noblesse Oblige: Charity & Cultural Philanthropy in Chicago, 1849–1929*. Chicago: University of Chicago Press, 1982.

Morris, William. "The Beauty of Life." In *Hopes & Fears for Art. Five Lectures by William Morris*, 71–113. London: Longmans, Green, and Co., 1911.

Polacheck, Hilda Satt. *I Came a Stranger: The Story of a Hull-House Girl*. Edited by Dena J. Polacheck Epstein. Urbana: University of Illinois Press, 1989.

Seigfried, Charlene Haddock. "Cultural Contradictions: Jane Addams's Struggles with the Life of Art and the Art of Life." In *Feminist Interpretations of Jane Addams*, edited by Maurice Hamington. University Park: Pennsylvania State University Press, 2010: 55–80.

Starr, Ellen Gates. "Art and Labor." Jane Addams and Residents of Hull-House. *Hull-House Maps and Papers: A Presentation of Nationalities and Wages in a Congested District of Chicago, Together with Comments and Essays on Problems Growing Out of the Social Conditions*, 130–137. 1895. Reprint, Urbana: University of Illinois Press, 2007.

———. Hull-House circular describing art loan program. October 29, 1892. University of Illinois at Chicago Hull-House Collection, Folder 507.

Thompson, E.P. *William Morris: Romantic to Revolutionary*. New York: Pantheon Books, 1977.

Trolander, Judith Ann. *Professionalism and Social Change from the Settlement House Movement to Neighborhood Centers, 1886 to the Present*. New York: Columbia University Press, 1987.

Turner, Frederick Jackson. "The Significance of the Frontier in American History." *Annual Report of the American Historical Association for the Year 1893*. Washington, DC: Government Printing Office, 1894: 197–228.

Warren, Louis S. *God's Red Son: The Ghost Dance Religion and the Making of Modern America*. New York: Basic Books, 2017.

White, Richard. "'Are You an Environmentalist or Do You Work for a Living?': Work and Nature." In *Uncommon Ground: Rethinking the Human Place in Nature*, edited by William Cronon, 171–85. New York: W.W. Norton, 1995.

———. *The Organic Machine: The Remaking of the Columbia River*. New York: Hill and Wang, 1995.

Wright, Frank Lloyd, "The Art and Craft of the Machine." *Brush and Pencil*. 8, no. 2 (May 1901): 77–81, 83–85, 87–90.

Chapter Three

Time Travelling with William Morris

John Plotz

A few years ago, I wrote a young-adult novel about William Morris, starring a pair of siblings, their pet bird, and a time-flexible Morris & Co. textile. The book is, to be charitable, goofy: *Phoenix and the Carpet* meets *News from Nowhere*. Thanks to its publisher's perfectly timed bankruptcy, it is also basically lost to history. As is often the case with first tries, I think I learned more from what went wrong than what went right.

I cannot sum up the pedagogical implications of that novel-writing year in a few words, but I do know it changed my classroom practice profoundly. First of all, the artisanal side of writing struck me forcefully. My original elevator pitch for *Time and the Tapestry* stressed Morris's manic enthusiasm and his hands-on ingenuity: "ADHD meets Etsy." Every chapter showcased, subtly or blatantly, another art or craft that Morris had taught himself: wallpaper, furniture, poetry, book design. Researching Morris as the invisible patron saint of the crafts revival opened my eyes wide to what his modern-day descendants have wrought. The weeks I spent taking typesetting classes (Oh, that poor printing press!) gave me an immense respect for the craftiness of craftwork—and made me realize just how terrible a teenage pottery counselor I had been, back at Camp Kabeyun. My various artisanal apprenticeships also opened my eyes to the crafty side of contemporary teenage experiments with Minecraft and other sorts of virtual world-building. It is easy to overlook the elements of material mastery, and free-form experimentation, in the computer design projects undertaken by the younger generation.

In addition, trying to channel Morris reassured me that goofiness sometimes pays off. *Time and the Tapestry* was field-tested by reading out bits at bedtime—if I got a giggle or a shriek, I kept that particular storyline alive. The talking blackbird loomed larger and larger in the story; debates between

Figure 3.1. One of Phyllis Saroff's beautiful illustrations for *Time and Tapestry*.
Reproduced courtesy of the illustrator.

Burne-Jones and Morris about Ruskin's legacy, not so much. Overall, the strongest influence on the composition process was probably Morris's optimism about art's power to bring about the future it foretold. Even his late fantasy worlds—impossible, magical, aloof and apart from our own world as they are—inspire new ways of thinking of what's possible with the right kind of effort. Pedagogically speaking, Morris struck me as a forerunner of what at my university is called "experiential learning"—thinking by doing.

Given Morris's hard-won optimism, though, I find myself second-guessing one key choice I made: to structure *Time and the Tapestry* as a wish-fulfillment plunge into the past. In *News from Nowhere,* Guest is constantly agog at bucolic, pacifist, socialist twenty-first century England. *Time and the Tapestry* also looked out of its own time for solace—yet it sent Jen and her kid brother Ed a century backward, landing them alongside Morris at various crises: painting the Oxford Union murals, fighting with Rossetti, visiting Iceland. It is true that Morris's earlier *Dream of John Ball* pinned its hopes on early medieval agrarian solidarity, but by 1890 Morris dared to dream and write himself forward out of the worst excesses of the imperialism and unregulated capitalism of his day. What does it mean that I set my sights backward to a time when such foresight, such utopic projections down the line, still seemed feasible?

When I recently taught *News from Nowhere* in a science fiction class alongside *1984* and various descendant dystopias, it got a decidedly dim reception. I was devastated at the time, but now I wonder if the same hidden drag that worked on *Time and the Tapestry* tugged at my students: a fear that the future's best days are behind it. The 2016 Presidential election took place the week before we turned to Morris, and I had to wonder: what was the point reading about beautiful young folks haying alongside a future Thames, when all you can see is a door into the dark? Dystopias are ascendant: *Hunger Games* is this decade's young-adult blockbuster, Orwell is back on bestseller lists. And when it comes to utopias nowadays, consider the arc that runs from *News from Nowhere* through its admitted successor, Ursula Le Guin's *The Dispossessed* to such implicitly post-*Nowhere* texts as the Kim Stanley Robinson *Red/Green/Blue Mars* trilogy (things get grimier and grimmer at every step—even sex-appeal gets ickier). All of which suggests there may be some downbeat general lessons from my students' recalcitrance and from my own difficulties translating Morris's sunny vision for a shadowy age.

The more I thought about my students' indifference (or was that hostility?) to *News from Nowhere*, the greater my sense of failure. It is true that today's most popular "hard" science fiction sells books by speculating in very tangible and direct ways about what today's inventions will look like in a decade: *Her* and *Oryx and Crake* were notable hits in my class. Introducing Morris into the syllabus, however, was part of my plan to make students think more capaciously about what speculation does in fiction. At least since Mary Shelley's *Frankenstein* (and arguably further back than that—what about Gulliver? Gilgamesh?) speculative fiction has worked by conjuring up distant impossible-seeming worlds that nonetheless offer a hint of present-day actuality beneath, viewed from a different angle. Frankenstein's creature is an imago of actual childhood, the Martians in a Wells invasion story are also, transparently, British imperialists laying waste to Tasmania. So why did Morris's joy in what agrarian socialism might do to upset the present balance of power make my students grumble and scoff? Perhaps for the same reason that my attempt to pay tribute to his inspired futurology succumbed to nostalgia.

EARTHLY PARADISES

However, not every lesson from my Morris-cloning project is quite so grim. The six months I spent trying to pass the dinner-table squeal test (*Ditch Ruskin; add more flying time!*) taught me how reliable, and how inspiring, a guide Morris could be. Morris's notion that "if others can see [the future] as I have seen it, then it may be called a vision rather than a dream" is at the heart of his democratic politics of solidarity, and he reminded me that the hope of making any vision plausible (making it realizable) depends upon gaining a sense of others' dreams. Only genuinely sharable dreams can possibly be translated into visions for futurity. Granted, my students couldn't share Morris's vision in November 2016. Had they come across it at some other moment, though, Morris's notion of how to throw yourself into an artwork without losing sight of your own surroundings might have kindled in them some kind of responsive glow.

While writing *Time and the Tapestry,* I found myself reflecting on all the things that I had learned from Morris himself about inventing dream worlds. The prologue of his early epic poem *The Earthly Paradise* (1868–1870), for example, offers up a telling metaphor for making sense of an artwork's semi-detached relationship to its own day and place:

> Folk say, a wizard to a northern king
> At Christmas-tide such wondrous things did show,
> That through one window men beheld the spring,
> And through another saw the summer glow,
> And through a third the fruited vines a-row,
> While still, unheard, but in its wonted way,
> Piped the drear wind of that December day.
>
> So with this Earthly Paradise it is,
> If ye will read aright, and pardon me,
> Who strive to build a shadowy isle of bliss
> Midmost the beating of the steely sea.[1]

The beating of the steely sea shakes the outside of the king's hall (and, implicitly, shakes the outside of Morris's own poem as well) but the "shadowy isle of bliss" is still visible and palpable within the hall. We can similarly think of Morris himself steering his readers toward some kind of complicated pas-de-deux between their actual world and the tangible, imaginable, almost touchable world within the artwork. The point of teaching Morris has never been to offer up one more fantasy realm (Narnia, meet Nowhere). Rather, the appeal is that Morris himself is well aware of just how shadowy this isle of bliss is.

My experience writing *Time and the Tapestry* gave me hope. And not just hope generally, but specifically tied to Morris's own peculiar charm—his capacity to remind his audiences that the delight of aesthetic experience always arises in part from a sense of connection, even of solidarity with those who were there before you. That feeling was especially strong because at the very same time (Fall 2011) I was also undertaking another strangely similar time-travel experiment. For as long as I can remember, I have wanted to read like the dead. Not just to read dead authors—something a little bit creepier. So when I learned about *What Middletown Read*, a database that tracks the borrowing records of the Muncie, Indiana Public Library between 1891 and 1902, I had some of the same feelings physicists probably have when new subatomic particles show up in their cloud chambers.[2] I wanted to find out what I could about the young readers of Morris's own day, in the hope I could figure out both what had changed and what had stayed the same over more than a century.

The database itself, as a feat of digital engineering, bedazzled me. Could you see how many times a particular book had been taken out? Could you find out when? And by whom? Yes, yes, and yes. We know, for example, that on Wednesday, February 3, 1892, a factory worker's son, Louis Bloom, ascended to the second floor of the Muncie City Building, turned left at the top of the stairs, entered the city library, signed the ledger kept by librarian Kate Wilson, and checked out *The Wonders of Electricity*. He came back the next day to return it and take out *Frank Before Vicksburg*; Friday it was Horatio Alger's *Ragged Dick*; Saturday *The North Pole: And Charlie Wilson's Adventures in Search of It*. Sunday, the library was closed; Monday, February 8, 1892 (his 13th birthday) he took out James Fenimore Cooper's *The Deerslayer*. If library records are usually the night sky of cultural history, a dim backdrop to action elsewhere, Louis's borrowing history is like a supernova.

I could not resist the fantasy of popping back into the past for a brief bibliographic séance—a kind of hermeneutics without suspicion. I gave myself a month to read as far as I could in the 291 books Louis Bloom had checked out over a decade. I would happily gather what external facts I could about Louis, but fundamentally his booklist would be my passport back in time. The experiment's limitations soon became apparent. As an effort to travel back in time, my Bloom month ended in failure. Though I was delighted when a power failure in our neighborhood meant I had to read *Elsie Dinsmore* for hours by a camping lantern, I never felt actually adrift. As I painstakingly checked to make sure that I'd gotten the same edition Louis would have been reading, I was aware of how far my pedantic antiquarianism was from what his own teenage first encounters must have been. Despite weeks of pleasant correspondence with his grandkids, despite time spent with photographs and archival records and letters, Louis Bloom remained by my experiment's end only a shadow, a dimly visible pair of shoulders, a motionless back of the head and protruding ears hovering before Horatio Alger's *Ben the Luggage Boy*, or Henry Mayhew's *The Story of the Peasant-Boy Philosopher*.

Yet some of my experiment's failures ultimately struck me as successes in disguise. The gap between our own era and the past can be bridged, imperfectly, by artworks themselves, to the extent that their aesthetic operations activate modern imaginations. Like me, Louis found a way out of his actuality; caught a glimpse of his own future in the world of mechanics and of physics, far from Muncie. Thanks to those books, he too had a telescope. Like mine, it was small and imperfect, with no guarantees about the accuracy of what he glimpsed through it. To understand what Louis Bloom felt opening up a book in Muncie, I had to grasp not only the space between me and the past I thought I had found, but also the gaps and glitches in his own life, the way that what Louis sought also eluded him, or receded from him as he pursued it. I won't go into detail about what happened when I temporarily took up residence in my daughter's classroom, and asked a half dozen Brookline second graders to read along with a Bloomington kid of the 1890's, one Nelly Perkins. But it was reassuring to know that they too seemed charmed by the idea of walking a few miles in Nelly's shoes; or at least, resting their elbows on the same books hers had rested on.

Still, given my confession about the guilty pleasure of looking backward, it is not surprising that what I took away from the experiment was mainly deep admiration for Morris's insistence on keeping his eyes turned future-ward. Writing *Time and the Tapestry* while trying to read like Louis Bloom taught me something new about the appeal of *News from Nowhere* with its attenuated, far-off vision of a deliberately implausible future. Just as my attachment to Bloom began with my realization that he to was trying (and failing) to break away from his own day and age, so too I never felt closer to Morris's Guest than the moment at which the whole of Nowhere starts to fade away, the moment when his beloved Ellen looks right through him.

What we share with those with whom we share nothing else is at least the sensation that they too knew what it was like to feel cut off, anchored in an actuality that allows no permanent escape to fantastical elsewheres. Knowing what teenagers were reading in the 1890's is a far cry from knowing what they were feeling and thinking. What I take from Morris is the same lesson that I take from trying to write a book about him, after him, and to him. Hearing voices from the past is difficult, but speaking to those who are gone is impossible. Our only addressees lie, as they always have, in the future.

That experience of connection in dislocation may relate to the hardest lesson of all that writing *Time and the Tapestry* taught me: when to stop learning and start forgetting. We are embarrassed by riches when it comes to William Morris—the well-meaning teacher can always be sure of finding a fact or three to fill in the background for any Morris moment. Part of telling a story—even about someone as multivalent and gregariously enthusiastic as Morris, and someone as well documented—is figuring out what to let go. The more details I sought to pack in—Emery Walker's poverty, Morris's socialist congresses—the less I had to say. What I love about the late Morris stories is the gaps and spaces they leave: not pictures but *designs*—life without and beyond us, a world protected from human meddling.

Perhaps the utopian gleam that my students could not see last November will come into clearer view with *The Sundering Flood* in my upcoming Fantasy class with a focus on that openness. And if it doesn't? Too bad. *News from Nowhere* is back on the syllabus for my fall 2019 SF class, germane as ever.

NOTES

1. William Morris, "Prologue," *The Earthly Paradise*, 1870.
2. Frank Felsenstein and James J. Connolly are the architects of the database: http://lib.bsu.edu/wmr/index.php.

I published a brief article in *Slate* discussing my experiment: http://www.slate.com/articles/arts/culturebox/2011/11/the_wondrous_database_that_reveals_what_books_americans_checked_out_of_the_library_a_century_ago_.html.

BIBLIOGRAPHY

Felsenstein, Frank and James J. Connolly, *What Middletown Read*, http://lib.bsu.edu/wmr/index.php.

Morris, William. *The Earthly Paradise*. London: F. S. Ellis, 1870.

Plotz, John. "This Book Is 119 Years Overdue," *Slate*, http://www.slate.com/articles/arts/culturebox/2011/11/the_wondrous_database_that_reveals_what_books_americans_checked_out_of_the_library_a_century_ago_.html.

———. *Time and the Tapestry: A William Morris Adventure*. Boston: Bunker Hill, 2014.

Chapter Four

"Work and Fun" and "Education at Its Finest"

Teaching Morris at Kelmscott House

Helen Elletson

Home of William Morris for the last eighteen years of his life, Kelmscott House is a fine example of Georgian architecture, situated by the River Thames in Hammersmith.[1] Today, it is the headquarters of the William Morris Society and its museum, which offers art, literacy, history, and citizenship sessions for school children based on its collection of original artifacts. In an intimate and friendly environment children can study firsthand such treasures of the Arts and Crafts movement as original Morris & Co. textile designs, wallpaper samples, stained glass, furniture, embroidery, and Pre-Raphaelite drawings, as well as seeing demonstrations of type-setting and printing on Morris's Albion printing press, originally used in the production of the Kelmscott Chaucer. This article is intended to showcase the range of educational opportunities provided for younger students at Kelmscott House. By passing Morris on to the next generation, we hope to keep his ideas and his creations alive for the future.

The majority of children who visit Kelmscott House are from the local area. They generally range from nine to eleven years old and they usually come as part of a lesson on the Victorians (Key Stage 2 History of the UK's national curriculum).[2] Morris is an obvious choice of study due to the variety of subjects with which he can be linked on the National Curriculum, and, because most visiting schools are from Hammersmith and Fulham, the importance of the local connection.

Visits begin with a brief introduction to the life and work of Morris, followed by a tour of the premises. The children then divide into groups to complete activities based on sketching items from the collection, including original designs, wallpaper, textiles, and furniture. They are asked to discuss the differences between the designs and the completed works, examine repeat patterns and give their own views of Morris's work.

The fact that pupils are studying Morris in the house where he lived has quite an impact. There is great satisfaction in seeing how much the children gain from the visits, their enthusiasm and obvious delight in their surroundings. Morris has proved to be an ideal Victorian personality to study and extremely popular with school teachers. The wide range of Morris's activities enables links to be made to the National Curriculum in many places, particularly Key Stages 1 and 2 but also at higher and further education levels. During a visit to the William Morris Society's premises at Kelmscott House, pupils are introduced to the history of Morris's life and work, his family, and his work as designer, environmentalist, writer, and socialist.

SCHOOLS WORKSHOPS FOR KS1 AND KS2

The following workshops are currently available:

1. Stained Glass (Key Stages 1 and 2, Art and Design/History)
    Pupils draw and "illuminate" a letter with specialist pens on acetate using Morris's interest in printing and medieval illuminated manuscripts as a starting point.
2. Textile Design (Key Stages 1 and 2, Art and Design/History)
    After an introduction on the importance of nature to Morris and looking at the construction of repeating designs, the children draw on "silk," inspired by Morris's natural designs. They can choose flowers, fruit, or leaves, focusing on three components only, to explore repeated pattern designing. Inspired by examples of Morris-designed textiles, they also look at wallpaper and fabric patterns, with a focus on repetition, symmetry, colors, and textures. At the end of the session the individual pieces are put together forming a large continuous block.
3. Victorian Object Handling (Key Stages 1 and 2, History)
    Pupils are shown a selection of Victorian objects, including a candle snuffer, carpet beater, candlesticks, embroidery sampler, ink pot, and photographs. They are encouraged to handle the objects carefully and discuss what they are made of and what they might be used for, what the modern equivalent might be (e.g., horseshoe for car tire, or candle for light bulb) with a worksheet as guidance for the session.
4. Storytelling (Key Stages 1 and 2, English)
    The pupils enact an adaptation based on either Morris's Icelandic Saga "Sigurd and the Dragon" or his retelling of the fairy story "Rapunzel," with costume and props.

5. Wallpaper printing (Key Stage 2, Art and Design/Math)

Students are introduced to block printing, a method used to print text, images, or patterns on textiles. Original Morris blocks are shown, the dye still visible in places, and the fact that each color to be printed needs a different carved block is explained and illustrated. Having seen the sample books for William Morris wallpapers, each pupil is able to experiment with blocks, applying paint and producing paper prints. They investigate printmaking techniques, and explore ways of combining and organizing shapes, colors, and patterns to make a decorative wallpaper piece.

The end of the session looks at the Kelmscott Chaucer and the Morris's Albion Printing press. Classes are fascinated by Morris's Albion hand printing press, which always provokes numerous questions. While listening to an account of how the press works, pupils can handle replica type and wood blocks of various illustrations and are shown examples of Kelmscott Press books, including a facsimile of the Kelmscott Chaucer.

Figure 4.1. A young student at Kelmscott House inking her press-print block of a passion flower; the design of which was developed from observation and inspired by William Morris.

Reproduced courtesy of Helen Elletson.

We discuss how Morris was inspired by the works of Chaucer and Icelandic sagas, and how he used the press to print his own books. Wooden letter blocks illustrate the printing process and show why the letter blocks are in reverse. The origin of uppercase and lowercase letters is explained—the type was stored in cases, the one with the capital letters stacked above the other. The whole printing process, from woodblock cutting to inking, is explained. The Albion press can be demonstrated during a class visit, including an explanation of how the blocks and type are held in place, how the paper is anchored, and how the printing mechanism itself works.

6. Citizenship (Key Stage 2, Citizenship/PSHE)

This module provides an analysis of the Morris & Co. workshops and Morris's writings on workers' rights and freedom of speech. Children are encouraged to think about justice, working conditions, and their environment. The program has cross-curricular links to English and history for Key Stages 2 and 3.

These six workshops make creative connections with the following curriculum subjects:

ENGLISH/LITERACY

Morris wrote and spoke widely on art, architecture, history, and politics. Kelmscott House is where Morris wrote some of his best known work, and seeing the original books and printing press brings the written word to life for the pupils. Reading Morris's words allows pupils to appreciate his views on art and society, and comparing his style of writing with contemporary writers acts as a springboard for their own stories and poems. Morris found writing difficult, saying, "I know what I want to say, but the cursed words go to water between my fingers"[3]—a sentiment with which many pupils (and teachers) will sympathize.

A project offered at the KS1 and KS2 level is based on the fairy tale "Rapunzel" by the Brothers Grimm, re-interpreted and illustrated by William Morris (c. 1858). The children study Morris's illustrations, encounter his printing press, and, working in small groups, recreate the tale in a series of tableaux with costume and props. Alternatively, the "Sigurd and the Dragon" workshop provides an introduction to Morris's love of Icelandic sagas. Pupils take on characters from the story (including Grani the horse and Fafnir the dragon) before acting out a version of the tale in front of their class. The adoption of roles also has a direct link to drama.

HISTORY

"What was it like to live here in the past?" and "What can we learn about recent history from studying the life of a famous person?" are very popular hands-on sessions that include role-play, handling original Victorian artifacts, and discussions of life as depicted in Ford Madox Brown's 1863 painting *Work*.

History Key Stage 2—Victorian Britain

This links with the National Curriculum program of study "how aspects of national history are reflected in the locality."[4] At a time when Britain was famous for its industrial achievements and its reputation as the "workshop of the world," Morris disliked factories and mass-produced goods, and his views are brought to life for students with an object-handling session. Documentation and photographs from the museum's collection along with local archive material, photographs, maps, and trade directories animate the session. Of especial interest are the records that provide a window into the lives of the servants at Kelmscott House. Reproductions of Morris & Co. catalogues also give comparisons of Morris's own handcrafted work with the typical Victorian mass-produced objects of poor quality. Many of Morris's customers had themselves made money from industrialized mass-production and the contradiction of purchasing Morris & Co. products is introduced to the pupils.

In Morris's book *News from Nowhere* (1890; 1891), the narrator wakes in the twenty-first century to find a new and better society. The ills of Victorian society have been left behind, the factories and slums have disappeared, the Thames is clean. Pupils find out what life was like in Hammersmith in 1890 for different classes of society, particularly for women and children. They discuss how much has changed and whether it is all for the better. Then the pupils imagine the kind of society they would like to see come about and write a story about it.

Art and Design: Key Stages 1, 2, and 3

Morris and those working with him (Philip Webb, Edward Burne-Jones, William de Morgan, and Dante Gabriel Rossetti) produced a wide range of arts and crafts objects and buildings. The study of these show how the visual elements of line, shape, pattern, texture, color, form, and space can be used to develop an appreciation of our diverse cultural heritage, enriching the pupils' own creative work.

By investigating Morris's style through original objects on display, pupils learn much about his prodigious output, including drawings, paintings, hangings, stained glass, lettering, furniture, tiles, fabrics, wallpapers, carpets, and printed books. Items from the Society's collection enable pupils to study pattern and texture, color, and images, and how shape, form, and space are represented in artifacts. By the end of this workshop, they are able to describe works of art, craft, and design and identify the materials and methods used by Morris & Co.

Design and Technology: Key Stages 1, 2, and 3

Morris's practical skill in many crafts and his knowledge of materials have particular application to the designing and making element of Key Stages 2 and 3. Morris stressed the importance of the making process. Children learn how he set out to study and revive craft techniques that the industrial process had superseded. They are able to see firsthand his block-printed wallpapers, naturally-dyed and indigo-discharged textiles, and hand-knotted carpets. They also see the Morris & Co. traditional rush-seated Sussex chairs. By understanding how Morris and his firm designed and made objects and where they were used, pupils learn the appropriate vocabulary to begin to describe production techniques and evaluate the quality of arts-and-crafts era artifacts.

The Society intends to develop and increase the range of practical workshops offered so that children can learn further about Arts and Crafts techniques. New activities in development include dyeing, embroidery, and weaving.

ENVIRONMENTAL EDUCATION

Morris is recognized as an environmental pioneer and campaigner. His hatred of the squalid cities and impoverished countryside of his day and his efforts to protect historic buildings offer an excellent opportunity to develop pupils' understanding of how environments are shaped, their qualities and vulnerability, and the opportunities and responsibilities for protecting and managing them.

Morris founded the Society for the Protection of Ancient Buildings and believed that buildings should be respected and repaired when necessary but not "restored." Pupils can discuss conservation areas in their locality: Are they worth preserving? Are there buildings that have fallen into disrepair which should be protected?

Children in their formal education rarely have the opportunity to discuss or learn about the future. In his introduction to *News from Nowhere* G. D. H. Cole wrote, "Morris was saying 'Here is the sort of Society I should like to live in. Now tell me yours.'"⁵ Pupils compare and contrast the area as it was in Morris's day with his utopian vision, where the ills of Victorian society have been left behind, the factories and slums have disappeared, the Thames is clean, and items which are made can be repaired rather than thrown away; this opens a discussion on a range of environmental issues. The fact that *News from Nowhere* begins in a fictional guesthouse set in the society's premises at Kelmscott House adds particular resonance for pupils.

EDUCATION FOR CITIZENSHIP

Morris was critical of his Britain in which there were huge extremes of wealth and poverty, inequality, and lack of democratic rights including freedom of speech. His writings convey his ideas of the rights and responsibilities of individuals to each other and the wider community. He felt society should provide fulfilling work for all, and his personal and political experiences provide many lessons on how citizenship can be achieved.

During Morris's lifetime adults could work up to eighty-four hours per week, or twelve hours per day. In 1847 this was limited to ten hours but, on average, adults still worked sixty-four hours per week, in often dangerous conditions. Morris tried to revive medieval craft techniques and organized workshops using the medieval guild model to stand up against the industrial processes and mass-producing factories that relied on wage labor to maximize profit. Morris favored handmade objects over the mass-produced versions made in contemporary machines. He said, "I am bound to act for the destruction of the system which seems to me mere oppression . . . we seek a change in the basis of society—a change which would destroy the distinctions of classes and nationalities."⁶

During Morris's time at Kelmscott House, socialism and politics played a key role in shaping his views on the future development of society. Morris was a founding member of the Socialist League, which held meetings in the Coach House where many prominent Victorians spoke: George Bernard Shaw—dramatist and Fabian Society member; Keir Hardie—founder of the Scottish Labor Party; Sidney Webb—Fabian Society and part of the intellectual wing of the Labor Party and his wife Beatrice Webb—economist; Gustav Holst—composer who conducted the Socialist Choir at Kelmscott House; Peter Kropotkin—an anarchist leader from Russia; Lucy Parsons—an African American freed slave whose husband was hanged for being an anarchist in Chicago; Annie Besant—socialist campaigner for women's rights who helped organize the Match Girls Strike of 1888; and Walter Crane—an artist who created a number of iconic socialist images.

The citizenship workshop, held in the Coach House, the actual meeting place of the Hammersmith branch of the Socialist League, investigates the views of these speakers and how they brought about change.

Key Stages 2 and 3: Citizenship Workshop

This workshop enables cross-curricular links with English, drama, and citizenship, and it incorporates the WMS's socialist ephemera collection. The workshop came out of a focus group with teachers, where it was recognized that citizenship is a subject that would meet a clear demand and it is also a theme we should be focusing on due to the strengths of our museum collection. The citizenship workshop highlights ethical debates around equality, freedom of speech, and the politics of Morris's socialism. Children are encouraged to think about justice and working conditions. Lectures that took place in the Coach House at Kelmscott House are analyzed, and pupils are asked to produce materials, including a poster, to publicize the events and explain their importance and relevance to the Victorian public. The spoken English element of this workshop enables pupils to understand the conventions for discussion and debate.

Following Morris's view to "Always think your design out in your head before you begin to get it on paper. You must see it before you can draw it, whether the design be of your own invention or Nature's,"[7] the pupils conceive their designs for the posters, inspired by nature, before drawing their patterns on large paper sheets. They then paint the design thickly with block paints before taking their sheet to the printing and binding station. This final activity involves folding the sheets horizontally and vertically to create a four-block print which illustrates how designs can be repeated infinitely. The paint is then quick-dried with a dryer and the sheets are finally bound onto notebooks. Participants can then glue, in a Kelmscott Press, paper, label, and stamp their initials onto their finished books, using rubber stamps and ink. The response from the children is enthusiastic from start to finish.

During the object handling session, pupils are asked to consider how mass-produced and handmade items are different. By making Morris's ethics and production methods relevant to today's consumer society, pupils examine the following themes: fair trade, labor rights, consumer power, and equality at work. This helps the pupils develop their communication skills by speaking in front of others and explaining the reasons behind the decisions made in the workshop. It also helps them to develop their confidence in discussing quite complex themes, including Morris's campaign for the right of free speech, usually to an impressively high standard. This provides pupils with the tools to challenge others' views and the confidence to hold reasoned justification for their own views.

NEW WORKSHOPS

Pattern and Symmetry (Math and Art Key Stages 1 and 2)

The Society is currently developing a new workshop inspired by the repeating patterns found in Morris's designs, therefore enabling math to be incorporated into our art sessions. Pupils examine shapes and patterns in the textiles and wallpapers on display in the Coach House, looking at symmetry and repeat patterns. They then create their own symmetrical design. The math element builds on the design and technology scheme of work, and provides the ideal opportunity for schools to develop their own schemes of work based on creating images using repeating patterns.

Materials and Their Properties (Science: Key Stages 1, 2, and 3)

Morris and his associates worked in natural materials such as wood, wool, silk, rush, and naturally produced dyes for textiles. By studying these objects in the context of Morris's home, pupils gain an understanding of where the materials originated, and they are helped to group and classify them. Children investigate patterns from around the world and identify key features and compare them, allowing for cross-curricular links with geography and math. Additionally, by incorporating dyeing procedures into school visits, vegetable dyes, such as indigo and woad, are explored in contrast to the industrial chemical dyes favored in the Victorian age. By investigating how vegetable dyes work, pupils learn about changing materials, physical processes, and chemicals. In this session we also discuss conservation of irreplaceable Morris textiles, and the devastating effects of light and environmental damage. Object handling is also utilized to prompt further discussion about materials, their uses, and specific properties and applications.

Arts and Crafts Hammersmith

Arts and Crafts Hammersmith (A&CH)[8] is a joint project between the WMS and the nearby Emery Walker House,[9] which aims to open up access to the rich collections of both organizations and the wider histories—personal, social, political—of the arts and crafts that are deeply rooted in this part of Hammersmith. Attracting new and more diverse audiences through the development of new learning and outreach initiatives is at the heart of this project. We particularly wish to demonstrate how Morris, and the Arts and Crafts movement, was influenced by different cultures in order to illustrate the relevance to our multi-cultural society. The WMS is working with primary and secondary school teachers to create a set of new learning materials to develop skills from our Arts and Crafts heritage, including lesson plans, worksheets, and curriculum resource packs—both physical and online. Specific plans include the development of a schools object-handling-loans box, outreach sessions for classroom activities, assemblies, and after school clubs, as well as lectures, specialist tours, and workshops for adults.

Teacher Training

The Society has been hiring out the Coach House at Kelmscott House, for the last fifteen years, as a venue for a Saturday morning art class for children aged seven to sixteen with an aptitude for art, run by an art education adviser. Pupils have been inspired by their surroundings and through being immersed in the Morris designs on display in the premises. This has led to special projects by the art class, focusing on Morris, and even leading one student to have an exhibition of her Morris-inspired artwork at the Society. The following is a selection of testimonies from students attending the Saturday art class:

Lilibet Williams: "It is inspiring to be surrounded by such wonderful pieces of artwork. I get inspiration from the colors and patterns that William Morris uses in his prints. I especially love doing printing ourselves in the same place where William Morris did his prints."

Ria: "Being surrounded by William Morris' artwork, puts me in the right mood to be ready to draw, paint or do anything artistic."

Tess Fontaine: "The amount of detail put into William Morris' prints really inspires you to work into your drawings and creates an atmosphere that drives us."

The Society has worked with the primary art adviser, Rosemary Bignell, to deliver an INSET (In-Service Training for Teachers) Day, *The Creative Curriculum: Printmaking in the Primary School through the Work of William Morris*. This practical course aims to develop teachers' skills and confidence in printmaking techniques through examining Morris's original working drawings, and investigating the processes he used to produce his designs for textiles and wallpapers.

Workshop sessions and presentations include:

- printmaking to examine form, shape, line, pattern, texture, and color
- using sketchbooks to collect visual research
- developing observational skills by working from direct experience of the natural world
- organization and management of the learning environment
- developing progression in printmaking throughout the primary school

- considering how links can be made with other curriculum subjects including math, history, science, and ICT

The course began with an explanation of how the Society's collection can be used by primary schools as a starting point for learning. The participating primary teachers and art and design coordinators investigated natural forms and collected information about shape, line, pattern, texture, and color from Morris's original designs. Using a viewfinder to select a design, they went on to experiment with arranging, ordering, and overlapping patterns in sketchbooks. Seasonal plants and flowers found in these designs were studied alongside the watercolors; this visual stimulus was a creative starting point for learning.

Teachers were then taught how to develop techniques using press print, experiment with mark-making, develop design by subtracting from the surface, and overlay prints using multiple colors. The course concluded with a plan for progression in printmaking within the classroom and for how to successfully evaluate pupils' work. In several local schools the teachers taught their classes using these newly acquired skills. The children produced work of a high quality that was displayed in the main entrance, thus sharing their work inspired by Morris with parents, teachers, and pupils.

Another unit focused on Morris and printmaking has been developed to be taught over one term. The children research the work of Morris and investigate how he developed his designs from visual research in the natural world. In one school, 120 children in Year 5 have been taught the Morris unit of work, resulting in 720 children benefiting over a six-year period. This is repeated in many primary schools. Therefore, thousands of inner-city children from different cultural backgrounds have been learning about their own heritage by understanding the importance of Morris as an influential designer.[10]

New Family Learning Activities at the William Morris Society

There was previously no provision for young people and nothing of an interactive nature at the Society's premises. Monitoring had proven that children and family groups spent very little time in the premises because there were no specific or shared activities geared toward younger family members. The Society has therefore worked hard to improve access directly through participation and a direct relationship with objects and interactives. The aim is to encourage repeat visits and direct involvement with the collection, making the premises and objects accessible in a way that was previously impossible.

This project aimed to introduce an exploration of Morris's work to children through a discovery trail in the form of a colorful and image-rich activity sheet to lead the child around the Society's rooms. In each room they encounter activities in order to bring to life Morris's work, and all these interactives are linked to the trail involving observation, touching, making, drawing, and investigating. There is a jigsaw of a ceramic tile to piece together; a "stained glass" effect activity where the child can create a beautiful Morris "window" from safe, smooth materials; and a printing activity for stamping a rubber image onto a pad to show the principles of block printing. There is also a felt activity for the visitor to place different colored felt onto a board to make a Morris pattern—this demonstrates very simply the complex process of wallpaper printing and the layering of designs to achieve a Morris-style pattern.

The felt wall hanging activity provides a simple replica of Morris's *Vine* embroidery, on display nearby. The background of the hanging is varied greens, to make it attractive to children, and the handmade felt is a tactile surface. The design incorporates a variety of separate flowers, leaves, bunches of grapes, and birds in order to imitate the original embroidery. A Velcro backing enables children to stick each piece directly onto the hanging, thereby designing their own wall hanging. The hanging is placed next to the original Morris embroidery so that the child has a direct comparison, which demonstrates, in a simple way, the complex process of textile making and the layering of designs as a playful example of one of the museum's best-loved Morris patterns.

The tile jigsaw puzzles are intended to reduce Morris's complex patterns to their simplest forms. The chosen designs have been enlarged so that one element of a repeat is featured to avoid making the puzzle overly complex. Child-friendly designs featuring birds have been chosen, and have proved very attractive to young visitors. This is an activity that young children can complete on their own, or with another family member, thereby increasing their confidence and rapport with objects in the museum.

One of the key objects in the museum is Morris's original printing press. It has, however, proved quite difficult to explain the book-printing process and so an activity that featured letters was required. It was decided to produce a stamping and block-printing activity situated next to the printing press and composing cases. This has enabled children to understand first hand why type letters are in reverse. Children stamp their own name with the ink pads to complete the activity.

The "stained glass" activity has always proved extremely popular, particularly after the addition of a light box to allow the backlit effect of a stained glass window. The aim was to create a safe method for children to design their own window pattern with replica lead lines, in imitation of the original Morris glass, which is displayed alongside. Simple bird, leaf, and flower shapes were made and smoothed down, and a black background used as a template allowing the child to place the shapes into the corresponding cutouts. This takes place on the surface of the light box, and when the unit is switched on it gives a wonderfully bright effect, showing the child's design to its best advantage. This has the result of making the complexity of a Morris design easier to understand for the youngest child.

These informal learning activities have made a huge difference to our organization and made a considerable impact on our educational service for early years. Before this project, the museum did not have any interactives whatsoever and the visit time for a family was under ten minutes. Now, due to the quality of resources, the average time has at least tripled and led to repeat visits, which were previously non-existent for family groups. The project has also been a catalyst in offering a new service to special educational needs, and to the youngest school groups.

FAMILY WORKSHOPS

For several years the Society has run family workshops over holidays and half terms. Activity sheets have been created and the purchase of arts and crafts equipment means workshops cover a wide range of crafts are possible, often with a seasonal theme. Additionally, the garden at Kelmscott House often serves as a source of inspiration and materials. Sessions have included:

Designing typefaces; decorative initial lettering and borders; poetry and creative writing; block printing wallpapers; textile designing; three dimensional flowers; recording nature in Morris's garden; fantastic animals based on William de Morgan; clay modeling; ceramic painting; felt creations; and "stained glass" windows. New workshops currently in development will focus on weaving, clay modelling, and jewelry making; all with the aim of bringing the work of William Morris to a new audience.[11]

FEEDBACK

The majority of feedback from teachers and visitors demonstrates that participants have been inspired by the workshops and learned new skills. Repeat visits have become common, which is very encouraging. Examples of feedback from visiting teachers are:

Carmel Raul, Year 5, Larmenier and Sacred Heart RC Primary School, November 4, 2010: "Support and materials etc. excellent, all staff so helpful.

Helen is a gem! Fantastic teachers, lovely with the children and really know how to get the best from them. We have been studying William Morris and his work in school, so this was an excellent extension and affirmation of the children's learning. We thoroughly enjoyed it and will be back!"

Sabina Carr, Year 2, Christchurch Primary School, July 17, 2014: "All of the historical knowledge supports the curriculum. The quality of the service is outstanding. My very challenging class loved the sessions and as a result behaved and learnt. The ladies are amazing! My class loved it!"

Bianca Lasi, Year 6, Lowbrook Academy, October 7, 2014: "The session supported the National Curriculum as it linked to Victorians and the Industrial Revolution."

Mr. Chris Bellis, Year 5, St Paul's Church of England Primary School, October 10, 2014: "Both art activities were enjoyable and linked to art objectives in curriculum. The adults who delivered the session were fantastic. Very informative and catered to the children's needs. Thank you for a great day. The children thoroughly enjoyed the visit and activities. It all linked fantastically well to our curriculum."

Mr. McLeod, Year 5, St Peter's Church of England Primary, November 16, 2015: "There were real items for children to study and discuss. Links to modern life to make learning real! Great detail and factual knowledge delivered in a child friendly way. Engaging content to get all abilities involved and interacting with resources. I really liked how the children were encouraged to verbally deliver their ideas."

Amy Periam, Year 4, Hotham Primary School, March 7, 2017: "Such beautifully prepared art resources, such a warm welcome. We really loved our trip—the class are obsessed with William Morris now! Thank you!"

We are confident that our future plans, and particularly new initiatives brought about as a result of the Arts and Crafts Hammersmith project, will encourage a new generation to be inspired by the work of Morris and the unique collections at Kelmscott House.

NOTES

1. Quotation from Lynne Emm; "We are delighted with the opportunities you have given our pupils and we urge you strongly to continue your outstanding and invaluable work—this is art education at its finest." Year 5 teacher at Berrymede Junior School, 2016.

2. The UK national curriculum was introduced in 1988 as a nationwide curriculum for primary schools and secondary schools. It covers what subjects are taught and the standards children should reach in each subject. For each subject and for

each key stage, programs of study set out what pupils should be taught and attainment targets set out the expected standards of pupils' performance. (Key Stage 1: Age 5–7, Key Stage 2: Age 7–11, Key Stage 3: Age 11–14, Key Stage 4:- Age 12–16) Academies, independent, and free schools do not have to follow the National curriculum but must teach a broad and balanced curriculum. https://www.gov.uk/national-curriculum.

3. Norman Kelvin and William Morris. *The Collected Letters of William Morris, Volume 2, Part A: 1881–1884*. Princeton: Princeton University Press, 1987. Feb. 10, 1881, letter to Jane Morris, 14–15.

4. Department for Education (2013) The national curriculum in England: history programmes of study. Available at: https://www.gov.uk/government/publications/national-curriculum-in-england-history-programmes-of-study/national-curriculum-in-england-history-programmes-of-study (Accessed: 28 August 2019).

5. G. D. H. Cole, (ed.) *William Morris. Stories in Prose, Stories in Verse, Shorter Poems, Lectures and Essays*. London: Nonesuch Press, 1942.

6. Norman Kelvin and William Morris. *The Collected Letters of William Morris, Volume 2, Part B: 1885–1888*. Princeton: Princeton University Press, 2014.

7. Art and the Beauty of the Earth, a lecture given at the Wedgewood Institute at the Town Hall, Burslem 1881 and in *The Collected Works of William Morris* vol. 22, ed. May Morris (London, Longmans Green and Co, 1915–1919).

8. Further information on this joint project, and all downloadable learning resources, can be found at: www.artsandcraftshammersmith.org.uk.

9. Emery Walker (1851–1933) was a friend and colleague of Morris. His home is a perfectly preserved, authentic Arts and Crafts interior, and is open to the public. Further information on Emery Walker's House can be found at www.emerywalker.org.uk.

10. Particular recent developments highlighting the diverse influences of the Arts and Crafts movement have been our partnership with the local Iranian Association, culminating in a Morris and Persian Carpet exhibition at Kelmscott House, a book on the cultural heritage of Persian carpets: http://www.iranianassociation.org.uk/wp-content/uploads/2018/04/18th-April-2018-3205-Cultural-Heritage-of-the-Persian-Carpet-2018.pdf; and an online film with interviews recorded at Kelmscott House: https://www.youtube.com/watch?v=sHd7jSdOVEw.

Another project highlighting the importance of Islamic art within the Arts and Crafts movement is nearing completion. This will involve the creation of new teachers' resource packs on art, maths, and symmetry. An online display of Islamic-inspired art within the Emery Walker's House collections can be accessed at: www.emerywalker.org.uk/islamic-art-collection.

11. Recent participants at our family workshops have provided the following feedback: Feedback from children: "It was really fun"; "I didn't want to leave"; "I learnt new things to do at home"; "it helped me with art at school"; "I was happy, excited, and fascinated about today"; "fantastic"; "when we finished it was really successful and they looked really good"; "already perfect"; "the best it can be"; and "we are doing printing at school, so it helped me with my art"; "I learnt that you can really

express yourself through art and creativity." Feedback from adults included, "lovely staff and atmosphere"; "the children loved being free to explore their own ideas"; "Both activities were engaging and suited to the age. She liked the fact that she could start weaving independently soon after the workshop started"; "great to have arts and crafts workshops"; "we just want more"; "please organize more of the same"; "friendly atmosphere"; and "it was perfect!"

BIBLIOGRAPHY

Bernard Shaw, George. *Morris as I Knew Him*. London: William Morris Society, 1966.

Bird, James. *Survey of London Vol. 6 Hammersmith*. London: London County Council, 1915.

Christodoulou, Stephanie. *Art and Maths in the Courtauld Collection*. London, The Courtauld Institute of Art, 2017.

Cole, G. D. H. (ed.) *William Morris. Stories in Prose, Stories in Verse, Shorter Poems, Lectures and Essays*. London: Nonesuch Press, 1942.

Drake, Jane. *William Morris: An Illustrated Life*. Andover: Pitkin Guides, 1996.

Hardy, Sarah and Khokhar, Amber. *Sublime Symmetry Teachers' Maths Resource Pack*. De Morgan Foundation, London, 2016.

Maxwell, Matilda. *William Morris, A Resource Pack for Teachers*. London: William Morris Society, 1996.

McCarthy, Fiona. *William Morris: A Life for Our Time*. London: Faber and Faber, 1994.

McKinstry, Susan Jaret. "Taking Our Eyes Out of Our Pockets: Teaching William Morris's Ideal Book," *The Journal of William Morris Studies* 17 (Summer 2007): 89–98.

Miles, Rosie. "Teaching Morris Online," *The Journal of William Morris Studies* 17 (Summer 2007): 54–72.

Morris, May. *William Morris: Artist, Writer, Socialist*. Oxford: Basil Blackwell, 1936.

Read, Alan. "Speech Sites." In *Architecturally* Speaking, edited by Alan Read. London: Routledge, 2000.

Rogers, David. *William Morris at Home*. London: Ebury Press, 1996.

Tames, Richard. *William Morris: An Illustrated Life of William Morris 1834–1896*. London: Shire Publications, 1995.

Veryaecke, Philippe. "Teaching News from Nowhere in France for the CAPES and the Agrégation in English Studies, 2004–2006," *The Journal of William Morris Studies* 17 (Summer 2007): 24–40.

Chapter Five

The Medievalism of William Morris
Teaching through Tolkien

KellyAnn Fitzpatrick

There would be no *World of Warcraft* without William Morris. Often heralded as the inventor of the fantasy novel, Morris's influence on the books, films, and games that constitute our contemporary fantasy genre is significant.[1] Most directly, Morris's literary medievalism shaped the writing of J. R. R. Tolkien: a writer whose work is widely acknowledged to be foundational for both contemporary academic medieval studies and popular fantasy.[2] In spite of Morris's contributions to the fantasy genre, my experience teaching Morris at the undergraduate level suggests that students initially recognize him—if at all—from his contributions to decorative design through Morris & Co. or from his status as a second-wave Pre-Raphaelite. Students often know Tolkien, however, either directly through his writing (such as *The Lord of the Rings* or *The Hobbit*), through film or game adaptations of his work, or through other fantasy texts that his work inspired. Tolkien, then, offers an often untapped resource for engaging students with Morris and his literary medievalism.

While I have not yet had the opportunity to teach a course devoted to Morris and Tolkien, I have found Tolkien a useful approach to teaching Morris to undergraduate university students in a special topics course on medievalism, a British literature survey course, and an upper-level course on nineteenth-century British literature. Even in cases where a segment of a course focused primarily on Morris, a brief outline of his connections with Tolkien has made a positive impact on the levels of interest with which my students read Morris's texts; individual research projects can open up additional avenues of inquiry into the relationship between the two writers. In this chapter I outline some of the ways that I have used these links between Tolkien and Morris's medievalism to teach Morris (to different degrees of detail) in courses where I could address both authors. I begin with a brief analysis of the role of medievalism in both Morris's and Tolkien's work; I follow with methods for using Tolkien to teach Morris's translations and creative prose.

MORRIS'S MEDIEVALISM AND TOLKIEN'S WRITING

Although the finer points of the term *medievalism* have been contested in recent academic scholarship, here I use it broadly to refer to the ways in which later ages interpret, reimagine, or appropriate the Middle Ages.[3] In this sense medievalism may take on many forms, from Victorian wall hangings that incorporate medieval design elements and themes, such as the Holy Grail tapestries produced by Morris & Co. (1890), to fantasy novels such as Tolkien's *The Lord of the Rings* in which world-building relies on medieval tropes, language, and narratives. Morris's relationship to medievalism is best introduced through the larger context of the nineteenth-century Medieval Revival in Britain.[4] Building on related movements such as antiquarianism, the eighteenth-century Gothic Revival in architecture, and Romanticism, the initial wave of the Medieval Revival is often associated with Walter Scott and works such as his novel *Ivanhoe* (1820). However, this unofficial movement evolved throughout the century and manifested in forms as varied as poetry (e.g., Tennyson's *Idylls of the King,* published between 1859 and 1885), painting (e.g., the works of Morris's fellow Pre-Raphaelites), social events, and even home décor. Importantly, ideas and values attributed to a medieval English past were mobilized for both conservative and progressive political thought, including Morris's socialism.[5]

A productive polymath, Morris's medievalism colored many aspects of his life, work, and politics. Visually, we see medieval themes and design elements in his tapestry and stained-glass designs, as well as in the Arthurian-themed painting *La Belle Iseult* (1858). Medievalism manifests in Morris's poetry, such as the Arthurian "Defence of Guenevere" (1858) and the epic poem *The Earthly Paradise*, which retells a selection of medieval Scandinavian myth.[6] In addition to the texts that I discuss in the sections below, in his prose Morris drew from the 1381 Peasants' Revolt for his 1888 *A Dream of John Ball* (a dream vision in which his sympathies clearly lie with the peasants), and wrote an essay devoted to "Gothic Architecture" (1889). Even Morris's own Red House (1859), which he designed with architect Philip Webb, incorporates medieval design elements as well as a side porch called "Pilgrim's Rest" that was purposely situated on the road that Chaucer's fictional pilgrims would have taken to Canterbury.[7] Morris also founded Morris, Marshall, Faulkner & Co. (1861) and its successor, Morris & Co. (1875); the firm produced many of his decorative designs and contributed significantly to the larger Arts and Crafts movement, which championed pre-industrial (often coded as "medieval") design and production values as an alternative to cheap, mass-produced, industrial-age wares. He translated these values to publishing when in 1891 he formed the Kelmscott Press, where he strived to turn out books that were themselves beautifully produced works of art. In doing so Morris turned to the Middle Ages not only for inspiration for his production principles and printing practices, but also for material, as one of the press's most notable achievements was a gorgeous 1896 edition of Chaucer's *Canterbury Tales*.

Morris was thus a product of and a prolific contributor to the nineteenth-century Medieval Revival, and the fruits of his labor would have been familiar to a young J. R. R. Tolkien. Although he is considered a twentieth-century author, Tolkien (1892–1973) was born in the nineteenth century, and while his interest in medieval language and history led him to a career as a philologist—most famously as Rawlinson and Bosworth Professor of Anglo-Saxon at Oxford—his interests in the creative possibilities of medieval language and history fueled his fantasy writing. This writing was also considerably influenced by Morris's works in form, content, style, and source material. In a 1914 letter to Edith Bratt, his future wife, Tolkien, while still an undergraduate student at Oxford, writes of introducing the Finnish epic *The Kalevala* to a fellow student. He then describes how he is attempting "to turn one of the stories—which is really a very great story and most tragic—into a short story somewhat on the lines of Morris' romances with chunks of poetry in between."[8] Morris, then, was a consciously chosen model for Tolkien's early creative writing, and this influence can be seen in many of Tolkien's more mature texts.

In the sections that follow, I demonstrate how Tolkien's fantasy fiction and academic essays can be used to teach Morris's medievalism. Although Tolkien's own creative writing is extensive, I focus primarily on his best-known fantasy fiction, *The Hobbit* (1937) and *The Lord of the Rings* (1954/1955), because the familiarity that students have with these works and their adaptations is what make them such excellent teaching tools. I have organized my teaching approaches according to selections of Morris's translations, historical novels, and romances/utopian fiction.

MORRIS'S TRANSLATIONS

Alongside his many other pursuits, Morris published works in translation. Although not as proficient or competent in as many languages as Tolkien (a professional philologist), Morris undertook translations from languages such as Old Norse (also called Old Icelandic), Old French, Greek, Latin, and Old English (also called Anglo-Saxon). Among his translations, the two that have the most relevance to Tolkien's work are his 1870 translation *Völsunga Saga: The Story of the Völsungs and Niblungs, with Certain Songs from the Elder Edda* (translated from Old Norse with Eiríkr Magnússon) and his 1895 translation of the Old English poem *Beowulf*.[9]

The *Völsunga Saga*, a thirteenth-century Icelandic prose text, primarily concerns the legendary hero Sigurd, his family, and his slaying of the dragon Fafnir. Although Morris later adapted some of the events of the *Völsunga Saga* into a long, narrative poem, his translation was perhaps most widely read through a condensed version that appeared in Andrew Lang's *Red Fairy Book* (1890), in which Lang directly cites the earlier prose translation as his source.[10] As Tolkien biographer Humphrey Carpenter notes, Tolkien was introduced to Lang's version as a young child and was captivated by the dragon Fafnir.[11] Scholars such as Jonathan Evans have linked this early reading experience to Tolkien's first known creative writing endeavor, citing correspondence in which Tolkien writes, "I first tried to write a story when I was about seven. It was about a dragon."[12] Morris's *Völsunga Saga* translation, then, not only helped introduce Tolkien to Icelandic saga and legendary dragons; it also likely influenced his early writing career.

A dragon also figures prominently in the Old English poem *Beowulf* in which the titular hero, after successfully killing the monstrous Grendel (and Grendel's mother) in his younger days, dies attempting to protect his people from a dragon. Morris's poetical translation was based on A. J. Wyatt's translation and published by the Kelmscott Press in 1895. We know that Tolkien was familiar with Morris's translation, as he specifically criticized some of Morris's antiquarian word choices in his essay "On Translating *Beowulf*," writing "Still less is translation of *Beowulf* a fitting occasion for the exhumation of dead words from Saxon or Norse graves. Antiquarian sentiment and philological knowingness are wholly out of place. To render *leode* 'freemen, people' by *leeds* (favoured by William Morris) fails both to translate the Old English and to recall *leeds* to life."[13] Indeed, while Tolkien emulated Morris's fictional style, he had different ideas about translating medieval texts proper.

While Tolkien did his own translation of *Beowulf,* and a comparison of the two translations (perhaps informed by Tolkien's "On Translating Beowulf") could serve as a productive individual research project for a student interested in translation and style; I instead suggest two of Tolkien's academic lectures (revised and published as essays) in conjunction with *The Hobbit*, as a means of tracing Tolkien's academic and creative medievalism to Morris's translation efforts.[14] The first of these, "*Beowulf*: The Monsters and the Critics," examines the role of the dragon in *Beowulf*, and even alludes to references in *Beowulf* to the events depicted in the *Völsunga Saga*.[15] This meditation on dragons can be used to emphasize the relationship among the *Beowulf* dragon, Fafnir, and the dragon, Smaug, in *The Hobbit:* a dragon who, like the *Beowulf* dragon, is interrupted from his slumber by a thief—the hobbit Bilbo Baggins. The essay also provides a fascinating look at the state of medieval studies in the early twentieth century and how it emerged from the nineteenth-century interest in the Middle Ages, which provides an excellent segue into how and why Morris would decide to translate a text such as *Beowulf* in the first place. The second essay I have taught in this context is "On Fairy Stories," in which Tolkien introduces the concept of a "Secondary world," or fantasy otherworld (and also further elucidates his love of Fafnir). Here Tolkien draws on texts such as *Beowulf* and the *Völsunga Saga* to establish this concept of a Secondary world, illustrating how the Middle Ages are foundational to his understanding of fantasy. In the following sections I further examine how medieval history and language inform fantastic elements in the creation of such Secondary worlds in both Tolkien and Morris.

MORRIS'S HISTORICAL FICTION

In 1889 Morris published *The House of the Wolfings*, followed the next year by *The Roots of the Mountains*. Based loosely on accounts of early medieval Gothic tribes, both romances are often considered a blend of historical novel and fantasy novel, as they use history as the basis for narrative and settings while also incorporating minor supernatural elements. *The House of the Wolfings* draws on history in its pitting of Gothic tribes against Roman legions and in references to Norse mythology; *The Roots of the Mountains* sees a later generation of Wolfing descendants fending off a Hun invasion from the settlement of Burgdale (the inhabitants of which are called "Dalesmen"). Both romances draw on extant linguistic convention in their naming practices. *The House of the Wolfings*, for instance, has a protagonist named "Thiodolf," and place names in both romances draw from old Germanic names such as "Mirkwood" and "the Mark." While drawing on history in these ways, Morris also introduces some supernatural elements. *House of the Wolfings,* for instance, pairs Thiodolf with the Wood-Sun, a woman who is descended from the gods (as is their daughter, the Hall-Sun); *The Roots of the Mountains,* while associating supernatural elements with nostalgia for the past, also creates the sense that their return is possible.

In addition to the distinct linguistic elements that Tolkien borrows from Morris's historical fiction (Mirkwood for the name of a forest in numerous texts; the Mark as a term for Rohan in *The Lord of the Rings*; Dale as a ruined city near Laketown in *The Hobbit*), Tolkien also follows Morris in that he appropriates the culture and language of a historical group of people in his fiction. This is most apparent in *The Lord of the Rings* in the Rohirrim, who are culturally and linguistically based in part on the Angle and Saxon tribes that settled in Britain beginning in the fifth century CE, and whose language is often characterized collectively as "Old English," the language of *Beowulf*. Although Tolkien freely admitted to the linguistic connection between the Rohirrim and the Anglo-Saxons, he refused any specific cultural or historic connections between the two.[16] Nevertheless, Tolkien's characterization of the Rohirrim evokes a number of elements found in Old English texts, such as the practice of a high-ranking lady offering a guest cup (as Wealhtheow does in *Beowulf* and Eowyn does in *The Lord of the Rings*) and the centralization of power in a celebratory hall (Heorot for the Danes of *Beowulf* and Medusheld for the Rohirrim).

Not all aspects of the Rohirrim can be linked to the Anglo-Saxons, especially the Rohirrim's skill with and adulation of horses, and although some scholars have pointed to historical Gothic tribes as an inspiration for the Rohirrim, another possible inspiration lies in Morris's portrayal of the Germanic tribes in *The House of the Wolfings* and *The Roots of the Mountains*.[17] Indeed, Tolkien admits that parts of *The Lord of the Rings* were inspired by Morris's historical fiction, writing in one letter that "The Dead Marshes and the approaches to the Morannon owe something to Northern France after the Battle of the Somme. They owe more to William Morris and his Huns and Romans, as in *The House of the Wolfings* or *The Roots of the Mountains*."[18] Tolkien clearly had both books in mind while writing *The Lord of the Rings*, and this can make a convincing case to persuade undergraduates who might be otherwise disinclined to read Victorian historical fiction.[19] When read in whole or in part, either novel serves an excellent introduction to how Morris used history and language to invoke a fantastic past.[20] Even Morris's writing style in his romances—archaic-style prose interspersed with poetry—is recalled in Tolkien's fiction, where elves and hobbits alike are known to break into song.[21] Morris's historical fiction, then, when read against Tolkien and supplemented with students' own experiences with the fantasy genre, invites students to witness how various manifestations of medievalism have made their way into contemporary fantasy.

MORRIS'S ROMANCES AND UTOPIAN FICTION

Morris followed his historical fiction with a series of purely fantastic novels, all of which bring readers into what Tolkien would consider to be a

Secondary world, albeit informed by cultural elements of medievalism. A combination of romance and utopian fiction, these novels include *News from Nowhere* (1890; 1891); *The Story of the Glittering Plain* (1891); *The Wood Beyond the World* (1894); *The Well at the World's End* (1896); *The Water of the Wondrous Isles* (1897); and *The Sundering Flood* (1897, published posthumously). Whereas Morris's historical fiction creates Secondary worlds that do not stray too far from historical possibility, these later works take many of the same techniques of medievalism used in his historical fiction—settings, characters, names, and social hierarchies borrowed from the Middle Ages—and employ them to create Secondary worlds of a much more fantastical nature.

Rather than assign one of these texts to an entire class, I suggest breaking students into groups with each group taking responsibility for presenting a different specified text to the class. This allows students to perform a close and nuanced reading of one book (with the support of their group) while opening up the class to a more sustained examination of Morris's fantasy writing. While instructors may focus student readings as needed, a suggested avenue of inquiry would include elements of medievalism as they inform various fantasy elements traceable to later fantasy works such as Tolkien's. While students will often enthusiastically start with obvious and direct linguistic borrowings (e.g., the wizard Gandalf and horse Shadowfax in *The Lord of the Rings* echo the king Gandolf and horse Silverfax in *The Well at the World's End*; the Undying Lands of Middle-earth recall the Acre of the Undying from *The Story of the Glittering Plain*), upon closer inspection students often identify how Tolkien drew on many other aspects of Morris's fantasy.

Tolkien's portrayal of elves, for instance, owes much to Morris's vision of immortals, such as those portrayed in *The Glittering Plain*. When the protagonist Hallblithe, who hails from England, finds his way to the Glittering Plain, he meets an immortal king whom Morris describes as follows: "His face shone like a star; it was exceeding beauteous, and as kind as the even of May in the gardens of the happy, when the scent of the eglantine fills all the air. When he spoke his voice was so sweet that all hearts were ravished, and none might gainsay him."[22] Tolkien's description of Elrond, Lord of Rivendell in *The Lord or the Rings,* is strikingly similar: "His hair was dark as the shadows of twilight, and upon it was set a circlet of silver; his eyes were grey as a clear evening, and in them was a light like the light of stars."[23] Tolkien's association of elves with immortality, with a set of magical islands set away from the mainland, and with an ethereal beauty often described through imagery such as evening and stars are arguably directly inspired by Morris.

Whereas Morris's Glittering Plain and its inhabitants are portrayed as a seemingly utopian (but ultimately dystopian) society that the protagonist rejects, Tolkien's elves constitute a straightforward ideal rather than a vehicle for critique. Nevertheless, both Morris and Tolkien's fantasy writings have been read as commentary on their own contemporary societies. In *News from Nowhere*, Morris describes a futuristic Utopia that is economically socialist but culturally based on the Middle Ages; this space serves as a means to critique nineteenth-century capitalism and industrialization. Tolkien's Shire, while conveying his nostalgia for an idyllic rural England, also showcases the dangers of twentieth-century industrialization when it is temporarily taken over by the fallen wizard Saruman and his proto-industrial regime.[24] These examples can serve as an excellent segue to a discussion of how fantasy writers like Morris and Tolkien used representations of the medieval to reflect, represent, translate, critique, and idealize not only the Middle Ages, but also their own contemporary societies.

Because Tolkien helped popularize the fantasy genre, I have been making the case that his works can be used to help students understand Morris's own contributions to the form, yet Tolkien can also become a bridge for understanding the influence of Morris's work in its own right, and I have found that the resourcefulness and inquisitiveness of my students often lead them to consider connections that I never would have realized on my own. Indeed, I hit upon Tolkien as a tool for teaching Morris somewhat by accident, when I found that students in my medievalism course took a keen interest in Morris's work after learning of his links to Tolkien. I even had students take up Morris's medievalism as the subject of their final research project, in which they were encouraged to trace contemporary instances of medievalism to an earlier source, and they made connections to texts far beyond those related directly to Tolkien. Students can thus be encouraged to trace the influence of Morris's medievalism to texts discovered through their own research (even beyond *World of Warcraft*), thereby inviting a communal knowledge-building around Morris that extends beyond the initial knowledge-set of the instructor.

NOTES

1. See Chester Scoville, "Pastoralia and Perfectability in William Morris and J. R. R. Tolkien," in *Tolkien's Modern Middle Ages*, eds. Jane Chance and Alfred K. Siewers (New York: Palgrave Macmillan, 2005), 93.

2. The influence of Morris's writing on Tolkien appears to be widely accepted among scholars; see Scoville, "Pastoralia and Perfectability," 93–95. For an excellent set of perspectives on the relationships among Tolkien, his fantasy, and medieval studies, see Jane Chance, ed., *Tolkien the Medievalist* (New York: Routledge, 2003)

and Tom Shippey, *The Road to Middle-Earth: How J. R. R. Tolkien Created a New Mythology* (New York: Houghton-Mifflin, 2003). For more on Tolkien's influence on table-top gaming (e.g., *Dungeons and Dragons*) and video games such as *World of Warcraft*; see Matt Barton, *Dungeons and Desktops: The History of Computer Role-Playing Game*. (Wellesley, MA: A. K. Peters, 2009); Gerald Vorhees, Joshua Call, and Katie Whitlock, eds., *Dungeons, Dragons, and Digital Denizens: The Digital Role-Playing Game* (London: Continuum, 2012); and Daniel T. Kline, ed., *Digital Gaming Re-imagines the Middle Ages* (New York: Routledge, 2014).

3. A solid summary of the debate over the term medievalism can be found in special sections of the journal *Studies in Medievalism* volumes XVII (2009) and XVIII (2009) dedicated to "Defining Medievalism(s)." See also David Matthews, *Medievalism: A Critical History* (Cambridge: D.S. Brewer, 2015).

4. For excellent resources on the British Medieval Revival, see Alice Chandler, *A Dream of Order: The Medieval Ideal in Nineteenth-Century Literature* (London: Routledge, 1970) and Mark Girouard, *The Return to Camelot: Chivalry and the English Gentleman* (New Haven, CT: Yale University Press, 1981). For a more recent perspective, see Michael Alexander, *Medievalism: The Middle Ages in Modern England* (New Haven, CT: Yale University Press, 2007).

5. See, for instance, Girouard's description of events such as the 1839 Eglinton Tournament (in which early Victorians attempted to joust in armor) and the 1842 medievally-themed ball given by Queen Victoria, in *The Return to Camelot: Chivalry and the English Gentleman*, 87–128.

6. While I comment on specific editions of Morris's works as appropriate, Morris's works themselves are available in a variety of editions of varying quality. For teaching purposes, I use (and highly recommend) *The William Morris Archive*, which is currently edited by Florence Boos and hosted at the University of Iowa at: http://morrisedition.lib.uiowa.edu/index.html. This excellent project allows students to access many of Morris's text in an electronic, searchable format; for some texts it also offers full images, which allows students to see, for instance, the layout of a Kelmscott edition of Morris's work. All references in this chapter to a Kelmscott edition of Morris's work have been taken from this resource.

7. Marcus Waithe, *William Morris's Utopia of Strangers: Victorian Medievalism and the Ideal of Hospitality* (Woodbridge: D. S. Brewer, 2006), 43.

8. Letter 1, "To Edith Bratt," in *The Letters of J. R. R. Tolkien*, ed. Humphrey Carpenter (1981; repr., Boston: Houghton Mifflin, 2000), 7.

9. William Morris and Eiríkr Magnússon, trans., *Völsunga Saga: The Story of the Völsungs and Niblungs, with Certain Songs from the Elder Edda* (London: Ellis, 1870), and William Morris and A. J. Wyatt, trans., *The Tale of Beowulf* (Hammersmith: Kelmscott Press, 1895).

10. William Morris, *The Story of Sigurd the Völsung and the Fall of the Niblung* (London: Ellis & White, 1877), and Andrew Lang, ed. "The Story of Sigurd," in *The Red Fairy Book* (1890; repr., New York: Dover, 1966).

11. Humphrey Carpenter, *J. R. R. Tolkien: A Biography* (1977; repr., Boston: Houghton Mifflin, 2000), 30. Carpenter refers to Tolkien's 1947 essay "On Fairy-Stories," in which he talks about Fafnir as "the prince of all dragons" and notes "I

desired dragons with a profound desire." See Tolkien, "On Fairy-Stories" in *The Monsters and the Critics and Other Essays*, ed. Christopher Tolkien (London: George Allen & Unwin, 1983), 135.

12. Jonathan Evans, "The Dragon Lore of Middle-Earth: Tolkien and Old English and Old Norse Tradition," in *J. R. R. Tolkien and His Literary Resonances: Views of Middle-Earth*, eds. George Clark and Daniel Timmons (Westport, CT: Greenwood Press, 2000), 23. Evans refers to Letter 163, "To W.H. Auden," June 7, 1955, in Carpenter, *The Letters of J. R. R. Tolkien*, 214.

13. J. R. R. Tolkien, "On Translating Beowulf" in *The Monsters and the Critics and Other Essays*, ed. Christopher Tolkien (London: George Allen & Unwin, 1983), 56. For a survey of critical reactions to Morris and Wyatt's translation, see Chris Jones, "The Reception of Morris's *Beowulf*," in *Writing on the Image: Reading William Morris*, ed. David Latham (Toronto: University of Toronto Press, 2007), 197–208.

14. J. R. R. Tolkien, *Beowulf: A Translation and Commentary*, ed. Christopher Tolkien (London: Harper Collins, 2014).

15. J. R. R. Tolkien, "*Beowulf*: The Monsters and the Critics" in *The Monsters and the Critics and Other Essays*, ed. Christopher Tolkien (London: George Allen & Unwin, 1983), 5–48.

16. J. R. R. Tolkien, *The Lord of the Rings*, 2nd ed. (Boston: Houghton Mifflin, 1994), 1110.

17. See Thomas Honegger, "The Rohirrim: 'Anglo-Saxons on Horseback'? An Inquiry into Tolkien's Use of Sources" in *Tolkien and the Study of His Sources,* ed. Jason Fisher (Jefferson, NC: MacFarland, 2011), 115–32.

18. Letter 226, "From a Letter to Professor L.W. Forster," December 31, 1960, in Carpenter, *The Letters of J. R. R. Tolkien*, 303.

19. Publishers have attempted to take advantage of this link. In 2003 Inkling Books published editions of *The House of the Wolfings* and *The Roots of the Mountain* each with the subtitle "A Book That Influenced J. R. R. Tolkien." In 2013 editions by the same press prefaced the actual title with the label "Tolkien's Warriors."

20. Morris's short story "The Folk of the Mountain Door" (published posthumously in 1914) can serve as a shorter alternative reading assignment and is particularly useful in showcasing his style. The story can be found in *Tales before Tolkien: The Roots of Modern Fantasy,* ed. Douglas A. Anderson (New York: Ballantine Books, 2003), 120–32.

21. Recall that Tolkien wrote of his attempt to pen "a short story somewhat on the lines of Morris's romances with chunks of poetry in between." See Letter 1 in Carpenter, *The Letters of J. R. R. Tolkien*, 7.

22. William Morris, *The Story of the Glittering Plain* (Hammersmith: Kelmscott Press, 1891), 82.

23. Tolkien, *The Lord of the Rings,* 221.

24. William Morris, *News from Nowhere* (1890; repr., Hammersmith: Kelmscott Press, 1892). For an excellent summary of the similarities between Nowhere and the Shire, see Scoville, "Pastoralia and Perfectability in William Morris and J. R. R. Tolkien," 96–97.

BIBLIOGRAPHY

Alexander, Michael. *Medievalism: The Middle Ages in Modern England*. New Haven, CT: Yale University Press, 2007.

Barton, Matt. *Dungeons and Desktops: The History of Computer Role-Playing Games.* Wellesley, MA: A. K. Peters, 2009.

Carpenter, Humphrey. *J. R. R. Tolkien: A Biography.* 1977. Reprint edition, Boston: Houghton Mifflin, 2000.

———, ed. *The Letters of J. R. R. Tolkien.* 1981. Reprint edition, Boston: Houghton Mifflin, 2000.

Chance, Jane, ed. *Tolkien the Medievalist.* New York: Routledge, 2003.

Chandler, Alice. *A Dream of Order: The Medieval Ideal in Nineteenth-Century Literature*. London: Routledge, 1970.

Evans, Jonathan. "The Dragon Lore of Middle-Earth: Tolkien and Old English and Old Norse Tradition." In *J. R. R. Tolkien and His Literary Resonances: Views of Middle-Earth,* edited by George Clark and Daniel Timmons, 21–38. Westport, CT: Greenwood Press, 2000.

Girouard, Mark. *The Return to Camelot: Chivalry and the English Gentleman*. New Haven, CT: Yale University Press, 1981.

Honegger, Thomas. "The Rohirrim: 'Anglo-Saxons on Horseback'? An Inquiry into Tolkien's Use of Sources." In *Tolkien and the Study of His Sources,* edited by Jason Fisher, 115–32. Jefferson, NC: MacFarland, 2011.

Jones, Chris. "The Reception of Morris's *Beowulf.*" In *Writing on the Image: Reading William Morris*, edited by David Latham, 197–208. Toronto: University of Toronto Press, 2007.

Kline, Daniel T. ed. *Digital Gaming Re-imagines the Middle Ages.* New York: Routledge, 2014.

Lang, Andrew. "The Story of Sigurd." In *The Red Fairy Book.* 1890. Reprint, New York: Dover, 1966.

Matthews, David. *Medievalism: A Critical History.* Cambridge: D.S. Brewer, 2015.

Morris, William. "The Folk of the Mountain Door." 1914. In *Tales before Tolkien: The Roots of Modern Fantasy,* edited by Douglas A. Anderson. 120–132. New York: Ballantine Books, 2003.

———. *News from Nowhere.* 1890 Reprint edition, Hammersmith: Kelmscott Press, 1892.

———. *The Story of the Glittering Plain.* Hammersmith: Kelmscott Press, 1881.

———. *Story of Sigurd the Völsung and the Fall of the Niblung.* London: Ellis & White, 1877.

Morris, William and A. J. Wyatt, trans. *The Tale of Beowulf.* Hammersmith: Kelmscott Press, 1895.

Morris, William and Eiríkr Magnússon, trans., *Völsunga Saga: The Story of the Völsungs and Niblungs, with Certain Songs from the Elder Edda.* London: Ellis, 1870.

Scoville, Chester. "Pastoralia and Perfectability in William Morris and J. R. R. Tolkien." In *Tolkien's Modern Middle Ages,* edited by Jane Chance and Alfred K. Siewers, 93–103. New York: Palgrave Macmillan, 2005.

Shippey, Tom. *The Road to Middle-Earth.* 3rd ed. New York: Houghton Mifflin, 2003.

Tolkien, J. R. R. "*Beowulf:* The Monsters and the Critics." In *The Monsters and the Critics and Other Essays,* edited by Christopher Tolkien, 5–48. London: George Allen & Unwin, 1983.

———. *The Hobbit, or There and Back Again.* 1937. Reprint edition, Boston, Houghton Mifflin, 1997.

———. *The Lord of the Rings.* 2nd edition. Boston: Houghton Mifflin, 1994.

———. "On Fairy-Stories." In *The Monsters and the Critics and Other Essays,* edited by Christopher Tolkien, 48–71. London: George Allen & Unwin, 1983.

———. "On Translating Beowulf." In *The Monsters and the Critics and Other Essays,* edited by Christopher Tolkien, 109–61. London: George Allen & Unwin, 1983.

Vorhees, Gerald, Joshua Call, and Katie Whitlock, eds. *Dungeons, Dragons, and Digital Denizens: The Digital Role-Playing Game.* London: Continuum, 2012.

Waithe, Marcus. *William Morris's Utopia of Strangers: Victorian Medievalism and the Ideal of Hospitality.* Woodbridge: D. S. Brewer, 2006.

Part II
POLITICAL CONTEXTS

Chapter Six

A Dream of William Cobbett?

Teaching Morris's John Ball *in an Interdisciplinary Course on Victorian Radicalism*

Linda K. Hughes and William M. Meier

This essay emerges from a hybrid graduate/undergraduate interdisciplinary course entitled "Radical Victorians," co-taught by historian William M. Meier and literary historian Linda K. Hughes, which enrolled advanced students in both disciplinary fields. The course framed nineteenth-century Britain as an ideal laboratory for students to engage with radical texts. The Victorian era's industrialization, urbanization, growth of democracy, imperial expansion, and revolutions in print culture all contributed to an exciting yet unsettled time that inspired new visions for the root-and-branch transformation of society. We placed Morris in a long (if highly selective) line of British radicalism, a "fellowship" of precursors and contemporaries, including Chartists, feminists, and socialists who simultaneously looked backward to a tradition of the ancient rights of the "free-born Englishman" and forward to dreams of revolutionary rupture and utopia. Our course thus involved comparison not only of Morris to other writers but also of the politics of *A Dream of John Ball* to a longer arc of radical texts and activism: prior to encountering Morris, students had read William Cobbett, Feargus O'Connor, Ernest Jones, Friedrich Engels, Karl Marx, Giuseppe Mazzini, and J. A. Hobson as well as numerous primary materials in the British and Irish press and secondary works by historians and literary scholars.

Morris made his appearance at mid-term when we assigned two of his texts. The first, *A Dream of John Ball*, serialized in 1886–1887 and important enough to Morris to become a Kelmscott Press book in 1892, narrates the author's time-travel to witness the 1381 Peasants' Revolt.

The second assigned text, a short introduction to the 1892 Kelmscott edition of John Ruskin's "The Nature of Gothic," contains Morris's musings on the relationship of art, labor, and politics (and, in the digitized internet

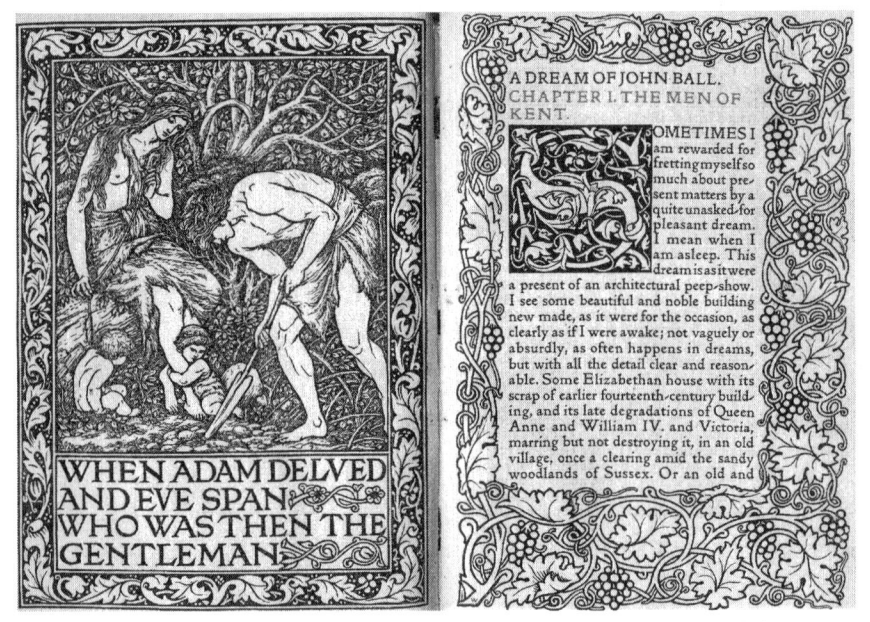

Figure 6.1. *A Dream of John Ball*, frontispiece and first page, Kelmscott Edition, 1892. Reproduced courtesy of the Mark Samuels Lasner Collection, University of Delaware Library.

version we assigned, Morris's commitment to design and to the "slow print" examined by Elizabeth Carolyn Miller in her monograph of that title, another of our course texts).[1] In the following week students also read *Commonweal* in the context of other digitized radical newspapers (see our syllabus in Appendix A). In these readings William Cobbett emerged as a crucial intertext for Morris, despite the curious silence about Cobbett in scholarly commentary on *A Dream*. In this essay, we begin by documenting how setting aside an author-centered approach to Morris in the classroom and instead reading him in a larger context of nineteenth-century radicalism illuminates the importance of Cobbett as an intertext for scholars, teachers, and students alike. We then describe in more detail how we framed *A Dream of John Ball* within our larger course structure and within our two-week discussion of Morris and *Commonweal* and the teaching challenges as well as benefits of our method.

After students had read *A Dream of John Ball* but prior to class discussion, we solicited five to ten minute responses at the beginning of class, stressing that their writing was not being graded. As the prompt for these comments stated, "To begin discussion we ask that you spend about 5 minutes writing out any and all connections you see between *A Dream of John Ball* and the earlier radicalisms we have studied." The most common link between Morris and other radicalisms (cited by all but one of our sixteen students) was the affinity students saw between *A Dream* and William Cobbett's *Rural Rides*, which we had read at the beginning of the semester. Students especially singled out Cobbett's love of rural life and the open countryside over the "Great Wen" London (Cobbett's term before it was Morris's) and the high value both placed on honest work and creativity. Insofar as this link is underrepresented in Morris studies, teaching and learning about Morris in the context of radicalism is a significant scholarly enterprise.

In August 1883 Morris sent a missive to one of his publishers, David White (of Ellis & White) to "lay hands for me on the works of William Cobbett— any or all of them."[2] His request apparently fulfilled, Morris ruminated on the great radical's writing and he was clearly drawn to Cobbett's vision of rural society as emblematic of a lost golden age; one early biographer even claimed that Morris knew *Rural Rides* "almost by heart."[3] In September 1883 he wrote to his daughter Jenny that "I have got a lot of W. Cobbet's [*sic*] books; such queer things they are, but with plenty of stuff in them . . . One little book called *Cottage Economy* is very amusing, and there is a chapter in it on the making of straw plait: the article on the pig is touching."[4] That fall he fired a letter to the editor of the *Daily News* to complain about "the malodorous and insanitary condition of the ditch which runs along the towpath from the Soap Works by Hammersmith-bridge," which "deprives those of us who value their health of the opportunity of walking in one of the most beautiful spots in the suburbs." Morris was especially incensed because "William Cobbett lived and wrote for some time on the farm . . . just south of this foul ditch. One might well wish that that master of plain-speaking were alive to address a few words to our present stink-and-pest breeders."[5] Certainly one discerns here Cobbett's contribution to Morris's environmental consciousness; but there is also a note of appreciation of Cobbett's writerly qualities of "amusing," "touching," and "plain-speaking."

Morris's contributions to the socialist periodicals *Commonweal* and *Justice* before, during, and after the serialization of *A Dream* in the former (November 1886 to January 1887), illustrate how closely he channeled Cobbett whenever he sought to defend the common men and women of England. Cobbett bookends *A Dream*: on the second page the narrator lays his dream scene amidst the un-enclosed landscape of "the sweeping Wiltshire downs, so well beloved of William Cobbett"; and in the penultimate paragraph of the novel he awakens in the "Great Wen." Strikingly, Morris had earlier (in 1884) framed an article in *Justice* in the exact same way: he invokes Cobbett and the Great Wen in the first sentence, and then, immediately following Morris's signature, he includes an extended quote from Cobbett. The occasion for this piece was the recent Lord Mayor's Show (the annual street parade heralding the inauguration of a new Lord Mayor of the City of London), which had staged a historical tableau of Sir William Walworth (Lord Mayor, 1380–1381) standing over the dead Wat Tyler.[6] Evidently the pageant got Morris thinking and gave him occasion to relate to readers for the first time his version of the story of John Ball, Wat Tyler, and the 1381 Peasants' Revolt. The article rewrites the Peasants' Revolt, with Morris seeking to counter the received story (he called it a "sort of nursery tale") and to rescue from condescension the depiction of "foolish and ignorant armed peasants, knowing not what they asked for." He refers to the episode instead as the "murder of Wat Tyler," who was martyred along with "his worthier associate John Ball." Morris concludes: "Nor will we say that he and John Ball died for nothing, however doleful is the story . . . of the stout men of Kent breaking up half in fear and irresolution, half deluded by the lies and empty promises of their masters, to whom, as ever, any course seemed good that enabled them to keep the people down."[7] Then follows the quote from Cobbett's 1829 *Advice to Young Men*, in which the old radical describes how much better off English laborers had been in the 1400s, especially regarding their high wages and the quality of their clothing (a preoccupation of Morris's in *A Dream*). Here Cobbett was both intertext and paratext.

When in December 1885 a laborer named Henry Smith was sentenced to one month's hard labor at Aldershot Police Court for taking food scraps, *Commonweal* damned the system that classified wasted food as property. Morris summoned the "Ghost of William Cobbett" to comment on the erosion of customary rights to subsistence, alleging that such a punitive law was retrogressive when compared to "the Scandinavian law that decreed a thousand years ago that he who stole from necessity of hunger was to go scot free."[8] In 1887 Morris again invoked Cobbett in an article on art and labor in which he claimed that medieval English working men were happier than their Victorian counterparts because "they practised that co-operation in their production of beauty; whereas we, as long as we are under the domination of the profit-grinders, cannot do so; and the result follows which I have so often spoken of, that art is a skinny drowsy skeleton amidst the stir and enormous riches of modern civilisation. . . . Again, along with William Cobbett, contrast the dungeon-like propriety of St. Paul's, the work of a 'famous' architect, with the free imagination and delicate beauty of the people-built Gothic churches, that were raised by masons who had no architect over them."[9] So Morris was not only reading Cobbett but actively drawing upon his method of using the past to critique the nineteenth century standard of living both in aesthetic and material terms.

Commonweal promoted Cobbett's political writings in its recommended reading list of "Books for Socialists" as a volume "being distinctly helpful to a right understanding of the social problem," and the journal frequently excerpted lengthy quotes from Cobbett's works.[10] In August 1886 Morris and his socialist comrade Ernest Belfort Bax identified Cobbett as a founding father of English Radicalism in their series of articles entitled "Socialism from the Root Up" published in *Commonweal*. Cobbett was "a man of great literary capacity of a kind, and with flashes of insight as to social matters far before his time." Though Morris and Bax thought him "clouded by violent irrational prejudices and prodigious egotism," he was "withal a peasant rather than a bourgeois—a powerful disruptive agent."[11] To envision Cobbett in this way—as a radical, idealistic peasant who could glimpse, albeit imperfectly, future social and political struggles—previewed Morris's engagement with the relationship between history, politics, and literature three months prior to publishing the first installment of *A Dream*. Though there is more room for research here, it is clear that by working through Cobbett Morris was situating himself in, and helping to craft, an indigenous tradition of Victorian radicalism. And by teaching Morris in a course in which students are also reading lengthy excerpts from Cobbett (see the September 2 assignment in Appendix A), students themselves are positioned to see the connections between these two nineteenth-century radical figures.

Given our students' backgrounds we were conscious that most would be reading Morris for the first time. Course members ranged from specialist graduate students with advanced skills to undergraduates who were very bright but had scant training in method or theory. Seven were English graduate students (3 MA, 4 PhD) specializing in rhetoric and in American, Irish, and British literature; five were history graduate students (2 MA, 3 PhD) whose primary research was in American, not British, history, and for whom the seminar was part of their field of transatlantic study. Moreover we enrolled one history undergraduate, one English undergraduate, and two undergraduates taking the course in fulfillment of Honors College colloquia (one an English, the other an environmental science major).

To equip our students with the necessary historical, literary, and theoretical tools we circulated weekly prompts that included reading questions, biographical sketches of the assigned authors, and short paragraphs outlining the context for the readings. For the week devoted principally to Morris, students read him alongside George Bernard Shaw's 1884 Fabian manifesto and Ruskin's "The Nature of Gothic." We also asked students to read background essays on *A Dream* by Florence S. Boos and Peter Wright, both on the website of the William Morris Archive, and several scholarly articles on Morris's rhetoric and the landscape of British socialism in the late nineteenth century.[12] When reading Morris's preface to Ruskin, for instance, we prodded students to consider: "What does art express, and why is it crucial to labor? What connections to earlier radicalism does Morris make? What do you think

Morris signifies by the term 'politics'?" Our questions for *A Dream* similarly emphasized political contexts: "How would you position Morris in the context of the radicalisms we've examined this semester, from Cobbett and the Chartists on through Marx and Engels?" Or again: "What specific tenets of socialism are evident in the novel?" We also queried, "What effect would you speculate the novel might have on those who subscribed to the penny paper?" (See Appendix A, week of October 28, and Appendix B, which reproduces the verbal portion of our prompt.)

Thus the structure of our syllabus, the nature of the week's secondary readings, and our prompting questions all prioritized Morris's place within the larger trajectory of nineteenth-century radical politics and radical print. If, on one hand, this enabled students' insight into the Morris-Cobbett relation, it also invited a less happy outcome: overdetermined readings of *A Dream of John Ball* shaped by scholarly frameworks they had encountered earlier. Despite our pairing of Ruskin and Morris, for example, not one student mentioned the impact of the former on Morris's experimental socialist novel in their free writing at the outset of the class period. Although this finding was not evident until we moved from in-class writing to class discussion, we were taken aback by the predisposition of so many students to read *A Dream* as propaganda rather than as a complex literary work. Students variously considered the text a mere vehicle for expressing radical ideas or an attempt to work out the implications of revolutionary socialism, while others discerned elements of Marxist class warfare and historical materialism. When we asked why students saw *A Dream* in this way, they cited the periodical context and argued that its serialization in the socialist journal *Commonweal* was proof enough of the novel's polemical purpose. Here students were drawing upon what they had learned earlier in the course from reading Ian Haywood, whose *Revolution in Popular Literature* argues that nineteenth-century popular radical writing was always propaganda.[13] This of course oversimplifies Haywood's complex argument; nonetheless, it is what students took away from their reading. We did our best during discussion to coax students to consider other dimensions of Morris's novel. But, given that one of our aims in teaching this text was to interest more students in Morris's work, we were disappointed in this outcome. From our experience we have learned anew to make explicit to students what we ourselves take too much for granted: the delights of Morris's experimentalism and literary play as well as his radical interventions in nineteenth-century politics. Just as for history students it is crucial to make them aware of differing, sometimes clashing historical interpretations of a given event or issue, so it can behoove us as teachers to remind humanities students of the multifaceted nature of specifically literary texts that can channel political ideation while simultaneously representing human emotion in the presence of political events and revolution, conveying the pleasures of design in literary structure and in resonant literary language, and imagining dreams of a better future that exceed political positions. As a practical strategy for achieving this end, we recommend having students read "An Aesthetic Ecocommunist: Morris the Red and Morris the Green," also by Florence Boos.[14] This essay not only connects Morris to current student interests in ecocriticism and activism but would also disrupt a purely Marxist reading of *A Dream* by students and offer a way into the aesthetic and humane qualities of the narrative.

In many other respects, however, we considered our teaching approach a resounding success. Because students had read a number of other radical writers for nine weeks, they were well equipped to see how readily Morris's work exhibited affinities with earlier radical writing. Among the political intersections that students cited between Morris's novel and the Chartist movement of the 1840s were workers' rights to the value of their own labor, the resort to physical force when necessary, workers' oppression as a result of the binary between monopolist land owners and laborers, the articulation of a set of demands that John Ball's followers (like Chartist leaders') planned to present to the monarch, and the movement's reliance on big meetings and radical action.

That we had previously read *Alton Locke*, the novel about a Chartist tailor authored by Christian socialist Charles Kingsley in 1850, also enabled students to connect John Ball the "rascal hedge-priest" and the narrator's opening dream vision to Kingsley's representation of religion and fellowship, since both novels endorse politically-engaged religion and spurn state churches predicated on hierarchy.

Even more students (all but three in the class) read *A Dream* in relation to socialism generally and Marx and Engels in particular. Some applied the same points adduced in relation to Chartism (class divisions and a labor-based theory of value) to Marxist thought. Additionally students commented on the prioritizing of community over the individual by both Morris and Marx. One history graduate student asserted that the novel presents the evolving relation of workers to other social groups over time in ways consistent with the terms on which Marx and Engels understood history; another succinctly encapsulated the convergence of Morris with Marx and Engels in the single phrase: "Eat the Rich!" An English graduate student, one of the few to focus on Morris's literary qualities, connected what she termed Morris's beautiful landscape descriptions at the outset to Engels's *The Condition of the Working Class in England*, since Engels also recounted the impact of industrialism on the environment. She noted as well the challenge posed both to the fictional John Ball and to nineteenth-century socialists of imagining a future radically different from the present. It is the challenge we still face today, and one that we can explore with students in a course featuring William Morris in company with other Victorian radicals.

APPENDIX A: COURSE SYLLABUS, "RADICAL VICTORIANS"
Engl./Hist. 50133
Seminar in Literature and History: *Radical Victorians*
Instructors: Dr. Linda K. Hughes and Dr. William Meier

Course description:

Nineteenth-century Britain was *the* cutting edge laboratory for experiments with modernity: industrialization, explosive urban growth, stable democratization, imperial expansion, and revolutions in print culture profoundly changed British society during the reign of Queen Victoria. Exciting yet unsettled times inspired new visions for the root-and-branch transformation of an already rapidly morphing nation. "Radical Victorians" examines these visions—some looking backward to a tradition of ancient rights of the "free-born Englishman," others forward to revolutionary rupture and utopia—to illustrate how Chartists, feminists, anarchists, and many others crafted progressive movements and communicated the promise of political regeneration to a wide public. In addition to exploring major political and ideological contours of nineteenth-century Europe, the course is grounded in an analysis of the relationship between power and print at a historical moment when mass circulation newspapers, popular novels, and poetry created new reading publics among the novel parties, social classes, and interest groups that evolved in a modernizing Britain.

"Radical Victorians" approaches these aims through interdisciplinary reading, research, and teaching in English and History. Enhanced command of interdisciplinary method is an integral part of this course; hence both a historian and literary scholar will lead discussions of common assigned readings to model how the two disciplines interpret and analyze primary sources. Both faculty members will also work closely with individual students to help craft research questions and topics for their final papers. Faculty and students will have the opportunity to enrich their own disciplinary approaches with new questions and methods, with a special focus on how we examine texts. Drawing upon the rich periodical databases and newspaper archives available through TCU Libraries will also stimulate discussion of how we can construct interpretations of the past through digital humanities. Because nineteenth-century Britain was a world power, students will be encouraged to connect the historical and literary landscapes of Victorian Britain to wider European, transatlantic, and imperial spheres.

During the semester students will complete:

1) Two 4–5 page papers based on periodical and archival investigation:
   The first paper is to curate a gathering of five poems from the *Northern Star*. Choose any that appeal to you from issues published 1837 to 1848 and write a headnote documenting how each poem exemplifies the "Chartist

revolution" identified by Haywood and the principles of Chartist poetry identified by Sanders. The second paper is to gather five articles from Irish newspapers on a topic related to British imperial violence (e.g., during the Indian rebellion of 1857) and discuss how these pieces mount an anti-colonial critique. Further details about these assignments will be announced in class.

2) Five short, 1-page primary source assignments:

Students will select one primary text related to the topic for the week and analyze it in light of the secondary reading for that week. Specific details for each assignment will be announced in class; due dates are highlighted in the course schedule below.

3) One long paper:

Fifteen to twenty pages based on a topic selected with the instructors' approval. The paper is based on intensive research in periodicals and digital historical archives and will make use of the interdisciplinary models of the course.

Reading list:

1) For purchase:
Norman McCord, *British History 1815–1914* (Oxford, 2007)
Elizabeth Carolyn Miller, *Slow Print: Literary Radicalism and Late Victorian Print Culture* (Stanford, 2013)
Charles Kingsley, *Alton Locke*
Olive Schreiner, *The Story of An African Farm*
William Morris, *A Dream of John Ball*
Niall Whelehan, *The Dynamiters: Irish Nationalism and Political Violence in the Wider World, 1867–1900* (Cambridge, 2015)

2) Reference works through TCU Libraries:
Oxford History of Popular Print Culture
Dictionary of Nineteenth-Century Journalism
Dictionary of Literary Biography
Oxford Dictionary of National Biography
C19 (including Wellesley Index to Victorian Periodicals)
Waterloo Directory of English Periodicals, 1800–1900

Course outline:

August 26: The Context of British Radicalism in 1815

Primary Sources:
- Percy Bysshe Shelley, "Mask of Anarchy" (1819)
- George Cruikshank, "Poor John Bull"
- George Cruikshank, "A Free Born Englishman!"

Secondary Sources:
- McCord, *British History 1815–1914*, pp. 9–17, 22–29, 34–50, 71–74
- James Epstein, "The Constitutional Idiom: Radical Reasoning, Rhetoric and Action in Early Nineteenth-Century England," *Journal of Social History* 23, no. 3 (Spring 1990): 553–74
- Glenn Burgess, "Introduction," in *English Radicalism 1550–1850*, eds. Glenn Burgess and Matthew Festenstein (Cambridge, 2007), pp. 1–16

September 2: William Cobbett and the Condition of England

Primary Sources:
- William Cobbett, excerpts from *Rural Rides*: Oct. 30, 1821, 1: 3–6; Nov. 11–12, 1821, 1: 26–28; Nov. 18–20, 1821, 1: 34–37; Sept. 25, 1822, 1: 92–97; Sept. 23, 1832, 2: 277–85 [also read the introduction by Asa Briggs, 1: v–x]

Secondary Sources:
- McCord, *British History*, pp. 79–89, 103–28
- Ian Haywood, *The Revolution in Popular Literature: Print, Politics and the People, 1790–1860* (Cambridge, 2004), ch. 4—esp. pp. 86–111
- Ian Dyck, "Cobbett, William (1763–1835)," *Oxford Dictionary of National Biography* [online via TCU Library; hereafter *ODNB*]
- Peter Jones, "Swing, Speenhamland and Rural Social Relations: The 'Moral Economy' of the English Crowd in the Nineteenth Century," *Social History* 32, no. 3 (Aug. 2007): 271–90

Primary Source Assignment #1 due:
Using the British Periodicals I&II and/or the 19th Century British Newspapers databases, choose one article by William Cobbett in his *Weekly Political Register* between 1819 and 1832 and analyze it using the approaches found in the Haywood and Jones readings.

September 9: Radicals in the Age of Reform

Primary Sources:
- Selected pieces from *Westminster Review* and *Monthly Repository*: W. J. Fox, "On Organic Reforms," *MR*, November 1835: 693–707; Z. [Robert Browning], "The King," *MR*, November 1835: 707–8
- Duke of Wellington, speech against reform, *Hansard*, Nov. 2, 1830
- T. B. Macaulay, "Reform that you may preserve," *Hansard*, March 2, 1831
- J.S. Mill on founding the *Westminster Review*, from chapter 4 of his *Autobiography*

Secondary Sources:
- McCord, *British History*, ch. 4–5
- H. S. Jones, "Philosophic radicals (act. 1830–1841)," *ODNB*
- Jose Harris, "Mill, John Stuart (1806–1873)," *ODNB*
- Haywood, *Revolution in Popular Literature*, ch. 5
- J. A. Phillips and Charles Wetherell, "The Great Reform Act of 1832 and the Political Modernization of England," *American Historical Review* 100, no. 2 (Apr. 1995): 411–36

Primary Source Assignment #2 due

September 16: The Chartist Movement

Primary Sources:
- Feargus O'Connor's *Northern Star* at ncse.ac.uk
- Ernest Jones, "Leawood Hall" (first published as "The Labourer: A Christmas Carol"), *The Labourer*, 1847.

Secondary Sources:
- Haywood, *Revolution in Popular Literature*, ch. 6 ["The Chartist Revolution"]
- Mike Sanders, *The Poetry of Chartism: Aesthetics, Politics, History* (Cambridge, 2009) [introduction]
- Malcolm Chase, *Chartism: A New History* (2007)
- John Belchem, "Radical Language, Meaning and Identity in the Age of the Chartists," *Journal of Victorian Culture* 10, no. 1 (2005): 1–14
- Gareth Stedman Jones, "Rethinking Chartism," in *Languages of Class: Studies in English Working Class History 1832–1982*, Gareth Stedman Jones (Cambridge, 1983), pp. 90–178

First 4–5 page paper due:
Curate a gathering of five poems from the *Northern Star*. Choose any that appeal to you from issues published 1837 to 1848 and write a headnote documenting how each poem exemplifies the "Chartist revolution" identified by Haywood and the principles of Chartist poetry identified by Sanders

September 23: The Anti-Corn Law League

Primary Sources:
- Ebenezer Elliott, "Corn Law Rhymes".
- Richard Cobden, speeches in Parliament [*Hansard* site]
- Charles Kingsley, *Alton Locke*

Secondary Sources:
- McCord, *British History*, ch. 5–6
- Miles Taylor, "Cobden, Richard (1804–1865)," and "Bright, John (1811–1889)," *ODNB*
- Peter Gurney, "'Rejoicing in Potatoes': The Politics of Consumption in England during the 'Hungry Forties'," *Past & Present* no. 203 (May 2009): 99–136
- Simon Morgan, "The Anti-Corn Law League and British Anti-Slavery in Transatlantic Perspective, 1838–1846," *Historical Journal* 52, no. 1 (March 2009): 87–107

September 30: Marx, Engels, and 1848

Primary Sources:
- Friedrich Engels, *The Condition of the Working Class in England* [introduction, The Industrial Proletariat, The Great Towns, Irish Immigration].
- Karl Marx, "The Chartist Movement," *New York Tribune*, Aug. 25, 1852.
- Giuseppe Mazzini, "Europe: Its Condition and Prospects," *Westminster Review*, January 1852
- Swinburne, "Dedication to Joseph Mazzini," *Songs before Sunrise*, 1871.
- Robert Owen, from *Revolution in the Mind and Practice of the Human Race* (London, 1849) [preface "To the Red Republicans, Communists, and Socialists of Europe"]
- Karl Marx and Friedrich Engels, *The Communist Manifesto*.
- Ruskin, "Unto this Last," *Cornhill Magazine*, Sept.–Nov. 1860

Secondary Sources:
- Ross McKibbin, "Why Was There No Marxism in Great Britain?" *English Historical Review* 99, no. 391 (April 1984): 297–331
- Gregory Claeys, "Mazzini, Kossuth, and British Radicalism, 1848–1854," *Journal of British Studies* 28 (1989): 225–61
- Robert Saunders, "The Politics of Reform and the Making of the Second Reform Act, 1848–1867," *Historical Journal* 50, no. 3 (Sep. 2007): 571–91
- McCord, *British History*, ch. 7–9

Primary Source Assignment #3 due

October 7: Empire (I): India and Ireland

Primary Sources:
- Ernest Jones, *The New World* (reprinted as *The Revolt of Hindustan*).

Secondary Sources:
- McCord, *British History*, pp. 310–11, 322–24, 399–414, 477–86

- Philippa Levine, "Britain in India," in *The British Empire: Sunrise to Sunset*, Philippa Levine (Harlow, UK, 2007), pp. 61–81
- Nicholas Owen, "The Soft Heart of the British Empire: Indian Radicals in Edwardian London," *Past & Present* 220, no. 1 (2013): 143–84

Second 4–5 page paper due: periodical assignment from Irish Newspaper Archive:
Gather five articles from Irish newspapers on a topic related to British imperial violence (e.g., during the Indian rebellion of 1857) and discuss how these pieces mount an anti-colonial critique.

October 14: Empire (II): Africa

Primary Sources:
- Olive Schreiner, *The Story of an African Farm*
- J. A. Hobson, *Imperialism: A Study* (London, 1902)

Secondary Sources:
- McCord, *British History*, 416–23
- P. J. Cain, "British radicalism, the South African crisis, and the origins of the theory of financial imperialism," in *The Impact of the South African War*, eds. David Omissi and Andrew S. Thompson (New York, 2002)

Proposals for long research paper due

October 21: Religion

Primary Sources:
- James Thomson, *City of Dreadful Night*
- Amy Levy, "A Ballad of Religion and Marriage"

Secondary Sources:
- Kevin Mills, "'The Truth of Midnight': Apocalyptic Insomnia in James Thomson's 'The City of Dreadful Night'," *Victorian Literature and Culture* 35, no. 1 (2007): 121–34
- Miller, *Slow Print*, ch. 5
- McCord, *British History*, pp. 259–64, 381–87, 514–17

Primary Source Assignment #4 due

October 28: Socialism and the Socialist Novel

Primary Sources:
- William Morris, *A Dream of John Ball*
- [G. B. Shaw], *A Manifesto, Fabian Tract No. 2* (London, 1884)

- Shaw, *Major Barbara*
- Ruskin, "On the Nature of Gothic," from *Stones of Venice* (1853)

Secondary Sources:
- Graham Johnson, "Making Reform the Instrument of Revolution: British Social Democracy, 1881–1911," *Historical Journal* 43, no. 4 (Dec. 2000): 977–1002
- Deborah Mutch, "Re-Righting the Past: Socialist Historical Narrative and the Road to the New Life," *Literature & History* 18, No. 1 (2009): 16–34

Preliminary bibliography and thesis statement for research paper due

November 4: The radical press/mass print

Primary Sources:
- Selected articles TBA from digitized historical newspapers: *Pall Mall Gazette, Daily Mail, Commonweal, Justice,* and *Reynolds's Newspaper*

Secondary Sources:
- Miller, *Slow Print*, ch. 1–4, 6

Primary Source Assignment #5 due

November 11: Terrorism

Primary Sources:
- Louisa Bevington, *Liberty Lyrics*
- Selected articles from *The Torch* [online via NCCO]

Secondary Sources:
- Niall Whelehan, *The Dynamiters: Irish Nationalism and Political Violence in the Wider World, 1867–1900* (Cambridge, 2015)

November 18: Feminism

Primary Sources:
- Butler, "An Appeal to the People of England" (1870);
- Sarah Grand, "The New Aspect of the Woman Question" (1894), *North American Review*
- Caird, "Marriage" (1888), *Westminster Review*
- George Egerton, "A Cross Line," *Keynotes* (1894).
- Amy Levy, "Magdalen" (poem), 1884 (posthumously published)
- Josephine Butler, "Lovers of the Lost," *Contemporary Review*, Jan. 1870

Secondary Sources:
- Antoinette Burton, *Burdens of History: British Feminists, Indian Women, and Imperial Culture, 1865–1915* (Chapel Hill, 1994), ch. 1, 5
- Janice Schroeder, "Speaking Volumes: Victorian Feminism and the Appeal of Public Discussion," *Nineteenth-Century Contexts* 25, no. 2 (2003): 97–117
- Laura E. Nym Mayhall, "Defining Militancy: Radical Protest, the Constitutional Idiom, and Women's Suffrage in Britain, 1908–1909," *Journal of British Studies* 39, no. 3 (July 2000): 340–71
- M. J. D. Roberts, "Feminism and the State in Later Victorian England," *Historical Journal* 38, no. 1 (March 1995): 85–110

Rough draft of research paper (min. 500 words plus full outline) due

APPENDIX B: EXCERPTS FROM COURSE PROMPT PREPARING STUDENTS TO READ *A DREAM OF JOHN BALL*
Socialism, Morris, Ruskin: Prompt for Week 10

William Morris, *A Dream of John Ball* (1886–1887, *Commonweal*; 1888, first bound edition; 1892, Kelmscott edition)

Read the *ODNB* entry on Morris for his biographical background. For images of Morris's socialist novel published during his lifetime, click on the appropriate links of the William Morris Archive edition of this text (http://morrisedition.lib.uiowa.edu/dream.html).

Peter Wright's and Florence Boos's introductions should provide the historical background you need to approach this text; Michelle Weinroth's article provides one possible interpretive framework for the novel.

Morris and Radicalism—how would you position Morris in the context of the radicalisms we've examined this semester from Cobbett and the Chartists on through Marx and Engels? What affinities or divergences emerge for you when you consider *A Dream of John Ball* in relation to the other poetry and fiction we've read?

In many of the other radical writings we've read, we've often found ideological or racist blind spots; what of Morris's novel?

Morris and Ruskin—Based on what you have read, what impression does Ruskin's essay on Gothic architecture leave upon Morris's representation of medieval England and medieval peasants in revolt?

Morris and Socialism—what specific tenets of socialism are evident in the novel? Do any elements seem inconsistent with socialism?

Morris and Readers of Radical Print—You can see the surrounding articles in *Commonweal* in the PDFs of the serial parts on the William Morris Archive. What effect would you speculate the novel might have on those who subscribed to the penny paper? (Some of course were litterateurs, but the journal sought a readership among workers as well.) Was *Commonweal* an effective venue for Morris's socialist novel?

Morris's legacy, and that of his novel—as you can tell from Fiona MacCarthy's *ODNB* entry on Morris, the single most famous of his socialist works is *News from Nowhere*, a utopian novel often characterized as an answer to Edward Bellamy's *Looking Backward*. Is there something about *A Dream of John Ball* that might limit its ability to "travel" across readerships and decades?

We are guessing that many of you are reading Morris for the first time. What features, values, or views stand out for you? Do you find elements relevant to twenty-first readers and students? Would you ever consider teaching Morris yourself if you were teaching a history or English class?

NOTES

1. Elizabeth Carolyn Miller, *Slow Print: Literary Radicalism and Late Victorian Print Culture* (Stanford: Stanford University Press, 2013).
2. Morris to White, Aug. 14, 1883, in *The Collected Letters of William Morris, Volume II, Part A: 1881–1884*, ed. Norman Kelvin (Princeton: Princeton University Press, 1987), 215.
3. J. W. Mackail, *The Life of William Morris*, (London: Longmans, Green and Co., 1899), 1:220.
4. William Morris to Jenny Morris, Sept. 4, 1883, *The Collected Letters of William Morris, Volume II, Part A: 1881–1884*, ed. Norman Kelvin (Princeton: Princeton University Press, 1987), 223. Cobbett's passage on the pig in *Cottage Economy* positioned the animal as indispensable to proper diet, proper cultivation of the land, and to public order: "A couple of flitches of bacon are worth fifty thousand Methodist sermons and religious tracts. The sight of them upon the rack tends more to keep a man from poaching and stealing than whole volumes of penal statutes. . . . They are great softeners of the temper, and promoters of domestic harmony": *Cottage Economy* (London: C. Clement, 1822), 116.
5. William Morris, "River Pollution in Putney," letter to the editor, *Daily News*, August 15, 1883, 6.
6. Contemporary accounts relate that this part of the procession "was received with groans and hisses": "Antiquarian News and Notes," *Antiquarian Magazine and Bibliographer* 6, no. 6 (December 1884): 294; "The Lord Mayor's Show," *Leeds Mercury*, November 11, 1884; "Lord Mayor's Day," *Daily News*, November 11, 1884. The *Pall Mall Gazette* noted that the image of Walworth killing Tyler "was not generally acceptable to the populace; indeed, some people had entertained the belief that the group would at the last moment have been omitted from the procession, so widespread apparently was the public agitation": "The Lord Mayor's Show Illustrated," *Pall Mall Gazette*, November 10, 1884. The *Penny Illustrated Paper* found the tableau "obnoxious . . . and especially inopportune at this crisis of a serious constitutional question": "Our London Letter," *Penny Illustrated Paper*, November 15, 1884. One paper even claimed that "but for the strenuous efforts of the police and military at Ludgate-circus the crowd would have demolished car, characters, and everything belonging to the ill-advised and offensive exhibition": "The Lord Mayor's Show," *Reynolds's Newspaper*, November 16, 1884.
7. William Morris, "The Lord Mayor's Show," *Justice*, November 15, 1884, 2.
8. William Morris, "The Husks That the Swine Do Eat," *Commonweal*, January 1886, 7.
9. William Morris, "As an Artist Sees It," *Commonweal*, September 10, 1887, 291.
10. "Books for Socialists," *Commonweal*, June 12, 1886, 88. See also "Worth above Wealth or Station" and neighboring column, quoting Cobbett on "Poverty is the great, the never failing badge of slavery," *Commonweal*, October 23, 1886, 237. Note also that William Sharman approvingly cited Cobbett as a source to prove the higher standard of living in medieval "Merrie England" as compared to modern, industrial England: William Sharman, "The Workhouse; or, John Poorman's Rest,"

Commonweal, January 1, 1887, 1–2. In its weekly "Revolutionary Calendar" of events that happened in that week in history, Cobbett's death was the occasion for a short biographical sketch that praised Cobbett's "thirty-three years of literary kicking" and his status as a "prose poet in praise of nature, and as a grammarian." "What he says may be wrong, but he never leaves you in doubt as to what he means . . . such a man would be a distinct gain to-day when jobbery and lying is rampant, but is handled with dainty touch of kid-glove." T[homas].S[hore]., "Death of Cobbett," *Commonweal*, June 16, 1888, 190.

11. William Morris and E. Belfort Bax, "Socialism from the Root Up. Chapter X.—Political Movements in England," *Commonweal*, August 28, 1886, 170.

12. Peter Wright, "*A Dream of John Ball*: Historical Introduction," *William Morris Archive,* http://morrisedition.lib.uiowa.edu/dreamJohnBallWrightHistoricalIntro.html; Florence Boos, "*A Dream of John Ball*: History as Fellowship," *William Morris Archive,* http://morrisedition.lib.uiowa.edu/DreamIntro.html; Boos, "The Socialist League," *BRANCH: Britain, Representation and Nineteenth-Century History*, ed. Dino Franco Felluga, published April 2015, http://www.branchcollective.org/?ps_articles=florence-boos-the-socialist-league-founded-30-december-1884; Michelle Weinroth, "Redesigning the Language of Social Change: Rhetoric, Agency, and the Oneiric in William Morris's *A Dream of John Ball*," *Victorian Studies* 52, no. 1 (2010): 37–63; Graham Johnson, "Making Reform the Instrument of Revolution: British Social Democracy, 1881–1911," *Historical Journal* 43 (December 2000): 977–1002.

13. Ian Haywood, *The Revolution in Popular Literature: Print, Politics and the People, 1790–1860* (Cambridge: Cambridge University Press, 2004).

14. Florence Boos, "An Aesthetic Ecocommunist: Morris the Red and Morris the Green," *William Morris: Centenary Essays*, ed. Peter Faulkner and Peter Preston (Exeter: University of Exeter Press, 1999), 21–45.

BIBLIOGRAPHY

Boos, Florence S. "An Aesthetic Ecocommunist: Morris the Red and Morris the Green." In *William Morris: Centenary Essays*, edited by Peter Faulkner and Peter Preston (Exeter: University of Exeter Press, 1999): 21–45.

———. "*A Dream of John Ball*: History as Fellowship." http://morrisedition.lib.uiowa.edu/DreamIntro.html

———. "The Socialist League, founded 30 December 1884." *BRANCH: Britain, Representation and Nineteenth-Century History*, edited by Dino Franco Felluga. http://www.branchcollective.org/?ps_articles=florence-boos-the-socialist-league-founded-30-december-1884.

Cobbett, William. *Cottage Economy*. London: C. Clement, 1822.

Haywood, Ian. *The Revolution in Popular Literature: Print, Politics and the People, 1790–1860*. Cambridge: Cambridge University Press, 2004.

Johnson, Graham. "Making Reform the Instrument of Revolution: British Social Democracy, 1881–1911." *Historical Journal* 43 (Dec. 2000): 977–1002.

Kelvin, Norman, ed. *The Collected Letters of William Morris,* Volume 2, Part A: *1881–1884*. Princeton: Princeton University Press, 1987.

Miller, Elizabeth Carolyn. *Slow Print: Literary Radicalism and Late Victorian Print Culture*. Stanford: Stanford University Press, 2013.

Morris, William. "The Lord Mayor's Show." *Justice*, 15 Nov. 1884, 2.

———. "As an Artist Sees It." *Commonweal*, Sept. 10, 1887, 291.

Morris, William, and E. Belfort Bax. "Socialism from the Root Up. Chapter 10.—Political Movements in England." *Commonweal*, Aug. 28, 1886, 170.

Weinroth, Michelle. "Redesigning the Language of Social Change: Rhetoric, Agency, and the Oneiric in William Morris's *A Dream of John Ball*." *Victorian Studies* 52, No. 1 (2010): 37–63.

Wright, Peter. "*A Dream of John Ball*: Historical Introduction." http://morrisedition.lib.uiowa.edu/dreamJohnBallWrightHistoricalIntro.html.

Chapter Seven

"Vive la Commune!"

The Imaginary of the Paris Commune and the Arts and Crafts Movement

Morna O'Neill

For seventy-two days in the spring of 1871, in the aftermath of the Franco-Prussian war, the city of Paris had a communal government. This event came to be known as the Paris Commune, and it would occupy a totemic place in the radical imagination in London at the end of the nineteenth century. The short-lived Parisian social republic demonstrated both the strength of revolutionary spirit and the vindictive forces that opposed it, while the Communards heroically sacrificed themselves for the cause.[1] Literary scholar Kristin Ross recently described the Commune as a powerful "imaginary," evoking the symbolic power of the event, one whose "centrifugal effects" outlasted the Commune itself and spread beyond Paris to London, St. Petersburg, and elsewhere.[2] For Ross, the force of these effects constitutes the prolonged temporality of the Commune: the afterlife of the Commune was "part and parcel of the event itself . . . it is a continuation of the combat by other means."[3] Viewing the Commune in this way—as a historical event as well as an imaginary—allows teachers of history, politics, literature, and art to mine fruitful interdisciplinary ground, as artists, writers, and thinkers continued to find inspiration in the Commune well into the twentieth century (indeed, Ross suggests that the Commune is important for our own political moment). While one could argue that William Morris was always already interdisciplinary in his pursuits and commitments, a consideration of the Commune in approaches to teaching Morris allows for a fuller contextual account of Morris's political and artistic ideals, and the vital points of overlap between them.

Arts and Crafts artists, designers, and activists William Morris and Walter Crane were partisans in the battle to revive the idea of the Commune as an example for English socialists in the 1880s. It is not surprising that Morris and Crane gravitated to the Commune, since the event presented a powerful case of the convergence of art and politics, particularly in the example of the French painter Gustave Courbet. As Linda Nochlin has pointed out, "For Courbet, the Commune was, all too briefly, the fulfillment of his dreams of a government without oppressive, domineering institutions," including those institutions that governed the display of art.[4] Courbet also played a vital role in the Commune's efforts to reform artistic practice through the creation of new Federation of Artists, a democratic organization that would replace the authoritarian institutions of the Second Empire. Art would be taken out of the hands of institutions and placed with the people, in what the Federation called "communal luxury," a "profusion" of art in the public sphere.[5] As the Manifesto states:

> By the word, by the pen, by the pencil, through popular reproduction of masterpieces, and through intelligent and edifying images that can be spread in profusion and displayed in the town halls of the most humble villages in France, the committee will work towards our regeneration, the inauguration of communal wealth, the splendors of the future and the Universal Republic.[6]

The evocative phrase "communal luxury," translated in the above passage as "communal wealth," is taken up by Kristin Ross as the title of her recent reevaluation of the Paris Commune, joining the social goals of the Commune with the category usually assigned to art objects. The Federation instituted free and open exhibitions of contemporary and historical art, as well as instruction in drawing and modeling from primary school onward. Chief among the reforms was the recognition of commercial artist and decorative artists as equal members as well as the individual recognition of a designer and maker. The emphasis during the Commune on the role of the artist and artisan in the creation of such objects shifts the focus from consumer to producer: in imagining a new social role for the artist, the "Universal Republic" promised by the Commune creates a new understanding of luxury.

William Morris and Walter Crane looked to the Paris Commune as both a statement of political goals and an articulation of the place of art and the artist in society. For this reason, a focused examination of the Commune can provide a valuable case-study that allows students to explore the social and political networks that bound socialists and artists together: they went to the same social events, shared ideas in person and in print, and considered how their work might be communicated to and received by "the public." Together, they established the Commune as an example of political activism for English socialists while they advocated and organized on behalf of the decorative arts and the rights of the artist as a worker. For Morris and Crane, this convergence of art and politics was especially vital between 1886 and 1891, the five years spanning the fifteenth and twentieth anniversaries of the Paris Commune. The connections between artistic activism and political activism are more than mere coincidences of a timeline. Morris presented the Commune as a viable example of social revolution, and Crane gave visual expression to this ideal with two cartoons, "Vive la Commune" from 1888 and "In Memory of the Paris Commune" from 1891. The first part of this essay will consider Crane's "Vive la Commune" to examine how it presents the artist and the artisan as active participants in this revolution, while the second part will consider how concerns with artisanal labor informed the establishment of the Arts and Crafts Exhibition Society and shaped the organization of their first three public exhibitions in 1888, 1889, and 1890. For Morris and Crane, the Paris Commune provided a model for collective action that was both political and artistic.

Figure 7.1. Walter Crane, "Vive la Commune," Cartoons for the Cause, 1886–1896, London, 1896.

Reproduced courtesy of Beinecke Rare Book and Manuscript Library, Yale University.

Figure 7.2. Walter Crane, "In Memory of the Paris Commune," Cartoons for the Cause, 1886–1896, London, 1896.

Reproduced courtesy of Beinecke Rare Book and Manuscript Library, Yale University.

London socialists did not commemorate the Commune until 1884, and even then, they combined it with a march to Karl Marx's grave in Highgate Cemetery to mark the first anniversary of his death.[7] Around the time of the fifteenth anniversary in 1886, however, efforts began to return the Commune to the contemporary. And, over the next five years, it would become an important commemoration on the radical calendar, as socialists sought to create their own set of traditions apart from the usual unifying social narratives of religion or nation. William Morris evoked the Commune as one manifestation of a utopian community in his poem cycle *The Pilgrims of Hope*, serialized in his socialist newspaper *Commonweal* beginning in March 1885.[8] These efforts coalesced in 1886, when organizations came together to celebrate the Paris Commune at the South Place Institute, and Morris co-authored *A Short Account of the Commune of Paris of 1871* with Ernest Belfort Bax of the

Social Democratic Federation and the Belgian journalist and anarchist Victor Dave. They hoped to wrest the Commune from what they called "mere myth," "at best a symbol or token of things which some fear most, others hate most, and from which some hope most," and inspire a new social revolution.[9]

The authors acknowledged the divisive nature of the Commune, even amongst radicals, through the separation of "some" from "others" in the catalogue of responses to the event. This division also refers to the growing debates between anarchists and socialists over the means of social change and the outlines of a new social model. Broadly speaking, anarchism emphasized the primacy of individual liberty and denounced the hierarchical apparatus of the state. Socialism, on the other hand, retained and reimagined the role of the state in the production and distribution of goods. Each group tried to claim the Commune for their cause, and yet Morris, Bax, and Dave position the Commune as a unifying event, as suggested by the joint authorship by socialists and anarchists. They offer a revisionist history of the Commune, one that seeks to unify radicals and counter a broader "anti-communist imaginary" in England.[10] At the same time, there is more than history at stake: "so it has been in past history, so it will be in the future."[11] Remembering the Commune was an important step toward the coming revolution.

Many texts appeared in the following years, each attentive to the challenge of evoking the Commune in the late 1880s: how to unify around a potentially divisive event and how to conjure the future from a vision of the past, even if that past was only fifteen years ago. Morris echoed these sentiments in an essay published in *Commonweal* in March 1887 entitled "Why We Celebrate the Commune of Paris:" "We honor them as the foundation-stone of the new world that is to be."[12] That same year, H. M. Hyndman, leader of the Social Democratic Federation, declared in a pamphlet the need to make "a commune of London."[13]

Such temporal shifts became a hallmark of English socialist rhetoric, and perhaps the most enduring example is William Morris's utopian novel *News from Nowhere* (1890; 1891). The time-traveling narrator William Guest visits a post-revolutionary future that resembles an idealized vision of the past, a strategy that allows Morris to avoid the degradations of the present capitalism system. This erasure bespeaks a larger philosophical conundrum, since, according to Matthew Beaumont, for Morris and other socialists "the present appears to represent a well-nigh insuperable phenomenological problem."[14] In order to avoid the industrialized, capitalist present, Morris's *News from Nowhere* engages in a "past temporality"—that is to say, its vision of the future relies upon an understanding of the medieval past.[15] As a result, Morris "excises" the nineteenth century from *News* and the manufacturing towns of England have disappeared in Morris's vision of the future. Similarly romanticized evocations of pre-industrial community and craftsmanship underpin most accounts of the politics of the Arts and Crafts movement, and this approach guided Morris's work in art and design, especially when we consider the ways in which he sought to bring the past—whether of Chaucer or block-printing wallpaper—into the present. The Commune proved to be particularly challenging in this regard, as an event of relatively recent history. As the Paris Commune receded further into history would its role as a harbinger of a new social order wane?

Walter Crane directly addressed these questions of temporality and activism, especially the activism of the artist, in his first cartoon to commemorate the Commune, "Vive la Commune" (Figure 7.1) published in *Commonweal* in March 1888. Two kneeling male figures flank a standing female figure, all posed on an arc. Like many of Crane's early political cartoons, this design accommodates the rectangular format of the printed sheet or newspaper page, while also seeking to enliven this geometry. Here, he explores the expressive potential of the white space; for example, the shading in the curl of the banner suggests the three-dimensionality of this pictorial space. It is as if the frame provides a window onto a living scene in the manner of a tableau vivant (such events were also a popular part of socialist celebrations). Furthermore, the design overrides its framework, as the tip of a Phrygian bonnet bursts through the top border and the clog of the figure on the viewer's left seems to push against the corner of the frame. The foreshortened rendering of the shoe in the right corner seems to penetrate the "fourth wall" of the page. Are these figures from the past, eager to step into the present struggle? Or are they new revolutionaries, inheritors of the Commune? The arc at the bottom of the page functions as a "counterbalancing curve" described by Crane in his later essay "On the Structure and Evolution of Decorative Pattern" (1892); this shape balances the curve of upraised arms. As he explains it, "in dealing with curves and angles" in design "we are really dealing with forms of a most expressive language, and one which cannot be clearly articulated even, unless we have something to say."[16] The arc here is expressive of the globe and the rising sun, both prominent emblems in socialist visual culture.[17] The form thus communicates a new beginning and the global importance of localized uprisings such as the Paris Commune.

The figures likewise address the individual and the universal, as they negotiate common ground between anarchists and socialists. In Crane's commemoration, the Commune is the collective action of individual types. The worker to the viewer's left appears as the figure of the artisan (Crane himself often worked in a similar smock) carrying a torch in his right hand and a flag in his left, while the figure on the right carries the tools of the manual laborer on his shoulder, the shovel and the pick-axe, as he brandishes his cap of liberty in his left hand. A woman stands at the center of revolutionary politics. As art historian Linda Nochlin has discussed, women proliferated in the imagery of the Commune as both allegorical figures representing Paris, or Revolution, or the Commune, as well as individual partisans. Crane's figures allude to the allegorical ideal as well as the prominent place of women such as Louise Michel in fighting for the Commune.

It is tempting to suggest that viewers identified this figure with Michel, the so-called "Red Virgin" of the Commune.[18] Michel visited London frequently, from 1881 until her death in 1905, and she remained for an extended period from 1890 to 1895. She and Crane knew one another by 1888, when they appeared together at the commemoration of the Commune in March, and he would later agree to support her efforts to establish a school.[19] The female figure in Crane's cartoon rehabilitates the legacy of the Commune for women revolutionaries. Carrying a banner rather than the torch, the image counters the popular perception of uncontrollable Commune *petroleuses*: working class women who set Paris aflame with homemade petroleum bombs.[20] Although the clogs and apron in the cartoon suggest a proletarian woman of 1871, the fall of the drapery and her bare outstretched arms recall the idealized allegorical embodiments that would populate Crane's later political cartoons. She wears a cap of liberty on her head, and around it, Crane has placed a laurel wreath, an ancient symbol of victory. She unfurls the banner of "Vive la Commune." Crane has borrowed this slogan from the event itself; in the waning days of the event, it was supposedly inscribed on the "Communard's Wall" at Pére Lachaise Cemetery which provided the bloody backdrop to the execution of Communards on May 28, 1871.

The use of the French imperative "live!" in the banner and in the title of the cartoon suggests that such commemorations give continued "life" to the Commune and make it "live again" for a new audience.[21] Indeed, the "Communard's Wall" would become a site of commemoration in Paris and the subject of later works of art by politically-engaged artists such as Ilya Repin, Felix Valloton, and Théophile Steinlen. The title might also be a specific reference for English socialists to a stirring memorial by the Communard Édouard Vaillant entitled "Vive la Commune!" published in the *Commonweal* for April 1885.[22] In this essay, the Commune is a harbinger of world-wide revolution, where "each day and in all lands the assault upon the old society becomes more general and more impassioned,"[23] a formulation that recalls Morris's unifying vision of the Commune as the foundation of a new society. An unsigned editorial with the same title reiterates the importance of the Commune in the March 17, 1888 issue of *Commonweal*; it appeared with the notice that Crane's cartoon would be given away with the March 24 issue.[24] A report of the Commune celebration notes that Crane's cartoon sold well at the event.[25]

The design of "Vive la Commune" acknowledges the role that artists can play in activating the past for the present. Crane positions the artist at the center of revolutionary politics through the prominent placement of the palette in the bottom center of his design. Covered with paint and displayed with paintbrushes, this tool of the trade is not an anonymous object, but one marked with Crane's characteristic hieroglyph signature, an intertwined "WC" that can also be read as the outline of a long-legged crane. Considerably larger than the other assembled objects of revolution (pen, book, coins), the artist's weapon almost overshadows another weapon: a gun rests on the very edge of the image.

The revolver here is one of the few instances where the means of revolutionary violence come to the fore in Crane's images, bringing a further poignancy to this work as a commemoration of past events. Although William Morris describes "how the change came" in *News from Nowhere,* the reader does not experience it firsthand but rather as a historical narrative. Crane's image, on the other hand, takes temporality as its motif: the palette is signed March 1888, the time of the image's creation, and it rests atop a book inscribed with the date "1871": perhaps this is one of the many histories that the Commune inspired, including the one published by Morris (the 1895 reprint featured Crane's image on the cover). Whereas *News from Nowhere* imagines a future that resembles the past, Crane's cartoon looks to the past as an inspiration for the future; it recalls Morris's own comments at the Commune commemoration of 1888: "The beginning of the end was perhaps not far off; the revolution was not something to come, we were in the midst of it."[26] Even as the print commemorates a past event and hopes for its long life or "vive," it insists upon the present moment and the role of the print itself in asserting that present.

The broad dissemination of Crane's cartoon suggests that the design successfully managed the contradictions between the past and the present. It first appeared in *Commonweal* in March 1888 advertised as "a picture for framing, printed on fine paper."[27] The image became a popular part of the annual celebration of the Commune, appearing in subsequent years as both a supplement and reprinted "on the ordinary paper of the publication," as in March 1889.[28] The following year, it decorated the handbill for a Socialist League commemoration on March 19, 1890 at the South Place Institute in East London.[29] Anarchist and socialist groups across Europe adopted the image as their own.[30] Throughout each iteration, the palette remains as a highly charged symbol of revolution and the ideal of the "universal republic," even without any specific reference to the Commune, as it is in a German example from 1890.[31]

For Crane, these revolutions were artistic as well as political. Yet Crane did not look to Courbet's realist aesthetic as a model, but rather to the idea of the Commune itself as a mode of artistic organization. Crane himself would later write about the renewal of art that will occur under "free federated communes."[32] His cartoons are about the collective, even as he began to think about the individual—the place of the individual in political agitation and the place of the individual in the craftsman's labor, as in the Arts and Crafts Exhibition Society (ACES). For artists such as Morris and Crane, the handicraft of the artisan provided an ideal link between the past, the present, and the hoped-for socialist future of art. Whether in painting or the decorative arts, it was a sign or declaration, so to speak, of the individual freedom of the worker—what Crane termed the "individuality of the workman's touch."[33] The artisan of the Commune cartoon, a product of Crane's own artistry, links the past of the Commune, the present of the Arts and Crafts movement, and the future.

As scholars such as Peter Stansky have argued, the establishment of the Arts and Crafts Exhibition Society in 1887 was a radical attempt to bring a new understanding of artistic labor to the fore.[34] "Vive la Commune!" appeared in March 1888 in Morris's *Commonweal*, and a month later, Crane, as president of the fledging society, published an open letter to ask for guarantors to invest in "the revival of arts and handicrafts."[35] Crane, in particular, allied the Arts and Crafts movement with the concurrent socialist movement. He would later describe the impetus for the Society in economic terms: it was a response to the restrictive exhibition policy of the Royal Academy, that "guild of popular picture painters" whose definition of art "applies almost exclusively to painting" and whose influence "has been to encourage an enormous over-production of pictures every year."[36] By over-producing pictures in the capitalist system, the artists of the Royal Academy flood the market and cheapen their products. In an open letter to supporters, Crane proposes to turn the logic of the marketplace, and the monopoly, on its head, asserting that "there is no existing exhibition of art which gives an opportunity to the designer and the craftsman as such to show their work under their own names, and give them at least a chance of the attention and applause which is not generally monopolized by the pictorial artists."[37] By naming the otherwise anonymous designer and maker and giving him or her a venue in the marketplace, the Society resisted the prevailing impulse to turn craft objects into mere commodities.

The radicalism of the Arts and Crafts movement, therefore, was not in making good design affordable or available to a broader audience. Despite some efforts, such as Morris's contribution to an exhibition in Manchester, the Movement did not seek out a working-class audience. This situation has led to the criticism that the Arts and Crafts movement was detached from workers' movements.[38] Such a critique overlooks the fact that it *was* a workers' movement. The artists were the workers. This position was not without controversy. Morris and one "Jim Allman," a workingman, engaged in a debate about this in the pages of *Commonweal* on September 10, 1887. According to Allman, the concerns of the artisan differ from those of the artist since "the artisan makes life possible; the artist makes it enjoyable."[39] True equality between artisan and artist will only come, he argues, with social equality. Morris responds with his statement "Artist and Artisan. As an Artist Sees It," where he argues that crafts are what unites both types of workers. If one looks back to the time before capitalism, "all craftsmen who made anything were artists of some kind, they only differed in degree." As he reminds his readers, "no one knows, for example, the name of the man who designed Westminster Abbey."[40] Although it was a partial and unsatisfactory solution for Morris, The Arts and Crafts Exhibition Society tried to address this issue in the capitalist period through naming.

By naming designers and makers, the ACES affirmed individual contributions even in collaborative efforts as they looked to pre-industrial models to resist the present capitalist marketplace. Yet in so doing, they were forced to confront the conflict between the aesthetic of individual designers and makers and the desire for a cohesive exhibition and identity. Initially, they favored an individualist approach to display, arranging objects in the first exhibition in 1888 according to artist, and then type of object.[41] The organizing committee acknowledged their struggle to balance a diverse array of individual artistic statements with the desire for a coherent exhibition. When C. R. Ashbee proposed, after the second exhibition in 1889, that the Society "should formulate the principles which guided its selection and should publish the same for the benefit of intending exhibitions," the committee rejected the proposal. They could not, or did not, want to agree on principles; to do so would limit what might be considered for exhibition.[42] Although the organization affirmed its commitment to artistic autonomy, it faced declining exhibition figures by 1890 (from 19,620 visitors in 1889 to 14,156 visitors in 1890), and they decided against staging an exhibition in 1891.[43] It seems that this interruption did not resolve the conflicts within the exhibition committee about what should be exhibited and how it should be displayed. Such debates can be traced back to one central issue: did the Society promote a group identity or did it merely provide an exhibition as a means for individual expression?

In its outline, this debate about how to organize the displays of the Arts and Crafts Exhibition Society mirrored the ones happening between anarchists and socialists over social organization, including how they commemorated the Paris Commune: collectivist, as espoused by many socialists, or individualist, as advocated by anarchists? And this debate was also a question of temporality: The Medieval guild model was in conflict with the modern desire for individual recognition. Yet again, Crane's art sought to bridge these conflicting perspectives. With his cartoon to mark the twentieth anniversary of the Commune, "In Memory of the Commune of Paris" (Figure 7.2), for example, Crane attempts to unite the individual and the collective and elide the past and the present by replacing the individual Communards with an angel.

The design appeared in the artistic journal *Black and White*, printed with a disclaimer that celebrated Crane as an artist but distanced the publication from his political views: "It is published as an example of Mr. Crane's artistic work and of his political views. The Commune is commonly regarded in England as a meaningless carnival of riot and vice. Mr. Crane and many of his fellow socialists regard it as an interesting attempt to establish an ideal form of government."[44] An angel looks down upon Paris with the cathedral of Notre Dame in the background. In the accompanying poem, Crane connected the ideals of the Commune, "a city FOR ALL AND EACH." The allegorical figure suggests an interest in the unifying collective, since she replaces the artisan, the proletariat woman, and the manual laborer of the earlier cartoon. Even though the angel wears the hammer of revolution in her belt, she is more allegorical, another step away from the realm of reality represented by the female Communard at the center of the earlier print. The cartoon no longer commands the Commune to "live!" but instead honors its memory.

The allegorical unity of this collective is in the past, perhaps acknowledging the increasingly divisive present. Crane's "In Memory of the Paris Commune" replaces the individuals of the earlier Commune cartoon with a unifying allegorical figure. This substitution accomplishes two goals: first, it situates the Commune in the historical past, and thus opens it up to the allegorical language usually favored by Crane in his political cartoons.[45] Second, it reimagines the Commune as a collective ideal rather than the product of individual action. The cartoon elides divisions in the movement and commemorates a moment claimed by a wide array of radical groups. But the future remains unclear, politically as well as artistically. Although Crane was willing to figure the Commune as a call to arms in 1888, by 1891, it was a past event to memorialize. Once it passed into the realm of history, the Commune could become part of a new international mythology of socialism advanced, in part, by the imagery that suffused Crane's other political cartoons.

When the Commune usually enters the art history curriculum, it is by way of Courbet. Most famously, Courbet led the commission of artists responsible for museums and galleries during the Commune. Their organization of the destruction of the monumental column in Paris's Place Vendôme celebrating Napoleon's victory at Austerlitz was a definite statement against the use of art as self-aggrandizing imperial pomp. It seemed to provide a real-world analog to his proclamation of artistic realism: "show me an angel and I'll paint one."[46] It is not surprising that Morris and Crane gravitated to the Commune, since the event presented a powerful case of the convergence of art and politics. By teaching the longer history of the Commune, one where its international importance and influence extends into British Arts and Crafts, and its embrace of the artist-worker, students gain a fuller understanding of the convergence of art and politics. They also have an opportunity to debate artistic approaches to political questions: while Courbet refused to paint angels, Crane figured the Commune itself as an angel. For teachers of William Morris today, such a response to the Commune provides an excellent opportunity to engage students in thinking through the expressive potential of different artistic media, and the politics they convey.

NOTES

1. Dennis Bos, "Building Barricades: the Political Transfer of a Contentious Roadblock," *European Review of History* 12, no. 2 (2005): 350.

2. Kristin Ross, *Communal Luxury: The Political Imaginary of the Paris Commune* (London: Verso, 2015), 1–2.

3. Ross, *Communal Luxury,* 6.

4. Linda Nochlin, *Courbet* (New York: Thames and Hudson, 2006), 87.

5. As discussed by Ross, *Communal Luxury,* 58.

6. "Manifesto of the Paris Commune's Federation of Artists" trans. Jeff Skinner, *Red Wedge Magazine*, http://www.redwedgemagazine.com/online-issue/manifesto-federation-artist-commune, accessed March 19, 2019.

7. See Anne F. Janowitz, *Lyric and Labour in the Romantic Tradition* (Cambridge: Cambridge University Press, 1998), 231.

8. See J. B. Wright, "'The Valiant Dead': William Morris and the Commune of 1871," *The Journal of the William Morris Society* 13, no. 2 (Spring 1999), 34–38.

9. "The Socialist Platform.—No. 4. *A Short Account of the Commune of Paris of 1871,*" by E. Belfort Bax, Victor Dave, and William Morris. London: Socialist League Office, 18, Farringdon Road, Holborn Viaduct, E.1. 1886. 20pp. http://www.marxists.org/history/international/social-democracy/paris-commune.htm, accessed May 8, 2012.

10. Matthew Beaumont, "Cacotopianism, the Paris Commune, and England's Anti-Communist Imaginary, 1870–1900," *ELH* 73/2 (Summer 2006), 465–87.

11. The Socialist Platform.—No. 4. *A Short Account of the Commune of Paris of 1871.*

12. William Morris, "Why We Celebrate the Commune of Paris," *Commonweal,* (March 19, 1887): 90.

13. H.M. Hyndman, *A Commune of London* (London: Social Democratic Federation, 1887).

14. Matthew Beaumont, "To Live in the Present: *News from Nowhere* and the Representation of the Present in Late Victorian Utopian Fiction," in *Writing on the*

Image: Reading William Morris, ed. David Latham (Toronto: University of Toronto Press, 2007), 121.

15. Philip Steer, "National Pasts and Imperial Futures: Temporality, Economics, and Empire in William Morris's *News from Nowhere* (1890) and Julius Vogel's *Anno Domino 2000* (1889)," *Utopian Studies* 19, no. 1 (2008): 55.

16. Crane, *Claims of Decorative Art* (London: Lawrence & Bullen, 1892), 40.

17. Jo Briggs has explored the symbolism of this shape in Crane's work; see Jo Briggs, "Imperial Analogies: Global Events, Local Visual Culture, 1899–1901" (PhD diss., Yale University, 2007), especially Chapter 1, "Global Doubt: The Consequences of an Analogy, Water Crane, *Stop the War*, and Socialist Imagery," 17–49.

18. Crane's cartoon appears next to Michel's reply to the "Enquête sur la Commune," ("Survey on the Commune" second série, published in *Revue Blanche* Tome 12 (April–June 1897), 300–301. Crane's cartoon appears on page 301.

19. See A. K. Donald, "Celebrating the Commune," *Commonweal*, (March 24, 1888): 92.

20. Gay L. Gullickson, "La Petroleuse: Representing Revolution," *Feminist Studies* 17 (Summer 1991): 240–66.

21. As such, Elizabeth Carolyn Miller has suggested that Crane's "Vive La Commune" ignores the present and instead merges "the past and the future" through the elision of the events of 1871 and the expectations of a future society. Elizabeth Carolyn Miller, "William Morris, Print Culture, and the Politics of Aestheticism," *Modernism/modernity* 15, no. 3 (2008): 477–502. See also Miller, *Slow Print: Literary Radicalism and Late Victorian Print Culture* (Palo Alto: Stanford University Press, 2014), especially 46–50.

22. Édouard Vaillant, "Vive La Commune!" *Commonweal*, (April 3, 1885): 1.

23. Vaillant, "Vive La Commune!" 1.

24. "Vive La Commune!" *Commonweal*, (March 17, 1888): 84.

25. A. K. Donald, "Celebrating the Commune," *Commonweal*, (March 24, 1888): 22.

26. As noted by A. K. Donald, "Celebrating the Commune," 22.

27. As noted in H. Buxton Forman, *The Books of William Morris Described with Some Account of His Doings in Literature and in the Allied Crafts* (London: Frank Hollings, 1897), 198. The April 7, 1888 issue of *Commonweal* notes "Price Twopence." In 2005 currency, this is equivalent to about fifty pence, according to the National Archive's currency converted. See http://www.nationalarchives.gov.uk/currency/results.asp#mid, accessed July 18, 2012. At the time, the print costs as much as one night's lodging or a pint of gin. As compared on http://www.oldbaileyonline.org/static/Coinage.jsp, accessed July 18, 2012.

28. Ibid., 198. Ernest Belfort Bax's *Short History of the Paris Commune* (London: Twentieth Century Press, 1895) uses Crane's cartoon as the cover.

29. Manchester, Labour History Archives and Study Center, People's History Museum. See, for example, an announcement of an anarchist public meeting in *Liberty* (March 1894): 24.

30. Anne-Marie Bouchard, "Figurer la société mourante. Culture esthétique et idéologique de la presse anachiste illustée en France, 1880–1914," PhD diss., McGill University, 2009.

31. *Der Sozialdemokrat*, the official organ of the German Social Democratic Party, used the cartoon on its March cover but it removed any reference to the Commune. The design now had a new slogan in the banner: "Unser die Welt, trotz alledem" ("Our World, In Spite of All This"). For *Der Sozialdemokrat*, see Andrew R. Carlson, *Anarchism in Germany:* vol. 1: *The Early Movement.* (Metuchen, NJ: The Scarecrow Press, 1972), 183–187. This slogan comes from a revolutionary moment that pre-dates even the Commune: Ferdinand Freiligrath's poem "Despite All This!" that memorialized the revolutions of 1848. The date on the palette now reads "Feb. 20, 1890," when Social Democrats won almost 20 percent of the vote in German elections. Ross discusses the popularity of the phrase "Universal Republic" during the Commune. See *Communal Luxury*, 22.

32. Crane, *Claims of Decorative Art* (1892), 16.

33. Walter Crane, "Presidential Address, Applied Arts Section," *Transactions of the National Association for the Advancement of Art and its Application to Industry, Liverpool Meeting 1888* (London: 1888), 87.

34. As suggested by Peter Stansky; see *William Morris, C. R. Ashbee, and the Arts and Crafts* (London: Nine Elms Press, 1984), 4.

35. Pamphlet dated April 16, 1888, in Archive of Art and Design, AAD 1/1–1980 to AAD 1/20–1980.

36. Walter Crane, "The English Revival of Decorative Arts," *Fortnightly Review* 58 (July 1892): 815–6.

37. Pamphlet dated April 16, 1888.

38. See, for example, Eric Hobsbawn, "Socialism and the Avant-Garde, 1880–1914 in the Period of the Second International." *Le Mouvement Social* 111 (April–June 1980): 190–99.

39. Jim Allman, "Artist and Artisan. As a Workman Sees it." *Commonweal*, (September 10, 1887): 291.

40. William Morris, "Artist and Artisan. As an Artist Sees it." *Commonweal*, (September 10, 1887): 291.

41. Minutes of the ACES, Thursday June 14, 1888. Report of the Select Committee responsible for arranging the first Exhibition. Archive of Art and Design, AAD 1/1-1980 to AAD 1/20-1980.

42. Tuesday, November 19, 1889. Ashbee also suggested that the Society should pursue a closer relationship with Trade Unions. The committee also rejected that proposal. Archive of Art and Design, AAD 1/1-1980 to AAD 1/20-1980.

43. Minutes for meeting December 6, 1890, Archive of Art and Design, AAD 1/1-1980 to AAD 1/20-1980. Crane resigned as President in 1890 and Morris served in that position from 1891 until his death in 1896, at which time Crane resumed the presidency, until his death in 1915.

44. Crane, "In Memory of the Commune of Paris," *Black and White* (April 1891): 274.

45. See Morna O'Neill, "Cartoons for the Cause? Walter Crane's *The Anarchists of Chicago*," *Art History* 38, no. 1 (February 2015): 106–37.

46. Quoted by Vincent van Gogh in a July 1885 letter to Theo Van Gogh, Ronald de Leeuw, *The Letters of Vincent van Gogh* (New York: Penguin, 1996), 302.

BIBLIOGRAPHY

Allman, Jim. "Artist and Artisan. As a Workman Sees it." *Commonweal*, September 10, 1887.

Bax, Ernst Belfort. *Short History of the Paris Commune*. London: Twentieth Century Press, 1895.

Bax, E. Belfort, Victor Dave, and William Morris. *A Short Account of the Commune of Paris of 1871*. London: Socialist League, 1886. http://www.marxists.org/history/international/social-democracy/paris-commune.htm, accessed May 8, 2012.

Beaumont, Matthew. "Cacotopianism, the Paris Commune, and England's Anti-Communist Imaginary, 1870–1900." *ELH* 73/2 (Summer 2006): 465–87.

———. "To Live in the Present: *News from Nowhere* and the Representation of the Present in Late Victorian Utopian Fiction," in *Writing on the Image: Reading William Morris*, edited by David Latham, 119–36. Toronto: University of Toronto Press, 2007.

Bos, Dennis. "Building Barricades: the Political Transfer of a Contentious Roadblock." *European Review of History* 12, no. 2 (2005): 345–65.

Bouchard, Anne-Marie. "Figurer la société mourante. Culture esthétique et idéologique de la presse anachiste illustée en France, 1880–1914." PhD dissertation, McGill University, 2009.

Briggs, Jo. "Imperial Analogies: Global Events, Local Visual Culture, 1899–1901." PhD dissertation, Yale University, 2007.

Carlson, Andrew R., *Anarchism in Germany:* Vol. 1: *The Early Movement*. Metuchen, NJ: The Scarecrow Press, 1972.

Crane, Walter. *The Claims of Decorative Art*. London: Lawrence & Bullen, 1892.

———. "The English Revival of Decorative Arts." *Fortnightly Review* 58 (July 1892): 815–6.

———. "In Memory of the Commune of Paris." *Black and White* (April 1891): 274.

de Leeuw, Ronald. *The Letters of Vincent van Gogh*. New York: Penguin, 1996.

Donald, A. K. "Celebrating the Commune." *Commonweal*, March 24, 1888.

"Enquête sur la Commune." *Revue Blanche* 12 (April–June 1897): 300–301.

Forman, H. Buxton. *The Books of William Morris Described with Some Account of His Doings in Literature and in the Allied Crafts*. London: Frank Hollings, 1897.

Gullickson Gay L. "La Petroleuse: Representing Revolution." *Feminist Studies* 17 (Summer 1991): 240–66.

Hobsbawn, Eric. "Socialism and the Avant-Garde, 1880–1914 in the Period of the Second International." *Le Mouvement Social* 111 (April–June 1980): 190–99.

Hyndman, H. M. *A Commune of London*. London: Social Democratic Federation, 1887.

Janowitz, Anne F. *Lyric and Labour in the Romantic Tradition*. Cambridge: Cambridge University Press, 1998.

Labour History Archives and Study Center, People's History Museum, Manchester.

"Manifesto of the Paris Commune's Federation of Artists" trans. Jeff Skinner, *Red Wedge Magazine*, http://www.redwedgemagazine.com/online-issue/manifesto-federation-artist-commune, accessed March 19, 2019.

Miller, Elizabeth Carolyn. "William Morris, Print Culture, and the Politics of Aestheticism." *Modernism*/modernity 15, no. 3 (2008): 477–502.

Minutes of the Arts and Crafts Exhibition Society, Archive of Art and Design, AAD 1/1-1980 to AAD 1/20-1980. National Art Library, London.

Morris, William. "Artist and Artisan. As an Artist Sees it." *Commonweal*, September 10, 1887.

———. "Why We Celebrate the Commune of Paris." *Commonweal*, March 29, 1887.

O'Neill, Morna. "Cartoons for the Cause? Walter Crane's *The Anarchists of Chicago*." *Art History* 38, no. 1 (February 2015): 106–37.

Ross, Kristin. *Communal Luxury: The Political Imaginary of the Paris Commune.* London: Verso, 2015.

Stansky, Peter. *William Morris, C. R. Ashbee, and the Arts and Crafts*. London: Nine Elms Press, 1984.

Steer, Philip. "National Pasts and Imperial Futures: Temporality, Economics, and Empire in William Morris's *News from Nowhere* (1890) and Julius Vogel's *Anno Domino 2000* (1889)." *Utopian Studies* 19, no. 1 (2008): 49–72.

Transactions of the National Association for the Advancement of Art and its Application to Industry, Liverpool Meeting 1888 (London: 1888).

Vaillant, Édouard. "Vive la Commune!" *Commonweal*, April 3, 1885.

"Vive la Commune!" *Commonweal*, March 17, 1888.

Wright, J. B. "'The Valiant Dead': William Morris and the Commune of 1871," *The Journal of the William Morris Society* 13 (Spring 1999): 34–38.

Chapter Eight

"Living in Heaven"
Hope and Change in News from Nowhere
David Latham

> To me you seem here as if you were living in heaven compared with us of the country from which I came.
>
> —William Morris, *News from Nowhere*, 176

My first experience with teaching *News from Nowhere* (1890; 1891) was not at all what I expected.[1] I had scheduled the book as the final text on our Victorian literature course, one intended to provide an inspirational resolution to the complex problems raised throughout the course. Earlier in the year we had read "The Defence of Guenevere" and "King Arthur's Tomb," poems about the triangular love relationships that lead to the decay of Camelot, a Celtic version of the fall from paradise and the hell that follows. With each poem and novel during that year I would repeatedly emphasize that the archetypal fall from paradise is one that each generation experiences, as most of us fall too quickly from hope and idealism to cynicism and despair, a fall that signals our transition from growth to death. The cynical attitude is the resort of those who are too lazy to struggle for more growth and who thus begin dying in their youth.

News from Nowhere would provide the antidote; it would inspire us to strive toward the restoration of paradise. But I was not prepared for the depth of cynicism in the class. The students rolled their eyes at the naivety of Morris's dream: "He can't be serious; it's Nowhere because it will never work; it's unreal; even the sunny weather would scorch the earth." Though I had defined the mythical fall as a generational fall from the short growth of youth to the lengthy decay of death, I had overlooked the subtle ways each generation may experience the fall differently. Morris's generation responded to the pessimism of the age by embracing art over religion, with Morris advocating that we all must live our lives as artists: "The repulsion to pessimism . . . is,

I think, natural to a man busily engaged in the arts."[2] My 1960s generation was ripe for *News from Nowhere*. John Lennon could sound cynical with his mocking of naive revolutionaries "carrying pictures of Chairman Mao" who "ain't gonna make it with anyone anyhow."[3] But Lennon echoed Morris in his anthemic "Imagine": "You may say that I'm a dreamer, but I'm not the only one. I hope someday you will join us and the world will be as one."[4] Lennon's lyrics sound like a direct response to Morris's dreamer at the end of *News from Nowhere*: "I lay in my bed at dingy Hammersmith . . . trying to consider if I was overwhelmed by despair at finding I had been dreaming a dream; and strange to say, I found that I was not despairing. . . . If others have seen it as I have seen it, then it may be called a vision rather than a dream."[5] Both Morris and Lennon anticipate and reject the cynical dismissal of such faith in the effort to pursue our hopes.

But how can a teacher who shares that faith make Morris's romance appeal to the conservative generation who have grown up during the wary "uh-oh" ('00) decade and this weary-teens decade of financially strapped part-timers? Yeats's description of the best "lack[ing] all conviction, while the worst are full of passionate intensity,"[6] appears to be taken to heart now as a defence for cynicism rather than a condemnation. Thus, starting with the presumption that students no longer share my faith in Morris's steadfast zeal, I propose to focus on the fundamental nature of hope and change. It is a focus that explores the relationship between the desire to dream and the probability of change, how the force of desire can turn the impossible dream into a probable reality. As Blake protested, "Every thing possible to be believ'd is an image of truth."[7] If we recognize the incredible transformations that have occurred in the world since Morris wrote *News from Nowhere* then we may ask ourselves why more easily achievable changes have not occurred and why we have failed to pursue such changes.

Where do we find our inspiration for thinking, for living, for improving the world? Not in the routine of our lives, but rather in the flight of our dreams: we find it self-referentially in the realm of the art we construct, the stories we imagine. Morris turns to the oldest story of our exile from the garden, and to the dream of returning from the wilderness of our modern wasteland to the lost paradise of our home. For Morris, paradise is not the overly determined order of a utopian city on a hilltop, but the green Edenic garden in a golden Arcadian valley. The Thames River valley provides Morris with a local image of his dream-vision, while its Edenic and Arcadian qualities provide the mythical context of his dream of a reunion of our brazen nature with the green and golden paradise associated with biblical and classical art.

Cynical readers might think it naive for Morris to ask us to dream of a utopian paradise where the weather is sunny and the people are healthy. But

Morris keeps his focus directed on this very discrepancy between reality and dream, never allowing us to forget this "contrast of the present with the future: of blind despair with hope."[8] Why are some dreams considered credible and others considered incredible? Let's examine five of Morris's envisioned transformations that cynical readers will likely dismiss as incredible, as naive dreams too impossible to ever realize: 1. Who can believe that fellowship might ever replace self-interest, that the principle of self-sacrifice for the good of the community might ever replace the practice of self-assertion of the individual, so that the communal values of socialism may spread from a fringe cult to a mass movement like a worldwide religion? We may just as well ask 2. who can believe that healthy, beautiful people will replace our corrupt social order, 3. that the sunshine will change our dreary weather, 4. that clean fish will renew our polluted rivers, and 5. that good people will enjoy working without the rewards that distinguish workers from loafers. As the years pass since Morris first raised these five issues in *News from Nowhere*, some of these ideal dreams have become seriously credible as achievable goals despite our growing cynicism.

Morris's choice of genre immediately establishes the serious framework for his dream. Any Victorian student schooled in the Classical tradition of literature would have known that the two major genres of prose (corresponding to the epic and tragedy in poetry) are the two practiced by Plato: the Socratic dialogue narrative and the ideal commonwealth narrative. These are the two elite genres of prose reserved for serious subjects. Morris thus reveals the serious intentions of his dream by combining these two genres, foregrounding the Socratic dialogue technique directly in chapter 11 and more subtly in chapters 12, 13, 14, 17, and 18. He thus challenges us to change the world by starting with the most profound of philosophical questions: What would it be like to live in heaven, to live a heavenly life on earth? Morris dares us to consider this as a practical question that every responsible adult should pursue rather than dismiss as a childish dream. The most radical writer in English literature wrote *News from Nowhere* as a revolutionary response to this fundamental question about the way we live our lives.

The subtext of Morris's narrative romance is not so much whether or not a heavenly utopia could ever become a reality; rather what horrifies Morris is that we no longer even wish for it to happen. Too many of us prefer to dream of some technological paradise, of unlimited data streaming, of drone-delivered consumer goods, of holding the winning lottery ticket. As Herbert Marcuse noted, "capitalism's real power is to make unthinkable the alternatives."[9] In a lecture on "How I Became a Socialist," Morris explains how the capitalist system has "reduced the workman to such a skinny and pitiful existence, that he scarcely knows how to frame a desire for any life much better." Art provides the answer: "It is the province of art to set the true ideal of a full and reasonable life before him, a life to which the perception and creation of beauty, the enjoyment of real pleasure that is, shall be felt to be as necessary as his daily bread."[10]

The first and last chapters of *News from Nowhere* frame the desire for this utopian ideal, as the narrator's friend repeats his anxious wish to envision "what would happen on the Morrow of the Revolution": "If I could but see a day of it; if I could but see it."[11] By the last chapter, his despair has turned to an affirmation of hope: "Yes, surely! and if others can see it as I have seen it, then it may be called a vision rather than a dream."[12] The transformation is achieved through a complex dream-vision wherein the reader is unsure who is speaking from the beginning through to the end.

Why is the narration so confusingly complex? The eight brief paragraphs of the opening chapter are interrupted eight times by these seemingly awkward phrases: "says a friend," "says our friend who tells the story," "our friend says." The story is thus introduced as a hearsay rumor: the narrator tells us about a friend who tells about another friend—"a man whom he knows very well"[13]—who returns home one evening after a disagreeable socialist meeting, falls asleep, and dreams about a heavenly future after a successful socialist revolution. The second speaker tells the narrator that he will narrate the third friend's dream "in the first person, as if it were myself."[14] To complicate the narration still further, the friend of the narrator's friend calls himself "William Guest," lives in William Morris's residence at Kelmscott House in Hammersmith, and identifies with Old Hammond's Victorian grandfather— "a genuine artist, a man of genius, and a revolutionist,"[15] Morris's accurate but uncharacteristically boastful description of himself. To summarize this narrative maze, Morris the author writes as a first-person narrator about a friend who tells about a friend named William who dreams about Dick and Old Hammond (who are Morris's own hypothetical descendants—his great-great grandson and grandson). Morris may be employing these multiple levels of narrative as part of his utopian strategy: the story of this dream-vision is a story to be passed from friend to friend, each spreading the word from one to another, as an apostle spreading the Word of the Bible, a socialist bible for the Morrow of a new world-order.

Dream-visions are a popular medieval convention for story-telling, but Morris updates his dream-vision by providing psychological explanations for such supernatural elements as time-traveling into the future. Telling us that after repeatedly wishing he "could but see" a vision of "the Morrow of the Revolution," Guest awakens the next morning "as if [he] had slept a long, long while, and could not shake off the weight of slumber."[16] But aside from suggesting that Guest is still asleep, Morris grounds his story humorously and linguistically in the all-too-real political quarrels that threaten to surrender the most idealistic dreamer to despair.

The story begins with an argument: a political discussion among six socialists means that there will be six different opinions, with each quarreler shouting damnation at all the others. Morris thus confronts head-on the cynicism of those who would argue that the heavenly ideals of socialism are impossible to achieve because of our selfish human nature. Morris seems to acknowledge that such discord is as inherent in our souls as it is in our language: much of the first chapter is a play on the *dis* prefix. "Sundering betwixt"[17] is a Morris phrase which serves well as the definition of this prefix. Discussion, discontent, discomfort, disgust, disgrace: with discord seemingly at the center of humanity, how could Morris ever dream of a utopia wherein the capitalist principles of competition are replaced by the socialist principles of cooperation, profit replaced by the principles of sharing, capital replaced by the principles of community, and exploitation replaced by the principles of neighborliness? Stewing over "the many excellent and conclusive arguments" which he should have said before leaving the meeting, Guest walks to the riverside where his remembrance of the discussion eventually "disappears" in the beautiful moonlight, as wind, sky, river, and elm refresh him from the fretful logic of rebuttals, leaving him with "a vague hope, that was now become a pleasure, for days of peace and rest, and cleanness and smiling goodwill."[18]

Chapter 2, "A Morning Bath," is a baptismal submersion in the now clean waters of the Thames, whereupon he enters his dreamland "wide-awake and clear-headed."[19] Having gone to bed calmed by the winter moon at night, he awakens with the summer sun shining through the morning, an archetypal progression wherein the natural renewal of the seasons is signifying a spiritual resurrection enabled by the dream of social revolution. Morris's utopia is a radical challenge to virtually every established social institution accepted by many as the irreversible condition of the world. When Guest meets the waterman on the Thames outside his house he finds himself confronted and confused by a new class order and new ecological order. Dick, the working-class waterman, is a handsome, muscular, refined, and well-dressed gentleman; a working-class gentleman is an oxymoron to the Victorian Guest. Despite his familiarity with the polluted docksides of London, Guest finds the Thames now flowing as a clean and healthy river full of salmon. The "smoke-vomiting chimneys" of the soap-works are gone.[20] "In spite of all the infallible maxims of [our] day,"[21] there is nothing supernatural and magical in finding beautiful people, sunny weather, and a salmon-filled river. Northrop Frye provides a rational explanation of the first phenomenon:

> Even as late as the First World War, if you looked at the officers and the enlisted men in the British army, they were just two different races of people. The officers had been brought up on protein foods, and they were all big and handsome,

and the enlisted men had starved and kept alive on very inferior foods, and they were all stunted and warped, and Morris saw all this around him and realized how much beauty could be in the world if there were more good health, and how much good health there would be if social conditions were equalized.[22]

The second phenomenon—the phenomenal change in the weather—has an equally rational explanation: the infamous London fog has largely disappeared with the coal-smoke from the chimneys that caused it, leaving England with much more sunshine than there was a century ago. Ironically, few of Morris's Victorian readers would have guessed that the weather could be improved more easily than the social conditions of laborers.

The idealistic Morris was not naive about the likelihood of easily revolutionizing our lives. In the serialized 1890 edition of *News from Nowhere* he cited the date for the new Hammersmith bridge without the "grimy sootiness" as 1971. When he revised his manuscript for publication as a book a year later, he pushed the date of the bridge forward to 2003. Unfortunately, we need to push the date still further into the future, as we watch the years pass with one generation after another doing so little to affect the change required to bring about a better world. The paragraph that recounts Guest's reaction when he hears this 2003 date provides us with a subtle suggestion as to why successive generations accept our lot in life, too soon abandoning our ideals, our dreams, our responsibilities to improve the world:

> The date shut my mouth as if a key had been turned in a padlock fixed to my lips; for I saw that something inexplicable had happened, and that if I said much, I should be mixed up in a game of cross questions and crooked answers. So I tried to look unconcerned, and to glance in a matter-of-course way at the banks of the river.[23]

The moment Guest realizes how different he is from his neighbors, the moment he recognizes that he does not belong in their world, he shuts up, padlocks closed his sense of difference, and immediately tries to conform, to adapt to the social order, to belong with the majority. This pressure to conform is what discourages each one of us from pursuing our ideals, from revolutionizing the world. Just as Guest tries "to look unconcerned" with the world he sees as shockingly lovely, we learn to look unconcerned with a world that is shockingly corrupt, an "ugly characterless waste."[24] We believe it easier to adapt and conform to this wasteland in order to avoid "cross questions and crooked answers." To carry on an explanation of our own contrary thoughts will too often lead us lazily to lose our resolve: "I should have begun to doubt myself."[25] Guest belittles "the service we should do for a fellow citizen" as a trivial matter that requires an exchange of cash,[26] whereas the true service for fellow citizens would require a concerted devotion of our lives to improve the world for our descendants.

The resemblances of utopian Nowhere with fourteenth-century architecture and clothing are not meant as an escape to some nostalgic past. Rather they are part of Morris's radical assault on our conventional ways of thinking, those allegedly "infallible maxims."[27] In this case, Morris is challenging our conventional maxims of history and progress. Morris's preference for the medieval age is a radical reversal of the maxim that modern civilization has been evolving in a progressive line since the Renaissance, when the re-discovery of models of learning from Classical Greece and Rome enabled our emergence from the "dark ages" of medieval ignorance. Morris is following the lead of John Ruskin, who argued in "The Nature of Gothic" chapter of his *Stones of Venice* (1853) that the conventional distinction between the artistic genius of the blueprint designer and the manual labor of the craftsman who carries out the designer's vision is a snobbish distinction which leads to the degradation of both the artist and the art. Ruskin presents the asymmetrical, irregular imperfections of the Gothic style as exemplifying the independence of the craftsman freed from an enslaved conformity to the symmetrical uniformity of the Classical style. The ideal artist carves his own Gothic gargoyle, while the slave copies identical Corinthian columns. For Ruskin, the designer and the craftworker must be one and the same, so that spiritual contemplation and common daily experience are inseparable. Praising "The Nature of Gothic" as "one of the few necessary utterances of the century," Morris developed from it the principles of the Arts and Crafts movement, by which he intended to unify art and work. As Morris explains, "art is the expression of man's pleasure in labour."[28] Without such pleasure in our work, beauty cannot be restored to our productions, and we shall continue to toil and live in pain. Thus, Morris added a radicalized ideology to Ruskinian aesthetics and Marxist economics. He spent a decade of his life lecturing tirelessly from trade-union halls to Hyde Park corner, campaigning for a socialist revolution that would save civilization by making art an integral and intrinsic part of life. According to Morris, art cannot continue to be marginalized as the exclusive culture of an elite class; art must not only be essential to the life of everyone, but, as the expression of our joy in living, art must also change from being a way of life for a few to becoming the essential way of all our lives.

Morris's preference for the craftsmanship of fourteenth-century art marked not only his resistance to the sophisticated pretension of the Renaissance; Morris also recognized that the myth of progress is a reactionary ideology, as it supports a passive faith in evolution that resists the need for revolutionary action. He campaigned against this laissez-faire attitude of capitalism, which promoted a passive acceptance of the status quo as if each of us should leave well enough alone so that the world will continue to follow along its supposedly progressive course of growth.

News from Nowhere is Morris's fictional demonstration of the contrary socialist principles for which he campaigned in his political lectures. One institution after another is no longer functioning in the new socialist society of Nowhere. The Houses of Parliament are now "a storage place for manure," as the proverbial bullshit of corrupt politicians is replaced by a legitimate "dung market," now valuable as a source for fertilizer.[29] The justice system is gone because there is no longer a need for inhumane prisons and gallows designed for punishing the criminal acts of desperate citizens and no need for illogical interference in divorce matters, as if married partners were objects to be bartered over. There does remain the occasional crime of passion, as "love madness" is not always coped with rationally, but the punishment for such crimes is the burden of remorse.[30]

It should not surprise us that so radical a thinker as Morris would envision many of his own interests as being no longer important for the society of the future. Much of what he held so dearly close to his heart—literature, paintings, historic architecture—is dismissed as something to be tolerated but scarcely considered important in the new society. First, an institutionalized education system is no longer needed because children are now allowed to learn whatever interests them, and adults continue to learn at their own pace. Guest worries that the children will never acquire a sense of discipline, but in Nowhere there is no obsession to determine what books children should learn, no effort to impose upon children what adults believe will do the most good. Instead, the adults shrug from worrying over the prospect of studying too many books: "After all, I don't know that it does them much harm, even if they do grow up book-students. Such people as that, 'tis a great pleasure seeing them so happy over work which is not much sought for. And besides, these students are generally such pleasant people; so kind and sweet-tempered; so humble, and at the same time so anxious to teach everybody all that they know."[31]

Though in his own life Morris founded the Society for the Protection of Ancient Buildings, in his utopia there is little use for the historic architecture he so passionately defended; the British Museum and St. Paul's Cathedral are merely tolerated in Nowhere: "You see, in this matter we need not grudge a few poorish buildings standing, because we can always build elsewhere."[32] Morris was a passionate student of history, but history holds little interest in Nowhere. Old Hammond understands why his interest in history is not shared by others: "I don't think my tales of the past interest them much. The last harvest, the last baby, the last knot of carving in the market-place is history enough for them. It was different, I think, when I was a lad, when we were not so assured of peace and continuous plenty as we are now."³³ Two of Morris's own principal prescriptions for life suggest an equation of architecture and literature:

> If I were asked what is at once the most important production of Art and the thing most to be longed for, I should answer, A beautiful House; and if I were further asked to name the production next in importance and the thing longed for, I should answer, A beautiful Book. To enjoy good houses and good books in self-respect and decent comfort, seems to me the pleasurable end towards which all societies of human beings ought now to struggle.³⁴

For Morris, this advice is intended as the first step for adding some heavenly light to our hellish world. But once a socialist paradise is achieved, then architecture and literature are merely two of the many elements that may interest us in our daily lives as artists. Books are not valued as mass-printed novels, but rather as exercises in beautiful calligraphy. To help us as readers of *Nowhere* to understand why reading is no more important for education or entertainment than "boating and swimming," Morris introduces the young Ellen as the spokesperson for the new social order.³⁵ Her grandfather is nostalgic for "the spirit of adventure" energizing the old novels that he misses in the books of the new utopian age. But as Ellen explains, people no longer need to escape in literature, for they are now free to experience directly the ideals of the world:

> "Books, books! always books, grandfather! When will you understand that after all it is the world we live in which interests us; the world of which we are a part, and which we can never love too much? Look!" she said, throwing open the casement wider and showing us the white light sparkling between the black shadows of the moonlit garden, through which ran a little shiver of the summer night-wind, "look! these are our books in these days!—and these," she said, stepping lightly up to the two lovers and laying a hand on each of their shoulders; "and the guest there, with his over-sea knowledge and experience;—yes, and even you, grandfather" (a smile ran over her face as she spoke), "with all your grumbling and wishing yourself back again in the good old days,—in which, as far as I can make out, a harmless and lazy old man like you would have pretty nearly starved.... Yes, these are our books; and if we want more, can we not find work to do in the beautiful buildings that we raise up all over the country (and I know there was nothing like them in the past times), wherein a man can put forth whatever is in him, and make his hands set forth his mind and soul."³⁶

The choice of a young woman as the spokesperson for Morris's utopia is yet another radical departure for a nineteenth-century author. Old Hammond serves as the conventional figure of the wise grandfather who guides Guest through a series of questions and answers about the Morrow of the Revolution, but it is the young feminist woman who serves as the climactic embodiment of the utopian future. Ellen is "as beautiful as a picture,"[37] rows a boat much better than Guest does, and is the wisest inhabitant of Nowhere. She is compared to a picture because she is designed to demonstrate her argument that those who inhabit the happy and healthy world of fellowship are living lives that are the embodiment of art. The air they breathe "is fragrant and clean as the ideal of the old pastoral poets."[38] Dick identifies the scene of Ellen in a hayfield with the fictional garden depicted in the pictures from storybooks: "'Look, guest,' said Dick; 'doesn't it all look like one of those very stories out of Grimm that we were talking about up in Bloomsbury? Here are we two lovers wandering about in the world, and we have come to a fairy garden, and there is the very fairy herself amidst of it.'"[39] Novels and fine art are no longer necessary to the lives of those who inhabit a paradisal garden. In such a paradise the weather and the seasons provide better drama. The theater of the seasons is a drama wherein people actively participate rather than sit for passive observation. As Dick explains, "I can't look upon it as if I were sitting in a theatre seeing the play going on before me, myself taking no part of it. . . . I am part of it all, and feel the pain as well as the pleasure in my person. It is not done for me by somebody else, merely that I may eat and drink and sleep; but I myself do my share of it."[40]

Morris thus redefines art as the central activity of our lives. "Art or work-pleasure, as one ought to call it,"[41] is identified with the skill of mowing hay, carving a pipe, or mending a road. Indeed, the "gang of men road-mending" looked "much like a boating party at Oxford would have looked in the days I remembered, and not much more troubled with their work."[42] Dick identifies the "pick-work" of the merry road-menders as "good sport."[43] Whereas once "the aim of all people before our time was to avoid work,"[44] there is now in the land of fellowship no longer a distinction between work and play; the activities required for roads, hayfields, and rowboats are enjoyed indeed as a playful sport. The sports analogy reminds us that people do enjoy work, as they share their time in communal exercises without monetary rewards, just as weekend amateurs will race hard to score a goal on the football pitch, not for money but for the fun of the game. Old Hammond explains this change in attitude towards labor:

> Art or work-pleasure . . . sprung up almost spontaneously, it seems, from a kind of instinct amongst people, no longer driven desperately to painful and terrible overwork, to do the best they could with the work in hand—to make it excellent of its kind; and when that had gone on for a little, a craving for beauty seemed to awaken in men's minds, and they began rudely and awkwardly to ornament

the wares which they made; and when they had once set to work at that, it soon began to grow. All this was much helped by the abolition of squalor which our immediate ancestors put up with so coolly; and by the leisurely, but not stupid, country-life which now grew to be common amongst us. Thus at last and by slow degrees we got pleasure into our work; then we became conscious of that pleasure, and cultivated it, and took care that we had our fill of it; and then all was gained, and we were happy. So may it be for ages and ages![45]

Unlike most stories of futuristic worlds, Morris's utopia has no technological wonders. "This is not an age of inventions," we are pointedly informed in Nowhere.[46] That was the mistake of the nineteenth century, when machinery was considered more important than equality:

This opinion, which from all I can learn seemed as natural then, as it seems absurd now, that while the ordinary daily work of the world would be done entirely by automatic machinery, the energies of the more intelligent part of mankind would be set free to follow the higher forms of the arts, as well as science and the study of history. It was strange, was it not, that they should thus ignore that aspiration after complete equality which we now recognize as the bond of all happy human society? . . . They soon began to find out their mistake, and that only slaves and slave-holders could live solely by setting machines going.[47]

Morris envisions a world that has reversed the nineteenth-century effort to invent "machinery that would supersede handicraft."[48] Enslavement to the machinery of the nineteenth century could produce only "abortions of the market," whereas the people of Nowhere are artists whose art is the desired product of the pleasure of creation.[49] *News from Nowhere* demonstrates that the business of art and fellowship concerns the quality of life that empowers heavenly people like Dick and Clara and Ellen to thrive on Earth.

The pattern of contrasts between the reality of the capitalist present and the dream of the communist future reaches a climax when it threatens Guest's image of Ellen. Guest identifies her as the ultimate embodiment of the new social order. Although Ellen invites him to stay in the future with her, she recognizes that he cannot escape his "never-ending contrast between the past and this present," telling Guest that she "must not let you go off into a dream again so soon. If we must lose you, I want you to see all that you can see first before you go back again." He reminds her that she had invited him to stay with her, but she immediately sees that he is already relapsing: "'Only, what were you thinking of just now?' I said falteringly: 'I was saying to myself, the past, the present? Should she not have said the contrast of the present with the future: of blind despair with hope?'"[50] The contrast between the hellish present of his world and the heavenly future of her world becomes unbearable when it affects Guest's perception of Ellen: "I was thinking of what you, with your capacity and intelligence, joined to your love of pleasure, and your impatience of unreasonable restraint—of what you would have been in that past. And even now, when all is won and has been for a long time, my heart is sickened with thinking of all the waste of life that has gone on for so many years!"[51] As reality intrudes upon Guest's dream, he is left haunted by the loss of so many potential Ellens who have been forced to suffer the fate of servants and slaves.

In the first chapter we were reminded that Guest's experiences already "began to shape themselves into an amusing story."[52] When, in chapter 23, Guest laughs about feeling left out of Dick's "tale," Dick replies: "You had better consider that you have got the cap of darkness, and are seeing everything, yourself invisible."[53] Now in the last chapter at the "haysel" feast, Guest fades from their view, becoming a distant observer of the future. If we ask ourselves before we start reading *News from Nowhere* why we find the hell of our lives so much more credible than the heaven of our dreams, the answer for our cynical students is obvious: "Just look around." But as we reach this last chapter our position should be reversed. It is Guest who fades as a phantom because the heavenly world of Nowhere is the more credible reality than the hellish nightmare into which Guest seems to be drifting. Returning to this hellish world, Guest encounters a Victorian neighbor, a "grimed"-faced figure, "eyes dulled and bleared," "body bent," "feet dragging and limping," "clothing . . . a mixture of dirt and rags."[54] In contrast to the "joyous, beautiful people left behind in the church,"[55] this figure surely must be a phantom from a nightmare. Such an incredible nightmare surely could never be allowed to become the normative reality of a wide-awake world. Most disturbing because it rings so pathetically true in its detailed contrast with Nowhere is the trace of real fellowship that is all but extinguished by the soul-destroying mastery and servility of the class system: as they cross paths, Guest's Victorian neighbor "touched his hat with some real goodwill and courtesy, and much servility."[56] The indomitable traces of the humanity of fellowship revealed in this nightmarish figure leave Guest "inexpressibly shocked,"[57] and they tear at the reader's heart, as we realize that this nearly broken figure was born with the same potential as Ellen. Moreover, we realize that would-be precursors of Ellen may never have the opportunity to reach such potential unless we in the present work toward a better future.

Morris concludes with Guest imagining what "Ellen's last mournful look seemed to say." It is a rallying call for revolutionizing the world by striving "to build up little by little the new day of fellowship, and rest, and happiness."[58] Significantly, this speech attributed to Ellen is not her own spoken words because Ellen is an unrealized dream; hence, her speech is Guest's impression of what someone like Ellen might wish to say but will not be empowered to say aloud until enough readers are inspired to join the struggle for a more heavenly world where future generations of Ellens may thrive. Morris thus appeals to our social conscience to awaken us from the wish for a single dream-lover, replacing the selfish wish with an empathy for all our fellow neighbors so that we will fix our sight on the effort to change the conditions of our world, never abandoning our hope that future generations will enjoy living heavenly lives here on Earth.

We have seen how four incredible transformations can be credibly envisioned concerning the ideals of weather, health, ecology, and labor. The ideal of fellowship is the remaining dream. In his youth Morris said that his "work is an embodiment of dreams in one form or another."[59] As his career makes clear, he did not mean a wistful dream from which we may never awaken, but a commitment to spread the word from one friend to another, to inspire others to share his hope for the harmony of fellowship. As Ellen's impatient dismissal of "books, books, books" suggests, our hopes and fears for art are misdirected toward idle entertainment: toward the escapist nature of Victorian novels in Morris's time, and toward modern movies in our own time. Such novels and movies are generally about the selfish desire for a single dream-lover. If we can change the weather and our health and our height, then we may answer, "yes, surely," we can find time to consider a different kind of art about a different kind of dream. Turning from the *Commonweal* political lecture to the Kelmscott utopian romance, Morris shifted his campaign to change the world as he endeavors to show us how the force of a shared desire can transform the realm of the stories we imagine into the reality of the lives we live.

NOTES

1. This article is an update to "Hope and Change: Teaching *News from Nowhere*," *The Journal of William Morris Studies*, 17 (Summer 2007): 6–23. Parts of the original essay are republished with permission.
2. William Morris, "Preface to *Signs of Change*," in *Collected Works of William Morris*, ed. May Morris (London: Longmans, Green, 1910–1915), 23: 2.
3. The Beatles, "Revolution," *White Album* (London: Apple Records, 1968).
4. John Lennon, "Imagine," *Imagine* (London: Apple Records, 1971).
5. William Morris, *News from Nowhere and Other Writings*, ed. Clive Wilmer (Harmondsworth: Penguin, 1993), 228. All subsequent quotations from *News from Nowhere* are from this edition.
6. W.B. Yeats, "The Second Coming," in *Selected Poetry* (London: Macmillan, 1964), lines 7–8.
7. William Blake, "The Marriage of Heaven and Hell," plate 8, in *Selected Poetry and Prose of William Blake*, ed. Northrop Frye (New York: Modern Library, 1953), 126.

8. Morris, *News from Nowhere*, 222.

9. Herbert Marcuse, *One Dimensional Man: Studies in the Ideology of Advanced Industrial Society* (Boston: Beacon, 1965), 141.

10. William Morris, "How I Became a Socialist," *News from Nowhere and Other Writings*, ed. Clive Wilmer (Harmondsworth: Penguin, 1993), 382–83.

11. Morris, *News from Nowhere*, 44.

12. Ibid., 228.

13. Ibid., 43.

14. Ibid., 45.

15. Ibid., 127.

16. Ibid., 45.

17. Ibid., 92.

18. Ibid., 44.

19. Ibid., 46.

20. Ibid., 48.

21. Ibid., 228.

22. Northrop Frye and Christopher Lowry, "A Conversation with Northrop Frye about William Morris," *Journal of Pre-Raphaelite Studies*, ns 10 (Spring 2001), 40.

23. Morris, *News from Nowhere*, 48.

24. Ibid., 208.

25. Ibid., 52.

26. Ibid., 49.

27. Ibid., 228.

28. William Morris, "Preface to *The Nature of Gothic*," *News from Nowhere and Other Writings*, ed. Clive Wilmer (Harmondsworth: Penguin, 1993), 367.

29. Morris, *News from Nowhere*, 69, 77.

30. Ibid., 188–89.

31. Ibid., 68.

32. Ibid., 69.

33. Ibid., 89.

34. William Morris, *The Ideal Book: Essays and Lectures on the Arts of the Book*, ed. William S. Peterson (Berkeley: University of California Press, 1982), 1.

35. Morris, *News from Nowhere*, 184.

36. Ibid., 175.

37. Ibid., 173.

38. Ibid., 177.

39. Ibid., 179.

40. Ibid., 225.

41. Ibid., 160.

42. Ibid., 82.

43. Ibid., 83.

44. Ibid., 200.

45. Ibid., 160.

46. Ibid., 192.

47. Ibid., 200.
48. Ibid., 200.
49. Ibid., 125, 127.
50. Ibid., 222.
51. Ibid., 222.
52. Ibid., 45.
53. Ibid., 179.
54. Ibid., 227–28.
55. Ibid., 227.
56. Ibid., 228.
57. Ibid., 228.
58. Ibid., 228.
59. William Morris, [letter of July 1856] *The Collected Letters of William Morris*, ed. Norman Kelvin (Princeton: Princeton University Press, 1984), 1:28.

BIBLIOGRAPHY

The Beatles. "Revolution." *White Album*. London: Apple Records, 1968.
Blake, William. "The Marriage of Heaven and Hell." In *Selected Poetry and Prose of William Blake*, edited by Northrop Frye. New York: Modern Library, 1953.
Frye, Northrop, and Christopher Lowry. "A Conversation with Northrop Frye about William Morris." *Journal of Pre-Raphaelite Studies*, ns 10 (Spring 2001): 35–42.
Lennon, John. "Imagine." *Imagine*. London: Apple Records, 1971.
Marcuse, Herbert. *One Dimensional Man: Studies in the Ideology of Advanced Industrial Society*. Boston: Beacon, 1965.
Morris, William. *The Collected Letters of William Morris*. Vol. 1, edited by Norman Kelvin. Princeton: Princeton University Press, 1984.
———. "How I Became a Socialist." *News from Nowhere and Other Writings*, edited by Clive Wilmer, 379–83. Harmondsworth: Penguin, 1993..
———. *The Ideal Book: Essays and Lectures on the Arts of the Book,* edited by William S. Peterson. Berkeley: University of California Press, 1982.
———. *News from Nowhere and Other Writings*, edited by Clive Wilmer. Harmondsworth: Penguin, 1993.
———. "Preface to *The Nature of Gothic*." In *News from Nowhere and Other Writings*, edited by Clive Wilmer, 367–69. Harmondsworth: Penguin, 1993.
———. "Preface to *Signs of Change*." In *Collected Works of William Morris*. Vol. 23, edited by May Morris, 1–2. London: Longmans, Green, 1910–1915.
Yeats, W.B. "The Second Coming." In *Selected Poetry*. London: Macmillan, 1964.

Part III

LITERATURE

Chapter Nine

Morris Matters

Teaching News from Nowhere *in a Seminar on Victorian Materialities*

Susan David Bernstein

The study of material objects has been a lively focus in literary and cultural criticism, with a variety of approaches to materiality.[1] Terms like "posthuman" and "nonhuman" theories in recent years seek to emphasize the significance of material things rather than person-centered criticism. For William Cohen, posthumanism offers "an understanding of the human as simultaneously located in its materiality and as attachable to (and coextensive with) other materialities . . . machines, animals, and the environment."[2] Also part of this pivot away from an exclusive focus on the human are animal studies and ecocriticism, print culture, book history and new media studies, and object-oriented ontology, one theoretical vector of the new materialisms. Bill Brown's 2001 article "Thing Theory" inaugurated a branch of study, shaped by Heidegger's distinction between things as ideas, objects as physical entities. In my graduate seminar, "Victorian Objects, Things, and New Materialisms," at the University of Wisconsin-Madison in spring 2016, William Morris's *News from Nowhere* was the perfect text for encompassing so many of these material threads. The serial publication in Morris's *The Commonweal* followed by the Kelmscott Press edition worked well with our exploration of print culture and the materiality of the novel's different forms, along with the periodical context and the Arts and Crafts aesthetics of the book itself. A class visit to the University of Wisconsin Special Collections made possible close-up interactions with the Collection's Kelmscott Press holdings. We also investigated Morris's novel in relation to the forms and uses of archives. As evidence of the significance of this part of the syllabus and how productive Morris proved for a course on the new materialisms, two students submitted seminar essays on *News from Nowhere*. One focused on Morris's use of red bricks in the novel and on his theory of architecture, realized in the construction of Red House;

this research emerged from the course assignment to present a "Thing Study" of a material object from a novel on the syllabus. The other essay argued that Morris's tapestry designs, along with his writing about decorative patterns, form a productive corollary for the narrative design of *News from Nowhere*. A third student offered a fascinating reading of *News from Nowhere* for a "thing case study" presentation on the river locks in the novel and the serial form of the novel. From this profile on the way William Morris "matters" in Victorian studies, I will take up each strand in the fabric of the course to show how *News from Nowhere* provided a generative location for investigating new materialisms and what this approach offers for Morris studies.

MORRIS AND MATTER THEORIES

Morris took the heart or center spot in the course syllabus calendar. The theoretical compass of this course, different from a "Victorian Things and Thing Theory" seminar I had taught six years earlier, took its bearings from Jane Bennett's *Vibrant Matter: A Political Ecology of Things*. Moving beyond the dichotomy of thing and object, Bennett makes a rousing call for a "vibrant materiality" of all matter, organic and inorganic, human and nonhuman, with all entities having "agential life." Arguing for a "distributive notion of agency"—that not only humans can affect change for better or worse—Bennett claims that "people, animals, artifacts, technologies, and elemental forces share powers and operate in dissonant conjunction with each other."[3] In some sense, Morris offers a perfect exploratory field for Bennett's "political ecology of things," especially in his socialist utopia *News from Nowhere* where objects are both aesthetically brilliant and without ranked and monetary value or special possession. As Bennett puts it, "Materiality is a rubric that tends to horizontalize the relations between humans, biota, and abiota" and prompts "a greater appreciation of the complex entanglements of humans and nonhumans."[4] The open-endedness of Bennett's "agentic swarm"[5] invited us to dwell on the variant and vibrant mattering of things for Morris.

The class framed questions too on theorizing matter through new materialisms. About this networked, liberally distributed agency, we recognized the privilege for us to repudiate a special human agency, to disavow as posthumanists an ontologically-centered position, while still enjoying a central place of agency as readers and theorists. How does this more democratic approach to agency, then, square with the extraordinary value given to first editions of, say, Morris's Kelmscott Press? If the *Commonweal*, priced at one penny per issue, supported the eradication of class distinctions along with wealth and private property, what about the Kelmscott version of the novel produced two years later in 1892, in a run of 300 copies, an aesthetic object rendered in Golden type along with a woodcut frontispiece of Kelmscott Manor?[6] As Florence Boos points out, "The exquisite intricacy of the Kelmscott Press's designs raises an obvious question. . . . *How*—if at all—can one possibly construe these works as examples of 'popular' art?"[7]

What would a new materialist approach to rare books and archives look like? New materialisms theorists Diana Coole and Samantha Frost urge expanding agentic power beyond "normative" human agency, and at the same time investigating human "material practices such as the way we labor on, interact with, and exploit nature."[8] As the seminar participants argued, it is difficult to disaggregate material stuff from labor and exchange values, especially ironic for a socialist artist like Morris.

A few questions posed by students set the stage for our semester investigations well before we encountered Morris. Posting online questions on the assigned reading, Aaron Vieth asked, "I am wondering how the veneration of original copies fits into the intersection of New Materialism and print culture/book history. We (some scholars, librarians, museum curators, collectors) imbue first editions with extraordinary value, and preservationists take extreme actions to protect the material of these first editions. Coole and Frost emphasize the active, creative, and productive capacity of material itself; how does the valuing and maintenance of particular materials by humans confirm or challenge this emphasis?"[9] In terms of the levelling of agency between humans and nonhuman matters, many voiced a robust skepticism around taking "agentic power" to extremes. Still, the consensus was that new materialisms opened up potentially new routes for conceptualizing the realm and significance of matter in the Victorian texts we explored, and for Morris, this framework was especially provocative with unexpected ways into and beyond the materialities of and about *News from Nowhere*.

THING CASE STUDIES

I asked everyone to present a "thing study" on any material object that intrigued them from an assigned literary text. Much like some of the thing theories we'd read, like Elaine Freedgood's "strong metonymic readings" in her *The Ideas in Things: Fugitive Meaning in the Victorian Novel*, students researched through online databases, such as *British Periodicals*, to find historical contexts for appreciating the materiality, agency notwithstanding, of their chosen objects. In addition to examples like Freedgood on mahogany in *Jane Eyre* (one student examined oak in *Wuthering Heights*), I assigned Karin Dannehl's "Object Biographies" in which she approaches the metal cooking pots, say, in an eighteenth-century home by formulating "biographical turning points or life cycles of the objects found in a kitchen,"[10] a combination of object biography with a life cycle model as conceptual tools for "handling the methodological challenges of an object-focused historical enquiry."[11] A decidedly historical approach, this one complemented other theories about thingness, including Susan Stewart on miniatures, Carolyn Steedman on archival "dust," and, when we reached the two weeks on Morris, Elizabeth Carolyn Miller on "extraction capitalism."

The two things students selected for the Morris portion of the syllabus were the Maple-Durham lock on the river and the red bricks of the buildings cited in the novel, as well the Red House, a building Morris co-designed with Philip Webb. Both sets of things—wooden locks and red-bricked houses—are located on or near the Thames in *News*. And both in different ways serve as things produced by what Dick tells Guest is "the practical aesthetics with my gold and steel, and the blowpipe and the nice little hammer."[12] But how do these materials unfold from a new materialist glance?

Aaron Vieth extracted his selection on the locks from a late chapter in the novel, when Guest takes the river boat journey up the Thames in Oxfordshire. Guest queries Dick on why "rude contrivances"[13] such as the Maple-Durham lock still survive in Nowhere. And Dick replies to Guest that these locks have replaced "your machine-lock, winding up like a watch" and instead date back to the original locks, "the simple hatches, and the gates, with a big counterpoising beam" that harmonizes with the natural environment and looks "pretty."[14] Vieth remarked that he had difficulty selecting an object in Morris's novel because so many objects aren't regarded with significance by characters where books and pipes are not precious possessions. He elaborated, "But the locks were interesting because they were used and not discarded. They were also much bigger than what we had discussed . . . also familiar to Guest in contrast to the modernized or medievalized objects elsewhere in the text. Consequently, it was interesting to think about the historical context for the locks because my thing study became a kind of echo for what Guest might have been thinking about the locks."[15] Vieth's presentation to the seminar focused on three aspects of the locks: the material mechanism including historical accounts and Bennett's idea of assemblages; historical narratives about the Thames along with the narrative implications of the locks in relation to the serial form (which was the initial form *News from Nowhere* took in the *Commonweal*); and the lock as a utopian and ecological space. On the historical context of Maple-Durham lock, Vieth found several articles from periodicals, including *The Ludgate Monthly* where the writer offers a travel guide for the locale of the landing-place near the lock: "The view here of the tumbling weir, with the mill and the church embowered in its nest of trees, forms a lovely scene, and is a favourite subject with artists."[16] In the middle of this three-part serial, "The River Thames: From Oxford to Kingston," the author capitalizes on the aesthetic pleasures that Dick points out to Guest in Morris's novel published three years earlier. The article includes picturesque sketches and photographs of the river and Maple-Durham lock, information about lodging, dining, fishing, all in keeping with the subtitle of *News from Nowhere or An Epoch of Rest, Being Some Chapters from a Utopian Romance*. Vieth's survey of the historical context made clear that this lock was part of the riverscape of a much treasured journey for those on holiday.

Taking a new materialist perspective, Vieth considered whether the lock could qualify as an assemblage, a key form in Bennett's *Vibrant Matter: An Ecology of Things*. Vieth directed the seminar to Bennett's definition of assemblages as "ad hoc groupings of diverse elements, of vibrant materials of all sorts. Assemblages are living, throbbing confederations that are able to function despite the persistent presence of energies that confound them from within."[17] Given that Bennett poses an electrical power grid as one example, Vieth speculated on the Maple-Durham lock in Nowhere as an assemblage of three diverse constituents: the material of the lock itself (the wooden gates closing and opening for boats, along with the elements of water, ropes, and hooks); the network of people who manage and who use the lock (lock-keepers, beggars with hooks, travelers in the boats); and the Thames itself (the raising and lowering of boats by the river leveling itself).

The next facet of Vieth's thing study addressed the lock in relation to the serial form of the novel. Not only did his historical account framework come from a serial on the Thames in the *Ludgate*, but *Nowhere* too was initially issued in serial parts. How do the locks function as a different kind of serial device, he asked. One answer to this question of analogy came from another periodical article Vieth found from 1890, the same year *Nowhere* appeared in serial form, which suggests that the locks function as "pleasing breaks" for those traveling up the river.[18] These gaps that punctuate the journey with pauses, Vieth proposed, have the same kind of form as serial publications with their embedded breaks between installments. So does the Thames itinerary break up into segments even in the serialized "From Oxford to Kingston" travel piece in the *Ludgate*. If the river itself is a kind of narrative, then the locks are also interruptions that facilitate progression through the plot. Taking a broader view for this thing study, Vieth finally considered the locale of the lock in relation to Morris's larger project. Could the river lock in particular encapsulate a utopian space, even a harmonizing ecological scene? To open this question, Vieth turned to Elizabeth Carolyn Miller's *Slow Print* where she quotes from Fredric Jameson's theory of Utopian fantasy that equates idealized space with "the momentary formation of a kind of eddy or self-contained backwater within . . . seemingly irresistible forward momentum."[19] Could Morris's seemingly inconsequential passage on Maple-Durham lock exemplify what Jameson calls a "pocket of stasis within the ferment and rushing forces of social change . . . an enclave in which Utopian fantasy can operate?"[20] Vieth in effect proposed that the river lock generated the material conditions for this "pocket of stasis" necessary for a utopian vision to flourish. Vieth also pointed to Morris's own attention to damming of the river as part of the operation of the locks, similar to the "self-contained backwater" of the utopian genre, which, at this point in *News from Nowhere,* has followed the Thames well beyond London. Concluding his thing study of the lock, Vieth highlighted this object in the novel's concluding chapter. Dick leads Guest through a field to a meadow above the river and then to the river itself "above the weir and its mill" where "we had a delightful swim in the broad piece of water above the lock, where the river looked much bigger than its natural size from its being dammed up by the weir."[21] This Jamesonian utopia of a "pocket of stasis" is the last moment of material pleasure, the shared "delightful swim" in the idyllic backwater shaped by the network of weir, mill, and lock, before Guest's journey back to his bed "in dingy Hammersmith."[22] Vieth's thing study unfolded different routes into the materiality, including the print publication of the serial form, of the Maple-Durham lock on the Thames River. With this versatile choice, Vieth elaborated on an assemblage crafted, maintained, and used by networks of humans yet entwined by the natural materials of the river, tides, banks, and the networks of people, and considered the metonymic possibilities of the river lock and its backwaters with two narrative forms of the serial and the utopian fantasy.

The second thing study for the seminar selected an object narrowly tuned to Morris's aesthetic craft, a material mentioned also in passing in Nowhere but salient in Morris's own architectural values: red bricks. Stephanie Klem began her presentation by noting the frontispiece for the 1892 Kelmscott Press edition of *News from Nowhere* which features the east front of Kelmscott Manor. The woodcut, designed by C. M. Gere, bears an engraved text at the bottom that draws together Morris's Gloucestershire house with his fiction: "This is the picture of the old house by the Thames to which the people of this story went."[23] This seminar session took place in Special Collections, University of Wisconsin, Madison, with the holdings of the Kelmscott editions—the magisterial *Works of Geoffrey Chaucer* (1896) including many illustrations by Edward Burne-Jones, and a collection of poems by Morris, *Poems by the Way* (1891). Although no one in the seminar chose to explore either volume in their researched papers, the Special Collections holdings offered an inviting archive of Morris objects.

Figure 9.1. *News from Nowhere* frontispiece.
Reproduced courtesy of the University of Wisconsin, Madison, Special Collections.

After the seminar perused these volumes, Klem presented her selection prompted by a longstanding interest in bricks and bricklaying by highlighting the four times "red bricks" appears in the text of *Nowhere*. William Guest mentions red bricks in chapters 2, 3, and 4, a hand-crafted material he uses to establish Nowhere's utopian and historically reversed revision of modern London. After noting that the waterman's clothing resembles "a costume for a picture of fourteenth century life"[24] he exclaims over the transformation of the urban mess along the river. Replacing the "soap-works with their smoke-vomiting chimneys"[25] and the noise and sight pollutions of the engineering and factory works, Guest is particularly impressed by the replacement of modern industrial bridges over the Thames by "a wonder of a bridge" with "stone arches, splendidly solid, and as graceful as they were strong."[26] As his amazed gaze shifts to the shore, Guest describes, "a line of very pretty houses, low and not large . . . mostly built of red brick and roofed with tiles."[27] In the next chapter, the Guest House too is "handsomely built of red brick with a lead roof,"[28] and in the fourth chapter he observes some more houses of red brick in Hammersmith beyond the river's edge, buildings "pretty in design, and as solid as might be, but countryfied in appearance, like yeoman's dwellings."[29] The final fleeting mention of red bricks comes as Dick and Clara and Guest approach Hampton Court, again from the Thames and pass by "quaint and pretty houses . . . dominated by the long walls and sharp gables of a great red-brick pile of building, partly of the latest Gothic, partly of the court-style of Dutch William."[30] Not only are these red bricks, like the locks in Vieth's thing study, part of a picturesque scene, but this material is transhistorical, used in architecture of both "the latest Gothic" and "Dutch William" going back to the seventeenth century. From here Klem posed questions for her project on the red bricks of William Morris, queries that again took root in historical context, in thing theory's signifying potential, and in new materialist interest in the vibrancy of matter. First Klem examined how Morris, along with other nineteenth-century architects, theorists, and art critics, conceptualized red bricks and how architects used this material in their practice. She cited Morris's 1891 lecture, "The Influence of Building Materials on Architecture," published in 1892, in which he emphasizes the importance of suitable materials as the foundation of architecture.

Klem posed several questions to guide her study of red bricks in Morris's novel and his aesthetic practice. Do red bricks appear in other literary texts or art criticism of the era? In *News from Nowhere*, do these appearances of red brick serve a strong metonymic function? The presentation examined Morris's Arts and Crafts Red House, which he designed with the architect Philip Webb, and occupied with family and friends from its completion in 1860 until it proved too expensive to maintain while living there. At the time, Klem explained, the house was viewed as remarkable precisely for the red bricks in contrast to the stuccoed villas in villages near London.[31] But Webb also had built other red brick houses before, and Klem told us how these contributed to the rise of the Queen Anne style. Ruskin theorized about red brick in *The Poetry of Architecture* (1873) in which he favored a medium and neutral red, over a bright red, as the ideal color of brick, a material that harmonized well with the landscape. Ruskin's discussion of not only the color, but the durability, adaptability, and locally sourced potential of this brick provided an interesting description alongside Bennett's "political ecology" of matter.

And Klem pointed out how Morris's description of red-brick houses seems to echo Ruskin's aesthetics in *News from Nowhere*. Klem identified other Morris sources to elaborate on this aesthetic, such as his poem "Golden Wings" that prompted critics to appreciate Morris's treatment of red brick in poetic descriptions. She concluded her study with a consideration of how Morris's red bricks, both in the novel and in his theory and practice of architecture, are consistent not with aestheticism but with Victorian realism.

HOW COURSE MATERIAL MATTERS: MORRIS ESSAYS

Finding red bricks to open up into so many approaches, Stephanie Klem chose to develop her thing study for the seminar paper due at the end of the course. Although I had suggested Klem consider Morris's use of red bricks in relation to a hybrid genre of utopian realism, she ultimately decided that Freedgood's thing theory of "strong metonymic readings" was most fruitful, and to this end Klem's essay aims to restore "fugitive meanings"[32] to red bricks in *News from Nowhere*. Klem concludes, "If red bricks are metonymically linked to conceptions of truth and reality in nineteenth-century discourses of art and architecture, their sudden appearance and disappearance in *News from Nowhere* suggests the desirability but inaccessibility of Morris's utopian dream."[33] The essay traced the uneven literary life of bricks in Victorian literature. For Dickens in *Oliver Twist, The Old Curiosity Shop,* and *Hard Times,* red bricks become blackened due to the effects of pollution, and contrast markedly with Morris's red-brick edifices. However, as Klem also notes, Morris describes grey stone bridges rather than red brick houses in the closing passages of the novel, a shift that might signal not only geographical distinctions but also changes in Guest's consciousness from utopian vision to apprehending that state as only a dream as he begins to wake to his present reality. In her conclusion, then, Klem opens up another matter in Morris, the grey stone bridge, as a structure that connects the vividness of utopian fantasy with the dimness of the industrialized contemporary scene of London.

An art history graduate student in the course, Lindsey Wells, became interested in a category of things from Morris's decorative arts—the tapestry—as a design blueprint for the writer's use of nature in *News from Nowhere*. What emerged from Wells's research included a seminar paper, "'A Thoughtful Sequence': Nature as Tapestry in *News from Nowhere*," which Wells then compressed into a presentation at the annual Modern Language Association conference in a session organized by the William Morris Society that brought into dialogue craft design and literary forms. In an extended abstract of her conference paper for the MLA session "Craft and Design in Literary Study," Wells calls attention to the imbrication of Morris's decorative art of weaving and literary craft as "expressions of a comprehensive, multi-disciplinary artistic philosophy."[34] Distilling the larger argument Wells crafted in her seminar paper, she argues, "Morris treats nature in *News from Nowhere* such that he recreates for his readers the experience of actually viewing one of his decorative designs. Through his manipulation of text as pliable raw material, he demonstrates how fiction is not only able to embody the same aesthetic principles as ornament, but also performs similar functions."[35] Wells's contention that tapestry craft and narrative design converge in principle and in function in *News from Nowhere* is shaped in part by the new materialism theories the seminar explored.

Rather than the "strong metonymic reading" of Freedgood's thing theory which Klem used in her treatment of red-brick houses in Morris's novel, Wells drew from Bennett's "thing power" and "heterogeneous assemblage" in her reading of Morris. By selecting a material object showcasing design features that mapped onto both Morris's depiction of nature in *News* as well as the very narrative weave and woof of the text itself, Wells made manifest the robust interpretive possibilities of new materialism. Bennett's definition of the agency of vibrant materials resembles Wells's own approach to the textuality of Morris's tapestries and narrative: "*Thing-power* . . . draws attention to an efficacy of objects in excess of the human meanings, designs, or purposes they express or serve" and as such thing-power prompts "thinking beyond the life-matter binary."[36] For Wells, Bennett's thing-power dovetails with Morris's ideas on the expressive affordances of tapestries, and especially how he understands the raw materials of woven craft, which in turn Wells compares with Morris's narrative designs. Following a quotation from Bennett's definition of thing-power, Wells explains, "This is precisely how Morris positions decorative tapestries in 'Some Hints on Pattern-Designing,' a lecture that treats beauty in raw materials and finished products as agentic force."[37] In addition to Bennett's thing-power with its distributive agency, the framework of new materialism suits Wells's reading of vibrant nature descriptions in the novel: "The environs of Nowhere are inclusive of *all* life forms and respectful of *all* material vitalities."[38]

The intertwining of craft and nature designs that fuels Wells's argument also glances at ecocriticism, likewise consistent with Bennett's new materialist theories and more specifically with Miller's reading of Morris. Writes Wells, "Morris shows readers a world in which raw materials are lovingly fashioned into articles of beauty, from silk gowns and gold pipes to steel buckles and stone bridges. As Miller has recently pointed out, he also uses *News from No-*

where to imagine a system of production that deliberately restricts its harm to the environment, unlike the mass-production of tawdry commodities in capitalist factories."[39] More implicitly perhaps, Vieth's attention to Morris's interest in pre-industrial materials for the lock on the Thames, and Klem's research on red bricks as locally sourced materials also suggest ecocritical stakes, a more recent iteration of Victorian thing theory where nature and human production converge. Although I could not assign *The Sky of Our Manufacture: The London Fog in British Fiction from Dickens to Woolf* (2016) because it was published after the seminar, Jesse Oak Taylor's exploration of anthropogenic climate change might prompt further ecocritical analysis of Morris's utopian Nowhere within and beyond London.

CODA: MAKING MORRIS MATTER

The objects these scholars chose to examine stay clear of the most obvious ones for an artist-writer invested in the craft of producing beautiful books through his own press. Yet in Nowhere books are rare not because they are valued for their creative or informational or aesthetic significance, but because in Morris's utopian society "machine printing is beginning to die out, along with the waning of the plague of book-making."[40] Books are for an imperfect world of want, as Ellen explains, "well enough for times when intelligent people had but little else in which they could take pleasure, and when they must needs supplement the sordid miseries of their own lives with imaginations of the lives of other people."[41] Sounding like a Marxist dismissal of religion for the needy masses here, Ellen instead claims that nature in various guises, like a moonlit garden, are their books, while Guest's gaze turns Ellen's face and body into his own reading pleasure.[42] A new materialist approach to the crumbling archive of Nowhere might also open up some fruitful questions about the novel's own bibliophobia, suggesting not all material things of the past are valued in Nowhere.

The choices of a lock on the Thames, red bricks, and tapestry provide different routes into how Nowhere matters, how the vibrancy of the material surfaces (and the flatness of characters, as scholars have noted) maps onto narrative forms, whether the seriality suggested by the river lock, the units that comprise a whole structure prompted by the bricks, or the patterns on the textile surface of threads with hidden ones on the flipside. In each selection, the object itself prompts the readers to make connections between theory, text, and context, and yet all three studies discovered ways in which the objects of choice mattered to the forms of Morris's narrative. For Vieth, the lock leads him to seriality; for Klem, the brick connects to the genres of realism and utopia; for Wells, the tapestry means descriptions of nature with the dimensions of beauty, imagination, and organization. The "agentic swarm" Bennett claims for our world of vibrant matter is also the world of Morris's Nowhere. Closing with a creed for her "political ecology of things," Bennett confesses this new materialist faith, "I believe that encounters with lively matter can chasten my fantasy of human mastery, highlight the common materiality of all that is, expose a wider distribution of agency, and reshape the self and its interests."[43] Likewise there are many Nowherean creeds about nature, about mastery, about making all things "common materiality," and about the effects of this utopian world on self, possession, and self-possession.

Teaching Morris's *News from Nowhere* in a graduate seminar, like mine, with a new materialities framework, is one of many paths for incorporating the novel. A general undergraduate survey course on Victorian literature or a methodology course for literary studies are other possibilities, especially given the range of topics Morris's career as a writer and decorative artist opens up. The variety of things Vieth, Klem, and Wells conceptualized from *News from Nowhere* attests to the scale and scope of new materialism, which dovetail with other current methods and fields such as ecocriticism and seriality studies. The category of objects—waterway technology, building material, interior decoration—also encompass a range of use values, including transportation, architectural construction, and beautification. I could envision every student exploring an object from Morris, with the abundance of vibrant materialities this novel encompasses.

NOTES

1. I am grateful to the students in my graduate seminar English 828, University of Wisconsin, Madison, in spring 2016, and especially to Lindsay Wells for her generous comments on this article.

2. William Cohen, *Embodied: Victorian Literature and the Senses* (Minneapolis: University of Minnesota Press, 2009), 132.

3. Jane Bennett, *Vibrant Matter: A Political Ecology of Things.* (Durham, NC: Duke University Press, 2010), 34.

4. Ibid., 112.

5. Ibid., 32.

6. One of the 300 Kelmscott Press editions of the novel sold in November 2013 through Christie's London for GBP 3,750. http://www.christies.com/lotfinder/Lot/morris-william-1834-1896-news-from-nowhere-or-5736046-details.aspx Accessed January 8, 2018.

7. See http://morrisedition.lib.uiowa.edu/BookArts/KelmscottPressIntro.html.

8. Diana Coole and Samantha Frost, "Introducing the New Materialisms," in *The New Materialisms: Ontology, Agency, and Politics*, eds. Coole and Frost (Durham, NC: Duke University Press, 2010), 4.

9. All the people I cite were graduate students at the University of Wisconsin in 2016. Vieth was in the PhD English Literary Studies program, while Klem and Wells were PhD students in the Art History Department.

10. Karen Dannehl, "Object Biographies: From Production to Consumption," in *History and Material Culture: A Student's Guide to Approaching Alternative Sources*, ed. Karen Harvey (New York: Routledge, 2009), 123.

11. Ibid., 123.

12. William Morris, *News from Nowhere*, ed. Stephen Arata. (Peterborough, UK: Broadview Books, 2003), 70.

13. Ibid., 210.

14. Ibid., 210. The Maple-Durham lock dates back to the eleventh century with a dam or weir presumably on this portion of the Thames in 1086, since a corn mill linked to the Thames is mentioned in the Domesday Book of that year. https://www.visitthames.co.uk/about-the-river/river-thames-locks/mapledurham-lock Accessed January 9, 2018.

15. Personal email from Aaron Vieth, December 17, 2016.

16. Phillip May, "Part II: Goring to Maidenhead, The River Thames: From Oxford to Kingston," *The Ludgate Monthly* (May 1893): 358.

17. Bennett, *Vibrant Matter*, 23–24.

18. "On the Tow-Path," *All the Year Round* 3, no. 77 (June 21, 1890): 585.

19. Elizabeth Carolyn Miller, *Slow Print: Literary Radicalism and Late Victorian Print Culture*. (Stanford: Stanford University Press, 2013), 36.

20. Quoted in Miller, 36.

21. Morris, *News from Nowhere*, 245.

22. Ibid., 249.

23. For more information on Morris's Kelmscott Press editions, including this frontispiece, see Boos.

24. Morris, *News from Nowhere*, 57.

25. Ibid., 58.

26. Ibid., 58.

27. Ibid., 59.

28. Ibid., 63.

29. Ibid., 73.

30. Ibid., 187.

31. Red House in Bexleyheath, London, is a National Trust property and open to the public.

32. Stephanie Klem. "Utopian Visions of Red and Grey: The Influence of Building Materials in William Morris's *News from Nowhere*. Paper submitted for English 828, UW-Madison, Spring 2016, 2.

33. Ibid., 17.

34. Lindsay Wells. "'A Thoughtful Sequence': Text as Tapestry in William Morris's *News from Nowhere.*" *Useful and Beautiful*. Published by the William Morris Society in the United States (Spring 2017.1): 22.

35. Ibid., 21.

36. Bennett, *Vibrant Matter,* 20.

37. Lindsay Wells, "'A Thoughtful Sequence': Nature as Tapestry in *News from Nowhere.*" Paper submitted for English 828, UW-Madison, Spring 2016, 9.

38. Ibid., 17.

39. Ibid., 4. Wells refers here to Elizabeth Carolyn Miller, "William Morris, Extraction Capitalism, and the Aesthetics of Surface," *Victorian Studies* 57 (2015): 402. Not only did the seminar read Miller's chapter on Morris in *Slow Print* as well as this article, she visited the seminar when we discussed Morris and delivered a talk on her recent work on extraction ecology and Hardy.

40. Morris, *News from Nowhere*, 69.

41. Ibid., 192–3.

42. Ibid., 192.

43. Bennett, *Vibrant Matter*, 122.

BIBLIOGRAPHY

Bennett, Jane. *Vibrant Matter: A Political Ecology of Things.* Durham, NC: Duke University Press, 2010.

Brown, Bill. "Thing Theory." *Critical Inquiry.* 28, no.1 (Autumn 2001): 1–22.

Boos, Florence. "Introduction: The Kelmscott Press." William Morris Archive. University of Iowa, http://morrisedition.lib.uiowa.edu/BookArts/KelmscottPressIntro.html.

Cohen, William. *Embodied: Victorian Literature and the Senses.* Minneapolis: University of Minnesota Press, 2009.

Coole, Diana and Samantha Frost. "Introducing the New Materialisms." In *The New Materialisms: Ontology, Agency, and Politics*, edited by Coole and Frost. Durham, NC: Duke University Press, 2010. 1–46.

Dannehl, Karen. "Object Biographies: From Production to Consumption." In *History and Material Culture: A Student's Guide to Approaching Alternative Sources*, edited by Karen Harvey, 123–38. New York: Routledge, 2009.

Freedgood, Elaine. *The Ideas in Things: Fugitive Meaning in the Victorian Novel.* Chicago: University of Chicago Press, 2006.

Klem, Stephanie. "Utopian Visions of Red and Grey: The Influence of Building Materials in William Morris's *News from Nowhere*. Paper submitted for English 828, UW-Madison, Spring 2016.

May, Phillip. "Part II: Goring to Maidenhead, The River Thames: From Oxford to Kingston," *The Ludgate Monthly* (May 1893): 356–64.

Miller, Elizabeth Carolyn. *Slow Print: Literary Radicalism and Late Victorian Print Culture.* Stanford: Stanford University Press, 2013.

Morris, William. *News from Nowhere.* Edited by Stephen Arata. Peterborough, UK: Broadview Books, 2003.

"On the Tow-Path," *All the Year Round* 3, no. 77 (June 21, 1890): 585–88.

Wells, Lindsay. "'A Thoughtful Sequence': Text as Tapestry in William Morris's *News from Nowhere.*" *Useful and Beautiful.* Published by the William Morris Society in the United States (Spring 2017.1): 21–22.

———. "'A Thoughtful Sequence': Nature as Tapestry in *News from Nowhere.*" Paper submitted for English 828, UW-Madison, Spring 2016.

Chapter Ten

Teaching *News from Nowhere* in a Course on "The Simple Life"

Michael Robertson

Over the past few years, I have taught *News from Nowhere* in three different settings: an upper-level honors seminar on utopia, a first-year interdisciplinary seminar on "The Simple Life," and a course on utopian literature at New Jersey's Northern State Prison, a maximum-security prison in Newark. The easiest, by far, was the prison. The incarcerated men, delighted to escape one night a week from the petty, numbing routines of prison life, came to class eager to talk about Morris's utopian ideals. They contrasted his egalitarianism to the hierarchy of Plato's *Republic*, commented on his continuities with Thomas More, seized on his disagreements with Edward Bellamy, and argued zestfully about his ideas on government, education, work, money, families and, of course, crime and punishment. All I had to do was play traffic cop, directing the flow of conversation and occasionally stepping in to unsnarl a jam.

The most difficult course was "The Simple Life," part of my college's required first-year seminar program. In principle, students can choose a topic that engages their curiosity. In practice, they must select six unranked courses from a long list, based solely on the titles. The result is that students frequently find themselves in a course that has nothing to do with their major and little to do with their interests.

When I initially began teaching in the first-year program, I offered a course focused on my research specialty at the time: Walt Whitman's poetry. It did not go well. I soon wised up and created interdisciplinary courses designed to appeal to students from varying backgrounds. "The Simple Life" has been the most successful. Last fall I inserted *News from Nowhere* into the syllabus for the first time. I was apprehensive about including a book that means so much to me both professionally and personally. My prison students did not all love the book, but they were eager to grapple with Morris's ideas. The honors students may have been baffled at times, but they responded to the novel's political, moral, and formal complexities. Would these first-year students from across the college—prospective majors in fields from engineering to nursing, from business to graphic design—be engaged enough to finish the book, much less consider its deliberately ambiguous vision?

The result was mixed. The students in that fall's class were a particularly difficult group, reluctant to drop the mask of indifference they had crafted in high school. I was in despair until, drawing inspiration from Morris's utopian conception of education, I changed my pedagogical approach. By the final class on the novel, students were conversing with an intellectual passion I had not seen all semester. Moreover, inserting Morris into the course helped me to see it in a powerful new context. *News from Nowhere* is generally taught in courses on Victorian literature or utopian studies, and it is most often read alongside works by Thomas Carlyle and John Ruskin or Thomas More and Edward Bellamy. "The Simple Life" course convinced me of the value of locating Morris within an alternative discursive tradition.

That tradition is not easily defined. As Fiona MacCarthy notes, "The Simple Life . . . has tended to be a very complicated concept."[1] MacCarthy simplifies the task in her book *The Simple Life* by focusing on the efforts of C. R. Ashbee and a small group of associates to establish an Arts and Crafts colony in the Cotswolds. Similarly, Vicky Albritton and Fredrik Albritton Jonsson's recent book on the simple life is limited to a circle of late nineteenth-century cultural radicals who were attracted to the Lake District by John Ruskin's ideals. The only near-comprehensive history of the concept is David E. Shi's *The Simple Life*, which is limited to the American tradition, and which largely sidesteps definition. Instead, Shi quotes Wordsworth's poetic lament for a supposedly simpler past: "Plain living and high thinking are no more."[2] *Plain living and high thinking* has become a definitional catchphrase.

I introduce the phrase to my students on the first day of the course and tell them that, rather than imposing a potentially procrustean definition of the simple life that the works we'll read must stretch to fit, we will define the idea collectively over the course of the term. I do, however, set some limits. I give them a brief excerpt from Antonio Gramsci's *Prison Notebooks*, introduce the concept of hegemony, and explain that the simple life needs to be seen as a form of counter-hegemonic praxis. We take up the hypothetical example of a tribe in the Amazon newly come into contact with South American anthropologists. Members of this tribe would certainly be living simply by our standards, with no tools more complex than a stone axe, no clothing except that which they make themselves, and no food except that which they hunt or gather. But they would not be living the simple life, since the simple life is a consciously counter-hegemonic tradition developed in opposition to dominant cultural ideology. Moreover, the simple life is not simply a set of practices or ideas but a form of praxis, which I explain as theoretically informed action toward social change.

When I was planning the course, I intended to follow the first day's attention to the concept of the simple life with some of the earliest examples of the simple life tradition, such as the community of goods established among first-century Christians and described in the biblical book of Acts. However, influenced by Tim Clydesdale's research on the educational experience of first-year college students, I decided instead to begin with a more recent and accessible text: Lauren Greenfield's documentary film *The Queen of Versailles*. The film follows David Siegel, a Florida-based real estate developer, and his wife Jacqueline, a former beauty queen, in their effort to build America's largest private home, a 90,000 square foot mansion. Greenfield offers a detailed, powerful portrait of the Siegels' consumption-driven lifestyle, their peculiarly American combination of *ancien régime* glamour—David sits for a photo session in an elaborate gilded throne—and Walmart kitsch: Jackie goes on shopping sprees at big-box stores, cramming her SUV with plastic toys for her eight children. They find the inspiration for their new home on a visit to Versailles and decide to reproduce the French palace outside Orlando, adding a bowling alley, a spa, and other amenities. Greenfield's film is not a simple satire of the nouveaux riches Siegels; instead, she creates a complex, nuanced portrait. Nevertheless, my students were uniformly appalled by the thoughtless lavishness that permeates the Siegels' lives, their compulsive spending and gaudy surroundings. *The Queen of Versailles* turns students into critics of consumption and increases their receptiveness to the counter-hegemonic values of simple living.

I follow Greenfield's film with a series of American texts that are central to the simple life tradition and that serve as useful preparation for *News from Nowhere*. First are excerpts from the journal of John Woolman, an eighteenth-century New Jersey Quaker. Woolman began his adult life as a merchant, but gave it up when his honesty, integrity, and hard work made the business a financial success. Woolman found that his devotion to trade and his burgeoning wealth were turning him away from Quaker values of simplicity and equality, and he devoted the remainder of his life to an informal traveling ministry among Quakers in the American colonies and Great Britain, demonstrating the ways in which seemingly harmless luxuries inevitably entangled consumers in systems of violence and oppression. The sugar with which they sweetened their tea came from Caribbean plantations dependent on slave labor; their fashionable clothes were made from slave-grown cotton and dyes. Woolman's crusade did not necessarily turn the people he encountered into apostles of the simple life, but it succeeded in drawing their attention to the inherent cruelties of slavery. Woolman is credited with inspiring Quakers to embrace abolitionism, and his posthumously published journal influenced generations of readers interested in simplicity.

Among them was A. Bronson Alcott, friend of Emerson and Thoreau and father of the writer Louisa May Alcott. Along with Charles Lane, a British philanthropist, Alcott established the utopian colony Fruitlands in rural Massachusetts in 1843. Alcott and Lane's prospectus for Fruitlands is a stirring manifesto on the political and spiritual necessity of simple living. Early advocates of animal rights, Alcott and Lane required prospective colonists not only to adopt a vegan diet but also to abstain from artificial lighting, which was fueled by whale oil. The Fruitlands colonists were required to abstain, in addition, from money, trade, private property, and warm baths. "Outward abstinence is a sign of inward fulness," the two Transcendentalists wrote.[3]

Thirty years later Alcott's daughter Louisa May, who was eleven when Fruitlands was established, published "Transcendental Wild Oats," a witty satire about her family's experience. The story reveals her admiration for her father's fervent idealism, but it is unsparing in its depiction of the incompetence, sexism, and self-righteousness that led to the community's dissolution after only seven months. My students read both the father's prospectus and the daughter's satire, an exercise that can result in a fruitful discussion on the promise and perils of the simple life. I tell my students about Peter Elbow's concept of both believing and doubting what one reads—a concept at the heart of the critical thinking skills that the first-year seminar program is committed to teaching.

This emphasis on believing and doubting is invaluable for reading the course's two major texts, *Walden* and *News from Nowhere*. *Walden* comes first. Thoreau's memoir makes a perfect prelude to Morris's utopian romance, since it engages in all of the central functions of utopian literature. Darko Suvin places *cognitive estrangement* at the heart of utopian fiction; the term is Suvin's version of Viktor Shklovsky's concept of *defamiliarization*, literature's power to disrupt readers' habitual blind acceptance of the status quo. What *News from Nowhere* achieves through plotting—the future world in which William Guest awakens serves to estrange him from nineteenth-century London, defamiliarizing its ubiquitous ugliness and inequality—Thoreau accomplishes through paradox. *Walden*'s opening chapter is shot through with paradox: "Men have become the tool of their tools"; "If I repent of any thing, it is very likely to be my good behavior."[4] Thoreau defamiliarizes the anxious material striving of his nineteenth-century neighbors, fulfilling one of utopian fiction's two principal forms of cultural work: offering a radical critique of contemporary society. The other is to provide a vision of a better world, which Thoreau achieves through his description of his two years' sojourn at Walden

Pond. Walden serves as a utopian space, an Arcadian retreat from antebellum America's chattel slavery, pervasive materialism, and burgeoning industrial capitalism. *Walden* is a paean to the simple life: "Simplicity, simplicity, simplicity!" Thoreau exclaims at one point. "I say, let your affairs be as two or three, and not a hundred or a thousand."[5] The book is not, however, an instruction manual. Students often exclaim, "But I don't want to go live in the woods!" I direct them back to the text, where Thoreau emphasizes, "I would not have any one adopt *my* mode of living on any account; . . . but I would have each one be very careful to find out and pursue *his own* way, and not his father's or his mother's or his neighbor's instead."[6] Utopian studies scholars emphasize utopian fiction's heuristic function; the greatest utopian fictions, such as *News from Nowhere*, stimulate readers' questions rather than offering a blueprint to be followed. In Lucy Sargisson's pithy formulation, "The function of utopia is not its own realization."[7] Similarly, *Walden*'s function is not to send readers into the wilderness but to stimulate their awareness of others'—and their own—lives of quiet desperation.

Morris himself knew something about quiet desperation. His daughter May said that Morris watched with amusement the vagaries of his friends and acquaintances who were attempting to live the simple life in fin-de-siècle Britain, but his essays and letters reveal a longing for Thoreauvian simplicity. "Look," he wrote plaintively to his friend Louisa Baldwin, "suppose people lived in little communities among gardens & green fields, so that you could be in the country in 5 minutes walk, & had few wants; almost no furniture for instance, & no servants, & studied (the difficult) arts of enjoying life, & finding out what they really wanted: then I think one might hope civilization had really begun."[8] The letter dates from 1874; sixteen years later he elaborated his utopian vision of the simple life in *News from Nowhere*.

I began my teaching of *News* in "The Simple Life" in the same way I had in my utopian literature courses for honors and prison students, with a brief background lecture on Victorian England and William Morris: his hatred of the era's savage inequalities; his delighted revelation when he first encountered the Gothic churches of northern France; his commitment to the "lesser arts" of architecture and design as a path toward a better future; his gradual embrace, spurred by his reading of Ruskin and Marx, of revolutionary socialism; and his journeys up the Thames from his house in Hammersmith to Kelmscott Manor. This seemed adequate background for reading *News*, but during the next class, it soon became clear that these first-year students needed more preparation. By the time they encountered Morris's romance, my utopian literature students had been steeped in speculative fiction, but nothing in "The Simple Life" had prepared students for the book's formal complexities, particularly in its opening pages, in which Morris changes narrators with sleight-of-hand deftness and challenges the conventions of literary realism. "What the hell's going on?" one asked. "This book really threw me off." In an effort to contextualize Morris's romance, I asked them what books or movies the novel reminded them of. None had read any utopian fiction, but almost all had read the young adult dystopian novel *The Giver*, and others brought up *Nineteen Eighty-Four, Brave New World*, and *The Hunger Games*. Elise, the class libertarian, suggested Ayn Rand's *Anthem*, and when one student mentioned *Spirited Away*, an animated children's film, everyone enthusiastically agreed. With the question of genre addressed, we were ready to talk about central issues in Morris's simple life utopia.

The students, however, soon turned as quiet and disengaged as they had been all semester. I had never encountered so difficult a group. I teach at a highly selective public college, and in every class I can count on at least a handful of curious, articulate students to spark discussion. These students were bright enough—their essays proved that—but they were remarkably reluctant to talk, resisting every effort in my pedagogical bag of tricks. They had been silent from the beginning, and they signaled their disengagement by behavior I'd never encountered before: frequently leaving their seats to throw something in the wastebasket, wandering out of the room for long bathroom breaks. I was initially baffled, then angry, then reflective. I realized that they were simply acting the way they were accustomed to from high school, when it was taken for granted that they had little interest in learning. These students weren't being sullen or disrespectful; rather, they were victims of authoritarian public schools. Their intellectual curiosity had largely been driven out of them, and they had resorted to a form of nonviolent noncooperation. To borrow a term from Paolo Freire, they had responded to the "banking" model of education by closing the deposit window.

William Morris would have sympathized with my students. "On the few occasions that I have been inside a Board-school," he wrote in *Commonweal*, "I have been much depressed by the mechanical drill. My heart sank before Mr. Mc'Choakumchild and his method."[9] Morris himself had not been subjected to the harsh utilitarian methods of *Hard Times'* Mc'Choakumchild and Gradgrind—he had, as he said, been born well off enough to be sent to a public school where the teaching methods were relatively benign and totally ineffectual—but he agreed with Dickens' critique. In *News from Nowhere* he anticipates the radical twentieth-century educational theorist Ivan Illich and portrays a "deschooled" society, where the notion of a *school* is applied only to herrings, where the desire to learn is assumed to be as natural as the desire to make beautiful things, and where children are left free to gain knowledge of the world about them. Faced with my reluctant students, I realized that I needed to figure out a more Morrisian pedagogy. Conditioned by years of utilitarian discipline, these students had resisted my most earnest efforts to engage them. I had to find a way to deschool my classroom, to move myself out of the way and allow them to teach themselves. The evening before the next class session, I came up with a plan.

At the start of the class, I divided the group in two and explained that we would be having a debate. Students by that point were accustomed to the believing/doubting method of inquiry that we had been using all semester, and I assigned one group to be believers, defending Morris's vision of a transformed society. The other students, the doubters, had to attack it as not only unworkable but undesirable. Each side broke into smaller groups to prepare their arguments—I wanted to be sure that every student was engaged in making the case—and when they reassembled I made an announcement. I explained that I was writing an essay about teaching *News from Nowhere*, that I needed to take notes on everything that was said, and that I would not be participating in, or even moderating, the discussion. And at that point I picked up my pen, bent my head over my paper, and did not look up for the rest of the class.

The next thirty minutes were the high point of the semester. Because I was not looking at the students, they could not raise their hands to be recognized, and they saw that it was pointless to address their remarks to the teacher. They had to talk to one another. If the ensuing conversation was occasionally chaotic, it was also lively and funny and earnest. And quite quickly, it turned profound. The doubters went first, and they brought up the episode of the pipe, when William Guest enters a shop tended by children and is handed a gorgeous, jewel-encrusted object. "It doesn't make sense that he can just take a pipe," Abby said. Looking at James, who was on the opposing side, she went on: "If James takes six pipes, and there are none for you, you'll be pissed off. And that's going to happen, because people are naturally greedy." Within minutes of the debate's commencement, the students were tackling a topic at the center of *News from Nowhere*: the nature of human nature. If I had been monitoring the debate, at this point I would have instructed the students to turn to chapter 14, where Guest brings up an objection to the future society based on human nature, and old Hammond roars back, "Human nature! What human nature? The human nature or paupers, of slaves, of slave-holders, or the human nature of wealthy freemen? Which? Come, tell me that?"[10] I might have gone on to mention the political theorist Barbara Goodwin, who argues that while the conception of humans as endlessly acquisitive is at the center of capitalist economics and liberal political theory, this view of human motivation is not necessarily true. But since I was busy taking notes, I had to rely on the students to counter Abby's assertion. After a while, they did. When Garrett, one of the doubters, said, "People are naturally lazy; we all want something for nothing," both Arianna and Mitchell came back at him. "We naturally want to build things and do things," both argued. People want to be happy, they said, and it makes us happy to create. These first-year students were not skillful close readers, and none of them referred to Morris's obstinate refusers, engaged in building a beautiful stone hall for the sheer pleasure of the work, but they had clearly absorbed Morris's ideas about the lesser arts and, to an extent, about the change from the Middle Ages to capitalist modernity. Later in the debate, Mitchell said, "In the past, before capitalism, people didn't always want to make the most money." Abby shot back, "You can't escape human nature." Channeling old Hammond, Mitchell replied, "But human nature isn't fixed. It changes when society changes." He went on, "In this society, the incentive to work is work. Once you introduce money into society, that becomes people's motivation."

The conversation was still going on when it was time for the class to end. "This was fun," Abby said as she walked out of the room. "We should do debates more often." We should, but it was near the end of the semester, and none of the few remaining topics lent themselves to the clear believing/doubting distinction of Morris's utopian romance. However, the students were able to continue their exploration of *News* in the essays they wrote after the debate. For that assignment, I asked students to defend or critique a specific element of Morris's simple life utopia; in a short essay, it was crucial that they be specific. I offered them a wide range of topics, including government, money, work, family, gender, marriage, and criminal justice. The most popular topic was education.

The students were equally divided between those enamored of Morris's deschooled society and those appalled by it. I found the latter essays particularly interesting. Elizabeth wrote as if it were perfectly natural for students to hate school. "Teaching children to read does not take away their freedom and happiness," she wrote. "It will expand their minds, making them happy in their later life. Children usually are not capable of understanding this, which explains why they dislike school." I recalled our reading of Gramsci from earlier in the semester; hegemony depends on the consent of the oppressed. Elizabeth and her peers, educated in hierarchical, authoritarian institutions, had come to believe that a coercive pedagogy, no matter how distasteful, was the only route to learning. The children of Morris's Nowhere, who learn to read as it suits them, seemed to them fantastic creatures. Other students, however, envied Nowhere's children and imagined themselves in their place. "Humans are a curious species," Zach wrote, and he delighted in Morris's portrayal of a world where children were free to follow their curiosity down a variety of paths.

Miguel Abensour famously wrote that the "education of desire" is at the heart of *News from Nowhere*. Utopia, he continued, opens a path for desire, teaches it "to desire better, to desire more, and above all to desire otherwise."[11] *News from Nowhere* can educate desire; so can a course on the simple life. *The Queen of Versailles* illuminates the nature of desire in a consumer society, the way it can drive frantic accumulation and a determination to possess the largest and gaudiest of toys. John Woolman, Bronson Alcott, and Henry David Thoreau all offer ways of desiring otherwise, of finding satisfaction in personal simplicity and in imagining a redefined, egalitarian prosperity. Introducing *News from Nowhere* into the course convinced me of Morris's central place in the simple life tradition; it also taught me the importance of simplicity in pedagogy. When I arranged the debating exercise for my students and then withdrew, their curiosity and zest for ideas could flourish. Less, as William Morris well understood, can indeed be more.

NOTES

1. Fiona MacCarthy, *The Simple Life: C. R. Ashbee in the Cotswolds* (Berkeley: University of California Press, 1981), 9.

2. David E. Shi, *The Simple Life: Plain Living and High Thinking in American Culture* (Athens: University of Georgia Press, 1985), 5. The phrase comes from Wordsworth's sonnet "Written in London. September, 1802."

3. Amos Bronson Alcott and Charles Lane, "On the Community at Fruitlands," in *The Blithedale Romance,* by Nathaniel Hawthorne, ed. William E. Cain (Boston: Bedford Books, 1996), 366. See also Richard Francis, *Fruitlands: The Alcott Family and Their Search for Utopia* (New Haven, CT: Yale University Press, 2010).

4. Henry David Thoreau, *Walden* (1854; Boston: Beacon Press, 1997), 34, 9.

5. Ibid., 86.

6. Ibid., 66.

7. Lucy Sargisson, "The Curious Relationship between Politics and Utopia," in *Utopia Method Vision: The Use Value of Social Dreaming*, ed. Tom Moylan and Raffaella Baccolini (Oxford: Peter Lang, 2007), 31.

8. May Morris, introduction to *The Collected Works of William Morris*, vol. 22 (London: Longmans, Green, 1915), xxiv; *The Collected Letters of William Morris*, ed. Norman Kelvin, vol. 1 (Princeton: Princeton University Press, 1984), 218.

9. William Morris, "Thoughts on Education under Capitalism," *Commonweal*, June 30, 1888, in May Morris, *William Morris: Artist, Writer, Socialist*, vol. 2 (Oxford: Blackwell, 1936), 498. On Morris and education, see Phillippa Bennett, "Educating for Utopia: William Morris on Useful Learning versus 'Useless Toil,'" *Journal of William Morris Studies* 20, no. 2 (2013): 54–72.

10. William Morris, *News from Nowhere*, ed. Clive Wilmer (London: Penguin, 2004), 118.

11. Miguel Abensour, "William Morris: The Politics of Romance," in *Revolutionary Romanticism*, ed. Max Blechman (San Francisco: City Light Books, 1999), 145–46.

BIBLIOGRAPHY

Abensour, Miguel. "William Morris: The Politics of Romance." In *Revolutionary Romanticism*, edited by Max Blechman, 125–61. San Francisco: City Light Books, 1999.

Albritton, Vicky and Fredrik Albritton Jonsson, *Green Victorians: The Simple Life in John Ruskin's Lake District.* Chicago: University of Chicago Press, 2016.

Alcott, Amos Bronson and Charles Lane. "On the Community at Fruitlands." In *The Blithedale Romance,* by Nathaniel Hawthorne, edited by William E. Cain, 362–66. Boston: Bedford Books, 1996.

Alcott, Louisa May. "Transcendental Wild Oats." In *The Blithedale Romance,* by Nathaniel Hawthorne, edited by William E. Cain, 366–76. Boston: Bedford Books, 1996.

Bennett, Phillippa. "Educating for Utopia: William Morris on Useful Learning versus 'Useless Toil.'" *Journal of William Morris Studies* 20, no.2 (2013): 54–72.

Clydesdale, Tim. *The First Year Out: Understanding American Teens after High School*. Chicago: University of Chicago Press, 2007.

Elbow, Peter. *Writing without Teachers*. New York: Oxford University Press, 1998.

Francis, Richard. *Fruitlands: The Alcott Family and Their Search for Utopia*. New Haven, CT: Yale University Press, 2010.

Freire, Paolo. *Pedagogy of the Oppressed*. New York: Herder and Herder, 1970.

Goodwin, Barbara and Keith Taylor. *The Politics of Utopia: A Study in Theory and Practice*. New York: St. Martin's, 1983.

Gramsci, Antonio. *Selections from the Prison Notebooks*. Edited and translated by Quintin Hoare and Geoffrey Nowell Smith. New York: International Publishers, 1971.

Greenfield, Lauren. *The Queen of Versailles*. DVD. Los Angeles: Magnolia Home Entertainment, 2012.

Illich, Ivan. *Deschooling Society*. New York: Harper & Row, 1971.

MacCarthy, Fiona. *The Simple Life: C. R. Ashbee in the Cotswolds*. Berkeley: University of California Press, 1981.

Morris, May. Introduction to *The Collected Works of William Morris*, Vol. 22, xi–xxxiv. London: Longmans, Green, 1915.

Morris, William. *The Collected Letters of William Morris*, Vol. 1. Edited by Norman Kelvin. Princeton: Princeton University Press, 1984.

———. *News from Nowhere*. Edited by Clive Wilmer. London: Penguin, 2004

———. "Thoughts on Education under Capitalism." *Commonweal*, June 30, 1888. In May Morris, *William Morris: Artist, Writer, Socialist*, Vol. 2, 496–500. Oxford: Blackwell, 1936.

Sargisson, Lucy. "The Curious Relationship between Politics and Utopia." In *Utopia Method Vision: The Use Value of Social Dreaming*, edited by Tom Moylan and Raffaella Baccolini, 25–46. Oxford: Peter Lang, 2007.

Shi, David E. *The Simple Life: Plain Living and High Thinking in American Culture*. Athens: University of Georgia Press, 1985.

Shklovsky, Victor. *Theory of Prose*. Elmwood Park, IL: Dalkey Archive Press, 1990.
Suvin, Darko. *Metamorphoses of Science Fiction*. New Haven, CT: Yale University Press, 1979.
Thoreau, Henry David. *Walden*. 1854. Boston: Beacon, 1997.
Woolman, John. *The Journal of John Woolman*. In *Quaker Spirituality: Selected Writings*, edited by Douglas V. Steere. Mahway, NJ: Paulist Press, 1984.

Chapter Eleven

Teaching Morris the Utopian

Deanna K. Kreisel

Literary utopias are boring. They are notoriously prosy and descriptive, stuffed with arcane topical political references and containing little character development and even less plot. Their dreariness, of course, makes perfect sense. Once you have set up your ideal society in a way that is rational, just, and self-sustaining, then you have guaranteed that nothing much will happen there; narrative interest requires conflict, strife, or tragic flaw. William Morris's *News from Nowhere* (1890; 1891) is, unfortunately, no exception to this rule (at least according to my undergraduates). And yet reading and teaching utopian thought—both political theory and literary texts—seems more important than ever in the current political moment, as the urgency of imagining alternative modes of social organization becomes increasingly apparent.

Teaching *News from Nowhere* in the context of a class on utopian and dystopian literature can bring out the fascinating contradictions, ambivalences, and visionary insights of this otherwise difficult text. The task of the instructor when teaching this novel is thus twofold: 1. to illuminate the great (if not immediately obvious) interest of the novel by drawing out its significance in the history of utopian thought; and 2. to encourage students to consider why the novel seems boring to begin with by reflecting on the literary elements "missing" from the text. The latter method may be used to model a formalist or even narratological reading practice, while the former can be used to teach more historicist methodologies.

There are obviously a myriad of ways to approach *News from Nowhere* in the undergraduate classroom, depending on course context, preparation level of the students, class size, and instructor predilection; in this essay I will discuss strategies for teaching the novel in a discussion-oriented course for English majors. My experience with teaching the novel is in an upper-level specialty-topics seminar on Victorian British utopias where we dedicated two weeks (or six hours of class time) to Morris. However, the techniques I discuss here could easily be used, with some tweaking, in a larger, second-year course or first-year seminar, or a more broadly conceived course or survey that includes a unit on utopian fiction. Ideally the students will have some familiarity with Thomas More's *Utopia* (1516). I asked my upper-level seminarians to familiarize themselves with it before class began, but the instructor may decide instead to assign some passages from More's text at the beginning of the course or unit in order to give students a sense of its mode of address, emphasis on description, contemporary political commentary, and relative plotlessness as a way into understanding its influence on later utopianists, and thus on Morris's own aesthetic choices.

It is helpful to at least include—perhaps through excerpting if the novel is taught in a shorter section on nineteenth-century utopianism—the two most important utopian source texts to which Morris was directly responding: Edward Bellamy's *Looking Backward* (1888) and Richard Jefferies's *After London* (1885).[1] Bellamy's novel describes an industrial socialist utopia where problems of production and distribution have been solved through technological means, while Jefferies's dystopian text describes a post-apocalyptic England that has returned to a feudalist, agrarian state. Students can readily see how Morris is responding to both works in *News from Nowhere* in his depiction of a quasi-Medieval economic organization as the solution to the contradictions of capitalism.

If the instructor has the luxury of an entire course on British utopianism, then the syllabus will include a wider selection of the literally hundreds of utopian and dystopian novels published in the nineteenth century; obviously anyone teaching such a class will already have decided opinions about which texts to teach, but my own course included Samuel Butler's *Erewhon* (1872), James DeMille's *A Strange Manuscript Found in a Copper Cylinder* (1888), Edward Bulwer-Lytton's *The Coming Race* (1871), and H. G. Wells's *The Time Machine* (1895) in addition to *News from Nowhere* and *After London*. This essay proceeds with the assumption that the instructor has included *News from Nowhere* as one among several utopian texts, and is teaching it in that context.

My seminar on Victorian utopias began with two weeks dedicated solely to theoretical reading before we turned to the literary utopias, which we read in roughly chronological order (we read *News from Nowhere* before *After London*, since I wanted to establish the parameters of the utopian novel before introducing dystopias). As we read each literary text our discussion reflected back on both the elements of the theoretical readings that we saw reflected or challenged in that novel, and on the intertextual conversation between that novel and the ones that had come before. *News from Nowhere* came after *Erewhon*, and before *Strange Manuscript*, *After London*, *The Coming Race*, and *The Time Machine*. The discussion that follows is constructed differently than the order in which we discussed the texts since I will, naturally, be drawing together the various threads of the class that were dedicated to *News from Nowhere*. I will begin with an overview of our theoretical reading, jumping back and forth between these texts and their subsequent reappearances in our later discussion of Morris, then turn to more detailed suggestions for class discussion of *News from Nowhere* in the context of broader utopian thought.

MORRIS AND UTOPIAN POLITICAL THEORY

The decision of whether or not to include primary theoretical readings will depend on the course context and preparation level of the students, but it would seem remiss not to address the rich theoretical history of utopianism in some fashion, particularly since Morris's political predilections were so closely tied to his literary production. One of the most compelling reasons to teach *News from Nowhere* in the broader context of utopian political theory is that it stages so clearly the tensions in the history of that theory. Morris's text is a perfect way into a broader discussion of the differences (and similarities) among literary utopias, concrete utopian experiments such as intentional communities, the "utopian strain" in political thought, and Marxist and socialist theory. In order to frame these distinctions and to draw out the unique place of *News from Nowhere* in the utopian tradition, it is necessary to assign a fair amount of background material as part of the course or unit.

Before diving into the course material itself, I began with an overview of the different manifestations of "utopia": literary genre, intentional community, strain of political thought, psychological impulse. Of course one of the greatest challenges of utopian theory has been to assay the relationship among these various versions of utopia. Presenting this challenge to students up front can help to focus subsequent discussion of the relationship between the theoretical and literary texts they will read. I made available as an optional reading the first two chapters of Fredric Jameson's *Archaeologies of the Future*, and summarized parts of the first chapter in my introductory lecture.[2] The book can be tough going for undergraduates (even for professors), but I like to give curious students at least a taste of recent theoretical work, and Jameson's first chapter is short and relatively accessible.

We started off our reading with two introductory essays—"The Concept of Utopia," by Fátima Vieira, in *The Cambridge Companion to Utopian Literature*, and Jorge Bastos da Silva's introduction to his edited volume *The Epistemology of Utopia*—and then moved on to primary theoretical readings.[3] We relied heavily on Ruth Levitas's excellent and accessible volume *The Concept of Utopia* as a guide through this material, moving back and forth between Levitas's explanatory overviews—which are also polemical in their own right—and excerpts from Marx's *Economic and Philosophic Manuscripts of 1844* and *Grundrisse*; Engels's *Condition of the Working Class in England*; Bloch's *Principle of Hope*; and Marcuse's *Eros and Civilization*.[4]

Levitas organizes her discussion of Marx and Engels around the foundational split between utopian socialism and classical Marxism, and how the epithet "utopian" came to denote, for the latter, impracticality and woolly-headed idealism. For most Marxist theorists, the construction of detailed blueprints for a specific future society has been seen as at best a distraction from the immediate and pressing tasks of social change and at worst an ideological, compensatory sop akin to religion. Levitas notes, however, that the "real dispute between Marx and Engels and the utopian socialists is not about the merit of goals or of images of the future but about the process of transformation"[5]—whether the workers' paradise will be brought about through revolution or through "an appeal to all classes on the basis of reason and justice."[6] Marxists claim that utopian socialism "entails an idealist model of social change, suggesting that the mere propagation of such [utopian] schemes will have a transformative effect."[7] In other words, the two central differences between Marxism and utopian socialism are: 1. whether the ideal society will be brought about through revolution or through persuasive tactics, including already-existing political processes; and 2. whether depictions of utopia can form a kind of counter-ideological force or are themselves always and inherently ideological.

Levitas stages an intervention into this long-standing debate by arguing that the differences between the two systems of thought are not as stark as they have been portrayed. As she points out, Marxism also indulges in blueprint-making, since "an outline of the principal features of communist society can be pieced together from the writings of Marx and Engels."[8] A productive classroom discussion can be built around the role of such blueprints in progressive social movements. Is the "utopian impulse" a necessary part of political action? Is it an inherent function of the human psyche, or is it historically contingent (or both)? What happens to the utopian impulse after utopia is achieved? (Is the lack of utopian desire the reason why utopias themselves seem boring?) It can be fruitful to ask students to think through these ideas at an early stage of the course, as they are central to the differences between psychoanalytic and classical Marxist takes on utopia that Bloch and Marcuse explore. (As a springboard for this discussion, I asked students on the first day of class to write a description of what their ideal society would look like, and then to imagine how it might be brought about.)

Levitas's chapter describes in detail the critique of utopian socialism by Marx and Engels, including their admiration of the work of Owen and Fourier and their split with those writing and organizing in their wake. However the instructor may decide to use this material—in full or excerpted form or as the basis for background lecture—it forms an excellent way into the sections from *News from Nowhere* that describe the revolution and how the new social organization came about (chapters 17–18). It can be helpful to ask students to reflect on where Morris seems to fit in the debate between Marxist and utopian-socialist theories of transformation, using the Levitas discussion as a guide, since both gradualist/persuasive (the importance of newspapers, the formation of unions) and violent/revolutionary (the massacre in Trafalgar Square) elements are present in his account of "how the change came."

After Marx and Engels, our theory unit turned to Marxist philosopher Ernst Bloch, whose work was enormously influential on later utopian theorists. Again we relied on Ruth Levitas's discussion as a guide alongside excerpts from Bloch's magnum opus *The Principle of Hope* (1954–1959). The central issue we focused on here is Bloch's notion of the "utopian impulse," and how it manifests itself as either concrete or abstract wishes. The former, which he also calls "anticipatory," refers to reality-directed schemas of social reform such as intentional communities and revolutionary praxis. The latter refers to compensatory wishes and daydreams and can be found in an array of cultural formations such as music, architecture, popular culture, myths, daydreams, and medicine. The former are social and the latter are selfish; the former are (or can be) properly Marxist while the latter are essentially ideological.

Yet Bloch is careful not to draw artificial or untenable distinctions. As Levitas points out, for Bloch the distinction between concrete and abstract utopia is one of function rather than form; both kinds of impulse can be found in different kinds of cultural production. When discussing this distinction with my students, I asked them to generate some examples of each kind of impulse; one of my favorite suggestions for an instance of abstract utopia was a bored office worker daydreaming about a tropical vacation, which another student countered with an example of concrete utopian impulse as the same worker circulating a petition for more vacation time for everyone.

This structuring distinction became very useful in our discussion of the end of *News from Nowhere*, when William Guest reflects on the meaning and purpose of the experience he has just had:

> I lay in my bed in my house at dingy Hammersmith thinking about it all; and trying to consider if I was overwhelmed with despair at finding I had been dreaming a dream; and strange to say, I found that I was not so despairing.
>
> Or indeed *was* it a dream? If so, why was I so conscious all along that I was really seeing all that new life from the outside, still wrapped up in the prejudices, the anxieties, the distrust of this time of doubt and struggle? . . .
>
> Ellen's last mournful look seemed to say, ". . . Go back and be the happier for having seen us, for having added a little hope to your struggle. Go on living while

you may, striving, with whatsoever pain and labour needs must be, to build up little by little the new day of fellowship, and rest, and happiness."

Yes, surely! and if others can see it as I have seen it, then it may be called a vision rather than a dream.[9]

"Hope" is a central term for Bloch, and discussion can be built around asking students to compare Ellen's (imagined) description of Guest's vision as adding hope to the struggle with Bloch's usage of the term. We supplemented our discussion of the ending with an analysis of the other parts of the novel where the concept of hope is invoked. In chapter 18, Old Hammond explains that hope is what enabled people to persevere during the chaos that immediately followed the revolution: "In the times which you are thinking of, and of which you seem to know so much, there was no hope; nothing but the dull jog of the mill-horse under the compulsion of collar and whip; but in that fighting-time that followed, all was hope."[10] It is instructive to compare this passage with the ending of chapter 21, when Guest claims that he did in fact indulge utopianist hope in the "time before," hope that he sees realized in Nowhere: "how often had I longed to see the hayfields peopled with men and women worthy of the sweet abundance of midsummer, of its endless wealth of beautiful sights, and delicious sounds and scents. And how, the world had grown old and wiser, and I was to see my hope realised at last!"[11]

In my class we also used our analysis of hope in the novel to discuss more fully the function of literary utopia as distinct from utopian impulse. What does Morris seem to suggest about the utopian possibilities (in the Blochian sense) of utopian literature? Literature more generally? What elements of the description of Nowhere would Bloch see as concrete versus abstract? How does the ending of the novel comment, ironically or otherwise, on this distinction? What is the difference between a "vision" and a "dream"? For Bloch, dreams are instances of anticipatory consciousness; is that the way the dream seems to function for Morris? As part of this discussion I read students a passage from Levitas's chapter on Morris: "The ambivalence between the need for a vision to inspire and mobilise, not simply to articulate desire but to express and create hope, and the danger that such a vision may mislead and disable by expressing the wish without the will and power to effect change, lies at the heart of the Marxist response to utopia."[12] The ending of *News from Nowhere*, with its oscillation between "vision" and "dream," is a perfect encapsulation of this tension.

The last major theoretical text we discussed in the introductory section was Herbert Marcuse's *Eros and Civilization* (1955). I included Marcuse because I wanted to give students a sense of the potential power of a psychoanalytic-Marxist analysis of utopia, particularly as a way beyond the impasse between liberatory and ideological views of utopian impulse. We read two chapters of *Eros and Civilization*, "The Origin of Repressive Civilization" (chapter 3) and "Phantasy and Utopia" (chapter 7); I supplemented these readings with an overview (in lecture) of Freud's description of the reality principle and its source in the resolution of the Oedipus complex.[13] We also read the Levitas chapter on Marcuse alongside the selections from his work.

For Marcuse, the reality principle contains first a necessary element—the control of anarchic selfishness in the process of socialization—and second a "surplus" element, whose function is to ensure dominance and hierarchy. As Levitas explains, different modes of production are associated with different modes of domination; for Marcuse, the version of the reality principle associated with advanced industrial capitalism, the "performance principle," has several salient features: 1. it "keeps people working longer and harder than is reasonably necessary given the forces of production"; 2. it involves the repression of sexuality; 3. it penetrates the psyche through the creation of false needs; 4. it ultimately entails the "progressive destruction of the human subject."[14]

In our discussion of *News from Nowhere*, we found Marcuse's idea of surplus repression and the distinction between real and false needs particularly useful. For Morris, the contradictions of surplus repression are resolved by the transformation of labor into pleasure. Marcuse discusses the fact that it is very difficult for subjects of modern capitalism to imagine "the liberation of Eros" that creates "new and durable work relations."[15] In the last pages of "Phantasy and Utopia," Marcuse works through the implications of an imagined—indeed, utopian—"non-repressive reality principle."[16] In my seminar we spent quite a bit of time discussing the ways in which Marcuse's discussion was anticipated by, and diverged from, the labor system described in Morris's novel. (If everyone in Nowhere loves working so much, why is the novel subtitled "An Epoch of Rest"?) Since many students seem to find the description of pleasurable work and the elimination of wages the most unbelievable part of *News from Nowhere*, Marcuse's analysis helps them at the very least to interrogate their resistance to this idea. In general, the psychoanalytic framework of Marcuse's analysis gave students another group of tools with which to think through the function of pleasure and desire in depictions of utopia.

DISCUSSING *NEWS FROM NOWHERE*

It may seem paradoxical, since I have already confessed that I find *News from Nowhere* and most other utopian novels to be generally clumsy in execution, but an excellent way into the novel on the first day of discussion is to begin with its formal properties. Who is the narrator of the novel? A deceptively easy question that often takes some time for students to fully unpack. I begin by asking students whose voice is speaking the opening words "Up at the League." It's a bit of a trick question, since there are three different personas at play in the first chapter: 1. "a friend," who reports the action of the chapter; 2. one of the other persons present at the Socialist League meeting (humorously referred to as a "section" in reference to his embodying one of the six different currents of opinion present), who will morph into the first-person narrator of the rest of the novel beginning with the second chapter, and will later be referred to as William Guest; 3. and, finally, the first-person narrator of the opening chapter, floating above the action and passing on the friend's report, who disappears thereafter. While a footnote in the Penguin edition dismisses this framing device as clumsy and "quickly dropped," I think it's worthy of class discussion; some focused questioning about the "friend" can yield interesting results relevant to the novel as a whole.

Why does the friend not participate in the meeting? ("For the rest," he reports, "there were six persons present, and consequently six sections of the party were represented."[17]) How does he have access to the events that take place immediately after the meeting, including the movements of the "section" (or Guest) and, most importantly, his thoughts, moods, and even memories? Why is the mysterious first-person narrator so insistent on reminding us that this private information about Guest is being reported by the friend—repeating the phrase "says our friend" four times in just a few paragraphs?[18]

And finally, what do we make of the odd transition at the very end of the chapter, when Guest takes over the narration? After Guest has gone to bed he lies awake for hours, thinking over the events of the meeting:

> He heard one o'clock strike, then two and then three; after which he fell asleep again. Our friend says that from that sleep he awoke once more, and afterwards went through such surprising adventures that he thinks that they should be told to our comrades, and indeed the public in general, and therefore proposes to tell them now. But, says he, I think it would be better if I told them in the first person, as if it were myself who had gone through them; which, indeed, will be the easier and more natural to me, since I understand the feelings and desires of the comrade of whom I am telling better than any one else in the world does.[19]

The winking suggestion seems to be that the friend and Guest might be the same person—a reading supported by the non-participation of the friend in the meeting—which parallels the extradiegetic identification of Guest with Morris himself. What, then, is the purpose of this three- (or even four-) degree distancing strategy? In what ways does it call into question the reliability of the information being reported to the intradiegetic listener (who is apparently acquainted with both the narrator and "our friend")?

In my experience, undergraduates discussing narratorial techniques like these will tend either to over-read—ascribing such moments to a deliberate authorial attempt to "build suspense," "call reality into question," or "keep the reader interested"—or under-read—dismissing them as accidental or bad writing. In other words, they will give either too much or too little weight to authorial intention. Spending some initial class time on these questions raised in the first chapter of *News from Nowhere* can thus help the instructor to set the tone for subsequent discussion. I recommend asking students who dismiss the narratorial framing device as clumsy to reflect on their expectations and terms of judgment, which can then lead into a productive discussion of the properties of utopian literature as a genre. (The instructor will want to keep this conversation focused by leading it back to specific examples in the Morris novel or other utopias they have read.) For students who insist on reading these moments as part of an authorial attempt to make the novel "interesting" (surely the least interesting thing one could ever say about a literary text), I suggest connecting these infelicities in the first chapter to moments later in the novel where the role and function of literature in utopian society are described.

The first such moment occurs in chapter 3, with the introduction of the character of Boffin. The narrator Guest notes the allusion to Dickens in his name, and upon asking about the elegantly dressed gentleman is told that the nickname is partly due to his being a dustman, partly due to his showy way of dress, and partly due to his "weakness" of "writing reactionary novels."[20] Boffin doubtless wants to talk further with Guest, according to his guide Dick: "as he thinks you come from some forgotten corner of the earth, where people are always unhappy, and consequently, interesting to a story-teller, he thinks he might get some information out of you."[21] This moment is instructive for two main reasons: 1. here Morris seems to suggest that happy people are *not* "interesting to a story-teller," which can lead to a productive discussion about the generic expectations of literary utopias; 2. it introduces an idea developed throughout the rest of the novel: that literature in general is unnecessary for a happy people, and will wither away as society progresses in economic and social justice.

An important passage to examine for this idea is the debate between Ellen and her grandfather in chapter 22 over the usefulness of literature; the instructor might ask the students to discuss this debate and the merits of each side as presented by the two characters. It is not as simple a question as it might appear! Certainly Ellen's view that books "were well enough for times when intelligent people had but little else in which they could take pleasure, . . . [but] in spite of all their cleverness and vigour, and capacity for story-telling, there is something loathsome about them"[22] seems the prevailing view of Nowhereans, whom Guest (and Morris) find thoroughly admirable and sensible in every other way. Given that students will know that *News from Nowhere* is written as an expression of Morris's hopes for an actually existing future society, it is difficult to escape the conclusion that he is throwing literary production under the bus, as it were.[23] Can this rejection of the frivolousness of literature be read as an explanation (or excuse) for the plotlessness of the novel in which it appears?

The discussion of the function of literature can lead into the larger question of the role of art in the novel: what is the utopian function of artistic production for Morris, and how does it compare to the theories of utopia discussed earlier? As Old Hammond opines in chapter 16:

> In the nineteenth century, when there was so little art and so much talk about it, there was a theory that art and imaginative literature ought to deal with contemporary life; but they never did so; for, if there was any pretence of it, the author always took care (as Clara hinted just now) to disguise, or exaggerate, or idealise, and in some way or another make it strange; so that, for all the verisimilitude there was, he might just as well have dealt with the times of the Pharaohs.[24]

Several important questions are raised by this passage. Morris seems to suggest here that escapist literature is no longer necessary in the perfect society; can we connect this claim back to the insistence on verisimilitude that seems to be borne out by the framing device of the novel? What does the novel's attitude toward realism seem to be? Where does *News from Nowhere*, as a novel, seem to fit in the taxonomy of art that Old Hammond sketches here?

Another crucial aspect of Morris's utopian vision is the role and status of women. Students will notice that Nowhere is not an egalitarian society by contemporary standards; Old Hammond attempts to defend the very traditional gendered division of labor by insisting that housekeeping has been given the respect it is due, without challenging the naturalization of that gendering: "it is a great pleasure to a clever woman to manage a house skilfully."[25] The instructor will want to spend some time on the historical context of the late Victorian period in order to illuminate Morris's *relative* progressivism. (One of my students insisted that *News from Nowhere* is actually a dystopia for women!)

A fruitful classroom conversation of this question would consider the overall sex/gender system of Nowhere, and how Morris reinscribes sexuality and desire as property relations: "Many violent acts came from the artificial perversion of the sexual passions, which caused overweening jealousy and the like miseries. Now, when you look carefully into these, you will find that what lay at the bottom of them was mostly the idea (a law-made idea) of the woman being the property of the man. . . . That idea has of course vanished with private property."[26] What elements of human desire might Morris's analysis be obscuring in this rather simplistic account? (Note that the idea did not vanish with the eclipse of the outmoded idea that women are property, but rather with private property itself!) We later learn that the major (if not sole) source of crime in Nowhere is sexual jealousy when Dick's friend Walter Allen recounts the story of the young man who accidentally kills a romantic rival with an axe after the latter attacked him in a jealous rage. A consideration of these two passages together can open into an examination of the role of sexual desire and its potential to constitute a type of utopian impulse in the novel; a return to Marcuse can help guide this discussion.

If Nowhere is dependent upon the maintenance of gendered labor, what other invisible structures does it rely upon for its economic maintenance? There is an implied colonial "elsewhere" in the novel that is depicted as a necessary prop to the seemingly self-contained and self-perpetuating economic system of Nowhere:

> Those lands which were once the colonies of Great Britain, for instance, and especially America—that part of it, above all, which was once the United States—are now and will be for a long while a great resource to us. For these lands . . . suffered so terribly from the last days of civilisation, and became such horrible places to live in, that they are now very backward in all that makes life pleasant. Indeed, one may say that for nearly a hundred years the people of the northern parts of America have been engaged in gradually making a dwelling-place out of a stinking dust-heap; and there is still a great deal to do, especially as the country is so big.[27]

Nowhereans have made labor so pleasant that there is now a shortage of work to do, and competition over it. The ironic (or perhaps not) reversal here is that the colonies have become a dumping-ground not for surplus British commodities, but for surplus British labor. Furthermore, Nowhereans have not abandoned the colonizing impulse of their nineteenth-century forbears: "Of course, also, we have helped to populate other countries—where we were wanted and called for."[28] What does it mean for Morris's utopian vision that it is still dependent upon a version of the kind of imperial exploitation that was the driving engine of nineteenth-century industrial capitalism?

As we worked our way through the novel, the discussion in my seminar built toward a broader conversation about how we might characterize the "thesis" of *News from Nowhere*, and how that thesis fits with broader utopianist thought. Why is there no more history in Nowhere? (Only Old Hammond retains a detailed knowledge of the past, and he is regarded as something of a crank.) Is the novel suggesting that the only reason we need knowledge production is alienation? *News from Nowhere* sets about breaking down familiar boundaries/hierarchies—which ones does it leave intact?

("Natural"/human-made; inside/outside; human/animal; etc.) What is the function of *trust* in the novel—to what underlying process or force do Nowhereans seem to be trusting to maintain their social organization? Human nature? The natural world? Is it the case that in utopia there is no longer any utopian impulse? Is it even possible any longer? What would it be like to live in a world without utopian desire?

One way of broadening the classroom conversation is to assign and discuss some more recent theoretical writings on utopia. In his influential recent work of "social science fiction" *Four Futures: Visions of the World After Capitalism* (2016), Peter Frase posits four outcomes of human civilization in the wake of climate change and mass automation: two possible utopias and two possible dystopias.[29] The two variables determining which future lies ahead—he takes as givens climate change and automation—are the discovery of an abundant source of clean energy and the development of egalitarian social structures. Interestingly, the factor separating the utopias of communism and socialism from the dystopias of rentism and exterminism is not energy but distribution. It is in our power as a species to create either heaven or hell on earth, and that power is political. As Morris himself understood, in order to work toward a utopian future we must be able to imagine it. At our particular historical moment, when increasing economic inequality, political instability, and scarcity of resources mean that we truly stand at a crossroads of utopia and dystopia, we need more than ever Morris's hopeful "vision rather than a dream."[30] What better time to reintroduce a generation of students to the hopeful possible future of an epoch of rest?

NOTES

1. "I remember [Morris] arriving from the train with Jefferies's book *After London* in his hands—which had just come out. The book delighted him with its prophecy of an utterly ruined and deserted London, gone down in swamps and malaria, with brambles and weeds spreading through slum streets and fashionable squares, and pet dogs reverting to wolfish and carrion-hunting lives. And he read page after page of it to us with glee that evening as we sat round the fire." Edward Carpenter, *My Days and Dreams* (London: Allen and Unwin, 1916), 217.

2. Fredric Jameson, *Archaeologies of the Future: The Desire Called Utopia and Other Science Fictions* (New York: Verso, 2005).

3. Fátima Vieira, "The Concept of Utopia," in *The Cambridge Companion to Utopian Literature*, ed. Gregory Claeys (Cambridge: Cambridge University Press, 2010), 3–17. Jorge Bastos da Silva, "Introduction: Revis(it)Ing the Rationales of Utopianism," in *The Epistemology of Utopia: Rhetoric, Theory, and Imagination* (Newcastle upon Tyne, UK: Cambridge Scholars Publishing, 2013), 1–6.

4. Ruth Levitas, *The Concept of Utopia* (Oxford: Peter Lang, 2011). Ernst Bloch, *The Principle of Hope*, trans. Neville Plaice, Stephen Plaice, and Paul Knight, 3 vols. (Cambridge, Mass: MIT Press, 1986). Herbert Marcuse, *Eros and Civilization: A Philosophical Inquiry into Freud* (Boston: Beacon Press, 1966).

5. Levitas, *Concept of Utopia*, 41.
6. Ibid., 60.
7. Ibid., 66.
8. Ibid., 46.
9. William Morris, *News from Nowhere: Or, an Epoch of Rest*, ed. David Leopold (Oxford: Oxford World's Classics, 2003).
10. Ibid., 113.
11. Ibid., 124.
12. Levitas, *Concept of Utopia*, 146. I did not assign Levitas's chapter on Morris to my undergraduates, since it was quite dense and contained a great deal more detailed discussion of mid-twentieth-century criticism than I felt they needed. I do recommend, however, that the instructor read it and perhaps make it available to particularly motivated students as an optional supplemental reading.
13. A discussion of teaching psychoanalysis to undergraduates—how, when, and why—would require another entire essay. I've found it helpful to take a few minutes the first day to discuss the historical and theoretical relevance of psychoanalysis. I address questions that invariably arise about Freud's misogyny and racism by explaining that many psychoanalytic critics, including feminist and critical race scholars, have found Freud's account of childhood psychosexual development a useful heuristic. I explain that the Oedipus complex can be read metaphorically rather than literally—as a narrative of the individual's accession to society and the workings of the reality principle—and as descriptive, rather than prescriptive. (As Marcuse himself writes, "We use Freud's anthropological speculation only in this sense: in its *symbolic* value." Marcuse, *Eros and Civilization*, 60.) I note that Freudian theory has been enormously influential, and that entire schools of feminist and postcolonial theory are indebted to psychoanalysis: at the very least, I point out, it is important to understand Freudian theory in order to be able to critique it.
14. Levitas, *Concept of Utopia*, 157–9.
15. Marcuse, *Eros and Civilization*, 155.
16. Ibid., 155.
17. Morris, *News from Nowhere*, 3.
18. Ibid., 4.
19. Ibid., 4–5.
20. Ibid., 19.
21. Ibid., 19.
22. Ibid., 130.
23. I have not included here much discussion of contextualizing *News from Nowhere* with other writings by Morris, since this topic will be thoroughly addressed by other essays in this volume. But the instructor teaching the novel in the context of utopian literature and thought might want to include Morris's essay "How We Live and How We Might Live" (1887).

24. Morris, *News from Nowhere*, 88.
25. Ibid., 52.
26. Ibid., 70.
27. Ibid., 84–85.
28. Ibid., 63.
29. Peter Frase, *Four Futures: Visions of the World After Capitalism* (Verso, 2016).
30. Morris, *News from Nowhere*, 182.

BIBLIOGRAPHY

Bloch, Ernst. *The Principle of Hope*. 3 Vols. Translated by Neville Plaice, Stephen Plaice, and Paul Knight. Cambridge: MIT Press, 1995.

Carpenter, Edward. *My Days and Dreams*. London: Allen and Unwin, 1916.

Frase, Peter. *Four Futures: Visions of the World After Capitalism*. New York: Verso, 2016.

Jameson, Fredric. *Archaeologies of the Future: The Desire Called Utopia and Other Science Fictions*. New York: Verso, 2005.

Levitas, Ruth. *The Concept of Utopia*. Oxford: Peter Lang, 2011.

Marcuse, Herbert. *Eros and Civilization: A Philosophical Inquiry into Freud*. Boston: Beacon Press, 1966.

Morris, William. *News from Nowhere: Or, an Epoch of Rest*. Edited by David Leopold. Oxford: Oxford World's Classics, 2003.

Silva, Jorge Bastos da. "Introduction: Revis(it)ing the Rationales of Utopianism." In *The Epistemology of Utopia: Rhetoric, Theory, and Imagination*, 1–6. Newcastle upon Tyne, UK: Cambridge Scholars Publishing, 2013.

Vieira, Fátima. "The Concept of Utopia." In *The Cambridge Companion to Utopian Literature*. Edited by Gregory Claeys, 3–17. Cambridge: Cambridge University Press, 2010.

Chapter Twelve

Teaching Guenevere through Word and Image

Pamela Bracken

> You may say . . . that you wish to read literature and to look at pictures; . . . but you must pardon me if I say that your interest in books in that case is literary only, and not artistic, and that implies, I think, a partial crippling of the faculties; a misfortune which no one should be proud of.
>
> —William Morris, "The Woodcuts of Gothic Books"[1]

Teaching William Morris is a joy to many Morrisians and a privilege to those of us whose work is focused on classroom instruction in the small liberal arts college environment. I can only imagine what my newly-minted PhD-self would have thought of the professor of English I have become, a generalist in almost every sense of the word, with interests in areas that seem at one level so far from my coursework in nineteenth-century British literature and my early scholarship on Morris and the Artworkers' Guild. My teaching of British Literature from 1765 to the present, my course in twentieth century world literature, and my recent offering in the graphic novel seem to stretch me in ways that make the word expertise impossible. And yet, I have found my recent pursuit of visual studies and word and image theory segues naturally with my work on William Morris, especially his Kelmscott Press. The Arts and Crafts movement with its tradition of illustrated texts readily connects to many of the ideas I find so provocative in this relatively new heuristic as it provides readers with "an ability to decode interactions between words and images."[2] Interdisciplinary in nature, this approach is true to the spirit of Morris's lifework in the literary and visual arts.[3]

Traditional English majors in traditional curricula often meet Morris through one or two consistently anthologized poems, particularly two of his most dramatic and narrative, "The Defence of Guenevere" and "The Haystack in the

Floods." While I am pleased to teach at least one of my favorite poems in Morris's oeuvre, the prospect of presenting Morris's Guenevere in the context of Browning's "Porphyria's Lover" or "Andrea del Sarto" has gone stale. A quick Google search reveals a surplus of material on the poem as a dramatic monologue, from web sources as diverse as Shmoop to The Victorian Web, where browsers can quickly discover that "The Defence of Guenevere" is "primarily a dramatic monologue, with occasional objective descriptions from a third-person narrator. The reader has no immediate access to the events in question, and can only make judgments based upon Guenevere's subjective account."[4]

Several years ago, longing for a fresh approach to Morris's rich and complex poem, I turned to the digital resources of the World Wide Web and began teaching Morris's poem as a verbal-visual artifact. I have now concluded that what began as temptation has now become necessity. In the visual culture of my undergraduate students, "The Defence of Guenevere" offers an interface of word and image. This rich marriage can be facilitated through the resources of digital texts and the exciting lens of word and image studies.

Florence Boos and Rosie Miles have written extensively and editorially about manuscripts and editions of "The Defence of Guenevere." Their work—Boos's in editing the William Morris Archive and Miles's in establishing the impossibility of separating "out the work's visual qualities from the verbal presentation of the text"[5]—sets the stage for approaching our visually-oriented twenty-first-century students with provocative questions: What were the origins and exigencies of the visual variants in the text of the poem? How do the visual adornments of the Kelmscott Press edition of the poem interact with the verbal performance of Guenevere, who is the narrative's primary speaker? With its rich imagery and striking textures, how has the poem been illustrated?

One of the first strategies I employ is to orient students to the borders and initials of Morris's Kelmscott Press edition of the poem (1892), readily available from the marvelous online William Morris Archive hosted by the University of Iowa and edited by Boos.[6] While projecting the image of the poem's first page from the archive, I point out the somewhat baffling *en media res* omniscient narrative frame. Guenevere's hair, thrown "backward from her brow" creates an immediate image of motion as well as sensuality. I then direct their attention from the text of the poem to the decorative and evocative border, pointing them to the constrained tension of the filigree as well as the tumultuous vines wrapping the text. This is the time to ask students to locate images of Morris designs and wallpapers on their laptops, images readily available on the web or made available through links on my university's Learning Management System (LMS). Though mostly unfamiliar with these engaging, organic shapes and swirls, my students are able to provide some useful adjectives for what they see: energetic, enthusiastic, enveloping.

Teaching Guenevere through Word and Image 177

Figure 12.1. *The Defence of Guenevere and Other Poems.*
Reproduced courtesy of the William Morris Archive, University of Iowa.

Returning to the Kelmscott Press image, they now see that Morris's characteristic visual patterning is revisited in the border before them. The key maneuver is to make students of literature, especially English majors conditioned to look only at words on a page, to connect the words of the poem's opening to the curving shapes and images surrounding them on the Kelmscott Press page. In this strategy I am guided not only by Morris himself, but by recent attention to composite textuality, work largely spearheaded by Jerome McGann and his expansive digital Rossetti Archive.[7] Before his project of digitizing Rossetti, McGann offered this challenge in *The Textual Condition* (1991):

> We must turn our attention to much more than the formal and linguistic features of poems ... we must attend to textual materials which are not regularly studied by those interested in "poetry": to typefaces, bindings, book prices, page format, and all those textual phenomena usually regarded as (at best) peripheral to "poetry" or "the text as such."[8]

As my students pay attention to the embellishments on the borders of the projected 1892 Kelmscott version of the poem and compare them with the unadorned version on the black and white pages of *The Norton Anthology* before them, they begin to see that the visual elements are as provocative as the meaning of the lines of poetry they have read. A few of my students are troubled by the erotic and sensory aspect of these lines (much like their original readers in the *Oxford & Cambridge Magazine*). Morris scholar Margaret Laurie, in her comprehensive edition of *The Defence of Guenevere* (1981) now available on the William Morris Archive, points out that early and initial readers did recognize Morris's verbal and visual artistry, but they did so pejoratively: "[Morris's] Victorian readership eagerly agreed to label him a mere escapist, weaving decorative but inessential tapestries in rhyme."[9] It is one of my aims to dispel current readers of such a pejorative perspective. Reading these decorative "weavings" is a priority.

I now encourage students to "decode interactions between words and images"[10] in the opening lines of the poem projected to the front of the classroom:

> But, knowing now that they would have her speak,
> She threw her wet hair backward from her brow,
> Her hand close to her mouth touching her cheek burned so,
> She must a little touch it (ll. 1–7)

Noting the erotics of the imagery, students readily turn to the phenomenon of the initial capital *B*, a printing convention unfamiliar to twenty-first-century readers familiar with both traditional, printed books and digital texts. I point out that the decidedly tangled capital replicates the tangled ideas in the text itself. Guenevere's apparent state of confusion, fear, defiance, and disability is reflected in the serpentine vines, leaves, and grapes wrapping the initial *B*. I inform my students that Morris the poet and Morris the designer meet in this capital. As Norman Kelvin described it in notes accompanying his *Collected Letters of William Morris*, "Morris designed several initials as well as other ornaments for the book, including a floriated 'B' ten times high."[11] When students express surprise at this ornamentation, I direct them to an instructional website at Khan Academy's "What is an Illuminated Manuscript?"[12] to highlight the basic conventions of the medieval manuscripts which were not only procured by Morris but also inspirational in his designs for the capitals of the Kelmscott Press.

To more fully interrogate the word-and-image relation, I draw further connections to the conventions of verbal poetry and the border art of the initial page in the Kelmscott Press. What few readers or critics fail to notice in currently anthologized presentations of the poem is the shift from the third person narrator to the first person dramatic voice of Guenevere, the poem's obvious eponymous hero and defendant. It is easy for my students to identify the quotation marks that indicate the poem's perspectival shift in the bland printed text. But while viewing the second page of the Kelmscott Press digital image, they cannot rely on conventional typography to identify the shift. As Guenevere begins to entreat, accuse, and shame her accusers in the lines David Latham refers to as her "printed voice"[13] on page two, the only indication of the shift on the Kelmscott page is a colon and an initial *O*:

> O knights and lords, it seems but little skill
> To talk of well-known things past now and dead.
> "God wot I ought to say, I have done ill,
> And pray you all forgiveness heartily!
> Because you must be right, such great lords; still
> "Listen, suppose your time were come to die,
> And you were quite alone and very weak;
> Yea, laid a dying (ll. 11–18)

Beyond the visual elements, Guenevere's verbal acrobatics in these lines confuse my twenty-first-century students. The words on these opening pages projected before them seem a confession to her male accusers. At the outset, my students suspect duplicity in Guenevere, but what the visual cues of the Kelmscott Press initial borders seem to do is to dramatize Guenevere's own confusion rather than attempt to make sense of it. In her editorial notes on the poem, Boos hints at the equivalence of Guenevere's verbal performance with the visual performativity of the layout of words on the page: "Oddly syncopated hyphenations at the ends of lines (e. g., "burn-ed," l. 6)—reinforce Guenevere's agitated mental state as she confronts the possibility of death."[14] Attention to such details is always at the center of a verbal-visual reading.

After being exposed to the opening pages of the illuminated Kelmscott Press *Defence of Guenevere*, my students often throw thoughtful questions at me. These have come to constitute an alternative line of visual inquiry: Why did Morris choose not to add illustrations to accompany his own Guenevere in The Kelmscott Press edition? For answers, I turn them loose for several minutes on the plentiful Morris material now available on the World Wide Web. An initial Google image search for Kelmscott Press editions of other works reveals that Morris's *Love is Enough, The Story of the Glittering Plain,* and *News from Nowhere,* as well as *Milton's Early Poems* and *The Works of Geoffrey Chaucer,* were all accompanied by illustrations. Why, with its rich imagery and striking textures, was the text of the poem not accompanied by more traditional illustrations? And what illustrations were later provided by artists?

Such questions can also be explored in the spirit of McGann's *The Textual Condition* (1991). Through the composite textuality available on the internet, my undergraduates can "attend to textual materials which are not regularly studied by those interested in 'poetry.'"[15] Exploring later illustrated versions of *"*The Defence of Guenevere" helps to make them aware of the kind of rich verbal-visual/word-image relationships that Miles describes as "[a] fascinating after-life through the response of illustrators to [Morris's] texts."[16] Images of Jessie King's illustrations for the John Lane Bodley Head edition of *The Defence of Guenevere* (1904) are readily available on Google Images. Another jewel is revealed in the Blackie and Sons edition of *The Early Poems of William Morris Illustrated by Francis Harrison* (1914), which is available in a virtual/digital format through the rich resource of The Internet Archive.[17] In both illustrators' works, students can "explore the word and image relation" in an even more detailed way.[18]

My students enjoy viewing King's various images of Guenevere through images I provide them from the internet. After having considered reflections of the text in borders and capitals, students enjoy a different approach to visual interpretation through the variety of King's illustrations. I project a few of these, asking students to recall the portion of text King is visualizing, and I encourage them to focus on the intriguing ways that the illustrations echo some of the shapes, swirls, and swags we saw in the capital and borders of the Kelmscott Press Guenevere.[19] For example, in King's image "A Great Angel Standing," the angel bearing dyes "not known on earth" from the early part of the poem appears to be casting out a net of stars toward a lavishly postered bed. The bed ornamentation is often the first part of the image my students notice, however. With reference back to the Kelmscott borders, they note the similarity in the curves and spirals on the bedpost, a strict vertical almost in the center of the panel. It is among one of the darkest and most concrete images in King's illustration of these lines of the poem.

> Suppose a hush should come, then some one speak:
> "'One of these cloths is heaven, and one is hell,
> Now choose one cloth for ever; which they be,
> I will not tell you, you must somehow tell
> "'Of your own strength and mightiness; here, see!'
> Yea, yea, my lord, and you to ope your eyes,
> At foot of your familiar bed to see
> "*A great God's angel standing*, with such dyes,
> Not known on earth, on his great wings, and hands,
> Held out two ways, light from the inner skies
> "Showing him well, and making his commands
> Seem to be God's commands, moreover, too,
> Holding within his hands the cloths on wands (ll. 21–33)

Few students leave the session satisfied by any explanation for the stars emanating out from the "cloths on wands." More ethereal than real, they may suggest the "light from inner skies" of line 30, or as a student more recently suggested, they are the equivalent of a visual effect before the invention of CGI. King's unique focus on the angel in the "choosing cloths" portion of the poem privileges the mystical/mythical over the tangible/concrete in the passage. In black and white rather than in color, the intensity of the verbal imagery is lost, and though the image is rather quaint to students, many of them express dissatisfaction with the pale lines and insubstantial shapes of "A Great God's Angel Standing." Morris's Guenevere deserves a more robust rendering.

Another King illustration I like to use is "The Wall of Stone." This illustration frames a later portion of the poem for students. In it, Guenevere's emotional turmoil is contained by a literal wall of stone, the enclosed garden trope of medieval romance.

> "I was half mad with beauty on that day,
> And went without my ladies all alone,
> In a quiet garden walled round every way;
> "I was right joyful of that wall of stone,
> That shut the flowers and trees up with the sky,
> And trebled all the beauty: to the bone,
> "Yea right through to my heart, grown very shy
> With weary thoughts, it pierced, and made me glad;
> Exceedingly glad (ll. 109–117)

With this image, I encourage students to read into King's visual interpretation of the scene, not just elements within the illustration but the illustration as an entire image. In this respect the border is significant. Like the walled garden behind her, Guenevere is enclosed in the image, entrapped by her own beauty and weary thoughts. Students have noticed many things in the illustration: the size of Guenevere in relationship to wall and tree, the static aspect of elements around the image, the flowing quality of Guenevere's hair and stole. Natural objects are dwarfed by this Guenevere. "She seems larger than her cage," one student insightfully notes. Though only a few of my undergraduates have training in graphic design, many of these twenty-first-century students read the image with an impressive vocabulary for shapes, motion, proportion, and even symmetry. The more organic shapes to the right and left of this Guenevere defy the lines of the poem. They are not shut up with the flowers and trees and sky (l. 13), students are quick to notice. What is tangible in the illustration as image is the wall of stone, cluttering up the middle portion of the image with what many perceive as painstaking detail and deliberateness. Its concreteness is at odds with the gracious curves and ethereal sweep of Guenevere's cloak and gown, a contrast worth noting. The figure of the wall, I often point out to students, is prevalent in many of King's illustrations for the volume.

If time allows in one exclusive session on "The Defence of Guenevere," I conclude with an exploration of an even later illustrated version of the poem, *The Early Poems of William Morris Illustrated by Francis Harrison* (1914), a real treasure, available in its entirety on the Internet Archive. Comparing images is one of the goals of this last activity, but more importantly with the Harrison illustrations, I relish the opportunity for my digitally-oriented students to virtually flip through the pages of this edition.

The first image I bring to my students' attention in this digital "visual book" is the title page. In many ways it imitates the more well-recognized Kelmscott Press title page. Harrison's design, an almost comics-like panel, includes an initial capital *T* enclosed by a profusion of leaves and vines. Students are quick to point out, however, that this title page actually includes Morris's Guenevere, rendered above and beyond the bordered title of the poem. When I ask students what is distinctive about Harrison's drawing of the heroine of the poem, they seldom miss the distinctive weaving of her hair into the vines behind her, rendered as if Guenevere has just emerged from the flora. My more text-literate students often prefer the earlier Guenevere-free Kelmscott Press title page to this one, and yet, after reading brief biographical headnote material in the Norton anthology, one or two almost always voice amazement that Morris's Kelmscott edition never provided an image of Guenevere, despite the sensitively articulated verbal images of "great eyes" (l. 54), "full lips" (l. 57), "long hand" (l. 121), and "long throat" (l. 230). Most of my students also confess to a pleasure in this visual adornment of the text, not only in the florid, organic border but also in the depiction of the long-tressed beauty of the poem.

At least one full-color illustration later in the digital text brings up a provocative question about illustration of texts and their interpretive integrity: to what extent is an illustrator held to a strict interpretation of a text and to what extent can a story, even a complex story-poem like "The Defence of Guenevere," be altered by an accompanying image? Harrison's illustration of the complex "choosing cloths" scene, for example, depicts the great God's angel—as did King's—but in a rich color palate zooming out to include not only him but the chooser as well. In the center foreground of the illustration, the figure appears male rather than female, leading students to question their own earlier reading of that scene from the poem. I usually take students back to the text. The gender ambiguity of the words underscores an intriguing rhetorical aspect of Guenevere's defense, which is her strategy of empathy. Though most readers, my own students included, recall the angel's test directed *to* Guenevere—"'One of these cloths is heaven, and one is hell,/Now choose one cloth for ever; which they be,/I will not tell you, you must somehow tell/Of your own strength and mightiness; here, see!'" (ll. 22–25)—Harrison's male figure, confronted by the angel, suggests a larger context: Guenevere inviting her accusers to imagine their own confrontation with a dramatic choice between heaven or hell. "Yea, yea, my lord, and *you* to ope your eyes,/At foot of *your* familiar bed to see" (ll. 26–27, emphasis mine). As Guenevere is describing a scene to Gauwaine and her accusers, Harrison's rendering of the scene reveals more illustrative accuracy than students normally recall. Though these two images merely scrape the visual surface of "The Defence of Guenevere" text on the Internet Archive, they do take students back to the verbal text, to the words of Guenevere as well as the intrusive narrator's external descriptions of Morris's evocative Guenevere.

My goal is to simulate a commonplace bookstore or library activity: checking out the illustrations in a book before exploring the words. This not uncommon action privileges the visual over the verbal, providing an immediate pleasure not shared by the higher order task of reading. I try to make an intentional activity out of a natural behavior. The value of this visual-textual exercise over a traditional word-only study of "The Defence of Guenevere" is measured by my students' responses to the poem. After years of struggling to make the poem come alive to my visually-sensitive readers, I found that bringing in the material-visual package to the exercise enriches their enjoyment. Students have responded with a new appreciation of Morris's visually rich text. Several have reported that their favorite poem in the Victorian archive is "The Defence of Guenevere." Others have encouraged me to apply similar kinds of visual reading techniques to other literary eras, as the inclusion of images has made them closer readers of the words as well as images. Thus, in addition to getting students to better appreciate Morris's poetry, I also get them to become better readers, achieving two objectives with one classroom activity.

NOTES

1. Reprinted in William Peterson, ed., *The Ideal Book: Essays and Lectures on the Arts of the Book by William Morris*. California: University of California Press, 1982: 37.

2. Penn Humanities Forum on Word and Image. Wolf Humanities Center University of Pennsylvania, 2005–2006. https://wolfhumanities.upenn.edu/annual-topics/word-image.

3. Elizabeth Carolyn Miller's work on Morris and the Kelmscott Press in *Slow Print* does much to provide an apologia for Morris's interest in the visual. In it, she points to his lecture "The Society of the Future" in which he praises "authors who appeal to our eyes . . . who tell their tales to our senses." Miller, *Slow Print: Literary Radicalism and Late Victorian Print Culture* (Stanford: Stanford University Press, 2013, 80–81.

4. Brian Eschrich. "Truth and Sincerity in 'The Defence of Guenevere.'" The Victorian Web, http://www.victorianweb.org/authors/morris/eschrich10.html.

5. Rosie Miles. "Illustrating Morris: The Work of Jessie King and Maxwell Armfield." *Journal of the William Morris Society* 15, no. 4 (Summer 2004): 109.

6. Florence Boos. "The Kelmscott Press." William Morris Archive, http://morrisedition.lib.uiowa.edu/Poetry/Defence_of_Guenevere/Images/guenevere1892/jpeg/pageflip1-50.html. Accessed January 23, 2018. Instructors should be aware that classroom computers will need to have an updated version of Flash in order to virtually turn the pages of the Kelmscott volume of "The Defence of Guenevere" from the William Morris Archive.

7. Jerome McGann, ed. The Rossetti Archive, http://www.rossettiarchive.org/.

8. Jerome McGann. *The Textual Condition* (Princeton: Princeton University Press, 1991), 13.

9. Margaret Laurie, ed., "The Defence of Guenevere and Other Poems." William Morris Archive, http://morrisedition.lib.uiowa.edu/guenevere.html.

10. Penn Humanities Forum on Word & Image, https://wolfhumanities.upenn.edu/annual-topics/word-image.

11. Norman Kelvin, ed. *The Collected Letters of William Morris*, vol 3. (Princeton: Princeton University Press, 1996), 374, n.1.

12. "What is an Illuminated Manuscript?" Khan Academy, https://www.khanacademy.org/partner-content/getty-museum/getty-manuscripts/a/what-is-an-illuminated-manuscript.

13. David Latham, "Writing on the Image," in *Writing on the Image: Reading William Morris*. (Toronto: Toronto University Press, 2007), 9.

14. Florence Boos. "The Kelmscott Press: Morris's Editorial Practice at the Kelmscott Press." *William Morris Archive*, http://morrisedition.lib.uiowa.edu/BookArts/KelmscottPressIntro.html.

15. Jerome McGann. *The Textual Condition*, 13.

16. Rosie Miles. "Illustrating Morris: The Work of Jessie King and Maxwell Armfield." *Journal of the William Morris Society* 15, no. 4 (Summer 2004): 111.

17. The Internet Archive, https://archive.org/details/earlypoemsofwill00morr.

18. Rosie Miles's work in this area encourages an active verbal/visual reading. This kind of reading is in fact established by William Morris's precedent. She contends that "for Morris the book that lacks any consideration of its visual aesthetic is an impoverished book . . . By the time of the Kelmscott Press Morris's conception of what it means to read has expanded beyond the mere taking in of a story through words alone. Reading means reading-and-viewing." Miles, "Illustrating Morris," 109–134.

19. Morris's influence on King's work is explained in Rosie Miles's "Illustrating Morris." King's training in Glasgow was based in Arts and Crafts principles, and as she puts it, "as such the influence and inspiration of Morris would have been everywhere felt" Miles, "Illustrating Morris," 109.

BIBLIOGRAPHY

Boos, Florence. "The Kelmscott Press." *William Morris Archive*, http://morrisedition.lib.uiowa.edu/BookArts/KelmscottPress.html.

Eschrich, Brian. "Truth and Sincerity in 'The Defence of Guenevere.'" *The Victorian Web*, http://www.victorianweb.org/authors/morris/eschrich10.html.

Khan Academy. "What is an Illuminated Manuscript?" https://www.khanacademy.org/partner-content/getty-museum/getty-manuscripts/a/what-is-an-illuminated-manuscript.

Latham, David. *Writing on the Image: Reading William Morris*. Toronto: Toronto University Press, 2007.

McGann, Jerome, ed. *The Rossetti Archive*, http://www.rossettiarchive.org/.

———. *The Textual Condition*. Princeton: Princeton University Press, 1991.

Miles, Rosie. "Illustrating Morris: The Work of Jessie King and Maxwell Armfield." *Journal of the William Morris Society,* 15 (Summer 2004): 109–35.

Miller, Elizabeth Carolyn. *Slow Print: Literary Radicalism and Late Victorian Print Culture* (Stanford: Stanford University Press, 2013.

Morris, William. *The Early Poems of William Morris*. New York: Dodge Publishing, 1914.

———. *The Collected Letters of William Morris*, Vol 3. Edited by Norman Kelvin. Princeton: Princeton University Press, 1996.

Penn Humanities Forum on Word and Image. Wolf Humanities Center University of Pennsylvania, 2005–2006. https://wolfhumanities.upenn.edu/annual-topics/word-image.

Peterson, William, ed. *The Ideal Book: Essays and Lectures on the Arts of the Book by William Morris*. California: University of California Press, 1982.

Chapter Thirteen

Morris and the Literary Canon

Michelle Weinroth

Admired in academic and non-academic circles alike, Morris's plethora of accomplishments never fails to impress. But of all his creative and political achievements, his design work elicits the most praise. He thus endures as a craftsman, enmeshed in the threads, and steeped in the dyes, of what he ironically called the lesser arts. Under the weight of this considerable reputation, his stature as literary figure has diminished,[1] garnering only ambivalent acclaim.[2]

To be sure, Morris's literary profile is not readily captured in a word. His multiple works have been unevenly appreciated.[3] In his day, *The Earthly Paradise* and *The Life and Death of Jason* won him great applause. Out of a colossal output, the first of these two works constituted the backbone of his literary popularity.[4] As for his Pre-Raphaelite poetry, it suffered from criticism or neglect early in his career, and though recognized decades later for its merits, it was never extolled.[5] Meanwhile, Morris's socialist verse was spurned for its propagandist motives.[6] If he was considered a serious successor to Tennyson as Poet Laureate, the nomination was a partial one, arising in default of convincing alternatives. According to Fiona MacCarthy, the shortlist was not impressive. She attributes Morris's nomination to the public's selective perception of him. In 1892, "he was still, in official eyes, the author of the *Earthly Paradise*,"[7] his socialist verse and political romances having been almost eclipsed from memory or deemed "negligible."[8] As for being invited to run for the chair of poetry at Oxford University, the recommendation was issued largely by Morris's circle of friends. And though he was considered a serious contender, he would not have been an "unopposed candidate," given his unorthodox politics.[9]

Residues of Morris's contested literary reputation in the nineteenth century have wafted downstream to us. Since the early twentieth century, his creative writing has been relegated to a minor category, his countless poems and medievalist romances having been dismissed as stylistically archaic, fanciful, vague, and naïve.[10] The Modernist poets, who discerned in his oeuvre the glint of a diamond in the rough, were also strangely those who cast these enduring aspersions.[11] Others, inspired by his ingenuity, gleaned fragments of his innovative oeuvre, but suppressed the politics of his creative legacy.

Morris thus features in a liminal space of English Studies,[12] at the edge of the Victorian Greats, even while his graphic oeuvre takes center-stage, embellishing multiple websites and academic works. If a number of his contemporary critics acknowledged his greatness as a poet, they typically harbored some niggling reservation about his eccentric mannerisms. "Morris was a great poet," they said, "*but*."[13] Scarcely a minor irritant, this "*but*" constituted a crucible of brewing discontent felt towards his medievalist archaisms[14] and radical politics, and it elliptically explains his scant presence within the literary canon.[15] Ambivalently embraced within contemporary English Studies, Morris is now applauded, now held at arm's length.

Much of this equivocal literary reputation can be attributed to the legacies of Matthew Arnold and the Leavises,[16] men and women who successively forged an enduring Anglo-American tradition of literary criticism, and one that (if only indirectly) impinged on Morris's status in the canon. Scholars who distanced themselves from that commanding heritage were inexorably subject to its abiding influence. For, as Fredric Jameson has argued, texts "come before us as the always-already-read; we apprehend them through sedimented layers of previous interpretations or—if the text is brand-new—through the sedimented reading habits and categories developed by those inherited interpretive traditions."[17]

Such an inheritance of reading habits poses a challenge for teachers acting as ambassadors of Morris's signature poetics. For if today's English students are (knowingly or not) the legatees of a hermeneutical tradition that once disparaged Morris's creative writing, but has since shaped the ways literary texts are habitually evaluated, how will his writerly merits be fairly appreciated? Will teachers find their heuristic efforts strained by this contradiction? To be sure, Morris's works are inextricably tied to the culture of his age. Yet, his unorthodox style begs a hermeneutical approach distinct from what has been customarily stitched into the interpretive practices of English Studies. How, under these conditions, will students adapt to his novelty, suspend their aesthetic tastes and preferred exegetical methods, and give Morris's "eccentric" poetics their due credit? Space does not allow me here to delineate an empirically tested pedagogical approach to answering such a query. I offer, instead, a critical portrait of Morris's marginality within the canon as a modest prolegomenon to any future teaching of his literary texts. Politics, aesthetic judgments, and disciplinary boundaries are at the heart of this preliminary groundwork.

A balanced appraisal of Morris's authorial oeuvre rests on revisiting his equivocal literary stature in the light of aesthetic values—values upheld by mainstream Victorian intellectuals and bequeathed to twentieth- and twenty-first-century academies.[18] In their capacity as literary critics, these nineteenth-century men often acted as gatekeepers, barring "disruptive" authors from the pantheon's inner sanctum. Morris was one such author. Having eschewed pretentions of "literariness," marked as these were by patrician privilege and a class society he tirelessly abjured, his reception in that temple of high art was predictably uneven. Close scrutiny shows that his creative works, so often deemed defective or damned with faint praise, were casualties of an intractable political conflict in literary culture, a tension obscured by a tendency to pathologize his stylistic peculiarities as endearingly quaint. Such a rift may account for why his reputation as a "minor poet" became entrenched. Morris's writings, however, were not blithely outlandish; they were conscious aesthetic protests against the linguistic regime and poetic tastes of the establishment. With his philosophy of the lesser arts, he challenged the practice of *belles-lettres*, deeming it one-dimensional and deficient, narrowly text-centered and impervious to the ethically grounded *poësis* of bookmaking: "you wish to read literature and to look at pictures," he wrote, "and . . . so long as the modern book gives you these pleasures you ask no more of it; well . . . your interest in books in that case is *literary only*, and not artistic, and that implies, I think, a partial crippling of the faculties."[19] (my italics).

Averse to the pretentiousness and dry scholasticism of the ruling academy, Morris publicly rejected the establishment of an Oxford chair in English literature, insisting that it would produce "merely vague talk about literature, which would teach nothing."[20]

> [M]ore damage has been done to art (and therefore to literature) by Oxford "culture" than centuries of professors could repair. . . . These coarse brutalities of "light and leading" make education stink in the nostrils of thoughtful persons to attempt to teach literature with one hand while it destroys history with the other is a bewildering proceeding on the part of "culture."[21]

Countering the academy's one-dimensional and dehistoricized appreciation of literature,[22] he advocated an enlarged hermeneutic, attentive as much to the ornamental production of books as to their verbal content.[23] He regarded the architectural design and materiality of the decorated tome as a sensuous disclosure of *creative* labor. Indeed, the ornamental book was a monument, writ small, to fulfilling human praxis, the cornerstone of his philosophy of ideal life. Seen in this light, Morris's authorial qualities may be grasped as incarnations of his political faith, untrammeled by his critics' disparaging claims that his poetics (across a range of works) were inelegant and spuriously archaic.[24] Such disparagement typified the mixed reviews of his classical translations (i.e., of Homer's *Odyssey*).[25] The "Homeric Question"—the controversy over how best to translate ancient Greek epics into mellifluous modern English—was the terrain on which nineteenth-century literary (and specifically poetic) style was strenuously debated and defined. Yet, it is precisely this heated exchange over literary aesthetics that allows us to reappraise Morris's creative merits, and confront the challenges involved in teaching his authorial qualities within the academy.

LITERARY STYLE AND THE HOMERIC QUESTION: HOMILIES AND HERESIES

The translation of Homer's *Odyssey* "was a growth industry in mid-nineteenth century Britain." No less than five major publications emerged in the 1860s alone.[26] Pursued largely by men of letters, this literary "mania" was more than a gentleman's pastime. The drive to render Homer into eloquent English constituted a nationalist impulse to affirm England's imperial glory. A host of impassioned writers, conscious of the past's auratic power, dipped their quills into the Homeric well to endow their collective Englishness with the eminence of classical erudition.[27] Such creative fervor, however, betrayed widespread ideological uncertainty.[28] Despite England's industrial supremacy, her halcyon days were on the cusp of decline. A formerly entrenched system of beliefs tottered as the Second Reform Bill (1867) spelled the rumblings of political change. With the publication of Darwin's *Origin of Species* (1859), religion was brought to the brink of self-doubt, a crisis expressed alarmingly by Matthew Arnold as an overpowering confusion felt "on a darkling plain . . . where ignorant armies clash by night" ("Dover Beach"). Literary art would thus step into the breach and become the new faith.[29] Novelists, poets, and literary critics were not disinterested public figures, but unofficial political apostles[30] seeking to restore nationalist cohesion with their belletristic works, and specifically with their choice of meter.[31] But what prosodic rule and what manner of poetic diction in translating Homer would achieve this exaltation of Englishness? There was no immediate consensus.[32] Instead, such questions were thrashed out in public exchanges, the most notable being between Matthew Arnold and Francis Newman.

The battle was waged primarily on prosodic grounds, but also on lyrical turf. While Arnold insisted that the translator emphasize rapid expression, "eminent plainness," and not least "nobility,"[33] Newman chose to highlight the demotic, gritty, and foreign quality of Homer's ancient idiom through the use of the ballad meter. His prosodic choice, against Arnold's preferred dactylic hexameter,[34] coincided with a subversive theory proposed in 1795 by the German F. A. Wolf that the Homeric epics were not authored by a genius bard but "originally a collections of folk lays,"[35] much like English balladry.[36] This Wolfian theory proved shocking to the Victorian intelligentsia.[37] Their prized values (e.g., genteel refinement, military heroism, exclusive male Englishness, and cultivated learning)[38]—exemplified in the reading, reciting, and translating of Homer—were scuttled by a "scandalous" idea: i.e., that Homer was not a singular poet incarnating cultural magnificence at the pinnacle of the social hierarchy, but a host of *common* folk, popular compositors of epic song.

The literati's dismay before Wolf's subversive claim makes clear that nineteenth-century classical translation was not a private activity pursued disinterestedly by men of letters; it was rather a poetic art tinged with nationalist zeal, made public, and deployed by cultural tribunes seeking political supremacy.[39] In their eyes, Homer was an exalted figure whose poetic prowess reflected their cherished ideals of superior English nationhood. For Arnold, in particular, the translation of ancient epics undergirded a bourgeois liberal hegemonic project, aimed at refurbishing England's frayed cultural fabric. Under his sway, each translator was expected to quash any suggestion that Homer, the supreme lyricist, was a band of boisterous songsters. Such an inference risked sullying the "pristine" morality and enlightenment that Arnold and his followers had assigned patrician Englishness.[40] Classical translation was thus more than an art of textual conversion; it was "a means to empower an academic elite,"[41] endow it with cultural finesse, and shield it from the "tumultuous" hoi polloi.[42]

In 1887, Morris ventured into this literary fray. Alongside his consuming political activism and artisanal projects, he, too, rendered the *Odyssey* into English. Like his literary peers, he was schooled in classical translation, yet his version of Homer was strikingly unorthodox. Celebrating the folkish character of the epic, he produced in his translation an archaic English correlative of the Greek popular voice by drawing on Anglo-Saxon and medieval roots that were linguistically affiliated to Icelandic sagas.[43] In this, he evoked a pre-modern Norse society of "upper barbarism"[44] marked by skaldic traditions, comparable to the Mycenaean bardic culture from which Homer drew his epic. Morris deployed an antiquarian style to convey the orality and lyrical vitality of a pre-modern society. Refusing the enslaved role of a Hermes, a messenger shackled to Arnoldian prescriptions, he asserted his creative autonomy by rendering the *Odyssey* in an archaic tongue. Here was an aesthetic gesture analogous to the spontaneous performance of every ancient bard who recounted the nation's saga from memory, but rose to sing the tale with added flourish and personal inflection.

In melding a Norse idiom with a Hellenic source text, Morris was not only affirming a creative approach to translation, but an ethics of reproduction. By underscoring the foreignness of the ancient Greek epics, their cultural and temporal remoteness, he was tacitly acknowledging the historical and linguistic impossibility of genuinely re-producing them as facsimiles. The past was largely unknowable. As Oscar Wilde said: "What he [Homer] was to his contemporaries we have, of course, no means of judging, but we know that the Athenian of the fifth century B.C. found him in many places difficult to understand."[45] As for Homer himself, he, too, was several centuries removed from the early bards of the Mycenaean age, whose songs bear no written record. For Morris, then, the sources of Homer's *Odyssey* were opaque, and could only be seized, or indeed conjectured, through an intermediary, a more proximate world of oral culture such as that of the medieval North.

Such an admission would call into question Arnold's preferred "domesticating" technique.[46] The latter produced the illusion that the lyrical works of Hellenic antiquity could be smoothly integrated into modern English,[47] regardless of insuperable chronological, ethnographic, or other disparities. Arnold called for a "mystical" transcendence of linguistic and cultural differences, and this in the interest of edifying the moderns (notably middle-class Victorians) and reaffirming their social order.[48] Morris's foreignizing method, like Newman's, sought to expose rather than occlude the otherness of the source text, so as to conserve its distinctiveness and tacitly repudiate the falsehoods of modern civilization. As such, it constituted a heretical rebuff of Arnold's homilies, which by the late nineteenth century became received doctrine.[49] But, predictably, as an iconoclastic intervention, Morris's version would not go unpunished. With the exception of rapturous praise from Wilde and the odd enthusiast, most reviewers poured scorn on his medievalist verbiage. "By this clumsy travesty of an archaic diction," wrote Mowbray Morris, "Mr. William Morris [. . .] has overlaid Homer with all the grotesqueness, the conceits, [and] the irrationality of the Middle Ages."[50] Similarly, Archibald Ballantyne described Morris's translations as "Wardour Street Early English,"[51] spuriously archaic and undignified. "Poems that talk about howes, and thrall-folk . . . are dialect and provincial."[52] "This is not literary English of any date,"[53] he railed.

With his reference to regional dialects, Ballantyne summarily traced the cartography of the literary canon, relegating Morris's poetic style to its hinterland. "Poems in which . . . thrall-folk seek to the feast-hall a-winter *do not belong to any literary centre. They are provincial . . . utterly without distinction; . . . unspeakably absurd*"[54] (my italics). The derogatory geographical allusion here betrays Ballantyne's adherence to the nationalist politics underlying Arnold's *On Translating Homer* (1861),[55] consensually deemed the how-to manual of nineteenth-century and, indeed, of twentieth-century, classical translation.[56] In situating Morris outside of the literary center, Ballantyne was effectively banishing Morris's writing from the *metropolitan* center where discourse was by definition "standard" or nationalist: (i.e., s*tanding in* for the nation at large).[57] The centrality of literary language rested on its proximity to official parliamentary speech. Steeped in public decorum, such discourse would serve as a benchmark for judging the linguistic peculiarities of a Morrisian idiom and stamping it as provincial, devoid of both political legitimacy and literary respectability.[58]

To gain entry into the "literary centre," a classical translation would have to be stylistically polished, purged of estranging elements from a remote past, and endowed with an aesthetic of poetic fluency attuned to the modern (notably middle- and upper-middle class) English ear. In this, it would not be a genuinely faithful recreation of the original Greek epic, but a simulation of an idealized antiquity, breathing grandeur into an imagined Englishness of "sweetness and light" (Arnold). Tied to a nationalist project, this preferred fluent style would act as the poetic correlative of Arnold's liberal ideal: a smooth-running nation-state, free of class friction and cacophonous social strife.

In 1887 the socialist Morris would refuse to embrace such a politics of style, one geared to obscuring society's flaws in the "native" melody of English speech. If the nationalist underpinnings of fluency in classical translation served to conceal the violence inherent in the modern nation-state, Morris would adopt a poetics of dissent to shatter that fiction, and this in accordance with his socialist objectives.[59] His use of archaisms in diction and syntax was among his more subtle conduits of political protest against Victorian literary taste and the institutions that buttressed the capitalist social edifice.

A POLITICS OF LETTERS

As a stark counterpoint to the Arnoldian doctrine, Morris's archaism could only be deeply troubling to the Victorian elite. It conjured the spirit of some seismic societal change. The antiquarian style was not an innocent or arbitrary choice. It would irk the literati's sensibility, but also shake their entire value system. In linking the popular authorship of the epic's composition to an egalitarian society, and in adopting the archaism as a key linguistic motif, Morris's translation flouted the idolatrous and class-based teaching of Hellenism. His "inelegant" poetic style scandalized his peers, unsettling their transmission of a high culture that he tirelessly sought to abolish, since it reflected society's concentration of wealth and value in an oligarchy of privileged men: politicians, figureheads of the literary academy, and not least their adulated epic heroes and genius bards.[60] In calling for a fair distribution of wealth within society, Morris adopted an archaic authorial style that was politically charged; implicitly it reflected his hatred of modern civilization and his irrepressible impulse to transform and re-cultivate it root and branch. But in the eyes of his literary peers, such political dissent was profoundly disturbing. His socialist values and activism were thus leveraged as a cudgel to slam, if not seriously challenge, his art.[61]

Consistent repudiation of Morris's authorial style fostered the longstanding fallacy that his writings were ideologically driven while canonical works were disinterested and impartial. But the evaluative criteria in Arnold's *On Translating Homer* were also politically invested; they were conceived to bring order to the nation through prosodic rules.[62] An aesthetic ideal of exquisite social harmony, incarnated in lyrical fluency and metrical markers of "nobility," was heralded as a linguistic bulwark against a looming tide of class strife. Implicit in this touted mode of translation was an attempt to eradicate the textual traces of an ancient "common" folk that might conjure up the specter of a "hostile" underclass and the dissolution of a "sweet" and "luminous" Englishness.

If Morris's *Odyssey* represented a threat to Arnold's middle-class liberalism, it was Wilde's defense of Morris's translation that raised serious questions about the technical feasibility of Arnold's prosodic prescriptions for coalescing a grand style with rapid expression. Loftiness, Wilde argued, is incompatible with speed. If Morris "has occasionally sacrificed majesty to movement, and made stateliness give place to speed . . . it is really only in such blank verse as Milton's that this effect of calm and lofty music can be attained, and in all other respects blank verse is the most inadequate medium for reproducing the full flow and fervor of the Greek hexameter."[63] Ultimately, Morris's objective was not governed by loftiness; his prosody highlighted the percussive vitality of creative labor rather than the leisure associated with aristocratic grace. Poignantly, Wilde remarked that Morris did not produce a "literary" translation, a "literate" conversion of Homeric poetry into elevated English; rather he worked according to the "metrics" and mnemonics of an oral and an artisanal tradition in which the skill of weaving a saga in song was paramount.[64] His oft-quoted line, "If a chap can't compose an epic poem while he's weaving tapestry . . . he'll never do any good at all,"[65] takes on new meaning in light of this "ambidextrous" practice. Morris's authorial qualities, both rhythmic and lyrical, are evocations of the *living art* of the people, a vibrant ancient culture of Saga-men. It is the voice of skalds, however rude and rough to the modern English ear, that he aims to broadcast in his version of Homer. And though his translation may "seem to many . . . more boisterous than beautiful, there is," as Wilde noted, "vigor of life in every line."[66]

Beyond reconstituting some semblance of a once ebullient oral culture, Morris's method of translation also reflects his materialist philosophy of history, a view consistent with Marx's claim in the *Grundrisse* (1857–1858) that an art born of an ancient mode of production cannot be veritably recreated under modern technological conditions. Similarly, Morris's syncretic translation underscores the impossibility of reproducing the epic of heroic times in the era of industrial capitalism. In this it answers Marx's rhetorical query: "Is Achilles possible with powder and lead? Or the *Iliad* with the printing press, not to mention the printing machine? Do not the song and the saga and the muse necessarily come to an end with printer's bar, hence do not the necessary conditions of epic poetry vanish?"[67]

For all its fidelity to the original Greek saga, Morris's line-by-line rendering[68] is more than a linguistic conversion, for it captures in rhythm and sonority the quintessential character of an ancient culture—its artisanal creativity and oral rituals. Uninhibited in exposing the historical vicissitudes separating antiquity from the modern author, Morris uses a medievalist Anglo-Saxon diction, calling attention to the remoteness of the source text. With sundry archaisms, he reanimates, by analogy, the Bronze-age bardic tradition, of which Homer's epic is the classic trace. His translation is thus a creative fiction, but a purposeful and self-conscious one, not a utilitarian, soulless facsimile, nor a technical conversion of "language into language," but a translation "of poetry into poetry"[69]—verse suffused with the Hellenic passion for the decorative arts: "a joy" fully shared by Morris "in the visible aspect of things."[70]

For all its pedantic requirements, Arnold's domesticating approach to rendering the Greek classics would not entail an ethnographic or historic fidelity to a mysterious Homeric past, but a devotion to a noble style, consonant with the ruling interests and tastes of the modern state. And this shift in priorities from antiquity to Victorian nationhood involved fostering the deceptive allure of smooth linguistic migration: an easy flow of classical verse into modern English.[71] Curiously, Arnold recognized the impossibility of reproducing the hexameter exactly as it was heard in ancient Greece. Yet he argued: "All we are concerned with is the imitation, by the English hexameter, of the ancient hexameter in its effect upon us moderns."[72] Esteemed classical translation was ultimately a metrical re-enactment of public school recitation and the aesthetic pleasure that such a performance would produce among men of letters and public schoolboys communing over shared sensibilities.[73] For these men of culture, Arnold claimed, were "docile echoes of the eternal voice, pliant organs of the infinite will," [74] and our "*best self*" by which "we are united, impersonal, at harmony."[75] Such aesthetic communion would become the model for achieving political calm and for quelling the "monstrous processions" (i.e., the Reform League's demonstrations for an expanded franchise) of 1866.[76] Arnold's use of Homer to create an aesthetic effect on the English intelligentsia was thus part of his somatic politics as an apostle of crowd management.[77]

If Morris's approach to translation involved an unabashed inventiveness, it would not be geared to affirming bourgeois liberalism, but to conjuring the paradigm of a would-be post-capitalist world: (i.e., fulfilling human activity, the productive life of ancient folk and the ethical bases of a communal society). In his eyes, gratifying (i.e., useful and decorative) work was the *sine qua non* of sustainable and salutary human coexistence. Wilde expressed this eloquently when he noted Morris's keen "sympathy with the Homeric admiration for the workers and the craftsmen in the various arts, from the stainers in white ivory and the embroiderers in purple and gold, to the weaver sitting by the loom and the dyer dipping in the vat, the chaser of shield and helmet, the carver of wood or stone."[78] Morris's aim was thus to portray *life* rather than to endorse the formalism of elite literature. His *Odyssey* can be seen as a tribute to the lesser arts, and a philological resurrection of the lost souls of time, whose mores, creative energy, and political organization left traces of an exemplary humanity, often buried under reams of official history. The latter, he would argue, recalled kings and warriors for their destructive deeds, but popular art salvaged from oblivion the life of the people.[79] Arguably, Morris's translation was a reenactment of popular art's redemptive historiographical gesture.

ON INTERPRETATION

Over the past decades, scholarship has increasingly emphasized the interpenetration of Morris's many expressive art forms. His prolific artisanal work, for one, has become the source material for deepening the study of his poetry and prose romances. Indeed, the constitutive elements of the decorative arts—floral designs, foliated letters, paratextual borders, heraldic color schemes—have been deployed as categories of literary hermeneutics. No longer seen as separate silos, distinct from his vast corpus of written works, Morris's multifarious artisanal creations have become a storehouse of critical tools, and notably for the interdisciplinary study of his writings. But if such approaches to probing Morris's work have enriched our understanding of his interlacing achievements, they have also, thanks to a reappraisal of his philosophy of craft, vindicated his iconoclastic poetics. This development counters the assumptions of an Anglo-American literary lineage (from nineteenth-century Arnoldian critics to their "descendants," F.R. Leavis & Co.) that repudiated Morris's "archaizing" quill,[80] and assigned him a backbench in English studies. Indeed, close scrutiny of his "lesser arts" lectures yields a more encouraging conclusion: i.e., that his "minor league" status was not the result of authorial inadequacy but of radical dissent[81] and creative ingenuity.[82] His was a rejection of the political premises underpinning the literary discipline itself, tied as it was to a society of egregious inequality.[83]

If certain nineteenth-century literary critics derided Morris's style, and deemed it "*not literary* English" (Ballantyne), their contemptuous reviews betrayed the disturbing nature of his archaism, sufficiently irksome to become the epitome of bad writing, of Wardour-Street English. Such intense reaction could only be the result of a deep sense of threat. And threat there was in Morris's verbiage. As the linguistic critique of modernity, it implicitly called for an unmitigated reconstitution of Victorian society, a demand for the supersession of antagonistic classes, both cultural and economic. Wilde, unlike his peers, endorsed Morris's style as *not literary*, precisely because it was *anti-literary* (anti-establishment) and condemned the iniquitous class division inscribed in the production of literarity itself—the verbal sign of privileged art set apart from the "artless" toil of the masses.

Such politically distinct and polar readings of "the literary" have left their mark on how critics treat Morris's authorial works today. For even as the evolving discipline of English studies radiates beyond single-author based scholarship and flourishes in the fields of cultural theory, questions of aesthetic value (what defines "good" or "genuine" literature) persist—often unresolved or simply eschewed—resurging in the ways students approach "literary" texts. Anthologies teach, if only tacitly, what is more or less worthy of study and, not least, the interpretive practices suited to those works. When Morris's creative writings are only sporadically included in the mainstream curriculum, students tend to regard his authorship more quizzically and more suspiciously than the perennially studied oeuvre of the Victorian "greats."[84]

If, at first read, Morris's foreign-sounding tongue leaves our students perplexed, repelled, or indifferent to his signature style, and if such an uneasy reception of his writing complicates our pedagogical task, we might take a leaf from Wilde's book. For in his enthusiastic review of Morris's Homer translation, Wilde plays the iconoclast's card, extolling Morris's emphatically non-literary style, and upholding its anti-establishment character as the measure of creative authenticity. In upending the canon's pyramid of aesthetic judgements, Wilde exposes the relative and contingent nature of literary value. Despite his espoused aestheticism, he reminds us that authorial style is rarely, if ever, a disinterested linguistic form; it always encodes a particular political perspective or interest. Class tensions invariably pierce through the mantle of aesthetic criteria, however esoteric and aloof these might seem at first blush.

To impart this knowledge to our students may not, in itself, guarantee a swift and immediate appreciation of Morris's authorial prowess, but it may nonetheless constitute a *significant* beginning, a launching pad for cultivating their aesthetic sensibilities in a quintessentially Morrisian vein, and for seeing his worth in a fresh light—removed from the precepts of "luminaries," who over the centuries have governed our thinking about that perennial question: "what is *good* literature?" or, more to the point, "what *exactly* is literature *anyway*?"

NOTES

1. Lionel Trilling and Harold Bloom, eds., *The Oxford Anthology of English Literature: Victorian Prose and Poetry* (New York: Oxford University Press, 1973), 617.

2. Jeffrey Skoblow, *Paradise Dislocated: Morris, Politics, Art* (Charlottesville: University Press of Virginia, 1993), xiv.

3. Karl Litzenberg, "William Morris and the Reviews: A Study in the Fame of the Poet." *The Review of English Studies*, os-XII (October 1936): 413–28.

4. Fiona MacCarthy, *William Morris: A Life for Our Time* (London: Faber and Faber, 2010), 632.

5. Delbert Gardner, *An Idle Singer and His Audience: A Study of William Morris's Poetic Reputation in England 1858–1900* (The Hague: Mouton, 1975), 18–26.

6. Ibid., 92–100.

7. MacCarthy, *William Morris*, 632.

8. Gardner, *An Idle Singer*, 108.

9. John Mackail, *The Life of William Morris*, vol. 1 (London: Longmans Green & Co., 1922), 346.

10. Peter Faulkner. "William Morris and the *Scrutiny* Tradition." *Journal of William Morris Studies* 16 (Summer 2006): 33–7; 39–41.

11. Peter Faulkner, *William Morris: The Critical Heritage* (London: Routledge, 1973), 23.

12. Carolyn Lesjak underscores this marginality: "(George) Eliot has maintained a central position in the literary canon while discussions of Morris, unlike those of, say, Carlyle or Ruskin or Arnold, have been limited by and large to more specialized sub-areas of literary interest, such as utopian or science fiction literature. Doubtless this difference reflects a break along literary-historical lines and the politics of canon-formation, with Arnoldian notions of an elevated bourgeois culture separate from and unsullied by politics qua politics marking the divide." *Working Fictions: A Genealogy of the Victorian Novel*. Durham, NC: Duke University Press, 2006, 142.

See also Faulkner, "William Morris and the *Scrutiny* Tradition," 34–35.

13. Litzenberg, "The Reviews," 421.

14. Susan Bassnett, *Translation Studies* (London: Routledge, 2002 edition), 105; MacCarthy, *William Morris*, 563.

15. Stephen Greenblatt et al., eds., *The Norton Anthology of English Literature*, vol. 4 (New York: W.W. Norton & Co., 2012 edition).

16. Faulkner, "William Morris and the *Scrutiny* Tradition," 31–45.

17. Frederic Jameson, *The Political Unconscious: Narrative as a Socially Symbolic Act* (London: Methuen, 1981), 9.

18. James Walter Caufield, *Overcoming Matthew Arnold* (Surrey: Ashgate, 2012), 29–40; Antony Harrison, *The Cultural Production of Matthew Arnold* (Athens: Ohio University Press, 2009), xi.

19. William Morris, "The Woodcuts of Gothic Books," 1892 in *William Morris: Artist, Writer, Socialist* 1, ed. May Morris (New York: Russell & Russell, 1966), 331.

20. Norman Kelvin, ed., *The Collected Letters of William Morris*, vol. 2 (Princeton: Princeton University Press, 1988), 589.

21. Ibid., 589–90.

22. Peter Faulkner, "Morris and the Study of English," *Journal of the William Morris Society* 11 (Autumn 1994): 28.

23. Morris, "The Woodcuts of Gothic Books," 320; 334–5.

24. Archibald Ballantyne, "Wardour Street English," *Longman's Magazine* 12 (Oct. 1888): 589.

25. Faulkner, *William Morris*, 293–311.

26. MacCarthy, *William Morris*, 563.

27. Nathanael Gilbert, "A Vision Rather than a Dream: The Production of Space in the Epic and Romantic Works of William Morris," PhD diss., Washington State, 2005, 10.

28. Amanda Hodgson, "'The Highest Poetry': Epic Narrative in *The Earthly Paradise* and *Idylls of the King*," *Victorian Poetry* 34 (Autumn, 1996): 340–3.

29. Terry Eagleton, *Literary Theory* (Oxford: Blackwell, 1983), 23–24.

30. Matthew Arnold, *Culture and Anarchy*, ed. Samuel Lipman (New Haven, CT: Yale University Press, 1994), 48.

31. Meredith Martin, *The Rise and Fall of Meter: Poetry and English National Culture* (Princeton: Princeton University Press, 2012), 4; 6–10.

32. Martin, *The Rise and Fall of Meter*, 6; William Whitla, "William Morris's Translation of Homer's *Iliad* I. 1–214." *Journal of Pre-Raphaelite Studies* 13 (Fall 2004): 97.

33. Matthew Arnold, *On Translating Homer* (London: Longman, Green, Longman, and Roberts, 1862), 16.

34. Ibid., 50.

35. Whitla, "William Morris's Translation," 75.

36. Frank M. Turner, "Homeric Question," in *A New Companion to Homer*, eds. Ian Morris and Barry Powell (Leiden: Brill, 1997), 126–29.

37. Cornelia Pearsall, *Tennyson's Rapture: Transformation in the Victorian Dramatic Monologue* (Oxford: Oxford University Press, 2008), 130.

38. Martin, *The Rise and Fall of Meter*, 4.

39. Yopie Prins, "Metrical Translation: Nineteenth-Century Homers and the Hexameter Mania," in *Nation, Language and the Ethics of Translation*, eds. Sandra Bermann and Michael Wood (Princeton: Princeton University Press, 2005), 229–256.

40. Arnold, *Culture and Anarchy*, 29–48.

41. Lawrence Venuti, *The Translator's Invisibility: A History of Translation* (London: Routledge, 1995), 110.

42. Gage McWeeney, "Crowd Management: Matthew Arnold and the Science of Society," *Victorian Poetry* 41 (2003): 93–111; Harrison, 17.

43. Whitla, "William Morris's Translations," 98–99.

44. See Lewis Henry Morgan's *Ancient Society* (New York: Henry Holt and Company), 1878.

45. Oscar Wilde, "Mr. Morris's Completion of the *Odyssey*." *Pall Mall Gazette* xlvi (November 1887): 3.

46. Venuti, *The Translator's Invisibility*, 106.

47. Prins, "Metrical Translation," 237.

48. Venuti, *The Translator's Invisibility*, 111–12.

49. Whitla, "William Morris's Translations," 84; Venuti, *The Translator's Invisibility*, 114–16.

50. Mowbray Morris, Unsigned article. *Quarterly Review* clxvii (October 1888): 407.

51. Ballantyne, "Wardour Street English," 589.

52. Ibid., 594.

53. Ibid., 589.

54. Ibid., 593.

55. Venuti, *The Translator's Invisibility*, 109–10.

56. Ibid., 116–17.

57. Krishan Kumar, *The Making of English Identity* (Cambridge: Cambridge University Press, 2003), 221.

58. Ballantyne, "Wardour Street English," 593–4.

59. Whitla, "William Morris's Translations," 81, 83, 84.

60. Alan Bacon, "Deliver Us from Two (or more) Professors of Criticism." *Journal of William Morris Studies* 9 (Autumn 1990): 32.

61. Gardner, *An Idle Singer*, 91–99.

62. Martin, *The Rise and Fall of Meter*, 4.

63. Wilde, "Mr. Morris's Odyssey." *Pall Mall Gazette* xlv (April 26, 1887): 5.

64. Ibid.

65. Mackail, *The Life of William Morris*, 192.

66. Wilde, "Morris's *Odyssey*," xlv (April 26, 1887): 5.

67. Karl Marx, *Grundrisse*, trans. Martin Nicolaus (Harmondsworth, Middlesex: Penguin Books Ltd., 1977), 111.

68. Whitla, "William Morris's Translations," 78; 80.

69. Wilde, "Morris's *Odyssey*," xlv (April 26, 1887): 5.

70. Ibid.

71. Venuti, *The Translator's Invisibility*, 36–51.

72. Arnold, *On Translating Homer*, 42.

73. Hugh Osborne, "Hooked on the Classics. Discourses of Allusion in the Mid-Victorian Novel," *Translation and Nation: Towards a Cultural Politics of Englishness*, eds. Roger Ellis and Liz Oakley-Brown (Clevedon, UK: Multilingual Matters, 2001), 120.
74. Arnold, *Culture and Anarchy,* 141.
75. Ibid., 64.
76. McWeeney, "Crowd Management," 94.
77. Ibid.
78. Wilde, "Morris's *Odyssey*," xlv (April 26, 1887): 5.
79. Morris, "Art of the People," 32.
80. Faulkner, "William Morris and the Scrutiny Tradition," 39.
81. Whitla, "William Morris's Translations," 98.
82. Jack Mitchell, "William Morris' Synthetic *Aeneids*: Virgil as Physical Object." *Translation and Literature* 24 (2015): 8–22.
83. Bacon, "Deliver Us," 32.
84. Lesjak, *Working Fictions*, 142.

BIBLIOGRAPHY

Arnold, Matthew. *Culture and Anarchy*. Edited by Samuel Lipman. New Haven: Yale University Press, 1994.

Arnold, Matthew. *On Translating Homer*. London: Longman, Green, Longman, and Roberts, 1862.

Bacon, Alan. "Deliver Us from Two (or more) Professors of Criticism." *Journal of William Morris Studies* 9 (Autumn 1990): 29–33.

Ballantyne, Archibald. "Wardour Street English." *Longman's Magazine* 12 (Oct. 1888): 585–94.

Bassnett, Susan. *Translation Studies*. London: Routledge, 2002 edition.

Caufield, James Walter. *Overcoming Matthew Arnold*. Surrey: Ashgate, 2012.

Eagleton, Terry. *Literary Theory*. Oxford: Blackwell, 1983.

Faulkner, Peter. "William Morris and the *Scrutiny* Tradition." *Journal of William Morris Studies* 16 (Summer 2006): 27–46.

———. "Morris and the Study of English." *Journal of the William Morris Society* 11 (Autumn 1994): 26–30.

———. *William Morris*: The Critical Heritage. London: Routledge, 1973.

Gardner, Delbert. *An Idle Singer and His Audience: A Study of William Morris's Poetic Reputation in England 1858–1900*. The Hague: Mouton, 1975.

Gilbert, Nathanael. "A Vision Rather than a Dream. The Production of Space in the Epic and Romantic Works of William Morris." PhD dissertation, Washington State, 2005.

Greenblatt et al., eds., *The Norton Anthology of English Literature,* Vol. 4. New York: W.W. Norton & Co., 2012 edition.

Harrison, Antony. *The Cultural Production of Matthew Arnold*. Athens: Ohio University Press, 2009.

Hodgson, Amanda. "'The Highest Poetry': Epic Narrative in *The Earthly Paradise* and *Idylls of the King*." *Victorian Poetry* 34 (Autumn 1996): 340–54.

Jameson, Fredric, *The Political Unconscious: Narrative as a Socially Symbolic Act*. London: Methuen, 1981.

Kelvin, Norman, ed. *The Collected Letters of William Morris* Vol. 2, Part B. Princeton: Princeton University Press, 1988.

Kumar, Krishan. *The Making of English Identity*. Cambridge: Cambridge University Press, 2003.

Lesjak, Carolyn. *Working Fictions: A Genealogy of the Victorian Novel*. Durham, NC: Duke UP, 2006.

Litzenberg, Karl. "William Morris and the Reviews: A Study in the Fame of the Poet." *The Review of English Studies*, os-XII (October 1936): 413–28.

MacCarthy, Fiona. *William Morris: A Life for Our Time*. London: Faber and Faber, 2010.

Mackail, John. *The Life of William Morris* Vol. 1. London: Longmans Green & Co., 1922.

Martin, Meredith, *The Rise and Fall of Meter: Poetry and English National Culture*. Princeton: Princeton University Press, 2012.

Marx, Karl. *Grundrisse*. Translated by Martin Nicolaus. Harmondsworth, Middlesex: Penguin Books, 1977.

McWeeney, Gage. "Crowd Management: Matthew Arnold and the Science of Society." *Victorian Poetry* 41 (2003): 93–111.

Mitchell, Jack. "William Morris' Synthetic *Aeneids*: Virgil as Physical Object." *Translation and Literature* 24 (2015): 1–22.

Morgan, Lewis Henry. *Ancient Society*. New York: Henry Holt and Company, 1878.

Morris, Mowbray. Unsigned article. *Quarterly Review* clxvii (October 1888): 407–408.

Morris, William. "The Woodcuts of Gothic Books." 1892. In *William Morris: Artist, Writer, Socialist* 1. Edited by May Morris, 318–38. New York: Russell & Russell, 1966.

———. "The Art of the People." 1879. *The Collected Works of William Morris* Vol. 22. Edited by May Morris, 28–50. London: Longmans Green & Co., 1910–1915.

Osborne, Hugh. "Hooked on the Classics. Discourses of Allusion in the Mid-Victorian Novel." In *Translation and Nation: Towards a Cultural Politics of Englishness*. Edited by Roger Ellis and Liz Oakley-Brown, 120–66. Clevedon, UK: Multilingual Matters, 2001.

Pearsall, Cornelia. *Tennyson's Rapture: Transformation in the Victorian Dramatic Monologue*. Oxford: Oxford University Press, 2008.

Prins, Yopie. "Metrical Translation: Nineteenth-Century Homers and the Hexameter Mania." In *Nation, Language and the Ethics of Translation*, edited by Sandra Bermann and Michael Wood, 229–56. Princeton: Princeton University Press, 2005.

Skoblow, Jeffrey. *Paradise Dislocated: Morris, Politics, Art*. Charlottesville: University Press of Virginia, 1993.

Trilling, Lionel and Harold Bloom, eds., *The Oxford Anthology of English Literature: Victorian Prose and Poetry*. New York: Oxford University Press, 1973.

Turner, Frank M. "The Homeric Question." In *A New Companion to Homer*. Edited by Ian Morris and Barry Powell, 123–45. Leiden: Brill, 1997.

Venuti, Lawrence. *The Translator's Invisibility: A History of Translation*, London: Routledge, 1995.

Whitla, William. "William Morris's Translation of Homer's *Iliad* I. 1–214." *Journal of Pre-Raphaelite Studies* 13 (Fall 2004): 75–121.

Wilde, Oscar. "Mr. Morris's Completion of the *Odyssey*." *Pall Mall Gazette* xlvi (November 24, 1887): 3.

———. "Mr. Morris's *Odyssey*." *Pall Mall Gazette* xlv (April 26, 1887): 5.

Part IV

ART AND DESIGN

Chapter Fourteen

Morris for Art Historians

Imogen Hart

William Morris occupies an ambiguous yet persistent place in art history. As a visual artist he appears in the literature as a peripheral contributor to various Victorian fine art movements such as Pre-Raphaelitism and Aestheticism. His influence as a writer is more widely recognized among art historians, who frequently cite his revolutionary views on art and labor. When the scope of art history is expanded to include the decorative arts, Morris is seen as the initiator (via both his writings *and* his objects) not only of the British Arts and Crafts movement but of a range of international developments in architecture, design, and the applied arts. Many artists have been remembered for their writings as well as their artistic output. Morris is unusual, however, in having been so prolific and influential in both areas that art historians are unsure which is the more important. Is Morris important for art history because he was an artist who made things? Or is he important for art history because of his ideas and how they have inspired later artists and audiences to think in different ways about the production of art and its value to society? Or both? Art historians have taken each of these three paths when writing about Morris. Correspondingly, students of art history may encounter Morris in any of these ways. A lecture on Morris might begin with a slide of Morris's *Vine* wallpaper (figure 14.1) or with a famous Morris quotation—such as, "I do not want art for a few, any more than education for a few, or freedom for a few"—or with the image and quotation together on the same slide.[1]

Whatever narrative art historians try to weave him into, he never quite fits. He was not a member of the Pre-Raphaelite brotherhood, but he belonged to the same social circle as those artists and his work shares many of the qualities associated with Pre-Raphaelitism.[2] Thus he might be included in a course on the Pre-Raphaelites, but it is unlikely that he would readily come to mind as a quintessential Pre-Raphaelite. Morris's art was undoubtedly embraced by major figures in the Aesthetic movement but, as scholars such as Peter Faulkner have argued, he did not embrace the tenets of Aestheticism in return.[3] Consequently one might teach Morris in a course on art and Aestheticism, but again, he would probably not be an exemplary figure. Morris often features in courses on art historical theories and methods. However, his focus on decorative art rather than fine art means that he sits rather awkwardly alongside the typical heroes of art theory whose primary concern is painting.[4] When Morris's art and writing are considered in the context of a more inclusive history of art that encompasses decorative art, they can become obscured by vague concepts of the ill-defined Arts and Crafts movement, as I have argued elsewhere.[5] A course on the Arts and Crafts movement would certainly include Morris, but there is a risk of bending his work to fit preconceived ideas about a movement. Finally, the frequent positioning of Morris as a point of origin in surveys of modern art implies that Morris is valued more for his influence on later artists than for his own work. Consequently a course on modern decorative art risks presenting a selective view of Morris that over-emphasizes the proto-modernist aspects of his practice. A course devoted to Morris alone might avoid all of these pitfalls, but it takes a courageous instructor to teach a course restricted not only to British art, but to a single British artist, and a Victorian one at that. Despite all the challenges that I have outlined here as to how to fit Morris into a typical art history curriculum, I hope to suggest in this chapter how the challenges of teaching Morris to art historians can, when faced head-on, provide pedagogical opportunities.

Teaching Morris has the potential to expand art history students' understanding of what art is. For many students, a class on Morris is the only time they are asked to engage closely with decorative art in their art history studies. It can be disconcerting to be presented with wallpaper and carpets and tiles when one is used to dealing with oil paintings and bronze sculptures and marble temples. Indeed, a student might be justified in asking why such things should be included in an art history syllabus. By way of explanation the following quotation may be offered. Morris argues in "The Lesser Arts of Life" (1882) that "not only is it possible to make the matters needful to our daily life works of art, but there is something wrong in the civilization that does not do this: if our houses, our clothes, our household furniture and utensils are not works of art, they are either wretched makeshifts, or, what is worse, degrading shams of better things."[6] This quotation reveals that the question of whether decorative objects were or were not art was one that Morris himself confronted. It is perhaps reassuring to find that one's hesitation on being asked to think of "household furniture and utensils" as works of art has been anticipated by Morris. Having acknowledged the issue, Morris attaches moral significance to it. If a civilization does not make "household furniture and utensils" works of art, "there is something wrong." The quotation then asks us to question our assumptions. It prompts us to reflect on what a wallpaper or a carpet or a tile is if it is not a work of art. If I didn't think of this as a work of art, we ask ourselves, what did I think it was? The quotation summarizes the implications of categorizing "the matters needful to our daily life" as "works of art." What is not clear from the quotation is what is required to make such objects art. A second Morris quotation, this time taken from "Art and Labour" (1884), sheds light on the matter:

> Well you must understand that by art, I do not mean *only* pictures and sculpture, nor only these and architecture, that is beautiful building properly ornamented; these are only a portion of art, which comprises, as I understand the word a great deal more; beauty produced by the labour of man both mental and bodily, the expression of the interest man takes in the life of man upon the earth with all its surroundings, in other words the human pleasure of life is what I mean by art.[7]

Here Morris reiterates that he is concerned with the question of what art is, and states that he aims to broaden the definition of art beyond pictures and sculpture and architecture. But instead of going on to tell us the kinds of objects he wants to include in the category "art" as he did in the first quotation—"household furniture and utensils," for example—Morris proposes a new conception of what art is that locates it in the process of making. Art, Morris says, is "beauty produced by the labour of man"; it is "expression"; it is, no less, "the human pleasure of life."

Putting these two quotations together, we have the following explanation for including wallpaper and carpets and tiles in the study of art history: "the matters needful to our daily life," such as "household furniture and utensils," should, no less than "pictures and sculpture," be sites where an artist "expresses" her or his "human pleasure of life" through "beauty produced by . . . labour." It follows that when there is "something wrong" with a "civilization," people do not "express" their "human pleasure of life" in "beauty produced by . . . labour," and the things they make are not "works of art," but are "wretched makeshifts" or "degrading shams of better things."

These two quotations help to demonstrate what is at stake in the decision to include or exclude things of everyday use from the discipline of art history. However, while they answer some questions, they raise new ones. Morris presents an argument for considering some "household furnishings and utensils" as works of art, but which ones? How do we sort the objects that are "works of art" from the "wretched makeshifts" and "degrading shams of better things"? How do we determine whether or not an object possesses "beauty" or "expresses" the maker's "human pleasure of life"? Can these qualities be identified in the object? Or do we have to know something about the circumstances of its production? One way of dealing with these questions is to use Morris's art as examples. If Morris believed that "the matters needful to our daily life" were "works of art" that "expressed" the "human pleasure of life," surely his views are represented in his own art? Though the notion that an artist's work embodies her or his ideas is often taken for granted, this solution raises questions of its own.

Take a selection of Morris objects in a range of media: the *Vine* wallpaper, the *Kennet* chintz, and a swan tile. None of these is a painting or a sculpture. They are made for domestic interiors and thus, potentially, fall under the heading of "household furniture." But they are certainly not "utensils" and it is hard to see how they could be considered "matters needful to our daily life." Unlike a knife or a cup or a chair, these objects do not have an obvious function. Their purpose is to add visual interest to an interior: in other words, they are purely decorative. These, then, do not seem to serve as examples of Morris's "matters needful to our daily life." Rather they are examples of Morris's incorporation of other media beyond painting and sculpture in the category of "art."

It is in fact hard to find an object made or designed by Morris whose primary purpose is functional rather than decorative. The most functional objects produced by his company, Morris & Co., were designed by other people. The chairs and tables were usually designed by Ford Madox Brown or Philip Webb (though sometimes painted by Morris), the glasses and metalwork by Webb or W. A. S. Benson. There are exceptions—Morris designed some furniture for his home in the 1850s, for example—but the majority of his own artistic output takes the form of pattern. In "Some Hints on Pattern-Designing" (1881) Morris tells us that pattern is "the ornamentation of a surface by work that is not imitative or historical."[8] Explaining "what reason or right this so-called ornamental art has to existence," Morris states, "I cannot allow that it is good for any hour of the day to be wholly stripped of life and beauty" and offers pattern as an "art with which to surround our common workaday or restful times."[9] Wallpapers and textiles allow "us to clothe our daily and domestic walls with ornament that reminds us of the outward face of the earth, of the innocent love of animals, or of man passing his days between work and rest as he does."[10] The vast majority of Morris's art, then, is not intended to perform a practical function; instead, its purpose is to introduce art into "daily and domestic" life.

So while Morris's art does not on the whole answer the question of what "the matters needful to our daily life" look like when they are "works of art," what it does do is open up a third category in between "pictures and sculpture" on the one hand and "household furniture and utensils" on the other.

The objects in this category are characterized by pattern and medium but also by their intended location: they are not destined for museums and galleries, but for "daily and domestic walls." Morris calls this category "lesser (I will not say worse) art" because he wants to distinguish it from "the best art" which is "the pictured representation of men's imaginings" whose purpose is to "stir our emotions."[11] He argues, "it is not so good to have the best art for ever under our eyes" because "we cannot always be having our emotions deeply stirred: that wearies us body and soul."[12] For ordinary life, Morris proposes we surround ourselves with "lesser art."[13] While Morris's comments on art and labor offered a definition of art that tied it to the process of production, we see here that consumption was equally important to Morris's concept of art. For Morris art is not only the "expression" of the "human pleasure of life" but also something that enriches people's living and working environments. A famous quotation of Morris's from "The Lesser Arts" (1877) sums this up: "To give people pleasure in the things they must perforce USE, that is one great office of decoration; to give people pleasure in the things they must perforce MAKE, that is the other use of it."[14] Studying Morris's art invites us to reflect on how art is (or is not) integrated into "our common workaday or restful times."[15] It reminds us to consider the context in which art is displayed and how it has been made. It encourages us to look for art in unexpected places. Most importantly, it trains us to look in different ways.

Take the *Vine* wallpaper (figure 14.1). A wallpaper sample is a challenging object for formal analysis. Should we draw attention to the holes in the top corners and the ragged edges or try to screen out these imperfections? Studying Morris's art often requires us to consider several objects alongside one another. For example, to study *Vine* we would want to look at a number of different samples to get a sense of the range of colors available. All of these samples are equally representative of the *Vine* wallpaper; none is the original. In search of an original we might consider Morris's pencil and watercolor design for *Vine* (1873, Victoria and Albert Museum). What this drawing helps to reveal is the boundaries of the motif, and how cleverly the repetition of the motif is disguised by the interweaving of the different elements of the pattern. To see how the pattern is meant to be viewed, we would want to see it hung in a room. Over a wide expanse of wall the scrolling vertical path of the vine becomes much more striking than in the specimens. Bearing in mind Morris's emphasis on the importance of context for the interpretation of art, we might want to find out how *Vine* was displayed closer to Morris's own time. A surviving photograph of the morning room at 1 Holland Park offers a glimpse of *Vine* amidst an array of decoration including Morris & Co.'s *The Forest* tapestry. *Vine* is barely visible, appearing here and there from behind the furnishings of the room and then disappearing again. The partial view

Figure 14.1. *Vine* wallpaper, designed by William Morris, 1873. Hand printed in distemper colors by wood block on paper by Jeffrey & Co.
Reproduced courtesy of Victoria and Albert Museum.

interrupts the structural logic of the wallpaper's design. *Vine* takes its place within an ensemble, a single component of an elaborate whole.

Comparable challenges arise when we try to study the *Kennet* chintz. Again, multiple colorways were produced, so we need to consult a variety of samples. In the case of the chintz, a flattened sample gives a misleading impression because many of Morris's textiles were meant to be displayed on walls hanging in folds. A photograph of Morris's home, Kelmscott Manor, reveals how these deep folds distorted the pattern. Named after a river, *Kennet* calls to mind the surface of water. Like reflections interrupted by ripples, the pattern disappears and reappears around the walls of the room. This was not something Morris, as the designer of the pattern, could control. The pattern is well suited to this display method, however; the narrowness of the motif means that the same section comes to the surface relatively frequently, making the repeat readily discernible, and suggesting that the disruption of the design by the folds was something Morris anticipated. For the *Kennet* chintz to be experienced as Morris intended, paradoxically, he had to relinquish control and leave its final effect to chance.

In both cases we have to consult a range of sources in order to understand the pattern. The essence of *Vine* or *Kennet* lies somewhere in between the preparatory drawing, the surviving samples, and the photographs of the pattern in use. *Vine* and *Kennet* are each composites of their many manifestations. The work of art is not a single object but a collective. Studying Morris trains the eye to compare and contrast, to see how forms morph between different media, how juxtaposition with other objects and spaces affects meaning. Because Morris's art demands to be viewed in the context of the interiors it was made for and displayed in, Morris leads us into the challenging territory of the history of the interior. One of the courses on which I teach Morris is called "Art and the Modern Interior." Just as Morris had many identities—poet, artist, socialist—the literature on the interior spans many disciplines: architecture, history, sociology, literature, and anthropology among them. An advantage of teaching Morris in this context is that students are able to draw on that literature in addition to the art history scholarship with which they may be more familiar. Neither Morris nor the interior can be fully encompassed by art history alone; both require a grounding in a wider discourse. Issues that take center stage when studying the interior—ephemerality, weighing up different forms of evidence, the relationship between image and space, the construction of identity—are also highly relevant to the study of art history. Morris provides an ideal case study for exploring all of these topics.

One important characteristic of the interior, certainly in Morris's case, is its collaborative nature. Morris was committed to a collaborative model of production. As he put it, "A work of art is always a matter of co-operation."[16]

This is true of individual objects such as the *Adoration* tapestry, which was designed in 1888 by Edward Burne-Jones, Morris, and John Henry Dearle and executed by weavers in Morris & Co.'s workshop at Merton Abbey, but interiors take this "co-operation" to a much larger scale. Red House, Morris's home from 1860 to 1865, which he designed together with architect Philip Webb, was decorated with art made by Morris and his wife, Jane, and their friends. The Green Dining Room at the South Kensington Museum (1867) was a team effort by the members of the recently formed Morris, Marshall, Faulkner & Co. These examples suggest how Morris's art does not conform to the notion of the lone genius artist. Sometimes we do not know which member of Morris & Co. was responsible for each part of an object or interior. We can see the collaborative aspect of Morris's work as an embodiment of his socialism, an example of cooperative, harmonious labor in practice. On the other hand, studying Morris—and particularly Morris interiors—draws attention to the way in which Morris's name acts as an umbrella for the labor of myriad individuals who have not enjoyed enduring fame. Many artists were represented in the Victoria and Albert Museum's exhibition to mark the centenary of Morris's death in 1996, but the exhibition was called simply "William Morris." Studying Morris provides an opportunity to critique the ways in which art history organizes information. By allowing Morris's name to stand for the work of many other artists, art historians, however inadvertently, reinforce unequal power relationships and reaffirm an art history that canonizes those with privilege.

Morris would not have wanted to eclipse his fellow artists. He would have wanted the work they produced together to be judged on its own merits. Morris did not share the Arts and Crafts Exhibition Society's preoccupation with making sure everyone involved in the production of an exhibit was named in the catalogue, including the designer and the executant. "After all, the name is not the important matter," he said in 1893. "If I had my way there should be no names at all."[17] Morris's perspective was not that of the art historian who wants to situate the work of art in its historical, social, and biographical context. He wanted to make art that would bring "life and beauty" to "our common workaday and restful times."[18] This brings us to something of a paradox. If we are truly to put Morris's theory of art into practice, we should consider only how it reminds us "of the outward face of the earth, of the innocent love of animals, or of man passing his days between work and rest as he does"—in short, we should be concerned only with its "beauty."[19] If we value his art only for its connection to the man whose ideas we are interested in, we have misunderstood what he believes art is for.

The topic of beauty can lead to much debate in the classroom. As Elizabeth Prettejohn has argued, art history has often been reluctant to engage with the issue of beauty, partly due to a widespread "view of beauty as irrevocably opposed to any form of responsible politics."[20] Morris's explicitly political understanding of beauty provides an opportunity to consider the radical potential of beauty. Indeed, the conviction that beauty, far from being a luxury, is essential to human happiness, underlies the Morris quotation with which we began—"I do not want art for a few, any more than education for a few, or freedom for a few."

Students studying Morris's art together with his writings naturally observe that his art *was* only available to "a few." They point out that Morris's art was often produced by laborers realizing his designs, and consumed by a wealthy clientele. This, they say, is a long way from "an art made by the people, and for the people."[21] A discussion on this subject provides a valuable opportunity to address questions of art-historical methodology. We often expect an artist's words to illuminate their art and use their art to illustrate their writings. Ideally, however, an art historical approach to Morris doesn't see his artworks only as illustrations of his political views (and therefore as failures when they don't live up to those expectations), but as works of art that are as complex as any other. Certainly, his art may be productively interpreted as directly related to his politics; Stephen Eisenman's "Class Consciousness in the Design of William Morris" is an excellent example of a text that does this successfully.[22] Nevertheless, because Morris's art and writings have both been so influential for artists, art theorists, and art historians, it is important to give them both equal weight when teaching Morris to art history students, and not to make them too reliant on one another, but rather to give them both room to breathe. We can value his writings and his art on their own terms; we can allow each to illuminate the other; but neither of them should set limits on the other.

A discussion about the tension between Morris's political ideals and artistic practice can raise other questions that are important for art history. Studying Morris encourages art history students to consider the economic conditions of art production and consumption. As Caroline Arscott points out, "within a capitalist era" the "alternative" to producing art for those who can pay a fair price is cheap art, meaning, in Walter Crane's words, "the cheapening of modern labour."[23] When Morris talks about "art made by the people, and for the people" he is looking forward to "to-morrow, when the civilized world, no longer greedy, strifeful, and destructive, shall have a new art."[24] The whole social and political system will need to be transformed before we have any right to expect such an art to exist. The challenges raised by this material invite us to think more broadly about art's relation to economic and political structures.

Exploring the perceived contradiction between Morris's writings and his artistic practice can encourage students to think critically about the category of "art" itself. Studying Morris prompts us to ask who art is for—who makes it, who can afford to buy it, who has access to it. If the answers to these questions vary at different times and in different places, are we right to think of "art" as something coherent and unchanging across time and space? Teaching Morris provides an opportunity to help students to be critical of the assumptions that structure the study of art history by enabling them to view the discipline from new perspectives.

NOTES

1. William Morris, "The Lesser Arts" (1877), in *Hopes and Fears for Art. Five lectures delivered in Birmingham, London and Nottingham, 1878–1881* (London: Ellis & White, 1882), 35.

2. See Imogen Hart, "The Designs of William Morris," in *The Cambridge Companion to the Pre-Raphaelites*, ed. Elizabeth Prettejohn (Cambridge: Cambridge UP, 2012).

3. See Peter Faulkner, "The Odd Man Out: Morris among the Aesthetes," *Journal of the Decorative Arts Society 1850 to the Present* 34 (2010), 76–91.

4. To illustrate this point, consider Michael Hatt and Charlotte Klonk's excellent *Art History: An Introduction to its Methods* (Manchester: Manchester University Press, 2006), which tests out each method on a single oil painting, Pablo Picasso's *Les Demoiselles d'Avignon* (1907, Museum of Modern Art, New York). When art history's methods are defined as ways of interpreting paintings Morris's thinking is not readily accommodated (intriguing as it may be to contemplate ways in which Morris's writing could be employed as a way of interpreting this painting).

5. Imogen Hart, *Arts and Crafts Objects* (Manchester: Manchester University Press, 2010).

6. William Morris, "The Lesser Arts of Life" (1882) in *The Collected Works of William Morris; with introductions by his daughter May Morris*, vol. 22 (London: Longmans, Green and Co., 1910–1915), 239.

7. William Morris, "Art and Labour" (1884), in *The Unpublished Lectures of William Morris*, ed. Eugene D. LeMire (Detroit: Wayne State University Press, 1969), 94–95.

8. William Morris, "Some Hints on Pattern-Designing" (1881), in *The Collected Works of William Morris; with introductions by his daughter May Morris*, vol. 22 (London: Longmans, Green and Co., 1910–1915), 175.

9. William Morris, "Some Hints on Pattern-Designing" (1881), 175, 177.

10. Ibid., 177.

11. Ibid., 176.

12. Ibid., 177.

13. Ibid., 177.

14. William Morris, "The Lesser Arts" (1877), 4.

15. William Morris, "Some Hints on Pattern-Designing" (1881), 177.

16. "Art, Craft and Life: A Chat with William Morris," *Daily News Chronicle* (October 9, 1893). Hammersmith and Fulham Archives, London, DD/341/319 a–c.
17. Ibid.
18. William Morris, "Some Hints on Pattern-Designing" (1881), 177.
19. Ibid., 177.
20. Elizabeth Prettejohn, *Beauty and Art 1750–2000* (Oxford: Oxford University Press, 2005), 9.
21. William Morris, "The Art of the People," in *Hopes and Fears for Art. Five lectures delivered in Birmingham, London and Nottingham, 1878–1881* (London: Ellis & White, 1882), 70.
22. Stephen E. Eisenman, "Class Consciousness in the Design of William Morris," *Journal of William Morris Studies* XV (2002), 17–37.
23. Caroline Arscott, "William Morris: Decoration and Materialism" in *Marxism and the History of Art: From William Morris to the New Left,* ed. Andrew Hemingway (London; Ann Arbor, MI: Pluto, 2006), 9.
24. William Morris, "The Art of the People," 70.

BIBLIOGRAPHY

"Art, Craft and Life: A Chat with William Morris," *Daily News Chronicle* (October 9, 1893). Hammersmith and Fulham Archives, London, DD/341/319 a–c.

Arscott, Caroline. "William Morris: Decoration and Materialism." In *Marxism and the History of Art: From William Morris to the New Left,* edited by Andrew Hemingway, 9–27. Ann Arbor, MI: Pluto, 2006.

Eisenman, Stephen E. "Class consciousness in the Design of William Morris." *Journal of William Morris Studies* XV (2002): 17–37.

Faulkner, Peter. "The Odd Man Out: Morris among the Aesthetes." *Journal of the Decorative Arts Society 1850 to the Present* 34 (2010): 76–91.

Hart, Imogen. *Arts and Crafts Objects.* Manchester: Manchester University Press, 2010.

———. "The Designs of William Morris." In *The Cambridge Companion to the Pre-Raphaelites*, edited by Elizabeth Prettejohn, 211–22. Cambridge: Cambridge University Press, 2012.

Hatt, Michael and Charlotte Klonk. *Art History: An Introduction to its Methods.* Manchester: Manchester University Press, 2006.

Morris, William. "Art and Labour." 1884. In *The Unpublished Lectures of William Morris*, edited by Eugene D. LeMire, 94–118. Detroit: Wayne State University Press, 1969.

———. *Hopes and Fears for Art. Five lectures delivered in Birmingham, London and Nottingham, 1878–1881.* London: Ellis & White, 1882.

———. "The Lesser Arts of Life." 1882. In *The Collected Works of William Morris; with introductions by his daughter May Morris.* Vol. 22, 235–69. London: Longmans, Green and Co., 1914.

———. "Some Hints on Pattern-Designing." 1881. In *The Collected Works of William Morris; with introductions by his daughter May Morris*. Vol. 22, 175–205. London: Longmans, Green and Co., 1914.

Prettejohn, Elizabeth. *Beauty and Art 1750–2000*. Oxford: Oxford University Press, 2005.

Chapter Fifteen

"William Morris, designer"

Morris and the History of Design as Social Engagement

James Housefield

Now more than ever it is time for teaching William Morris, especially within design. In an era when design is celebrated as a key facet of our zeitgeist, renewed study of Morris and his work becomes increasingly necessary, or even urgent.[1] The work Morris began is with us today, carried on by groups as diverse as interior designers, participants in the maker movement, and radical craft practitioners. Teaching aspiring artists and designers about Morris offers significant opportunities to integrate history into contemporary life. Although his art and design rarely delivered political messages, Morris's contributions were political by imagining an economy very different from that of industrial capitalism. Morris's work was grounded in a consideration of the types of relations it produced: considering how we make things, how we treat the natural world, and how we treat one another. Seen in this context, Morris's forays into utopian fiction are a logical extension of his embrace of design. Both paths imagined a different future than the world in which he lived, conceiving new roles of author and designer in questioning how to shape that future and actively build these newly envisioned worlds. Designer and author shape social relations through the act of creation. Morris reminds us that by looking *beyond* the objects of design we can recognize histories of social relations embedded within these objects. We can thus reveal stories of social engagement in the work designers do. This essay examines historiographical transformations of our interpretations of Morris and design, as a contribution to recognizing his role in shaping today's understanding of the social roles of design and designer.

DESIGN AND UTOPIA: OR, CREATION AS POLITICAL STATEMENT

On January 27, 2017, millions of people marched in solidarity protesting the misogynistic statements and politics of the newly inaugurated forty-fifth president of the United States. What began as the Women's March on Washington became known simply as "the Women's March," its broader name emphasizing the shared message uniting marchers around the world. Despite the dispersed locations of the protest sites and the demographic diversity of those marching, a distinct object unified the protesters visually and socially. Within days, *Time* magazine featured a dramatically iconic photograph of this object on the cover of its February 6, 2017 issue. A month later, London's V&A museum had ushered the design into its collections. This handcrafted object, known to individuals and groups as the "pussyhat," offers urgent and potent lessons about the relevance of Morris in the twenty-first century. We can begin with contemporary objects and practices like the pussyhat, looking back to understand the history that made possible such acts of design-as-resistance. Alternately, we can begin with Morris and project forward from his time to our own to draft a lineage of contemporary art and design. Yet we, as educators, need to provide the contexts in which our students can connect the dots. Powerful cultural traditions can help us elucidate the urgency of contemporary design only when we have a shared consciousness of the social questions and movements that paved the way for today's creators. Morris is recurrently relevant.

To write or speak of Morris as a designer insists on a deliberate anachronism. The career of designer as we know it today did not exist in his own time. Yet in 1883 he inscribed his membership card to the Democratic Federation with the identifier "William Morris, designer." Biographer John William Mackail interpreted this as a statement of labor solidarity: "it was on his status as a workman that he based his claim to admission into the fighting rank of a working-class movement."[2] By asserting his role in society as that of a designer, Morris underscored his vociferous belief that the work of a designer includes the redesign of society itself. Design, for Morris, was a utopian profession. Morris was not only a designer of objects, interiors, and architecture. Through his writing, speeches, example, and actions he was a designer of social systems—inspiring the design of educational systems and of a new business model with "the firm," Morris & Co. When Morris designed the Democratic Federation's membership cards he balanced the motto "Liberty Equality Fraternity" with three additional words of injunction: "educate," "agitate," "organise." To transform society would require them all.

What can designers today learn from the example of Morris? Morris remains timely for his creativity, his inspiration to others, and his emphasis on the potential roles creators might play in beautifying or redefining society. Design in the twenty-first century employs an array of tools ranging from those of graphic design or the design of interfaces to architectural design and the design of experiences. Following the late twentieth-century traditions of human-centered design, today's designer is motivated often by utopian goals akin to those Morris espoused. Designers today are as likely to redesign the world and promote social change as they are to design a book, furnishing, or interior. By investigating how this holds true, students and teachers additionally benefit from the opportunity to analyze the heritage of today's discipline of design through historiography.

HISTORIES OF TASTE: RECURRENTLY RELEVANT MORRIS

Although the designs he created fill museums and continue to be sold successfully on the market, the work of Morris has not always enjoyed unequivocally positive reception. Early twentieth century audiences began to lose interest in the medievalism that was central to the designs and thinking behind work done by Morris and the firm. While others debated whether Morris's patterns and politics had fallen out of fashion, Walter Gropius and his colleagues at the Bauhaus sought inspiration in Morris. The Bauhaus—arguably the most influential school of art and design that emerged during the twentieth century—emphasized handwork, like Morris, yet also embraced the machines and industrial production Morris despised. What emerged from the Bauhaus and other contemporary art movements of its time (1919–1933) encompassed a functionalist aesthetic that seems the logical conclusion of the "golden rule" Morris espoused in "The Beauty of Life," a manifesto delivered to the Birmingham Society of Arts and School of Design, February 19, 1880. "Have nothing in your houses that you do not know to be useful, or believe to be beautiful" anticipated the functionalism that characterized much of the architecture and design of the early to mid-twentieth century.[3] What changed between 1880 and 1919? An embrace of the machine and the possibilities of "machine art" changed attitudes from the time of Morris to that of Gropius.

Nikolaus Pevsner's *Pioneers of Modern Design: From William Morris to Walter Gropius* offers an ideal text to introduce students to the changing and enduring historical impact of Morris, his ideas, and his work. First published in 1936 as *Pioneers of the Modern Movement*, Pevsner's text holds up despite its age. Pevsner's book established the significance of Morris for generations that followed. Reading Pevsner can be a tool for introducing students to historiography, a history of taste, and the varieties of meaning that the generations immediately following Morris found in his work. Pevsner's book bears reading in its entirety. The first chapter of *Pioneers of Modern Design* gives an excellent overview of the work and impact of Morris, before elaborating in greater depth on Morris and his contemporaries in the second chapter. Pevsner makes clear that the question of the machine and its impact on society forged the greatest difference of opinion between Morris and those he influenced at the turn of the twentieth century. Students who read sections of "The Beauty of Life" by Morris and the first chapter of Pevsner's *Pioneers* should be well prepared to discuss this transition and changing attitudes about the machine. A lively discussion will prepare them for recent movements that once again question societal embrace of the machine.

VARIETIES OF TOTAL DESIGN

In Pevsner's summation, "the campaign of William Morris's lifetime was directed against the complete lack of feeling for the essential unity of architecture."[4] Unity, in this sense, denotes continuity between a building's exterior and its interior that is carried out by the design of all elements within the structure. Morris demanded that skilled craftsmanship should replace the shoddy creations churned out by industrialized production. For Morris, personally, this meant learning new crafts and techniques, and studying the art of the past in order to create anew. He founded "the firm" of Morris, Marshall, Faulkner & Co., Fine Art Workmen in Painting, Carving, Furniture, and the Metals (1861–1875)—later to be known simply as Morris & Co.—to put these ideals of architectural unity and skilled craftsmanship into practice on a commercial scale. For Pevsner, the founding of the firm "marks a new era in Western art."[5]

Through the firm Morris promoted an ideal of architectural unity to rival the German concept of the *Gesamtkunstwerk* or "total work of art." Morris's form of total design promoted visual and conceptual coherence for all elements of an interior space, unifying interior with exterior and the totality of the building. The firm's showroom displays famously demonstrated the stylistic unity a buyer could achieve in decorating an interior with the furniture, art objects, wall coverings, tapestries, and other objects on offer there. The international Arts and Crafts movement and Gustav Stickley's Craftsman movement, in North America, would not have been imaginable without the writings of Morris and the example of the firm. As Pevsner notes, the example of Morris & Co. was also powerful for Art Nouveau creators who sought stylistic unity and set the stage for the modern creators associated with the Dutch movement of De Stijl, the German Bauhaus and Deutscher Werkbund, and the International Style in architecture. Unlike Morris, these latter groups embraced the machine. Yet their machine aesthetic depended upon Morris's ideals of craftsmanship and the central importance of "honesty" in materials, construction, and style. Today, corporations from IKEA to Apple have adopted Morris & Co.'s holistic approach to architectural unity, even adapting it to corporate identities designed to reinforce consumer perceptions of a unified aesthetic.

THE DESIGNER IN SOCIETY: PLEASURE IN LABOR OR UNHAPPINESS AND DEGRADATION

Pevsner's protégé, Reyner Banham, could summarize the impact of Morris with a single phrase, attributing a "predisposing cause" of modern architecture to Morris and his cohort: "the sense of an architect's responsibility to the society in which he finds himself, an idea of largely English extraction, from [A.W. N.] Pugin, [John] Ruskin, and Morris."[6] An examination of writings by Ruskin and Morris illuminates what made Morris both like and unlike his contemporaries. Morris signaled the importance of Ruskin as a catalyst for his own thought on many occasions, but rarely as clearly as he did in 1892, when he reprinted the chapter on "The Nature of Gothic" from Ruskin's *The Stones of Venice* in an elegant edition from the Kelmscott Press. Morris commented:

> For the lesson which Ruskin here teaches is that art is the expression of man's pleasure in labour; that it is possible for man to rejoice in his work, for, strange as it may seem for us to-day, there have been times when he did rejoice in it; and lastly, that unless man's work become again a pleasure to him, the token of which change will be that beauty is once again a natural and necessary accompaniment of productive labour, all but the worthless must toil in pain, and therefore live in pain, so that the result of thousands of years of man's effort on the earth must be general unhappiness and universal degradation; unhappiness and degradation, the conscious burden of which will grow in proportion to the growth of man's intelligence, knowledge, and power over material nature.
>
> If this be true, as I for one most firmly believe, it follows that the hallowing of labour by art is the one aim for us at the present day. If politics are to be anything less than an empty game, more exciting but less innocent than those which are confessedly games of skill or chance, it is toward this goal of the happiness of labour that they must make.... Ruskin ... has done serious and solid work towards that new-birth of Society, without which genuine art, the expression of man's pleasure in his handiwork, must inevitably cease altogether, and with it the hopes of the happiness of mankind.[7]

Morris raged against the industrial production of machines that damaged human lives and promoted an aesthetics of ugliness. Building upon Ruskin, he predicted that these would be symptomatic of society's decline while also precipitating further degradation. At the core, what distinguished and distinguishes Morris from others is the utopian notion that *we can, and must, remake the world through design*. To accomplish this would require a wholesale redesign of the systems of education, production, and dissemination of design.

DESIGN IS DANGEROUS: REDESIGNING DESIGN EDUCATION

Today's designer has not completely fulfilled the charge of Ruskin and Morris to remake the world. Indeed, design risks perpetuating the unhappiness against which Morris inveighed. Since the 1960s, a recognition of design's real and potential dangers has propelled the field to embrace challenges to redesign the designer's goals. These included new approaches to design education, and new methods. The most dominant paradigm to frame design practices in the twenty-first century has been the "human-centered design" (HCD) framework or method. HCD emerged out of the late 1960s writings of Victor Papanek and others. Papanek's opening paragraphs in the preface to *Design for the Real World* cut to the heart of design's dangers. In their indictment of the then-dominant system and provocation for a new approach to design education, Papanek's words bear comparison to manifesto-like statements by Morris:

> There are professions more harmful than industrial design, but only a very few of them. And possibly only one profession is phonier. Advertising design, in persuading people to buy things they don't need, with money they don't have, in order to impress others who don't care, is probably the phoniest field in existence today. Industrial design, by concocting the tawdry idiocies hawked by advertisers, comes a close second . . . By designing criminally unsafe automobiles that kill or maim nearly one million people around the world each year, by creating whole new species of permanent garbage to clutter up the landscape, and by choosing materials and processes that pollute the air we breathe, designers have become a dangerous breed. And the skills needed in these activities are taught carefully to young people.
>   In an age of mass production when everything must be planned and designed, design has become the most powerful tool with which man shapes his tools and environments (and, by extension, society and himself). This demands high social and moral responsibility from the designer.[8]

Design reform begins with critical assessment and educational reform. If designers are not the ones taking the lead in critically rethinking the pitfalls and social ills their work produces, others will surely take the opportunity to do so. Today the design profession is still young; the job title of "designer" has yet to approach the century mark. Now is the time to call for renewed attention to the ethics of design, echoing the emphasis Morris placed on art, craft, labor, and industry—and the impact they have on the quality of life for us all.

Papanek's ideas transformed the field of design from the 1970s to the present and led to the development of HCD. In its name and practices, this approach distinguishes itself from designs that were motivated by profit. Human-centered design depends on communication with the audiences who would use a design in order to better fulfill their personal and social needs.

Papanek's critique of advertising and planned obsolescence as tools to promote false desires ("wants" as distinguished from "needs") echoes the exhortations of Morris while resonating with the antimaterialist sentiments of the emerging youth culture and counter-culture of the 1960s. Consulting *people* (rather than accountants and bankers) promoted new ethnography-based research methods with which a designer might conduct her work. By the early twenty-first century, contemporary designers increasingly took their lead from the sort of revolutionary design objects promoted by exhibitions like the Cooper Hewitt Museum's "Design for the Other 90%" and a traveling exhibition-on-wheels of objects designer Emily Pilloton curated to represent what she called a *Design Revolution*. Pilloton's exhibition took divergent physical forms in the Airstream Travel Trailer she drove across North America to display the objects for diverse communities, and in a printed book titled *Design Revolution: 100 Products That Empower People.*

Pilloton's voice echoed Morris in its criticism of the ways that design and production remain complicit with the degradation of society despite publicity otherwise. "As a whole," Pilloton wrote, "today's world of design (specifically product design) is severely deficient, crippled by consumerism and paralyzed by an unwillingness to financially and ethically prioritize social impact over the bottom line. We need nothing short of an industrial design revolution."[9] Pilloton designed pages twenty-nine through thirty of her book to be removed and distributed, thus enlisting designers in the service of this revolution. These pages present "The Designer's Handshake," a commitment to be signed by those agreeing "to try, to the best of [their] ability, to commit and adhere to the following principles within [their] work and life as a designer."[10] This manifesto calls for designers to remain aware and vigilant about the work that they do and its impact on society. Pilloton's words have had a tremendous impact on a generation of design students for whom happiness depends, in part, on ethical behavior and social engagement.

At the heart of Pilloton's book is a call to arms to change the systems in which design has traditionally operated, echoing the transformations that

Morris put in place as "designer." Pilloton has taken to heart the message that the designer must be aware of her role in society, complementing her work as a designer with a commitment to education through "Project H." Founded by Pilloton in 2008, Project H uses design education as a means to give young people tools for personal development, empowerment, and self-actualization. Through teaching in the secondary school of Bertie County, North Carolina, and subsequently in Berkeley, California (at Realm Charter School and Girls Garage), Project H students integrate core subject learning with socially transformative "design and build" projects. Girls Garage, the most recent venture of Pilloton's Project H, integrates design, engineering, and other skills with tools of social justice, to "equip girls with the confidence and tools to build anything they can imagine and to grow alongside one another and their communities."[11] For Girls Garage, as for Morris, social change begins with design.

Multiple benefits accrue to society at large in addition to the specific individuals who study with Pilloton through Project H and Girls Garage. Chief among these benefits is the opportunity for design to spark a conversation about how a society educates its youth for the work they will do across the arc of their lives. For Pilloton, design education is a catalyst for social justice that begins with self-awareness and individual empowerment. Emily Harris read *Design Revolution* early in her education and later worked alongside Pilloton as a teaching assistant at the University of California, Davis, and in Girls Garage. Harris developed the concept of Adventure Thinking by reflecting on her experience as a designer and building upon Pilloton's integration of design with education. Adventure Thinking moves aspects of the classroom into nature where participants face challenges that balance wilderness adventures (hiking, rock climbing, and more) with creative activities toward the goals of self-discovery through design. Participants in Adventure Thinking seminars use their hands to make what they design, emphasizing an element of handcraft from the ideas of Morris even when they work with industrial tools, including welding torches. To put Adventure Thinking into practice, Harris has developed She's Rogue, a platform through which she conducts workshops, weekend retreats, and longer courses that blend creativity with adventure. She's Rogue engages personal transformation and social activism simultaneously, empowering young female professionals through overcoming "adventure" challenges and urging new forms of creative making. By focusing on designers at an early or mid-career stage of their working lives, She's Rogue layers new experiences upon a designer's work and life experience, to promote dialogues about the role of design education in society. An embrace of "making"—whether through Girls Garage, She's Rogue, or some other outlet—promises to remake society at large by

"William Morris, designer" 227

Figure 15.1. Participants in an Adventure Thinking seminar, led by Emily Harris, work together to learn welding skills for a design-and-build project. Adventure Thinking integrates design education with adventure challenges to promote personal awareness, empowerment, and cultural change.

Photo by Genesia Ting and reproduced courtesy of Emily Harris and She's Rogue.

integrating craft with education. On a larger plane, activists worldwide have embraced handwork and craft as tools to promote conversations about the redesign of society.

RADICALLY SLOW (MORRIS 2.0): CRAFT, CONVERSATION, AND ACTIVISM

Morris's ideas remain alive today in groups that integrate design and craft with social activism. These groups fall under no single rubric, although many embrace the mantle of craft activism. Although no individual, group, or image can adequately encompass the diversity of craft activism, one image has become nearly iconic: a work by Marianne Jørgensen and the Cast Off Knitters titled *Pink M.24 Chaffee*. When displayed outside the Nikolaj Contemporary Art Center in Copenhagen, as part of the exhibition "TIME" (April 27–June 4, 2006), some 4,000 pink squares engulfed a M.24 Chaffee tank. The ubiquitous presence of the M.24 Chaffee in military occupations from late World War II through the Cold War made it clearly recognizable. Jørgensen's collaborating knitters from around the world connected with each other through word of mouth and the Cast Off Knitters group (begun by Rachael Matthews, London, 2000). The resulting convergence of soft knit fibers and hard metal prompted political conversations about Denmark's decision to join the United States and the United Kingdom in war against Iraq. Since the close of the twentieth century, knitting, yarnbombing, and other crafts have increasingly become tools to promote political conversations.

Those teaching William Morris would do well to find local groups that promote crafts, including craft activists. Sponsor marathon readings of Morris while crafters listen, work, and eventually respond to the ideas that remain vital today. Ask the crafters about the importance of handwork across the spectrum of their personal and social lives. How does manual labor reward them, and what are its limitations? What role does quality play in contemporary craft? What materials do they use, and from what origins do the materials and makers come? Does it matter whether the craft supplies they use were made by machine? Alternately, do they propose a larger do-it-yourself approach that might encompass the raising of agricultural fibers through to spinning and production? The responses will inevitably be as illuminating as they are specific to the time and place in which the groups gather. Use word of mouth and social media to find crafters. They'll likely come from corners as diverse as the Maker Movement and back-to-the-land agriculturalists.

Craft and handwork took distinctly political turns in the first decades of the twenty-first century. In the United States, the 2016 presidential election pitting Hillary Clinton and Bernie Sanders against Donald Trump led to many groups using craft to promote political agendas and conversations—especially in the wake of Trump's ascent to the presidency. Women worldwide knitted hats and marched to protest Trump's inauguration, as the opening paragraphs of this essay recounted. Pink hats, handmade by crafters, became a ubiquitous presence in the Women's Marches of January 2017 and 2018, worldwide. During and after the marches the hats served as political markers or visual statements of solidarity with women standing up against gender discrimination. "Femininity, whether it's in a man or a woman, is really disrespected in our society," Krista Suh, a cofounder of the Pussyhat Project, remarked in a film made by *The Atlantic* magazine's digital edition and promoted on YouTube. "What we're trying to do with this project is embrace pink, embrace the name 'pussyhat,' and not run away from that."[12]

Yet the hats were also a polarizing symbol, as I learned in conversations with students at the University of California, Davis. Some embraced the project, knitting their own hats and sharing the pattern and photographs on social media. Others criticized the hats as exclusionary. "Do you think all women have vaginas? Do you think all women have pink vaginas?" one student queried, asserting that the hats symbolized "transmisogyny, racism, colorism, and queer-antagonism." Another student noted, "Pussyhats alienate trans women and nonbinary folk from feminist circles by equating specific genitalia with womanhood. There are many women who do not have vaginas, and by parading the vagina as a symbol for feminism we steer further from intersectionality. While it's an interesting movement that has picked up a lot of steam during women's marches, it would be unfair to discuss Pussyhats without mentioning white feminism and how small things (such as a Pussyhat or phrases like 'Pussy Power') can subtly alienate members of the community." Another expressed concern that the hat "became a gimmick [used] by white people and women taking a perfect opportunity to create content for social media." As a gimmick, its political power was tainted; as an exclusionary statement, it was offensive.

Krista Suh explained to NBC News that the hats were not intended to promote discrimination. "I never thought that by calling it the 'pussyhat' that it was saying that women's issues are predicated on the possession of the pussy," Suh remarked.[13] Suh clarified that the Pussyhat Project was inspired by Donald Trump's vulgar comments allegedly recorded on Access Hollywood (2005), audio recordings of which were leaked during the presidential campaign leading up to the November 2016 election. The Project, said Suh, thus sought to reclaim the word to empower those who identify as female. The divergent responses to the Pussyhat Project within my own classes make it clear that the hat is not a universal symbol; its political messages can be interpreted variously. However, the crafted hats are unequivocally powerful vehicles for igniting conversations about the roles of craft and design in society, and the pathways to greater equity and gender equality in redesigning society itself.

Like the Pussyhat Project, "Nasty Women" drew its name from derogatory comments Trump made on the campaign trail ("Such a nasty woman," he was recorded saying in reference to his political challenger Clinton during a televised debate). A series of "Nasty Women" exhibitions brought together groups of designers, artists, and craft activists in localized regional displays. Exhibitions became instruments to spur conversations about gender equity and civil liberties, and to highlight the lack of public funding for groups such as Planned Parenthood that support women's health and reproductive rights. Alongside the promotion of these rights, the "Nasty Women" exhibitions promoted inclusivity rather than exclusive or biological definitions of womanhood.

One activist group came together in Davis, California, in March 2017, seeking to create work to submit to an iteration of the national "Nasty

Women" exhibitions of that spring, and chose to name themselves the Cliterate Collective. Primary members of the Cliterate Collective include Alicia Decker, glenda drew, Alyssa Goldsmith, Julia Boorinakis Harper, Belinda Huang, Naomi Acuña Pryor, Ariel Robbins, and Sinead Santich. The group's website outlines their mission:

> Cliteracy is a project of "The Cliterates," a collective of California-based artists, to serve as a practice of creativity and tool for the reclamation and celebration of our bodies. Building on the history of feminism, Cliteracy pushes social practice into new territory through the re-emergence of Stitch'n'Bitch feminist fibre collectives/groups. We create an inclusive, safe and explorative space for participants to create new visual work that contributes to and amplifies a critical conversation about gender, beauty, equity, discrimination, violence, reclamation and celebration, while contributing to a movement through practice that is joyful, connected, community-based and empowered through the arts.[14]

Following their participation in the Oakland, California, "Nasty Women" exhibition, the collective continued to meet and craft work for public exhibition. With events in Sacramento and Davis, they created craft work, particularly embroidery, in public and invited the public to participate in crafting. In October 2017, the Cliterate Collective paired a temporary exhibition of their work with a participatory crafting event held on the Event Plaza of the Jan Shrem and Maria Manetti Shrem Museum of Art at the University of California, Davis. Crafters added their works to the glass walls of the museum when they completed them, each embroidered fabric fitting into a hexagonal space within a matrix designed by glenda drew and the Collective in advance of the event. The museum's exterior walls thus became a space for public exchange. The temporary exhibition was one of several held in conjunction with the annual conference of Imagining America, an organization that promotes community-engaged scholarship. Works from the Cliterate Collective's participatory exhibition were eventually sold, and the proceeds donated to a local community group, Empower Yolo. A regional community service for Yolo County, California, "Empower Yolo provides twenty-four hour crisis intervention, emergency shelter, confidential counseling, training, legal assistance, and other services for individuals and families affected by domestic violence, sexual assault, stalking, human trafficking, and child abuse."[15] Through community donations, the Cliterate Collective made a public statement that connects to the craft activities the Collective pursues.

Although there are many ways that craft activists and contemporary designers prolong the Morris legacy, the ability to prompt conversation about social change may be the most significant. Despite the embrace of the machine in the arts and design of the past century, the return to handwork in the present-day

Figure 15.2. Members of the Cliterate Collective staged a participatory public craft event and temporary exhibition at the Jan Shrem and Maria Manetti Shrem Museum of Art, University of California, Davis, as part of the Imagining America 2017 National Conference (October 2017).
Photo by Belinda Huang and reproduced courtesy of glenda drew and the Cliterate Collective.

signals that the ideas of Morris continue to thrive. Elizabeth Carolyn Miller's elegantly argued 2013 book, *Slow Print: Literary Radicalism and Late Victorian Print Culture*, situated Morris in ways that illuminate the significance of craft activists like the Cliterate Collective today. Miller's book viewed the radical challenges Morris leveled against society through the aspect of print culture. A printed page, for Morris, was a work of art and craft that ideally required and expressed unalienated labor. To produce and to read such pages requires time. Pages from the Kelmscott Press required time for the making of type, and typesetting. They required time in the printing by hand, using time-honored techniques. They required time for the beautiful treatment of beautiful words from Morris, Ruskin, Chaucer, and others. The resulting pages and books from the Kelmscott Press and its like posed a radical alternative to the rapidly printed and cheaply disseminated books whose acidic papers soon yellowed and became brittle. Where the cheap papers of their day have self-destructed, Morris's have slowly grown into their age and matured.[16]

By comparison to industrial production, craft is slow. Like the juxtaposition of slow print to fast, or that of fast food to slow (in the contemporary

Slow Food movement), a deliberate choice to embrace a slow tempo is a politically charged decision. The paragraphs above have emphasized the roles of craft and contemporary design in prompting social conversations. Such conversations begin with the slow processes of crafting, education, and human-centered design. The art of the Cliterate Collective is as much a fleeting social and relational art produced in the crafting sessions as it is an art that can hang upon a wall or decorate an embroidered fabric. Conversations that unfolded during temporary public participatory crafting inevitably engaged the topics of human sexuality, rights, and civil liberties that the Cliterate Collective considers an essential aspect of their work. Because craft can be taught without need for expensive tuition, it can be a means to promote an equitable "playing field" for creative activities in which, over time, all who are dedicated to their craft can gain mastery. Because craft takes time, it opens social space for conversation. Its slow tempo offers an alternative to the rapidity of social media and communications that operate on sound bites. Slow craft denies immediate gratification and embraces delayed results. A return to the tempo of craft is a radical proposition for remaking today's world. Craft can be a manifesto for a new life: slow life.

Writing in *The Art Newspaper*, in early spring 2018, Jori Finkel queried: "Has the time come for craft to be accepted into the art canon? The unprecedented number of panels devoted to the topic at the College Art Association annual conference of art historians in Los Angeles . . . suggests this is already well underway."[17] Examples of craft from the time of Morris to the present day fill museums worldwide. Within the collections of London's V&A, the museum that also features the Green Dining Room whose decoration Morris designed (1866), crafts of our own times like the pussyhat are enshrined, preserved, and displayed. Future years and future generations will determine whether the pussyhat will be forgotten, deaccessioned, or balanced by designs that are more overtly inclusive. No matter its future, the hat stands as a reminder: Morris was correct to insist on the roles that designer and designs play as leaders in conversations about the shapes we seek to give to our lives and our society.

NOTES

1. The author extends special thanks to glenda drew, Talinn Grigor, Emily Harris, and Corrie Hendricks for conversations about the relevance of Morris and forms of craft activism during the revising of this essay. Comments from Jason Martinek, Liz Miller, and anonymous reviewers greatly improved the manuscript. Thank you to you all.

2. John William Mackail, *The Life of William Morris*, vol. 2 (London: Longmans, Green, and Co., 1901), 87.

3. William Morris, "The Beauty of Life," in *Hopes and Fears for Art* (London: Ellis & White, 1882), 108

4. Nikolaus Pevsner, *Pioneers of Modern Design: From William Morris to Walter Gropius* (London: Peregrine Books, 1986 edition), 20.

5. Ibid., 22.

6. Reyner Banham, *Theory and Design in the First Machine Age* (Cambridge, MA: MIT Press, 1980 edition), 14.

7. John Ruskin, *The Nature of Gothic*. (Hammersmith: Kelmscott Press, 1892), i–v.

8. Victor Papanek, *Design for the Real World: Human Ecology and Social Change* (Chicago: Chicago Review Press, 2005 edition), ix–x.

9. Emily Pilloton, *Design Revolution: 100 Products That Empower People* (New York: Metropolis Books, 2009), 10.

10. Ibid., 29.

11. See http://girlsgarage.org.

12. Atlantic Documentaries, "How Pink 'Pussyhats' Took Over the Women's March." *The Atlantic*, (January 25, 2017): https://www.theatlantic.com/video/index/514301/pussyhat-takeover/. Accessed February 1, 2017.

13. Julie Compton, "Pink 'Pussyhat' Creator Addresses Criticism Over Name," NBC News (February 7, 2017): https://www.nbcnews.com/feature/nbc-out/pink-pussyhat-creator-addresses-criticism-over-name-n717886. Accessed December 7, 2017.

14. "What is Cliteracy?" http://fembroidery.com/. Accessed December 2, 2017.

15. Empower Yolo, http://empoweryolo.org/. Accessed December 2, 2017.

16. Elizabeth Carolyn Miller, *Slow Print: Literary Radicalism and Late Victorian Print Culture* (Stanford: Stanford University Press, 2013).

17. Finkel, Jori. "Scholars Weave Craft into the Art History Canon at College Art Association," *The Art Newspaper*, February 22, 2018, https://www.theartnewspaper.com/news/scholars-weave-craft-into-the-art-history-canon-at-college-art-association. Accessed February 22, 2018.

BIBLIOGRAPHY

Atlantic Documentaries, "How Pink 'Pussyhats' Took Over the Women's March." *The Atlantic*, January 25 2017, https://www.theatlantic.com/video/index/514301/pussyhat-takeover/. Accessed February 1, 2017.

Banham, Reyner. *Theory and Design in the First Machine Age* (1960). Second edition. Cambridge, MA: MIT Press, 1980.

Compton, Julie. "Pink 'Pussyhat' Creator Addresses Criticism Over Name," NBC News, February 7, 2017, https://www.nbcnews.com/feature/nbc-out/pink-pussyhat-creator-addresses-criticism-over-name-n717886. Accessed 7 December 2017.

Empower Yolo, http://empoweryolo.org/. Accessed 2 December 2017.

Finkel, Jori. "Scholars Weave Craft into the Art History Canon at College Art Association," *The Art Newspaper*, February 22, 2018, https://www.theartnewspaper

.com/news/scholars-weave-craft-into-the-art-history-canon-at-college-art-association. Accessed 22 February 2018.

Hendricks, Corrie. *Yarn Bombing, Radical Fiber Art, and Birdie Sanders: The Socialist History and Visual Language of Craft Activism*. MA Thesis (art history), University of California, Davis, 2017.

Mackail, John William. *The Life of William Morris*, Vol. 2. New edition. London: Longmans, Green, and Co., 1901.

Miller, Elizabeth Carolyn. *Slow Print: Literary Radicalism and Late Victorian Print Culture*. Stanford: Stanford University Press, 2013.

Morris, William. "The Beauty of Life." In *Hopes and Fears for Art*. London: Ellis & White, 1882, 71–113.

Orso, Anna. "Some Say Women's March Pink Hats Aren't Inclusive. Philly Organizers Say Wear What You Want," *Philadelphia Inquirer and Daily News*, January 16, 2018, http://www.philly.com/philly/news/some-say-womens-march-pussyhats-arent-inclusive-philly-organizers-say-wear-what-you-want-20180116.html. Accessed 21 January 2018.

Pevsner, Nikolaus. *Pioneers of Modern Design: From William Morris to Walter Gropius* (1936). Third edition. Prescott, AZ: Peregrine Books, 1986.

Pilloton, Emily. *Design Revolution: 100 Products That Empower People*. New York: Metropolis Books, 2009.

Ruskin, John. *The Nature of Gothic*. Kelmscott Press, 1892.

She's Rogue, https://www.shesrogue.com/. Accessed 7 December 2017.

"What is Cliteracy?" http://fembroidery.com/. Accessed 2 December 2017.

Chapter Sixteen

William Morris and the Intersection of the Histories of Art and Design

Julie Codell

> "When they are so parted, it is ill for the Arts altogether: the lesser ones become trivial, mechanical, unintelligent, incapable of resisting the changes pressed upon them by fashion or dishonesty; while the greater . . . unhelped by the lesser, unhelped by each other, are sure to lose their dignity of popular arts, and become nothing but dull adjuncts to unmeaning pomp, or ingenious toys for a few rich and idle men."
>
> —William Morris, "The Lesser Arts"[1]

In the last few years historians of design and historians of art have begun a dialogue about their commonalities and differences. These histories were distinct in the past despite efforts to bring these disciplines closer by the Victorian Arts and Crafts movement, Roger Fry's modern Omega Workshop, and the German Bauhaus movement. Recent crossover studies on jewelry, fashion, and interior design have begun to spring up and indicate areas in which the two histories can find common discourses such as global markets and mobility in the trade of both fine and craft arts. In this chapter, I focus on how Morris, in his attempt to integrate art and craft, culturally "elevated" crafts by applying the presumed traits of high art to design and to the furnishings his firm produced. These suppositions were, and still are, that the so-called "higher" or "fine" arts had relations to the past that marked and embodied a changing history and that they expressed social relations and values. These characteristics were denied crafts, which were seen as mechanical, decorative, and marked by fixed, unchanging traditions, all trivializing traits. Crafts were also demeaned out of their social association with manual labor, working classes, and colonized cultures.

While "decorative art" is an ambiguous term with wide-ranging applications from architectural sculpture to any of the handicrafts, objects designated design, or craft objects are as expressive and embodying of cultural values as painting, sculpture, or architecture.[2] This infusion of crafts with fine art assets in recent studies of interiors, furnishings, and textiles, furthermore, offers critiques of vital cultural concepts such as authenticity, originality, appropriation, and replication.

Another distinction was the mode of production. Painting and sculpture were considered unique in their production, singular, and most importantly, not anonymous, as craft production has largely been until the eighteenth century when the artisans and craft factories became identified within a rising nationalism and signed by makers' names. Craft objects, whether mechanically manufactured or handmade, are consumed on a mass scale, compared to the one-off "creative" production of the fine arts. These distinctions of production were added to the Victorian association of crafts with working-class Britons and colonial peoples to contain the subordination of craft to art.

Since my students may be from disciplines of art history, design, or other humanities disciplines, I have the opportunity to do several things. Historically, I can place Morris in the contexts of overlapping Victorian debates: about architecture and ornaments, about design and industrialization, and about cultural hierarchies of class and empire. Morris's self-imposed mission was to "restore aesthetic values to craftsmanship" to bring together craft and aesthetics, the latter located in fine arts discourses and increasingly in late-Victorian debates about crafts and manufacturing.[3] In class we examine Morris's application of assumptions about the nature and significance of the fine arts to craft production, applying fine arts' changing histories of style and content as distinct from the notion of craft tradition as fixed, and art's expression of contemporary social relations. Morris sought painters, such as Ford Madox Brown and Edward Burne-Jones, willing and even eager to create furnishings for both Morris, Marshall, Faulkner & Co. (1861–1875) and its successor Morris & Co. (1875–1940).[4] The Pre-Raphaelites, in general, rejected the separation of art and craft and much has been written on their attitude.

Curiously, however, there is less written on Morris's revaluation of craft through an application of fine art values. His textiles and furnishings are the subject of much curatorial study and collecting, but the links between ideologies of craft and of high art are rarely analyzed or brought together in many studies. Yet what Morris understood from his experiences in all his areas of endeavor—architecture, painting, and poetry—was that crafts, too, had changing histories and technologies that tied them to a dynamic cultural expression. While Indian and Middle Eastern objets d'art were much admired and collected by the Victorians from the 1851 Great Exhibition on, this admiration was tempered by underlying imperialist notions of British modernity versus the backwardness of colonial artisans. Admiring Indian crafts and sensitive to imperialist attitudes, Morris sought to transfer high art values to crafts to elevate them in the Victorian aesthetic hierarchy and to inspire admiration for artisans and, indeed, for all laborers.

MORRIS AND THE VICTORIAN MOMENT OF DESIGN

Morris's contribution to bringing art and design histories together was partly an outgrowth of earlier efforts by civil servant and inventor Henry Cole (1808–1882), architect and designer Owen Jones (1809–1874), and others who organized the 1851 Great Exhibition.[5] This exhibition was anticipated by the 1835–1836 Parliamentary Select Committee of Arts and Manufactures and the 1836 founding of the Government School of Design, created to investigate state-sponsored design education as distinct from the Royal Academy's fine arts curriculum. Jones's *Grammar of Ornament* (1856) was comprehensively illustrated by over one hundred colored folio plates of designs from around the world and since antiquity. In creating a grammar, Jones shifted the function of ornament from narration to a kind of fixed linguistic structure, removing it from history by universalizing designs in a quasi-scientific order.[6] While this reconfiguration also appears imperialist in its range and promise of control over world cultures, Stacey Sloboda considers Owens' book and design principles a reflection of a cosmopolitanism in mid-century British culture that cultivated an openness to other cultures.[7] Sloboda argues that the internationalism of the later Victorian period begins in mid-century and grows out of the Great Exhibition, reflected in Jones's "model for a new style of British design that was at once radical, orientalist, cosmopolitan and modern" and was itself an outgrowth of "political radicalism, imperial expansion, and the growth of nationalism of the period."[8] In this regard his work anticipated Morris and echoed A. W. N. Pugin and John Ruskin in recognizing the "lack of integrity between style and culture," though, unlike the others, Jones favored industrial materials and machines.[9]

What differentiated Morris's efforts from Cole's or Jones's efforts was that Morris sought a historical precedent for this aesthetic joining of high art and design, while Cole and Jones sought to find universal principles linking craft with manufacture. Jones noted, "[n]o improvement can take place in the Art of the present generation until all classes, Artists, Manufacturers, and the Public, are better educated in Art, and the existence of general principles is more fully recognized."[10] His reference to artists was to artisans and to

"Art" was to design principles. Unlike Jones's universalism, Morris wanted his designs to provide a familiar, even local nature with common plants and believable patterns of growth in simple wallpapers such as *Daisy* or *Jasmine*. In deliberate opposition to the theories of the South Kensington School of Design, Morris emphasized the process as well as the product. His chintzes, carpets, tapestries, and embroideries were produced using natural vegetable dyes and time-consuming skills he had to learn from books and objects.

Furthermore, unlike Jones's advocacy of the "conventionalizing of natural forms" along with repetition and a belief in underlying principles beneath the variety of forms in the world, Morris sought less to conventionalize natural forms than to maintain their distinctness. His designs individualized images, making the plants and birds in his designs identifiable, as they were often distinctly British and interrelated in an ecology represented by his designs. His patterns were based on British flora and fauna and inspired by the British vernacular or domestic craft traditions. *Strawberry Thief* was inspired by an incident in the Kelmscott garden, in which thrushes stole fruit from underneath strawberry nets. *Willow* was inspired by trees along the river where Morris used to fish.

While Jones's concept of nature was universalized and fixed, Morris's nature remained distinct, identifiable, and linked to both nation and locale. While understanding nature as observable, Jones denied the historicity of nature, something Morris did not deny, but sought to revive, as he sought to revive older plants or to display British birds and garden paraphernalia, such as trellises. Jones did comment on specific plants, for example, according to "systematic botany (the study of kinds and relationships) and according to structural botany (the study according to structure and parts)," describing leaves, for example, as in perfect proportions in their shapes, while grouping styles by cultures and shared formal principles.[11] Yet, Morris worked in the opposite direction of Jones, by emphasizing the locality, rather than the universality, of his images.

In "The Nature of Gothic," John Ruskin decried the division of labor in industry that prevented workers from using their imagination and enjoying their work. This idea was central to Morris's craft production as well. As a practitioner of crafts, which Ruskin was not, Morris was involved in the founding of the National Association for the Advancement of Art and Its Application to Industry in 1887, along with other artists and some industrialists. This step represented an understanding of the symbiotic relationship between art that could improve industry, and industry that could disseminate good art and good taste to a mass public. Despite its intentions, however, the Association lasted three years and had very few industrialists among its members.[12]

Morris did share the taste of Jones and Cole, as reflected in the 1852 "Chamber of Horrors" exhibition displaying poor quality designs marked by an illusionism declared unfit for decorative objects. As Sloboda notes,

> To ornament is to put something in its proper social relation, to enact its status or its function through the marking of the surface. In this way, decoration has a performative aspect—it calls into being that which it represents. According to Jones and his colleagues, unreformed mid-nineteenth-century design failed to perform its modernity, tending instead to provide naturalistic illusions that were unrelated to either the circumstances of production (the machine) or its intended site (flat architectural space). Their brand of design reform was concerned with this performative aspect of decoration and saw flat, geometric forms abstracted from nature as an enactment of imperial and industrial, or in their words, "scientific," modernity.[13]

In terms of the "flat" aesthetic, Morris, too, rejected popular illusionism in rugs and wallpapers, as bad as using one material to imitate another material, another popular Victorian manufacturing practice. Nikolaus Pevsner claimed a modernism for Morris's innovative designs in his crafts and typography, arguing that Morris and contemporaries like Christopher Dresser's paramodern style—flat and colorful with geometricized or organic curvilinear forms—anticipated Art Nouveau and later modernisms like Fauvism.[14]

Beyond style, Morris's modernism expanded to inject agency into crafts. Alfred Gell noted that the specifics of ornamentation have agency to bind people to things, an idea that also levels differences between craft and art. For Gell, all art, decorative or "fine," have social agency as part and parcel of complex social relationships in a culture. Thus, crafts, like paintings or sculpture, can be read and interpreted for meaning and for the expression of social and power relations.[15] As scholars have noted, Morris's attention to crafts was part of his overall social critique, recognizing as he did that craft production was part of Victorian power relations and the social network, despite his frustration with largely serving wealthy clients. It was generally understood that painting and sculpture conveyed complex meanings related to, embodying and expressing, power and networks, while crafts were only "ornamental," rather than essential to an idea or structure, a denigration underlined by crafts' association with colonized societies and factory production.[16]

One class-related issue is certainly the nature and role of luxury items in the context of Morris's well-to-do clientele.[17] In this regard, Morris's furnishings-turned-luxury items were a continuation of the sale of high-end furnishings from 17th- and 18th-century France, a growing business among antique dealers from the early 19th century. But despite the vagaries of the market and manufacturing that Morris regretted, he, like Ruskin, considered the separation of the intellectual act of design from the manual act of physical creation as both socially and aesthetically damaging. Morris insisted that no work should be carried out in his workshops before he had personally mastered the appropriate techniques and materials himself, a model of this union of mind and hand. Morris feared that "without dignified, creative human occupation people became disconnected from life."[18] He angrily perceived the irony of his failure to bring art to working people. Visiting his client, ironmaster Sir Isaac Lowthian Bell, Morris exclaimed furiously, "I spend my life ministering to the swinish luxury of the rich."[19]

In the Victorian period, despite disingenuous explanations about the value of painting and sculpture that had developed since the Renaissance to raise the status of painters and sculptors and proclaim their activities as intellectual, rather than manual labor, one vital difference between crafts and art in the Victorian period was social class. The pitiful showing of British goods in 1851 led Cole to conclude that design schools, intended to train the working classes in craft skills and keep that training distinct from the fine art training in the Royal Academy, had failed and needed an overhaul. Indeed, by the end of the century, after the golden age of painters' successes and the publicly displayed wealth of artists such as John Everett Millais and Frederic Leighton, photographed in the press and in books in their large studios, there was a flood of people identifying themselves as artists. Marcus Huish expressed annoyance over this and encouraged readers to seek employment in crafts or other professions, lest art production be overrun by amateurs, public taste decline, and competition impoverish all artists. In "Whence This Great Multitude of Painters?" (1892), Huish, editor of *The Art Journal*, lamented the excessive number of painters in a limited market, the blurred distinctions between professional and amateur, and the government's failure to encourage the working classes to attend design schools. This last theme resurrected a mid-century debate over the assignment of the lower classes to design schools and of the middle and upper classes to the fine arts: "now there is hardly a household of which one member does not belong either professionally or as an amateur, to the artistic community. Fifty years ago the two hundred artists who exhibited at the Royal Academy and Water Colour Societies comprised almost every member of the profession; now the list of exhibiting artists extends to nearly five thousand names and it increases by hundreds yearly."[20] Societies and galleries together were listed in *The Year's Art* (edited by Huish), complete with an alphabetical list of British artists that between 1888 and 1909 had doubled in number.

As Rosemary Hill points out, even choosing a career in crafts "was a critical gesture against the hierarchies of work and class and economics that dominated the social landscape," especially for someone from Morris's class and for the teenage Morris who refused to enter the 1851 Great Exhibition with his family.[21] The fine arts and crafts have had distinctly different social, aesthetic, and cultural identities that reflect social hierarchies, economics, and politics. Morris's experiences in painting and architecture brought fine art presumptions into craft discourse. As Ray Watkinson recognized, Morris's success owed much to his early career training in the fine art of architecture. His merging of political and manufacturing ideas reflected his awareness that craft design was an "activity of society."[22] Morris borrowed from the emerging historicism of Victorian architecture and the growing interest in the histories of art and architecture that dominated such late-century publications as the interdisciplinary arts and literature journal, *The Century Guild Hobby Horse*, edited by architects Arthur Mackmurdo and Herbert Horne.[23] Architecture gave Morris a model to redefine the social relations of design and to bring design into an autonomy distinct from its subordination to architecture, modeled on the autonomy of painting in domestic settings. As Ann Compton notes,

> Taking up handicraft was not only an enactment of the ideal of unity between the arts but also a means of reclaiming an area of architectural practice deemed to have been lost. In the 1880s and 1890s architects lamented the specialism in their profession meant [*sic*] that "in the good decorative branches of craftsmanship, the architect is deprived of a good deal of his own work . . . furniture and decoration which properly belonged to him." Some practitioners went further than viewing handicraft as a means of reconnecting the profession with its past, and claimed their efforts reinvigorated the work of traditional sculptors and craft practitioners.[24]

This total art-work vision, this *Gesamtkuntswerk* ambition of architects, was embedded, too, in Morris's production of objects and his cultural transformation of craft.

Morris, architect Philip Webb, and others sought to endorse the vernacular tradition in regional architecture that was geographically and historically local, as opposed to the more common Victorian revivalism of a grammar of past styles. This insistence on the importance, and even existence of craft history, was Morris's attempt to redeem what was lost due to "specialism." Place was important to Morris, as was the historicity of craft processes in his developing vegetable dyes as an alternative to the alkaline dyes, and in 1875 spending time working on these dyes in Leek carrying out experiments at Thomas Wardle's Hencroft works. For Morris, craft tradition was not a fixed language or determined by unchanging technological practices and motifs to be repeated or imitated over and over, but was fluid, ever-changing, and fitted to cultural and social circumstances: "Tradition with Morris was something living . . . the appearance of the object was changeable, indeed, historically flexible . . . he did not completely reject the machine, but more its use by contemporary producers. He stressed the function of the machine to free the labourer from heavy and dull work, thus enabling him to be more creative and to enjoy more leisure," as exemplified by his moving from manual to more machine production, from illumination to book printing, and from embroidery to wallpaper.[25] Many good designers, including followers of Morris, did not share his resistance to industrial manufacturing but sought to use industrialization to create well-designed products. Innovative designer William Arthur Smith Benson, a follower of Morris who was not averse to industrial manufacturing, noted that Morris created "the only school of design which was not an empty echo of passed [sic] systems."[26] Benson here contrasted Morris's approach to craft production and vitality with Victorian design schools intended to improve manufacturing and to attract working-class students, while treating design as mechanical copying, rather than as creative and imaginative.

A second presumption of the fine arts was a developmental historical awareness of relationships from present back to past, from past to present, and from past and present to the future, a linearity that dominates the understanding of painting and sculpture still (e.g., that Renaissance or Victorian art derived from classical antiquity). Fine art embraced a structure of allusion, in which a work overtly or implicitly alluded to past art. Aware, perhaps painfully aware, of the canon of past artists, which weighed heavily on Victorian artists' anxieties of influences, painters and sculptors learned by copying and studying the art of the past. Victorians were attracted to and haunted by Renaissance art, increasingly available in the National Gallery and by an emerging neo-classicism that came to dominate Aestheticism, inspired in large part by the presence of the British Museum's Elgin marbles that so many Victorian artists studied at length.

Morris applied this historical awareness to crafts. In crafts, traditions and skills were often passed down in families, but industrialization led to a deskilling, as skills were lost and factories took over the manufacture of craft objects. Morris actively sought out the skills and materials of past craft production, probably inventing a few in his resistance to industrialism, but, in any case, trying to revive and modernize whatever passed as "tradition." The improved status of crafts and the decorative arts was wide-ranging in Morris's companies' production of painted furniture, mural decoration, metalware, glass, embroidery and hangings, jewelry, hand-painted tiles, and wallpaper. Morris's zeal was a multi-pronged reply to the poor quality of manufacturing design, the previous government schools promoted by Henry Cole, and the global collection of crafts in the South Kensington Museum gathered from the imperial appropriation of objects that re-situated these objects' places from the colonies to Britain in the museum's narrative of objects. His insistence on historical change and social content in crafts was tied to his understanding of architecture and of restoration as requiring a full knowledge of past styles and technologies in order not to leave behind "history in the gap," in carrying out restoration.[27] Morris in his lecture on pattern-designing, perhaps one of the most "minor" arts, recognized this dual historicity:

> The first is archaic, in style at least, if not always in date. It is mostly priestly and symbolic; lacking, willingly or not, the power of expressing natural facts definitely and accurately . . . limited, incomplete, often grotesque in its form, its bodily part. The other ancient art is only priestly and symbolic accidentally . . . since this priestly symbolism clung to it, it . . . used it and expressed it; but would as willingly and easily have expressed purely intellectual or moral ideas. . . . [I]t has perfectly attained the power of expressing what thoughts it allows itself.[28]

Morris combined historical identity of art with a notion of authenticity or genuineness that was associated with craft production. Characteristic of the relationship between creator and artwork was the belief that great art expressed the artist's ardent beliefs. This was an ideal but not the reality: Renaissance artists creating religious works were not necessarily religious themselves (e.g., Perugino, according to Georgio Vasari's *Lives of the Artists* [1550], a text popular with Victorians). Crafts were presumed not to express personal beliefs and their authenticity was a matter of technical skills. But artisanal individual expression was acknowledged in Ruskin's ideal medieval carver in *Stones of Venice*. Michaela Braesel's notion of authenticity in relation to time and art history offers a wider understanding of Morris's transformation of crafts by historicity and expressivity:

> Here the term not only means the concept of fitness to material, production and purpose, as it was so influential for the designers of the 20th century, but also fitness to time. The first aspect is referred to as "integrity," the second as "expressive authenticity" . . . concerned with the inherent values of a work of art and its meaning for its contemporary audience . . . the actual relevance of the work of art to its own time in a period that favoured imitations and variations of historical styles.[29]

This consciousness embodied by the material object—that it relates to its own time and comments on that time and that relationship—is one of the foremost features that defined the fine arts, distinguished it from craft, and suggested the agency of the artwork that expressed this contemporaneity. Morris brought this consciousness into the making of craft objects; he defied the idea that furnishings' relationship to time was capricious or merely fashionable. Morris brought furnishings into a temporal relationship with their own period, while also harking back to a Renaissance time when artists not only made paintings, but also designed furniture, wall decoration, and tapestries. Bringing art history to bear on his craft production, "Morris established in his work a close correspondence between practical methods and historical period."[30]

Late-century fine arts, too, in turn, were affected by Morris's innovative views about the significance and historicity of crafts. Martina Droth describes the effects on the New Sculptors of the 1880s of the elevation of decoration into fine art discourses:

> Following a period of strict containment in the earlier part of the century, when sculpture was identified largely with classicizing principles, broader influences began to permeate its parameters, setting out new aesthetic preferences. . . . By employing forms and characters drawn from decorative arts and crafts, sculpture in the late nineteenth century began to be redefined on different terms. Unlike neoclassical sculpture, which operated within a rarefied, self-contained sphere, . . . that underlined its separateness from the world, the New Sculpture reached outside conventional boundaries and actively engaged with the material world, thus addressing, rather than staying aloof from, contemporaneous political and critical issues affecting art practice.[31]

More recently, the material turn across disciplines has opened the door to many new studies by art historians of interiors, furnishings and objets d'art. Michael Yonan argues,

> for viewing material culture not as a methodology but rather as a meta-methodology, an ontological awareness that can inflect many critical techniques used to explain objects of all kinds . . . the scholarly project of material culture has potentially valuable things to gain from some traditional concerns of art history, but that these paradoxically may have little to do with "art" as a category of human manufacture. Rather, art history can form a model for examining the materiality of diverse sorts of objects well beyond the category of high art.[32]

NOTES

1. Morris, "The Lesser Arts," *The Collected Works of William Morris*, vol. 22, edited by May Morris, 3–4. Cambridge: Cambridge University Press, 2012.

2. Christina M. Anderson and Catherine L. Futter, "The Decorative Arts within Art Historical Discourse: Where Is the Dialogue Now and Where Is It Heading?" *Journal of Art Historiography* 11 (December 2014): 2.

3. Peter Stansky, *Redesigning the World: William Morris, the 1880s and the Arts and Crafts* (Princeton: Princeton University Press, 1985), 3.

4. I will be using design and craft as one category, even though they are not identical, of course, but their interests and discourses are overlapping, while both areas remain quite distinct from art history still.

5. Cole was a leading member of the commission that organized the Great Exhibition of 1851, and after the exhibition closed he was made secretary to the School of Design, which became, in 1853, the Department of Science and Art. Under its auspices was the South Kensington (now Victoria and Albert) Museum, with Cole as its director until 1873.

6. Rémi Labrusse, "Grammars of Ornament: Dematerialization an Embodiment from Owen Jones to Paul Klee," in *Histories of Ornament from Global to Local*, eds. Gülru Necipoğlu and Alina Payne (Princeton: Princeton University Press, 2016), 321.

7. Stacey Sloboda, "'The Grammar of Ornament': Cosmopolitanism and Reform in British Design," *Journal of Design History* 21, no. 3 (2008): 223–24.

8. Sloboda, "Grammar," 225.

9. Ibid., 225.

10. Owen Jones, *Grammar of Ornament*. 1856. (New York: DK Publishing, 2001), 37. Cited in Sloboda, "Grammar," 28.

11. John Kresten Jespersen, "Originality and Jones's 'The Grammar of Ornament' of 1856," *Journal of Design History* 21, no. 2 (2008): 150.

12. Martin J. Wiener, *English Culture and the Decline of the Industrial Spirit, 1850–1980*. 2nd ed. (Cambridge: Cambridge University Press, 2004), 179.

13. Sloboda, "Grammar," 227–28.

14. Nicholas Pevsner, *Pioneers of Modern Design: From William Morris to Walter Gropius*. Rev. ed. (London: Penguin, 1960), 12–57.

15. Alfred Gell, *Art and Agency: An Anthropological Theory* (Oxford: Clarendon, 1998), 24.

16. See Julie Codell, "Indian Crafts and Imperial Policy: Hybridity, Purification and Imperial Subjectivities," in *Material Cultures, 1740–1920: The Meanings and Pleasures of Collecting*, eds. Alla Myzelev and John Potvin (Aldershot: Ashgate, 2009), 149–70, on these issues of imperialism and the restructuring of Indian craft production, a concern of Morris's, as well, since he greatly admired Indian crafts.

17. As Adrian Rifkin notes, the art world, including Jones, tried "to imagine and to produce a kind of field of force that will hold the anarchistic processes of production and consumption in an ideal order. The cost of art here will balance out with the cost of education there, as taste and social order interweave themselves through the profitability of skill and sales, and knowledge of and contentment with one's place in the social structure . . . that left the commodity status of the object at the centre of different and conflicting political and social desires. One has only to recall the role of luxury objects in the life and work of William Morris, and in particular the class play of their de-fetishization in *News from Nowhere*. . . . The integrity of luxury consumption was inscribed at the very centre of the processes of coming to know, to organize, and to oppose the industrial system" (Adrian Rifkin, "Success Disavowed:

The Schools of Design in Mid-Nineteenth-Century Britain (An Allegory)," *Journal of Design History* 1, no. 2 [1988]: 101, fn 2).

18. Fiona MacCarthy, "Morris, William (1834–1896)," in *Oxford Dictionary of National Biography* (Oxford: Oxford University Press, 2004); online ed.

19. Fiona MacCarthy, *William Morris: A Life for Our Time* (New York: Knopf, 1995), 210.

20. Marcus Huish, "Whence This Great Multitude of Painters?" *The Nineteenth Century* 32 (1892): 720.

21. Rosemary Hill, *The Eye of the Beholder: Criticism and Crafts*. The 2001 Peter Dormer Lecture (London: Royal College of Art, 2001), 6. I wish to thank Rosemary Hill for generously sharing a copy of this lecture that is now out of print.

22. Ray Watkinson, *William Morris as Designer* (London: Trefoil, 1990), 68.

23. Julie Codell, "*The Century Guild Hobby Horse*: 1886–1894," *Victorian Periodicals Review* 16 (1983).

24. Ann Compton, "Building a Better Class of Craft Practitioner," in *Art Versus Industry? New Perspectives on Visual and Industrial Cultures in Nineteenth-Century Britain*, eds. Kate Nichols, Rebecca Wade, and Gabriel Williams (Manchester: Manchester University Press, 2016), 194.

25. Michaela Braesel, "William Morris and 'Authenticity,'" *Reading Matters: William Morris's Legacy* 15 (2009), University of Quebec. Accessed April 3, 2019, http://www.uqtr.ca/AE/Vol_15/ReadingMatters/Reading_matters_Braesel.htm.

26. W. A. S. Benson, "William Morris and the Arts and Crafts," *National Review* 34, no. 199 (1899): 268.

27. This comment is cited by Peter Burman, "Defining a Body of Tradition: Philip Webb," in *From William Morris: Building Conservation and the Arts and Crafts Cult of Authenticity, 1877–1939*, ed. C. Miele (New Haven, CT: Yale University Press, 2005), 79–80, and comes from the Manifesto of SPAB often credited to Morris but profoundly influenced by, if not co-authored by, Philip Webb.

28. William Morris, "The History of Pattern-Designing" in *The Collected Works of William Morris*, vol. 22, edited by May Morris (Cambridge University Press, 2012), 210.

29. Braesel, "Authenticity."

30. Ibid.

31. Martina Droth, "The Ethics of Making: Craft and English Sculptural Aesthetics c. 1851–1900," *Journal of Design History* 17, no. 3 (2004): 223.

32. Michael Yonan, "Toward a Fusion of Art History and Material Culture Studies," *West 86th: A Journal of Decorative Arts, Design History, and Material Culture* 18, no. 2 (2011): 234.

BIBLIOGRAPHY

Anderson, Christina M. and Catherine L. Futter. "The Decorative Arts within Art Historical Discourse: Where Is the Dialogue Now and Where Is It Heading?" *Journal of Art Historiography* 11 (December 2014): 1–9.

Benson, W. A. S. "William Morris and the Arts and Crafts," *National Review* 34, no. 199 (Sept. 1899): 268–71.

Braesel, Michaela. "William Morris and 'Authenticity,'" *Reading Matters: William Morris's Legacy* 15 (2009), University of Quebec. Accessed April 3, 2019, http://www.uqtr.ca/AE/Vol_15/ReadingMatters/Reading_matters_Braesel.htm.

Burman, Peter. "Defining a Body of Tradition: Philip Webb." In *From William Morris: Building Conservation and the Arts and Crafts Cult of Authenticity, 1877–1939*, edited by C. Miele, 67–99. New Haven, CT: Yale University Press, 2005.

Codell, Julie. "*The Century Guild Hobby Horse*: 1886–94," *Victorian Periodicals Review* 16 (1983): 43–52.

———."Indian Crafts and Imperial Policy: Hybridity, Purification and Imperial Subjectivities." In *Material Cultures, 1740–1920: The Meanings and Pleasures of Collecting*, edited by Alla Myzelev and John Potvin, 149–70. Aldershot: Ashgate, 2009.

Compton, Ann. "Building a Better Class of Craft Practitioner." In *Art Versus Industry? New Perspectives on Visual and Industrial Cultures in Nineteenth-Century Britain*, edited by Kate Nichols, Rebecca Wade, and Gabriel Williams, 181–98. Manchester: Manchester University Press, 2016.

Droth, Martina. "The Ethics of Making: Craft and English Sculptural Aesthetics c. 1851–1900," Special issue on relationships between design, craft and art, edited by G Lees-Maffei and L. Sandino. *Journal of Design History* 17, no. 3 (2004): 221–35.

Gell, Alfred. *Art and Agency: An Anthropological Theory*. Oxford: Clarendon, 1998.

Hill, Rosemary. *The Eye of the Beholder: Criticism and Crafts*. The 2001 Peter Dormer Lecture. London: Royal College of Art, 2001.

Huish, Marcus. "Whence This Great Multitude of Painters?" *The Nineteenth Century* 32 (1892): 720–32.

Jespersen, John Kresten, "Originality and Jones's 'The Grammar of Ornament' of 1856," *Journal of Design History* 21, no. 2 (Summer 2008): 143–53.

Jones, Owen, *The Grammar of Ornament*.1856. New York: DK Publishing, 2001.

Labrusse, Rémi, "Grammars of Ornament: Dematerialization an Embodiment from Owen Jones to Paul Klee," in *Histories of Ornament from Global to Local*, edited by Gülru Necipoğlu and Alina Payne, 320–33. Princeton: Princeton University Press, 2016.

MacCarthy, Fiona. *William Morris: A Life for Our Time*. New York: Knopf, 1995.

———. "Morris, William (1834–1896)." In *Oxford Dictionary of National Biography*. Oxford University Press, 2004; online ed., Oct. 2009. Accessed Nov. 24, 2018.

Morris, William. "The History of Pattern-Designing." In *The Collected Works of William Morris*, Vol. 22, edited by May Morris, 206–34. Cambridge: Cambridge University Press, 2012.

———. "The Lesser Arts," *The Collected Works of William Morris*, Vol. 22, edited by May Morris, 3–27. Cambridge: Cambridge University Press, 2012.

Pevsner, Nicholas. *Pioneers of Modern Design: From William Morris to Walter Gropius*. Rev. ed. London: Penguin, 1960.

Rifkin, Adrian. "Success Disavowed: The Schools of Design in Mid-Nineteenth-Century Britain (An Allegory)," *Journal of Design History* 1, no. 2 (1988): 89–102.

Sloboda, Stacey. "'The Grammar of Ornament': Cosmopolitanism and Reform in British Design," *Journal of Design History* 21, no. 3 (Autumn 2008): 223–36.

Stansky, Peter. *Redesigning the World: William Morris, the 1880s and the Arts and Crafts*. Princeton: Princeton University Press, 1985.

Watkinson, Ray. *William Morris as Designer*. London: Trefoil, 1990.

Wiener, Martin J. *English Culture and the Decline of the Industrial Spirit, 1850–1980*. 2nd ed. Cambridge: Cambridge University Press, 2004.

Yonan, Michael, "Toward a Fusion of Art History and Material Culture Studies," *West 86th: A Journal of Decorative Arts, Design History, and Material Culture* 18, no. 2 (Fall–Winter 2011): 232–48.

Part V

DIGITAL HUMANITIES

Chapter Seventeen

Morris for Many Audiences
Teaching with the William Morris Archive
Florence Boos

Over the years I have introduced Morris's works to a variety of groups—political gatherings, undergraduate and graduate students, conference attendees, and general cultural audiences. As a teacher I've assigned his essays, shorter and longer poems (among them *Sigurd the Volsung* and *The Pilgrims of Hope*), early prose tales such as "The Story of the Unknown Church" and long prose narratives such as *The Water of the Wondrous Isles,* and even his comic skit, "The Tables Turned, or Nupkins Awakened." Audience matters; graduate students have seized on all of these eagerly and have submitted essays on such topics as gender ambiguity in "Concerning Geffray Teste Noire," Morris's Icelandic diaries as an exploration of masculinity, or "The Unknown Church" as a response to the Crimean War.

For my most numerous audience, however, that of undergraduate students, my attempts to present Morris's literary works have met with varying degrees of success: the medieval settings can seem remote; rhymed poetry can elicit impatience; women's domestic roles in *News from Nowhere* evoke feminist censure; and even in an age of science fiction, *Nowhere*'s call to remake our future can discomfit those partial to marriage plots and conflict. In each situation, however, some students seem to take Morris's artistic aims and political insights to heart, and for these his works embody ideals seldom found elsewhere in the curriculum. In what follows I will describe approaches and teaching aids that have worked well and others I am still developing or would like to attempt. These share some common elements: they are highly visual; they present questions or puzzles to answer; they emphasize the interdisciplinary aspects of Morris's work; they focus on the details of a specific text; and/or they take the form of a project or group effort. Most of these approaches rely on online materials accessible to all teachers of Morris from the online William Morris Archive or from the art galleries and study questions available on my teaching website.[1]

THE DEFENCE OF GUENEVERE AND RELATED ARTWORKS

When teaching *The Defence of Guenevere,* before we discuss any of the poems, I ask one of the students to present a brief biography of Morris, after which I show slides of Morris and Co. textiles, tapestries, stained glass, and illuminated manuscripts.[2] Explaining all the available images would consume more than a class session, so for brevity I select out a few examples of the Firm's earlier and later styles, asking students if they can imagine any possible correlations between Morris's designs and his poetry (e. g., patterns of entrapment and release). Viewing examples of Morris & Co. stained glass enables them to see the Arthurian and romance interests of Morris's generation of Pre-Raphaelites, as in the 1862 "Tristram and Isoude" sequence. And as preparation for "The Defence of Guenevere" and "King Arthur's Tomb," we consider the many embedded symbols in Morris's painting of Jane Burden in "La Belle Iseult," in which Iseult stands by her bed gazing toward her opened breviary, as she holds open her unclasped belt with its serpentine buckle. After discussing "King Arthur's Tomb," it seems helpful to compare Morris's version with Dante Gabriel Rossetti's watercolor, "Arthur's Tomb," in which Arthur's eerily lifelike effigy gazes stonily at the lovers as Lancelot reaches awkwardly toward a reluctant Guenevere. Students find Morris's poem more sympathetic to the lovers, and its presentation of their agonized quarrel adds psychological nuances less available in a drawing.

The poem that seems to evoke the most immediate response, however, is "The Haystack in the Floods," and I have found no visual equivalent for its grim narrative of frustrated desire and butchery set amid the Hundred Years' War. Students are interested in Jehane's rejection of Godmar's "offer" to spare the life of her lover Robert in exchange for accepting his advances, and this prompts debate on what may be her motives and why an alternate choice could have seemed even worse.[3]

THE KELMSCOTT PRESS

After reading any selection from Morris's 1858 *The Defence,* it seems natural to consider how the older Morris reinterpreted his youthful work after a gap of thirty-four years. The Kelmscott Press version of *The Defence* is startling in its bold rearrangement of text features: its disregard of line and stanza breaks, its

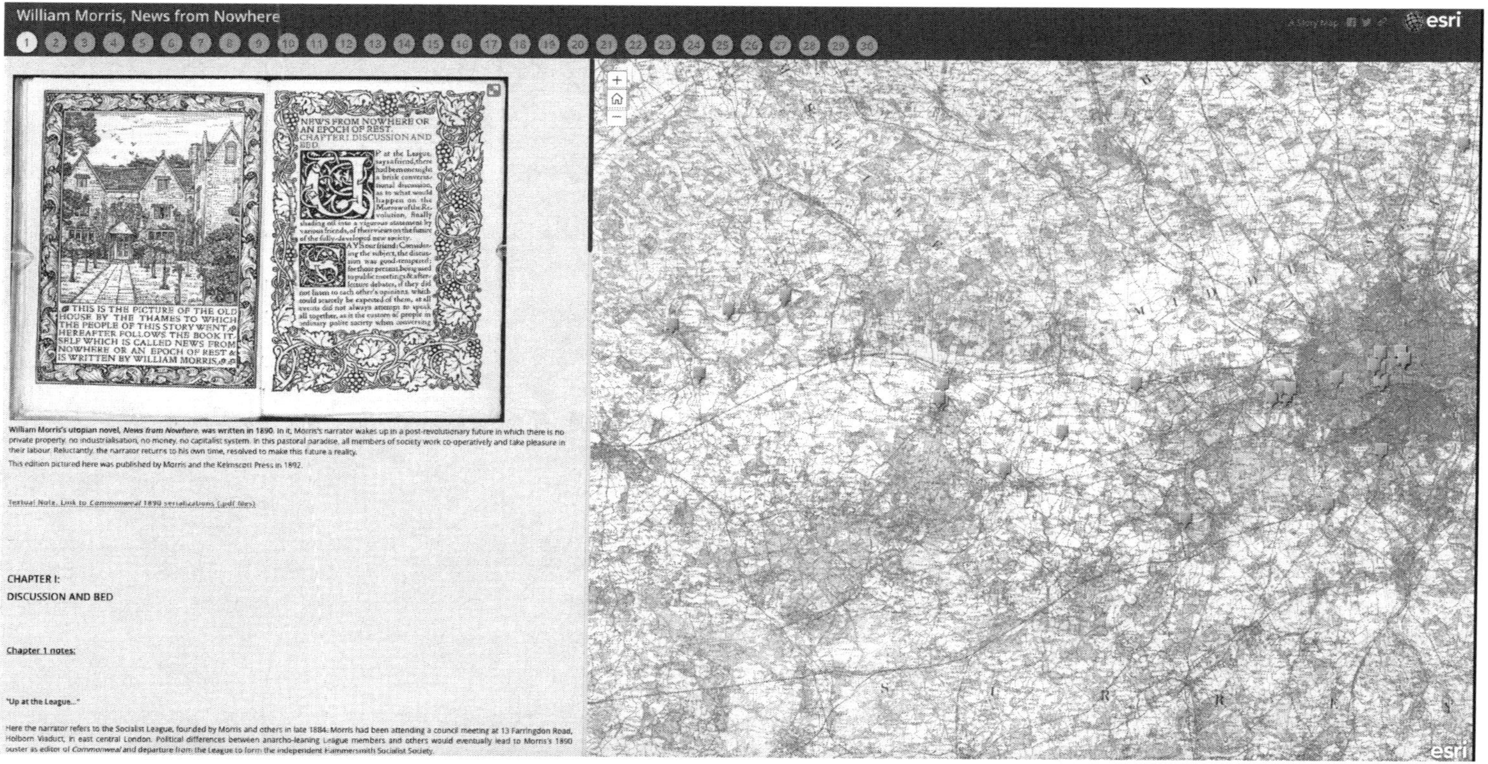

Figure 17.1. Map of the route traced in *News from Nowhere*, designed to illustrate each stage of Guest's journey, be keyed to the text, and include scroll-over notes.

Reproduced courtesy of the William Morris Archive.

rearrangement of white space, and its use of vivid black, white, and red coloring to suggest intensity and violence, as well as its exhibition of the familiar Kelmscott Press features of non-serif font, ornamented initials, and the careful placement of leaves and other ornaments to limit white space.[4]

The examination of selected Kelmscott Press pages leads to a discussion of what aesthetic goals may have prompted Morris's typographical innovations, and how the worlds of art and typography had changed between 1858 and 1892. At this point I show students selections from my gallery of Kelmscott Press images, pointing out the increasing sophistication of the lettering, borders, and title pages between 1891 and 1896, as well as Morris's rare experiments with blue and red lettering and his care to preserve symmetry and balance within each opening (double-spread page) of the text. All this segues into examining the symbolism and artistry of the title page of the iconic Chaucer, in which the medieval tax collector is refashioned as a solitary poet who listens to singing birds within his rural garden, as he stands by a well imaging his sobriquet as "the well of English undefiled." In conclusion I then show some of the Kelmscott Press's large decorated word initials, and I find students enjoy puzzling out the letters in such tours de force as "Whan," "Whilom, "Then," and even the mildly parodic "O Hateful."

VISITING SPECIAL COLLECTIONS: THE MOST POPULAR CLASS SESSION OF THE SEMESTER

Viewing slides of Kelmscott Press books provides an excellent preparation for visiting the Special Collections department (if one is available). For this visit the librarian and I select samples of nineteenth-century books for display, including illustrated volumes of poetry and fiction as well as periodicals, fine press books, and of course, everything published by Morris or issued by the Kelmscott Press. The librarian and I provide some background on nineteenth century printing technologies (changes in paper, bindings, and techniques for illustration), and explain why Morris reacted against earlier nineteenth-century print formats. We also describe his use of vellum and other bindings, the choice of ink and paper, the creation of decorative initials and a colophon, and his elegant patterning of spaces, text, and ornament within each page and opening.

At this point the students examine each book. I prepare a handout of questions to help focus their thoughts (see appendix A) and assign a one page response essay. These responses have been gratifyingly enthusiastic, exhibiting a sense of personal discovery. In this day of digitization, seeing and handling an antiquarian book can give surprising pleasure, and for some students this visit may have been their first chance to examine a nineteenth-century book.

NEWS FROM NOWHERE IN ITS NINETEENTH-CENTURY SETTING: AN ILLUSTRATED JOURNEY

North American students who have never seen London or visited England can lose much of the humor and pleasure of Guest's travels through a city and countryside well-known to *News*' original audience. Moreover much of the utopian meaning of the text is conveyed through exhibiting the many ways in which *Nowhere*'s imagined future London and Oxfordshire countryside both resemble and differ from their 1890 counterparts. To help bridge this gap, along with others I have created an illustrated *News from Nowhere*.[5] Presenting at least part of this sequence in class enables a teacher to explain some of the text's many contemporary allusions.

At a basic level, it is important to understand *News*'s sociology and geography, as the characters make their way eastward from Morris's Hammersmith home (the Guest House) through the more prosperous Kensington and from thence to crowded Piccadilly, after which they pass through the central gathering place of Trafalgar Square, visit the more intellectual reaches of Bloomsbury and the British Museum, and at length navigate what would have been in the 1890s an impoverished region of tenements and open sewers. And finally, the sequence during which Dick, Guest, Ellen, and Clara row northwest up the Thames enables students to see concrete examples of the bridges, waterways, buildings, and landscapes that Morris wished to preserve.

Several of the characters' observations are rendered clearer by images: why did Morris find the underground railway so dirty and noisy, for example (for this, see the photograph of a nineteenth-century train interior); why was Guest surprised at the absence of poor "country" people in Hammersmith market (see the image of contemporary farmworkers); or what may have prompted his recuperation of the Palace of Westminster as a hub for recycling (photograph of the Houses of Parliament and discussion of why Morris might have disapproved of Charles Barry's design). Other places in the text require more complicated explanations, however, and these are much aided by images: Chapter 10's references to Fourierism and phalansteries are helped by some knowledge of what a phalanstery would have looked like; and Old Hammond's remarks on the blending of town and country are more meaningful in the context of contemporary ideas on how to mitigate the contrasting limitations of both urban and rural life, as publicized later in the decade by Ebenezer Howard in his *Garden Cities of Tomorrow*.

Old Hammond's forceful attack on the waging of imperialist wars to feed the "World Market" and his references to explorer Henry Morton Stanley are usefully glossed by understanding that the latter's forays into "darkest Africa" were on behalf of the notoriously brutal King Leopold of Belgium, ruler of the Belgian Congo; the illustrated *News* depicts the king and Stanley, the latter with a black servant.

In the context of US mass incarceration and for profit prisons, one of *News from Nowhere*'s most relevant contributions is its repeated condemnation of the use of imprisonment as a means of social control, as in chapter 7, where Dick exclaims after learning that nineteenth-century governments have imprisoned peaceful protesters, "And how could [people] look happy if they knew that their neighbors were shut up in prison . . . Prisons indeed! O no, no, no!"[6] Morris's critique here always elicits some protest from my students, who are inured to a high level of imprisonment, but it also prompts discussion of the flaws of our current severe drug laws and excessively punitive penal system. The illustrated *News* depicts drawings of prisoners on a treadmill and the interior of a nineteenth-century prison.

Finally, it would be difficult to appreciate the book's conclusion without a sense of the exterior of Kelmscott Manor, as in chapter 31 Ellen places her arms on one of its lichened walls and exclaims, "Oh me! O me! How I love the earth, and the seasons, and weather, and all things that deal with it and all that grows out of it—as this has done!"; or its interior, the site of Guest's profoundly sad reflections on human history: "And even now . . . my heart is sickened with thinking of all the waste of life that has gone on for so many years!"[7] Likewise the painful rupture of the final dinner scene is mirrored in the simplicity of the small Kelmscott Church and its surrounding cemetery, where six years later Morris himself would be interred. The series thus ends fittingly with a photograph of Kelmscott church and the gravestone designed by Philip Webb for his friend.

Although the illustrated *News from Nowhere* has been upgraded since its inception, the quality of images could use further updating, and I hope to continue to improve it. As the next section indicates, I am also working on a version of the illustrated *News* that will link to a larger digital map of Guest's journey.

A COURSE BASED ON THE WILLIAM MORRIS ARCHIVE

As one of the great nineteenth-century theorists of work and pleasure, Morris observed in "The Society of the Future" that there were two approaches to a problem, "the analytical [theoretical] and the constructive [creative]," and that he himself favored the latter method.[8] A digital archive would seem an ideal site for combining these two approaches: the setting of abstract "analytic" goals and their practical "constructive" application. Moreover in the spirit of Morris such a project should be cooperative, as he advised, "[F]ind out what you yourselves find pleasant, and do it. You won't be alone in your desires; you will get plenty to help you in carrying them out, and you will develop social life in developing your own special tendencies."[9]

In 2016 the Iowa Digital Studio suggested that I offer an English department graduate course in the Digital Humanities using the William Morris Archive as the basis for student projects. In what follows I will describe the mixed results.

My goals for the course were multiple. Although I wanted students to enjoy acquiring some new techniques, I also wished them to learn to appreciate editing as a process. More importantly, I hoped to inspire enthusiasm for the complexity of Morris's texts, and for the added value of approaching them in multiple contexts: through examining his processes of composition, learning from the insights of earlier commentators, researching their literary or mythological contexts, or pondering the philological implications of his word choices. I hoped that in experiencing the difficulties of digital editing, they might also come to grasp its importance and to set about conceiving and designing such projects on their own.

To these ends, we read and discussed several articles on editorial and digital scholarship by Jerome McGann, Elena Pierazzo, Johanna Drucker, and others. I then walked them through the William Morris Archive in detail, explaining what problems we had faced and noting the many items still needing correction or implementation. We also benefitted from a session offered by a visiting scholar, Matthew Hannah, who demonstrated the use of Juxta, a versioning program that simplifies the comparison or collation of textual variants; and Voyant, a software program which enables analysis of word frequency and juxtapositions in attractive visual forms. In addition, the project manager of the Whitman Archive, Stephanie Blalock, visited our class to demonstrate the purposes and nature of TEI-coding, usefully laying out some uncertainties and obstacles which the Whitman Archive had faced in applying its principles. A Digital Studio presentation explained some of the features of Omeka, a file management and indexing program that after June 2020 will house the William Morris Archive, and a digital librarian explained to the graduate students how to use features of Arcgis, a map-creating program.

Each graduate student was asked to create a project during the semester. My own preference would have been for class members to complete an edition of one of the Archive's yet unedited texts, working either singly or collaboratively to prepare as many of the following as possible: an introduction, a corrected text, annotations, transcriptions of earlier drafts, a list of variants, and supplemental materials such as contemporary reviews, critical commentaries, or maps. Since a digital edition can be completed in stages, the addition of even a few of these elements would nonetheless have constituted progress toward a future completed work. Such a project, I believed, would have the advantage of actual use value; it would offer immediate practice in editing; and ideally it could become part of the Archive and thus provide its creators with a digital publication.

As it happened, the graduate students chose to prepare in collaboration a map of the route traced in *News from Nowhere*, designed to illustrate each stage of Guest's journey, be keyed to the text, and include scroll-over notes. As they began, they quickly learned to use basic features of the necessary mapping programs, and they readily created an initial map of the relevant sites as they now exist through Google, and keyed these places into an Excel list of places and images. At this point, however, the project foundered: delay was caused by the search for perfect maps of 1890 London and Oxford, allegedly only available in downloadable form from the National Library of Scotland, and which when obtained were, in the end, far too detailed for use. Moreover the enjoyment of map programs in theory didn't translate to the ability to find the relevant 1890s-era images to include; most of the annotations remained unwritten, and even the completed ones couldn't be uploaded until someone could determine how to deal with the characters' multiple returns to the same place. I myself could only provide editorial material, and in the end, everyone was dependent on the digital librarian's technical expertise to upload their material. Clearly the way of the digital is strewn with delays, and at semester's end the map-cum-commentary remained unfinished.

At the course's conclusion, to my relief the students politely claimed that all their efforts had been rewarding and educational. I believe that they did benefit from experimenting with several software programs and exploring the steps needed to create a text-linked map, and doubtless they gleaned something about the physical environs of the imagined future Nowherean society. I couldn't avoid the recognition, however, that for these students technology had constituted its own end, taking precedence over content. And although in some metaphysical sense the journey and not the arrival matters, surely one measure of success is the completion of a usable product.

Perhaps not coincidentally, the course's one clear accomplishment was created using a slightly older technology. Doctoral student Kyle Barton created a twitter account that posted several times weekly and garnered 412 followers. @MorrisArchive successfully publicized our efforts, and its #OTD [On This Day] feature also promoted some of Morris's interesting lesser-known writings. In the period surrounding the 2016 elections, it may also have made its own modest contribution to the wider political discourse, as Mr. Barton observes:

> We had not intended on using [the Twitter account] to recirculate Morris's political observations. However, while curating daily tweets we began lifting from Morris's "Notes on News" his brief, almost proto-tweet entries from *The*

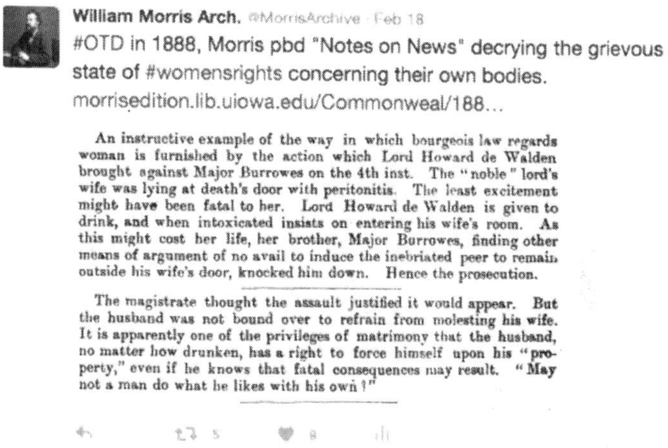

Figure 17.2. MorrisArchive Tweet, February 18, 2017.
Reproduced courtesy of the William Morris Archive.

Commonweal in which he reflected on the political problems of his moment. We quickly discovered just how relevant Morris's words remain. . . . Morris's thoughts on protest, police violence, and civil rights—amongst other issues—urgently speak to us of his moments and ours. They allow us to share his outrage, commitment to resistance, and hope.[10]

FINAL REFLECTIONS

In association with the North American Victorian Studies Association and several academic libraries, Dino Felluga and others have set up a pre-packaged template for creating a short scholarly edition with an associated timeline at COVE (Central Online Victorian Educator), and if sent the materials they will help upload them.[11] If I were to attempt a digital graduate course again, or indeed any course with a serious digital component, I would suggest the cooperative editing of the poem "The Defence of Guenevere," or any other short selection, as a text in COVE, with annotations, variants, critical references, and a timeline. The students who contributed materials to a composite and uploaded site would have a sense of completion; a link to their edition could be placed on the Archive; and the world would have a useful teaching aid. Along the way students would experience the complexity of a single Morris text as it reaches out to multiple contexts in the medieval, artistic, and contemporary worlds. Such a project would form a pragmatic compromise between the ambition to join the world of digital editing within a limited timeframe, and the need to provide commentary as well as develop specific technological skills. Kyle Barton and I have prepared a pilot version of a *Defence* poem, "Concerning Geffray Teste Noire" in such a COVE edition; once one learns the correct protocol for uploading, preparing the notes and illustrations is relatively straightforward and enjoyable.

Despite setbacks, I remained convinced that of Morris's works, *News from Nowhere* would most benefit from an annotated digital map to be used as a teaching aid. With some technical help I have continued to develop this, and a version of *News from Nowhere* created in the program "Story Maps" (storymaps.arcgis.com) is now available on the William Morris Archive.[12] Ideally, such an interactive map might inspire many short writing assignments at several levels of difficulty; at the simplest, beginning students might be asked to answer such questions as, "What stage of Morris's journey most interested you, and why?" Though such queries were of course asked and answered long before the advent of modern computers, I hope that contemporary students may pursue these answers more readily when enabled to trace Guest's journey in vivid topographical, pictorial, and digital form.

APPENDIX 1: SAMPLE ASSIGNMENT FOR SPECIAL COLLECTIONS

Please look through all the volumes on display, paying special attention to features of binding, page design, fonts, illustrations, paper quality, and choice of text. Four of the books are forgeries—Robert Browning's *Cleon* and *Gold Hair*; and Elizabeth Barrett Browning's *The Runaway Slave* and *Sonnets*.

For your next ICON posting, please write an essay in which you respond to several of the following questions:

What are some differences in the materials used for the bindings, and their quality and style? Do you notice changes as the century progressed? Is there a pattern to which kind of bindings and covers were used for which type of works?

What do you notice about the use of illustrations, and how does this change over the course of the century? What are some especially fine examples of illustrations and illustrated books?

Do the illustrations supplement and enhance the text, or are they on different or general subjects? (You might give an example of each.)

Notice especially the illustrations by Arthur Hughes, George Cruikshank, John Everett Millais, and Gustav Doré. Which types of subjects did each tend to illustrate?

What do you think of the quality of pictures in the *London Illustrated News* and other periodicals? Why did such illustrations cease to be used?

What do you notice about the paper used? The ways in which the pages are sewn into the binding? Are some of these bindings too tight or too loose?

Be sure to look at several examples of William Morris's Kelmscott Press books. What do you think may have prompted him to establish a press to make handmade books? What is different about these books? (e. g., the paper, ink, fonts, colophons, choice of texts) What seem to have been some of his principles of design?

Compare Kelmscott Press books published earlier and later in the Press's existence (1891–1896). What changes do you notice? Are there ways in which Kelmscott Press books may have influenced later book design?

After examining the forgeries, can you guess why the well-known bibliographer Thomas Wise may have chosen to issue these particular books in postdated editions rather than say, Tennyson's *Poems* of 1842 (which contained "The Lady of Shalott" and "The Lotus Eaters")?

What would be some motives for issuing a forgery? How might they have been detected?

Please select a volume, or volumes, that you find especially interesting, and describe its notable features.

NOTES

1. http://morrisedition.lib.uiowa.edu [after June 2020, http://morrisarchive.lib.uiowa.edu]; and http://victorianfboos.studio.uiowa.edu.
2. https://victorianfboos.studio.uiowa.edu/art-galleries ["William Morris and the Decorative Arts," "The Pre-Raphaelites"].
3. https://victorianfboos.studio.uiowa.edu/william-morris-defence-guenevere; and https://victorianfboos.studio.uiowa.edu/william-morris-haystack-floods.
4. http://morrisedition.lib.uiowa.edu/Poetry/Defence_of_Guenevere/Images/guenevere1892/jpeg/pageflip1-50.html.
5. http://morrisedition.lib.uiowa.edu/NewsNowhere_Illustrated/production/NewsfromNowhere/index.html; and http://morrisedition.lib.uiowa.edu/news.html [after June 2020, http://morrisedition.lib.iowa.edu/news.html].
6. See http://morrisedition.lib.uiowa.edu/NewsNowhere_Illustrated/production/NewsfromNowhere/chapter07.html.
7. See http://morrisedition.lib.uiowa.edu/NewsNowhere_Illustrated/production/NewsfromNowhere/chapter31.html.
8. William Morris, "The Society of the Future," in *The Political Writings of William Morris*, ed. A. L. Morton (London: Lawrence and Wishart, 1979), 190.
9. Ibid., 194.
10. Kyle Barton, "Morris in Our Times," *Useful and Beautiful* (2017.1): 17–18.
11. See https://editions.covecollective.org.
12. http://morrisedition.lib.uiowa.edu/newssupple.html, "An Argis Story Map." I am indebted to Sean de Vega for his help in completing this digital edition.

BIBLIOGRAPHY

Barton, Kyle. "Morris in Our Times," *Useful and Beautiful* (2017.1): 17–18.
Boos, Florence, ed. *The William Morris Archive*. http://morrisedition.lib.uiowa.edu; after June 2020, http://morrisarchive.lib.uiowa.edu.
Drucker, Johanna. "Humanistic Theory and Digital Scholarship." In *Debates in the Digital Humanities*. Minneapolis: University of Minnesota Press, 2012. http://dhdebates/gc.cuny.edu/debates/text/34.
Folsom, Ed. "Database as Genre: The Epic Transformation of Archives," *PMLA* 122 (2007): 1571–9.
Jockers, Matt. "Part 1," *Macroanalysis: Digital Methods and Literary History*, 3–32. http://search.lib.unc.edu/search?R=UNCb8103406.
McGann, Jerome. "Database, Interface, and Archival Fever," PMLA 122 (2007): 1588–92.
———. *A New Republic of Letters*. Cambridge: Harvard University Press, 2014.
McGann, Jerome, Sherry B. Orner, and Nicholas B. Dirks. *The Textual Condition*. Princeton: Princeton University Press, 1991.

Morris, May, ed. *The Collected Works of William Morris.* London: Longmans, 1910–1915.

Morris, William. "La Belle Iseult," 1858. The Tate Gallery.

———. "The Society of the Future." In *The Political Writings of William Morris*, edited by A. L. Morton, 188–203. London: Lawrence and Wishart, 1979.

Pierazzo, Elena. "Traditional and Emerging Editorial Models." In *Digital Scholarly Editing: Theories, Models and Methods*, 11–36. London: Routledge, 2015.

Rossetti, D. G. "Arthur's Tomb," 1860. The Tate Gallery.

Chapter Eighteen

William Morris on Social Media
A Personal Experience, 2007–2017

Tony Pinkney

I started what I believe to be the first-ever blog on William Morris in October 2007, just after the publication of my book *William Morris in Oxford: The Campaigning Years 1879–1895*. At the time of writing this piece (December 2017), my blog has just clocked up its first decade in existence, having now reached a tally of 400 plus posts. The first four years' worth of posts from it appeared in print as *William Morris the Blog: Digital Reflections 2007–2011* from the Kelmsgarth Press in 2011, and a second volume of selections from subsequent years may come out in due course. Within that decade of activity on the blog I also had two busy stretches of tweeting on matters Morrisian, from August 2011 to September 2012 and again from August 2013 to June 2014; these tweets remain available through a link on the blog site itself. I also made two small Morris-related films that were posted up on YouTube (more on these below). There are other Morris blogs out there now, and some strong digital Morris archives have been developed too. But this overall package of digital activity—blogging, tweeting, YouTube—constitutes at least one intensive attempt to make Morris and matters Morrisian a current force out in the realm of cyberspace. It expands the notion of "teaching Morris" well beyond the formal boundaries of the school classroom or the university seminar. As Raymond Williams used to insist about culture, however, there is no extension that is not simultaneously a transformation. So taking Morris out into the digital sphere is not just a spatial expansion, from the face-to-face relations of the classroom to the mass-anonymity of the global internet, but will also potentially transform the very meaning of teaching too, since notions of transmission, content, and reception all enter new, gray areas in this process.

With the completion of the *William Morris in Oxford* book, I felt that I had come to the end of the line with conventional, scholarly, historicist work on

Morris. In the new mediascape we inhabit in the early twenty-first century, that genre no longer felt at the cutting edge of what one could or should do with Morris, so I was eagerly on the lookout for new writing possibilities, for what Fredric Jameson in his *Adorno* book terms "the possibility of forms of writing and *Darstellung* [presentation] that unexpectedly free you from the taboos and constraints of things learnt by rote and assumed to be inscribed in the nature of things."[1] The first such venture for me was the notion of a sequel to *News from Nowhere*, picking up Morris's characters at the end of that work and taking their stories forward, sexually, culturally, and, above all, politically. I can see now, with the benefit of hindsight, that such an idea was not just a bright glitter in my own inventive eye, but was rather part of the much broader impact that the discipline of creative writing has had on traditional English studies over the last twenty years or so. There is no doubt a general lesson here: new writing possibilities, new forms, styles, and genres are not just conjured into being by sheer force of will and fiat, but must somehow inhere in material transformations that are taking place around you.

So it was that the computer on my office desk clamantly made its presence felt in these matters. Yes, one could use it as a tool to write in conventional scholarly ways, but it was also, through internet access, opening up new writing modes of its own—blogs and tweets, among others—with the possibility of a potentially global audience, perhaps particularly among the young, who were so much more attuned to these new communication technologies than I was. One might thus not just find new forms for writing about Morris, but also reach, and perhaps even politically activate, new constituencies of readers in the process. I came up with a title for this new digital venture—"William Morris Unbound"—which both paid its due to conventional historicist concerns (the Shelley reference) but also signalled the more writerly Jamesonian notion of getting free "from the taboos and constraints of things learnt by rote and assumed to be inscribed in the nature of things"—and on October 9, 2007 I got under way and wrote the world's first Morris blog post.

Of course, however new your writing platform and however distinctive the formal determinations it exercises upon you, you necessarily bring a whole package of aims, themes, and hopes to the new medium (which may or may not interact well with it in practice). I had half a dozen such expectations, as I recall. First, that I would regard the Morrisian canon as open-ended, as not yet finished, as subject to further creative writing not by the man himself now, obviously enough, but by us (this principle constituting, I suppose, a radicalization of my previous idea of a *News from Nowhere* sequel). Second, that I would view the blog, which is so much more nimble a form than the conventional academic essay or book, as an ideal forum to explore eccentric, serendipitous bypaths in and around Morris's work, thereby picking up the spirit of Fiona MacCarthy's inspirational remark that "my aim has been to reclaim Morris in the detail of his idiosyncrasy and *strangeness*."[2] Thirdly, that I would want to apply Morrisian values and politics to the present, to where and how we were living now, rather than exploring them historically in the 1880s where they first have their formulation; after all, if they are not "portable" in this sense (to borrow John Plotz's good word), we might as well not be bothering with them in the first place. In later years, this desire for contemporaneity honed itself down to the desire to reintroduce the term "communism" into debates around both Morris's own and our current politics.[3] Fourthly, that I would, in a modest way, explore the capacity of the blog form to incorporate visual images with written text, to play the two modes off against each other, so that one could, as it were, be both Morris and Burne-Jones at once. Fifthly, that I would do my best to make use of the interactive facilities a blog provides, and hopefully encourage active comment and debate around the posts I sent out into the digisphere (there was also a faint hope here that some of that response might come from a younger, more tech-savvy audience than conventional Morrisians). Another general orientation, somewhat in the background but also part of the impulse to pull Morris into the present, was that I should try to relate his work to issues in contemporary literary and cultural theory.

Well, even with general orientations, you have still got to start writing, so what form does that actually take on the new platform? Though there are no constraints of length built into a blog post—such are the glories and temptations of cyberspace!—there may nonetheless be constraints of audience attention; and I certainly had a sense from the beginning that relative brevity was important. On the other hand, you wouldn't just want to produce a very short academic essay either. I had two related formal models loosely in mind, both deriving from my early formation as a modernist scholar: the Japanese haiku, so influential upon Imagist poetry in the early twentieth century, and the modernist epiphany more generally. How might one find a blog equivalent to these, a short, tightly organized form that would shift the gears of perception and release an expansive charge of mental energy and insight? I am not sure that I have consistently lived up to this aim in my 400 or so posts; others will have to judge that rather than me. Indeed, I have a feeling that too often my posts have taken the form of a 300-word, three-paragraph intervention that rather too comfortably takes the form of thesis-antithesis-synthesis across its three divisions. This old Hegelian triad certainly does not seem entirely apt to the digital platform upon which it unfolds itself, perhaps because cyberspace, being neither present nor absent in conventional binary terms, adheres to what we might term a "logic of spectrality" that is not dialectizable. I belong to a postmodern and post-structuralist academic generation that in principle does not like syntheses, that would rather enjoy (or endure) the crackling friction of binary opposition that will not readily resolve itself on a supposedly higher plane. So how I consistently came to produce such triadic blog artefacts is something of a mystery to me.

I made a point, (at least in the earlier years), of religiously keeping the statistics for hits on my blog, so in the light of those I can offer some objective as well as subjective indicators as to how it was faring across the decade. For the first three years "William Morris Unbound" was receiving up to two thousand hits a month, which I was reasonably pleased with. Toward the end of 2012, the figures began to grow noticeably, and across 2013 they started to reach ten thousand hits a month. At the end of that year, a sudden jump to 16,390 hits for December prefigured quite extraordinary figures for much of 2014, of which I give some key samples: May = 77,006; June = 121,400; July = 125,176; August = 163,815; September = 138,168; October = 185,652. I still can't quite believe this last figure, which was the highest the blog ever scored. Numbers declined thereafter, and settled around twelve thousand hits a month by the end of 2015. The question then becomes qualitative rather than just quantitative: what kind of attention to the blog did these numbers really indicate?

That question about what the number of hits represents can probably never be fully answered: how many of them were real readers, how many just automated bots, and even when they were actual readers, what quality of attention or impact was involved? So one better way of approaching this issue might be to ask about the formal responses that these blog posts provoked across the years. The story there is very mixed. Two or three regular early commentators gradually fell away, although in later years one or two others suddenly joined the debate (I am especially grateful to Kotick for sustained commentary in recent times). And I was always very heartened by people who added their own comment on a particular topic that had meant something to them (I did my best always to reply to these, though if they were posted long after the original post itself I may not have noticed them). But over the decade of blog activity I have to concede that it has not managed to create the volume of debate and interchange that I had initially—perhaps utopianly—hoped for. At times I have felt that I was pumping stuff out there, to which there was little response. If that is then a tribute to my personal stubbornness, to have kept that up for ten years or so, one must also register the disappointment that the Morrisian "fellowship" the new medium had seemed to promise did not really materialize. Whether this was somehow my failing, a problem with the medium itself, or due to other factors altogether, who knows? Again, I am probably not the best person to make a judgment on this.

One early decision that needed to be made about the blog was whether to allow advertising to run on it. Given that Morris's own last public speech, on January 31, 1896, was to the Society for Checking the Abuses of Public Advertising, the answer might seem evident enough. However, after some rumination, I did allow advertising on the site, hoping first that it might afford some appropriate content, second that it would widen the network of connections that the blog was making, and third that it might even provide a modest trickle of income that might help sustain the blog itself (in terms of visiting exhibitions to report on, and so on). The first of these aims was partially achieved: "Coolest Political T-shirts in the UK" (May 2015), "Willow Bough Bedding Sets" (June 2015), and "Stained Glass Sidcup" (June 2012) all seem apt enough. But there was plenty of cultural and even political drift here too. Whether "Lose 4 Stone in 3 Months . . . Britain's Hottest Diet" (June 2012) was some kind of reference to Morris's ample girth, I do not know; but by the time we got to "China Top Ranked MBA" (April 2015), we had moved very far away from Morrisian purity (just as I sometimes find myself lecturing on Morris's communism in Lancaster University's Management School lecture halls).

The early numbers of hits on the blog were good enough to make me feel that I ought to give it more permanent form, which I accordingly did in *William Morris the Blog: Digital Reflections 2007–2011*. Such a move, from blogosphere to print, may not be as innocent as it seems, however. To distrust the impermanence of cyberspace in this way reveals, it could be argued, one's own personal formation in the print era; a young millennial, utterly committed to the world of the digital from birth, would probably not share such anxieties. And then one might wonder whether there is a certain Freudian effect of *Nachträglichkeit* or retroactivity here too: did the eventual possibility of book production, even if not consciously formulated at the time, secretly shape the construction of those blog posts from the very start, pulling one back from the form-shaping momentum of the new platform in its own right toward more conventional models? This, too, is something that a commentator from outside will have to make a judgement on. One interesting institutional sidelight might be worth registering here, though. My university department refused to put the Morris blog book into the ensuing Research Excellence Framework exercise, on the ground that it was not weighty enough, either in its intellectual content or in its place of publication. My argument that a 300-word blog post that floated some striking new idea was at least as intellectually worthy as a 6000-word scholarly article that simply spelled out the very same idea at plodding length across a wider variety of Morris texts was brushed cavalierly aside. So a commitment to work in digital humanities, however contemporary it may appear, risks disadvantaging you notably when research is judged according to much more traditional scholarly conventions (though it may be that the newer category of "Impact" will ultimately be more permissive here).

I once put up a post entitled "*The Earthly Paradise*: The Greatest Hits" (November 25, 2010), which attempted to establish, in a slightly ad hoc manner, which were the most anthologized of the twenty-four tales that comprise Morris's *magnum opus*. It might be helpful to turn that title self-reflexively upon my own Morris blog, and pluck out a couple of instances of what, for me at least, are its highlights, posts that achieved the goals I set myself either at the beginning of the enterprise, or as it matured and evolved in subsequent years. So I would offer, as personal favorites, from the early years, "Olympics 2012—William Morris-Style" (July 1, 2012), which ranges widely across Morris's writings to construct an alternative Olympics. Item seven here is: "shooting arrows either at a prisoner's buttocks (*The Well at the World's End*) or to kill a chaffinch on the twig one hundred yards away (*The Roots of the Mountain* again)." So this would be an example of that whimsical, exploratory mode inspired by aspects of Fiona MacCarthy's biography; and, as a general point of literary principle, I did try to give the late romances some significant prominence in my blog. My good friend Dorothy Coles, then in her 99th year, once described these to me as "the bits of Morris that even Morrisians don't read," and I wanted to do my small part in redressing that neglect.

From the later years, I would offer "Theses for a William Morris Communism Network" as exemplary. It was posted on October 10, 2014 and—in militant rather than whimsical mode—presents four theses that attempt to put this key political notion back into circulation. Thesis three reads, in part: "The return of communist thinking in our own time once again makes visible this neglected but central dimension of Morris, while his own political activism, artistic work and utopian writing make available new resources to the communist revival of the early twenty-first century. There is thus now the possibility of an invigorating conversation between communisms past and present." Communism was a notion that imposed itself upon me in the course of these blog years; it certainly was not there among my founding aims and hopes as listed above, though perhaps, in ways I hadn't fully seen at the time, it may have been implicit in them. Coming up with a "top ten" best hits from those 400 plus posts between 2007 and 2017 would take more time than I have available to me, so I wish my reader good hunting among them, should he or she be inclined to embark on that.

There were a couple of moments across this decade when I felt that even blog posts, prompt and flexible though they are compared to publication in traditional outlets like newsletters or journals, were not immediate enough; and I then turned to the idea of tweeting about Morris, to widen still further his visibility on contemporary social media. Tweets with their (then) restriction to 140 characters posed even more sharply than blog posts a paradox about Morris: how could an author as prolix as this, who had written something as massive as *The Earthly Paradise* and one of whose late romances was known among his own family as "the Interminable," possibly be fruitfully discussed in such miniature forms, mere tiny haiku and they were to his own Victorian epic proclivities? A consoling thought, though, was the fact that, in his political writing for *Commonweal* Morris himself had offered brief, hard-hitting "Notes on News," which one might loosely regard as the blog posts or extended tweets of their own time.

It was in fact a political emergency that set me tweeting about and around Morris: the police killing of minor criminal Mark Duggan on August 4, 2011 and the subsequent riots—probably *uprisings* is a better word—in London and other cities that followed this. Though I did offer some extended analysis of these on the blog, and of the extreme retributive class-based "justice" they aroused, they also seemed to require a nimbler, more immediate mode of response than such posts; and tweeting seemed ideally designed for this, with the 140 character requirement acting as a strict discipline on one's cultural or political thoughts. The first of my 790 tweets, posted on August 17, 2011, reads: "England today: economic crisis, mass unemployment, last week's riots and violence, current right-wing backlash. William Morris, we need you!" Perhaps the unacknowledged literary model in the background there, it suddenly occurs to me, was Wordsworth's 1802 sonnet to Milton.

But if tweeting begins as an incisive way of expressing opinion on current events, it very quickly, I found, became a quite adversarial form; you almost at once find yourself rebutting what you consider false views, either from the field of current politics (where your adversaries give as good as they get) or in the domain of what one might consider limited or reductive uses of Morris himself (where the people you criticize can get quite hurt and disturbed, seemingly unaware as they are that Morris himself has this more political and combative side). Moreover, once you get out there in the Twittersphere, hunting down what you consider Morrisian or wider political error, there is absolutely no end of it; and you could spend day and night engaged in all sorts of local skirmishes. But at their best, I hope these brief posts were generating Morrisian ideas from current political events, so I would offer as exemplary my tweet on December 5, 2013: "Shocking police violence against London students today. 'Police Violence 1887–2013' is a good Morris topic for a Kelmscott House exhibition."

To complete the survey of digital activities around Morris over the years, I should also note the two small films that I made with the help of my son (who contributed the technological expertise) and then posted to YouTube. The first of these was a modest little effort, filmed in my son's college room in Oxford, promoting the *William Morris in Oxford* book; it has so far had 4,115 viewings. The second, however, was longer and more venturesome, since it gets out and about in order to tell the story of Morris's visit to Lancaster on November 2, 1886 and of the local branch of the Socialist League that was set up in the wake of that visit. I always alert students on our second-year Victorian literature course to its existence, hoping that in this way I can make them feel that Morris is not just a dusty antiquarian figure, but someone who impinges at least on their own locality, and perhaps even on their own cultural and political concerns. We could now surely do with a whole host of such filmlets, made by people in towns and cities that Morris visited during his indefatigable lecturing tours.

Where am I now, then, as I contemplate a possible second decade of blogging about and around Morris? Should that be my project for the next ten years (during which, by the way, I shall certainly retire from Lancaster University, so I won't be subject to the oppressions of the Research Excellence Framework any longer). I am very much in two minds about this. Toward the end of that first decade, I had my sixtieth birthday and my first grandchild was born, so I certainly feel a good deal further away from the political and cultural concerns of young people than I was when I started blogging in 2007. The recent Brexit vote has exacerbated that distance in ways I don't myself yet fully understand; I am from a white, working-class family in Essex, and can therefore feel working-class populist concerns viscerally as well as analyzing them intellectually and critically. Moreover, blogging itself now feels rather an old form. Things move with frightening rapidity in cyberspace, so blogging has long since been overtaken by platforms such as Facebook, Instagram, WhatsApp, and probably several others that I haven't yet even heard of (although tweeting has been given a new lease on life by President Donald Trump, so perhaps I abandoned that mode prematurely).

And perhaps more generally, we have come to feel that cyberspace is less liberating than it seemed in the early days of, say, the Arab Spring. Today, as Jodi Dean, one of our recent prominent theorists of communism, has argued, blogging may bind us to the compulsive circuits of "communicative capitalism" rather than emancipating us from them.[4] I have certainly personally felt, in relation to my own digital activities, that these can become addictive, quite apart from their political effectivity or otherwise; and walking around my university campus, where every student seems glued to their smartphone screen and oblivious to the wider world, might well make one think twice about the wisdom of adding further content, even of a Morrisian nature, to such outlets.

Thomas Hardy's fine poem "The Superseded" seems to me very germane here: there are times when you just need to let things go, without too much ado or regret. Other Morris blogs have come and gone across these years— I think back fondly to "William Morris Fan Club," produced by Mo from Boston—so why shouldn't mine too? And the Morris Society now has—after some teething troubles in the early years—its own well-established blog, so perhaps that will do in terms of the representation of Morris and his concerns in cyberspace?

On the other hand, my third-year half-unit course on "Utopias and Utopianism," which has for some years failed to recruit enough students to run, does actually have a working complement for spring term 2018, so perhaps there is a political spark here that one should keep trying to fan into something more active. These students would have been signing up for this course in the spring of 2017, so the fact of this module coming back into circulation at that time may have been an early indication of the "Corbyn surge" among British young people that we later saw more generally. Of course, I would prefer that that new generation were doing their own blogging and tweeting about Morris rather than passively receiving that from me (perhaps they already are, on platforms I don't even know about—the Momentum social media campaign certainly played a notable role on Jeremy Corbyn's behalf in the 2017 British general election). But perhaps, too, I shouldn't give up while there is still a possibility of political contact and influence with that digital constituency. For it seems unlikely that these idealistic youngsters are going to spontaneously arrive at the notion of Morrisian communism without some prompting from older heads, so there may still be a necessary task of political education here. For me, then, the jury is still out over future blogging and tweeting; we shall see.

NOTES

1. Fredric Jameson, *Late Marxism: Adorno, or, the Persistence of the Dialectic* (London: Verso, 1990), 52.

2. Fiona MacCarthy, *William Morris: A Life for Our Time* (London: Faber and Faber, 1994), vii.

3. For further discussion of this issue, see my "'The Only Word He Was Comfortable With': William Morris and the Return of Communism," *Journal of William Morris Studies*, 22, (2017): 36–47.

4. See Jodi Dean, *Blog Theory: Feedback and Capture in the Circuits of Drive* (Cambridge: Polity Press, 2010).

BIBLIOGRAPHY

Dean, Jodi. *Blog Theory: Feedback and Capture in the Circuits of Drive.* Cambridge: Polity Press, 2010.

Jameson, Frederic. *Late Marxism: Adorno, or the Persistence of the Dialectic.* London: Verso, 1990.

MacCarthy, Fiona. *William Morris: A Life for Our Time.* London: Faber and Faber, 1994.

Pinkney, Tony. "'The Only Word He Was Comfortable With': William Morris and the Return of Communism," *Journal of William Morris Studies* 22 (2017): 36–47.

Chapter Nineteen

Digital Design with William Morris

Amanda Golden

In an age when the value of humanities is in question, when we ask how teaching literature and art can be more relevant, particularly with regard to time periods before our own, it is in the nineteenth century that we find William Morris's aesthetics, which, this essay demonstrates, can become a model for students' engagement with visual art and technology. This was the case in my "Victorian Technology and Art" course at the Georgia Institute of Technology, where Marion L. Brittain Postdoctoral Fellows teach multimodal composition with a WOVEN (Written, Oral, Visual, Electronic, and Nonverbal) framework. Teaching students to formulate complex arguments across a range of modes and media,[1] Brittain Fellows' courses include a series of projects that combine different forms of communication, achieving "multimodal synergy."[2] Morris is a forerunner in blending visual and textual media, and digital experiments give new life to not just his prints, but also the meaning he brought to the appearance of texts.

VICTORIAN TECHNOLOGY AND ART

The theme of Victorian Technology and Art invites students to investigate the past and present of scientific and artistic production. While the first half of the course emphasizes technology and the second half explores art, the course as a whole pursues the ways that technology and art overlap. With regard to the course texts, this also means reckoning with the imagination as science figures alongside the supernatural in Rudyard Kipling's "Wireless" (1902), Robert Louis Stevenson's *Dr. Jekyll and Mr. Hyde* (1886), and George Eliot's *The Lifted Veil* (1859).

Using technology draws students closer to the art of language. Throughout the term, students completed blog postings interpreting primary and secondary texts that enabled their strengthening of analytical and critical reading of texts. In class, students used technology in other ways, teaching them that their ideas can inform further reading of a text. Annotating *The Lifted Veil* using the site PoetryGenius offered an opportunity for students to be among the first to interpret the story on this site, which is filled with commentary, ranging in quality, on other texts.[3] Often commenting on quotations they had analyzed in previous writing assignments, the students were able to see that they have voices to add to the conversation, shaping it for others.

This attention to language prepared students to interpret novels like *The Picture of Dorian Gray* in more ambitious ways. As an alumna of the course put it, "being able to analyze content in the way that English classes analyze literature teaches critical thinking and trains technical minds to uncover deeper meanings and detect patterns."[4] The idea of patterns is twofold when it comes to Morris, as the students' Digital Dorian e-book projects urged them to blend visual and textual patterns, bringing Morris's art and that of his contemporaries to the pages of Oscar Wilde's novel.

DIGITAL DESIGN WITH WILLIAM MORRIS

The second half of the course took on the tantalizing and harrowing poetry and art of Dante Gabriel Rossetti, John William Waterhouse, Christina Rossetti, John Everett Millais, and Morris. Students came to know the camaraderie that shaped Pre-Raphaelite artistic endeavors and the medieval themes to which they were attracted. In their projects, students brought this terrain to bear on Wilde's *Picture of Dorian Gray*, imagining themselves as a Dante Gabriel Rossetti or a William Morris, illustrating Wilde's text in their e-books.[5] Morris's range proved to be the most useful for this task, as students brought a tone and color scheme to their e-books, availing themselves of Morris's adornment of spaces ranging from the domestic to the textual.

In preparation for this project, students completed an in-class assignment putting into practice some of the concepts they encountered in Imogen Hart's "The Designs of William Morris" from *The Cambridge Companion to the Pre-Raphaelites* and Elizabeth Carolyn Miller's introduction to *Slow Print: Literary Radicalism and Late Victorian Print Culture*. The former contextualizes the style and subjects of Morris's art and the latter his aesthetic contributions, particularly regarding typography. Working in groups, students selected digital images of Morris's designs for wallpaper and typography, creating decorated versions of ten to twenty lines of Christina Rossetti's "Goblin Market" or Alfred Tennyson's "The Lady of Shalott," which we had previously read.[6] In doing so, the students used Microsoft Word or Google Documents to combine text and images, and then shared the reasoning behind their design choices with the class. As a result, the students interpreted the poems in new ways and learned to access late-nineteenth-century visual materials online.

The research for this task involved surveying the online selection of Morris wallpaper and typography as well as artifacts of the Arts and Crafts movement using Google Images. I reminded students to check for the authenticity of what they found, as it could have been Morris-influenced rather than Morris-produced, but even so, their searches sampled Morris's visual register in popular culture, digitally, at the present moment. The students also learned of the William Morris Archive,[7] and a subsequent assignment asked them to use the *Yellow Nineties Online* (via NINES).[8] While the *Yellow Book* was actually published a few years after *Dorian Gray*, its aesthetic also came to play a role in students' e-book projects, especially as Dorian receives a different "yellow book," J. K. Huysmans's *À rebours* (1884).[9]

When students came to design their e-books, each group had a chapter of *Dorian Gray* on which to focus and free rein regarding the format with which to display two to three annotated pages and a cover for their e-book. The design was to extend to all elements of the book, including its typography, and to draw on examples from Morris, the Arts and Crafts movement, and *The Yellow Book*. Each group accompanied its digital project with a written rationale, addressing the arguments the e-book makes and the design choices, and analyzing quotations from the chapters and secondary sources we read. The rationale permits students to strengthen their argumentative skills, making a case for how the visual, digital, and textual dimensions of their project create meaning. In doing so, they address how their project interprets the text, analyzing passages from the pages that they included. Further, each group gave a presentation in which they not only explained to the class how their project makes meaning, but they also incorporated an activity that engaged the class, teaching them about an aspect of their project. The activities, one of which was a Buzzfeed-style quiz regarding *Dorian Gray*, were themselves multimodal, adding a creative component to the presentations and enabling students to strengthen and blend not only oral and nonverbal, but also electronic and visual communication skills.

The range of Morris prints that students selected led to interestingly varied visual aesthetics among their e-books. Using a Wix website, one group illustrating chapter two of *Dorian Gray* had a leafy green and blue Morris background against which they set their annotated text.[10] Their project takes the overall reading experience into account, and the students selected colors and backgrounds that would enable the communication of their ideas about Wilde's text. The layout of this site, and the students' customization of it, echoes the considerations of earlier book designers, particularly illuminated medieval texts with glosses.

Depicting chapter five of *Dorian Gray*, another group used iBooks Author to include a wide range of illustrations from Morris's typography along with audio commentary that they had recorded. In their rationale, the students elaborated on their decisions to incorporate the different Morris images, developing interpretations alongside the text of Wilde's novel. They chose to pair Morris's "Strawberry Thief" wallpaper pattern, for instance, with the moment when James Vane warns his sister Sibyl that Dorian "wants to enslave [her]." Her response is, "I shudder at the thought of being free."[11] The students explained that the "Birds on the upper position of 'Strawberry Thief' facing each other with their beaks opened could represent Sibyl and James arguing, while the birds on the bottom part with closed beak and birds facing away from each other could represent how stubborn and different their ideas are." During their presentation, the students also introduced their research into the flowers Morris depicted in a particular image, linking it with a passage in the novel that anticipates Sibyl's death. In this project, the reasoning behind students' decisions ranged from the presence of birds and the purpose of flowers to the tone of a passage and its implications in the novel. In each instance, students drew connections between Wilde's text and visual work that was the product of a similar artistic world.

One paradox of working with digital versions of Morris's prints is that they run counter to his own ethos. As Miller reminds us in *Slow Print*, Morris "produced unique objects using preindustrial methods . . . [and] handmade materials."[12] Students were not working by hand, rather they were adopting a collage method to adorn pages of text using existing images and digital platforms, such as iBooks Author. In doing so, however, their task was to create a new whole, and this fits with a different effect that Morris had. Miller reminds us that his projects demonstrated a cohesiveness that critics have often overlooked as he "exploited aspects of each print medium to critique the political effects of mass print culture."[13] While students may not have shared Morris's political aims, their use of digital media collects facets that had not before been joined in quite that way to accomplish a goal of their own design.

Searching Google brings forward images of Morris's work from different periods in his career, such as wallpapers and typography. Had Morris illustrated an edition of *Dorian Gray* or "Goblin Market," it may have demonstrated more harmony in approach, but the students' digital scaveng-

Figure 19.1. William Morris's "Strawberry Thief" pattern.
Reproduced courtesy of the Victorian and Albert Museum.

ing and piecework speaks to new research methods and modes of engaging materials. In her essay "Resistance in the Materials," Bethany Nowviskie remembers an interviewer "explaining the embodied frictions . . . when you move scholarly editorial practice, born in book culture, from print to digital media: 'You can't have art,' said William Morris . . . 'without resistance in the material.'"[14] Nowviskie interprets this "resistance" as different forms of productivity in the digital humanities. Working from scratch, she specifies, "our tools had one thing in common: overwhelmingly, *their own users* had made 'em, and understood the continual and collective *re-making* of them, in response to various resistances encountered and discovered, as a natural part of the process of their use."[15] Margaret Konkol underscores in her article "Public Archives, New Knowledge, and Moving Beyond the Digital Humanities/Digital Pedagogy Distinction" that "students can and do create new knowledge,"[16] which is the case regardless of the degree of technological creation, whether collage or code, short or long term.

The type of resistance of which Nowviskie writes can mean the frustration of beginning to learn new coding languages or of not being able to work as one might want with new materials. One advantage of working with the types of web, e-book, and presentation software that we did in our class was that their flexibility allowed the students to feel facility working with them and to then experiment with the digital environments they had created. These programs were also password protected or could remain offline or shared in a limited way. This is important because students can have room to experiment without their work being available to the public. If students choose to do so, they can create work that is accessible online. The sites or resources students use, however, may not be maintained in the future. Students might have more control over the long-term availability of their projects if they created and coded them. For student purposes, however, a shorter frame may be ideal, allowing them to complete projects that they may not desire to return to in the future.

While working entirely from raw materials by coding may have been closer to Morris's own techniques, the time spent learning coding may not have left enough time for students to spend with novels like *Dorian Gray*. Instructors often need to prioritize one skill over another, and using existing images and software enables students to accomplish a different range of tasks. Even in a short time frame, Morris's accessibility, in terms of available materials and the fact that his work speaks to a multimodal approach, enables students to interpret the language and technology of his time (including fine printing) by adapting that of our own.

Morris's work introduces students to the effort and creativity that he brought to reviving craft and decorating daily life. Following his example, from web design to the organization of an essay, students can gain greater control over the design of their work, marshalling its elements to different effects. In the process, students also find a new connection with the past and its aesthetics, becoming more curious artists themselves.

NOTES

1. http://victoriantechnologyandart.weebly.com/, accessed Jan. 3, 2018. Regarding WOVEN, see WOVEN*Text*, Version 2.2, Bedford/St. Martin's Press, http://ebooks.bfwpub.com/gatech.php.

2. Rebecca Burnett and L. Andrew Cooper, "Multimodal Synergy," WOVEN-*Text*, Version 2.2, Bedford/St. Martin's Press, http://ebooks.bfwpub.com/gatech.php. Brighton Kamen, an alumna of this course discusses the value of communication

in writing courses at Georgia Tech in her article "Do Not Disparage Your English Class at Tech Just Yet," *Technique*, September 15, 2017, http://nique.net/opinions/2017/09/15/do-not-disparage-your-english-class-at-tech-just-yet/, accessed May 2, 2018; hereafter cited in the text as "Kamen."

    3. http://victoriantechnologyandart.weebly.com/in-class/annotating-eliot, accessed April 19, 2018.

    4. Kamen, "Do Not Disparage," http://nique.net/opinions/2017/09/15/do-not-disparage-your-english-class-at-tech-just-yet/.

    5. http://victoriantechnologyandart.weebly.com/project-2.html.

    6. See http://victoriantechnologyandart.weebly.com/in-class/illustrating-with-william-morris.

    7. http://morrisedition.lib.uiowa.edu/, accessed April 19, 2018.

    8. http://www.1890s.ca/Default.aspx, April 19, 2018.

    9. Joris-Karl Huysmans, *Against Nature (À rebours)* (1884), "Decadent novel À rebours, or, Against Nature," The British Library, https://www.bl.uk/collection-items/decadent-novel-a-rebours-or-against-nature, accessed May 14, 2019. Joris-Karl Huysmans, Against Nature (À Rebours), trans. Robert Baldick (New York: Penguin Books, 2003).

    10. http://dgray31.wixsite.com/doriangray, accessed April 19, 2018.

    11. Oscar Wilde, *The Picture of Dorian Gray*, 1890, ed. Michael Patrick Gillespie (New York: Norton, 2006), 140.

    12. Elizabeth Carolyn Miller, *Slow Print: Literary Radicalism and Late Victorian Print Culture* (Stanford: Stanford University Press, 2013), 26.

    13. Ibid.

    14. Bethany Nowviskie, "Resistance in the Materials," in *Debates in the Digital Humanities*, eds. Matthew K. Gold and Lauren F. Klein (Minneapolis: University of Minnesota Press, 2016), http://dhdebates.gc.cuny.edu/debates/text/66, accessed April 19, 2018.

    15. Many students are practicing the type of production of which Nowviskie is speaking, in digital and physical forms ranging from Jentery Sayers's Makers' Lab at the University of Victoria to Amy E. Elkins's Make it New: Modern Art & Literature course at Emory University, https://modernartandliterature.wordpress.com/, accessed April 19, 2018.

    16. Margaret Konkol, "Public Archives, New Knowledge, and Moving Beyond the Digital Humanities/Digital Pedagogy Distinction," *Hybrid Pedagogy*, September 8, 2015, http://hybridpedagogy.org/public-archives-and-new-knowledge/, accessed April 19, 2018.

BIBLIOGRAPHY

Burnett, Rebecca, and L. Andrew Cooper, "Multimodal Synergy." WOVEN*Text*. Version 2.2. Bedford/St. Martin's Press, http://ebooks.bfwpub.com/gatech.php.

"Decadent novel *À rebours, or, Against Nature*," The British Library. Accessed May 14, 2019, https://www.bl.uk/collection-items/decadent-novel-a-rebours-or-against-nature.

Drucker, Johanna. *The Visible Word: Experimental Typography and Modern Art, 1909–1923*. 1994. Chicago: University of Chicago Press, 1996.

Elkins, Amy E. "Make it New: Modern Art and Literature." Emory University. Accessed April 19, 2018, https://modernartandliterature.wordpress.com/.

Hart, Imogen. "The Designs of William Morris." In *The Cambridge Companion to the Pre-Raphaelites*, edited by Elizabeth Prettejohn, 211–22. New York: Cambridge University Press, 2012.

Huysmans, Joris-Karl. *Against Nature (À rebours)*. Translated by Robert Baldick. New York: Penguin Books, 2003.

Kamen, Brighton. "Do Not Disparage Your English Class at Tech Just Yet," *Technique*, September 15, 2017. Accessed May 2, 2018, http://nique.net/opinions/2017/09/15/do-not-disparage-your-english-class-at-tech-just-yet/.

Konkol, Margaret. "Public Archives, New Knowledge, and Moving Beyond the Digital Humanities/Digital Pedagogy Distinction." *Hybrid Pedagogy*. September 8, 2015. Accessed April 19, 2018, http://hybridpedagogy.org/public-archives-and-new-knowledge/.

Miller, Elizabeth Carolyn. *Slow Print: Literary Radicalism and Late Victorian Print Culture*. Stanford: Stanford University Press, 2013.

Nowviskie, Bethany. "Resistance in the Materials." In *Debates in the Digital Humanities*, edited by Matthew K. Gold and Lauren F. Klein. Minneapolis: University of Minnesota Press, 2016. Accessed January 3, 2018, http://dhdebates.gc.cuny.edu/debates/text/66.

Wilde, Oscar. *The Picture of Dorian Gray*. 1890. Edited by Michael Patrick Gillespie. New York: Norton, 2006.

Index

A&CH. *See* Arts and Crafts Hammersmith project
Abensour, Miguel, 156–57
ACES. *See* Arts and Crafts Exhibition Society
Addams, Jane, 5, 14, 20, 25–27; founding principles of, 30–31; and the Hull-House Labor Museum, 26, 30, 32–35; on relation of labor and art, 28–29. *See also* Hull-House
Adorno (book by Jameson), 266
Adventure Thinking (developed by Harris), 226
Advice to Young Men (Cobbett), 82
"An Aesthetic Ecocommunist: Morris the Red and Morris the Green" (Boos), 85
Aestheticism movement, 207, 208, 242
After London (Jefferies), 162
Albion printing press, 49, 51–52
Albritton, Vicky, 150
Alcott, A. Bronson, 152, 157
Alcott, Louisa May, 152
Allman, Jim, 108
Alton Locke (Kingsley), 85
American Settlement House movement, 5, 25–35
anarchism, 103

The Ancient Classical Drama (Moulton), 15
"Andrea del Sarto" (Browning), 176
Anthem (Rand), 154
Anti-Corn Law League, 89–90
Apple (company), 223
Archaeologies of the Future (Jameson), 163
archaism of William Morris, 188, 193–98
architecture, 165, 213, 221, 236; as a craft, 236; flat architectural space, 239; Georgian architecture, 49; Gothic architecture, 66, 82, 94, 140, 153; "The Influence of Building Materials on Architecture" (Morris), 140; medieval architecture, 121, 138, 141; and Morris, 52, 122–23, 140–41, 153, 189, 207, 209, 220, 222, 223, 241, 243; Society for the Protection of Ancient Buildings, 54, 122; unity of, 222–23. *See also* Red House (designed by Morris)
À rebours (Huysman), 277
Arnold, Matthew, 188, 190, 193
on the translation of Homer, 190–93, 194, 195–96
Arscott, Caroline, 215

art and design curriculum: at Kelmscott House and Museum, 50–51, 53–54, 57; Morris and the history of design as social engagement, 6, 219–32; Morris and the intersection of the histories of art and design, 235–44; "Morris for Art Historians" (Hart), 6, 207–16; "Victorian Technology and Art" course and digital design with William Morris, 7, 275–80
"Art and Labour" (Morris), 209
"Art and the Modern Interior" course (Hart), 213
art history, teaching William Morris in: and the history of design as social engagement, 6, 219–32; Morris and the intersection of the histories of art and design, 6, 235–44; Morris for the art historian, 6, 207–16
The Art Journal, 240
The Art Newspaper, 232
Art Nouveau movement, 222–23, 239
"The Arts and Craft of the Machine" (Wright), 29
"Arts and Crafts" (Veblen), 16
Arts and Crafts Exhibition Society, 101, 107, 108, 214
Arts and Crafts Hammersmith project, 57–58
Arts and Crafts movement, 14, 277; in Chicago at Hull-House, 5, 25–35; highlighting Morris's abilities in *Time and the Tapestry*, 41; and histories of art and design, 235; influence of different cultures on, 57–58; Jane Addams drawing on principles of, 35; medievalism in, 66–67; and modes of production, 236; Morris's place in, 26, 28, 207–16, 208, 222, 235–44; *To-Morrow: A Magazine for Rational Thinkers/A Handbook of the Changing Order* promoting, 19; in the Paris Commune, 5, 99–110; politics of, 104; radicalism of, 107–8; Ruskin's place in, 26, 121; teaching Morris at Kelmscott House and Museum, 5, 49–62; and tradition of illustrated texts, 175; and Triggs, 15, 16, 19
Arts and Crafts Society of Chicago, 16; founded at Hull-House, 14, 29
Artworkers' Guild, 175
art-work vision, 241
Ashbee, C. R., 108, 150
The Assembly of the Gods (Lydgate), 14
The Atlantic (magazine), 228
authenticity: of crafts, 236, 243; of Morris, 197, 243

Baldwin, Louisa, 153
Ball, John (as a fictional character in *A Dream of John Ball*), 82, 85
Ballantyne, Archibald, 192–93, 197
Banham, Reyner, 223
Barnett, Samuel and Henrietta, 26
Barry, Charles, 255
Barton, Kyle, 258–59, 260
Bauhaus movement, 221, 222–23, 235
Bax, Ernest Belfort, 83, 102–3
Beaumont, Matthew, 103
"The Beauty of Life" (Morris), 221, 222
Bell, Isaac Lowthian, 240
Bellamy, Edward, 94, 149, 150, 162
Bellis, Chris, 62
Bennett, Jane, 134, 136, 137, 140, 142, 144
Benson, William Arthur Smith, 210, 242
Beowulf: Morris's translation of, 68, 69; Tolkien's translation of, 68
"*Beowulf*: The Monsters and the Critics" (Tolkien), 68–69
Bernstein, Susan David, 5, 133–44
Besant, Annie, 55
Bignell, Rosemary, 58
Birmingham Society of Arts and School of Design, 221
Black and White (journal), 109
Blake, William, 116
Blalock, Stephanie, 257

Bloch, Ernst, 164, 165–66
blog on William Morris, 265–73
Bloom, Louis (reading habits of), 45–46
Bodley Head (publisher), 180
Boffin (fictional character in *News from Nowhere*), 169
Boos, Florence S., 6, 83, 85, 94, 135, 176, 179, 251–61
Borges, Jorge Luis, 2–3, 4, 7
Bracken, Pamela, 6, 175–83
Bratt, Edith, 67
Brave New World (Huxley), 154
Breckinridge, Sophonisba, 30
Brexit, 272
British Museum, 122, 242
British Periodicals (database), 135
Brittain, Marion L., 275
Brothers Grimm, 52
Brown, Bill, 133
Brown, Ford Madox, 53, 210, 236
Browning, Elizabeth Barrett, 261
Browning, Elizabeth Grennan, 5, 25–35
Browning, Robert, 14, 176, 261
Browning and Whitman: A Study in Democracy (Triggs), 15
Bulletin (of William Morris Society), 15
Bulwer-Lytton, Edward, 162
Burden, Jane, 252
Burne-Jones, Edward, 41–42, 53, 138, 214, 236, 267
Butler, Samuel, 162
Butler Art Gallery in, 28
Buzzfeed, 277

The Cambridge Companion to the Pre-Raphaelites, 276
The Cambridge Companion to Utopian Literature, 163
Canterbury Tales (Chaucer). *See* Kelmscott Press, Kelmscott Chaucer
capitalism: industrial capitalism, 31, 167, 195; and Morris, 1, 43, 72, 103, 108, 121, 162, 171, 219; Ruskin on, 27–28
Carlyle, Thomas, 15, 17, 150

Carpenter, Humphrey, 68
Carr, Sabrina, 62
Cast Off Knitters, 227–28
Central Online Victorian Educator, 259–60
The Century Guild Hobby Horse (Mackmurdo and Horne, eds.), 241
"Chamber of Horrors" (1852 exhibition), 239
The Changing Order (Triggs), 19
Chapters in the History of the Arts and Crafts Movement (Triggs), 15
Chartist movement, 79, 84, 85, 86–87, 94; in course syllabus for Radical Victorians, 89, 90
Chaucer inspiring Morris, 49, 51, 52, 66, 67, 104. *See also* Kelmscott Press, Kelmscott Chaucer
Chicago, teaching Morris in, 4; Browning on American Settlement House movement and Morris, 5, 25–35; Helsinger on Triggs and Moulton's teachings, 5, 11–20
Chicago Public School Art Society, 28
citizenship curriculum at Kelmscott House and Kelmscott House Museum, 52, 55–56
Clara (fictional character in *New from Nowhere*), 125, 140, 170, 255
"Class Consciousness in the Design of William Morris" (Eisenman), 215
Cleon (Browning), 261
Clinton, Hillary, 228
Cliterate Collective, 229–30, 231, 232
Clydesdale, Tim, 151
Coach House at Kelmscott House, 55, 56, 57, 58
Cobbett, William, 79, 80–81, 82–83; and Chartists, 84, 94; in course syllabus for Radical Victorians, 88
Codell, Julie, 6, 235–44
cognitive estrangement, 152
Cohen, William, 133
Cole, G. D. H., 3–4, 54–55
Cole, Henry, 237, 239, 240, 242

Coles, Dorothy, 270
collaboration and Morris, 213–14
Collected Letters of William Morris (Kelvin), 178
College Art Association, 232
Collegiate Socialist Society, 19
The Coming Race (Bulwer-Lytton), 162
The Commonweal (socialist newspaper), 5, 80, 127, 134; Morris and "Jim Allman" debate in, 108; Morris commentary on education, 154; Morris commenting on William Cobbett, 82–83; "Notes on News" column by Morris, 258–59, 271; political cartoons of Crane in, 104, 105–6, 107, 109; serializing *A Dream of John Ball*, 81, 84; serializing *News from Nowhere*, 133, 136; serializing *The Pilgrims of Hope*, 102; "Why We Celebrate the Commune of Paris" (Morris), 103
Compton, Ann, 241
The Concept of Utopia (Levitas), 163–64
"The Concept of Utopia" (Vieira), 163
"Concerning Geffray Teste Noire" (Morris), 251, 260
The Condition of the Working Class in England (Engels), 84, 164
Cook, George Cram, 15
Coole, Diana, 135
"Coolest Political T-shirts in the UK" (from Pinkney's Morris blog), 269
"co-operative individualism, 16–17
Cooper-Hewitt Museum, 225
Corbyn, Jeremy, 273
Cottage Economy (Cobbett), 81
Courbet, Gustave, 100, 106, 109–10
COVE. *See* Central Online Victorian Educator
Cox, Ada Beall (Trigg's second wife), 15
"Craft and Design in Literary Study" (Wells), 142
crafts: craft activism programs, 227–32; craft education at Kelmscott House and the Kelmscott Museum, 5, 49–62; distinguished from fine arts, 243; infusing and elevating crafts with fine arts, 236, 244; Morris's attempts to integrate art and craft, 235–44; Morris's historical awareness of, 242–43. *See also* Arts and Crafts Exhibition Society; Arts and Crafts movement; decorative arts
The Craftsman (magazine), 14, 17
Craftsman movement in North America, 222
Crane, Walter, 55, 215; Crane and Morris and the Paris Commune, 99–110; political cartoons of, 101, 102, 104, 105–6, 107, 109
The Creative Curriculum: Printmaking in the Primary School through the Work of William Morris, 58–59
curriculum: Adventure Thinking (developed by Harris), 226; classes and workshops at Kelmscott House and Museum, 50–61; course syllabus for Radical Victorians, 86–94; finding hope and change in *News from Nowhere*, 115–27; "Project H" (founded by Pilloton), 226; She's Rogue workshops and retreats, 226; teaching medievalism of Morris through Tolkien, 65–72; teaching *News from Nowhere* focusing on Morris as a utopian, 161–72; teaching *News from Nowhere* in a course on "The Simple Life," 149–57; teaching *News from Nowhere* in a seminar on Victorian Materialities, 133–44

Daily News (newspaper), 81
Daisy wallpaper (Morris), 238
Dannehl, Karin, 135–36
Darrow, Clarence S., 19
Darwin, Charles, 190
Dave, Victor, 103
Dean, Jodi, 272

Dearle, Henry, 214
Decker, Alicia, 230
decorative arts, 100, 107, 244; defining, 236; elements of, 196; and Morris, 141, 142, 144, 207–8, 239, 242, 244; recognition of, 100, 207, 242. *See also* Arts and Crafts Exhibition Society; crafts; furnishings and furniture; tapestries; textiles; tiles as art; wallpaper
defamiliarization, 152
The Defence of Guenevere (Bodley Head's edition of), 180
The Defence of Guenevere (Laurie), 178
"The Defence of Guenevere" (Morris), 66, 115, 252; as an exercise in cooperative digital editing, 259–60; teaching through word and image, 6, 175–83
DeMille, James, 162
Democratic Federation. *See* Social Democratic Federation
de Morgan, William, 53
design: dangerousness of design and "Human-Centered Design," 224–27; "Digital Design with William Morris" (Golden), 275–80; Morris and the intersection of the histories of art and design, 6, 235–44; redesigning design education, 224–27; total design, varieties of, 222–23
design and technology curriculums: "Digital Design with William Morris" (Golden), 7, 275–80; at Kelmscott House and Museum, 54; "Morris for Art Historians" (Hart), 6, 207–16
"The Designer's Handshake," 225
"Design for the Other 90%" exhibition, 225
Design for the Real World (Papanek), 224
Design Revolution: 100 Products That Empower People (Pilloton), 225, 226
Design Revolution exhibition, 225

"The Designs of William Morris" (Hart), 276
De Stijl movement, 222–23
Dewey, John, 14, 16, 17, 30
Dick (fictional character in *News from Nowhere*), 118, 119, 124, 125, 126, 136, 137, 138, 140, 169, 255, 256
Dickens, Charles, 141, 154, 169
"Digital Design with William Morris" (Golden), 7, 275–80
digital humanities and the teaching of Morris, 6–7, 182, 256–59; blogging about Morris, 7, 265–73; use of digital design, 7, 275–80; use of to teach "The Defence of Guenevere," 176, 179–80; use of Twitter to post for William Morris Archive, 258–59; using the William Morris Archives, 251–61. *See also* types of digital media, (i.e., blogs, e-books, Twitter, YouTube, etc.,)
Digital Studio (Iowa), 258
"dis," as a prefix, 119
The Dispossessed (Le Guin), 43
Dr. Jekyll and Mr. Hyde (Stevenson), 275
A Dream of John Ball (Morris): focus on agrarian solidarity and the peasants, 43, 66, 82; the teaching of in a course on Victorian Radicalism, 5, 79–94
"A Dream of William Cobbett? Teaching Morris's *John Ball* in an Interdisciplinary Course on Victorian Radicalism" (Hughes and Meier), 5, 79–94
dreams, *News from Nowhere* exemplifying, 115–27
Dresser, Christopher, 239
drew, glenda, 230
Droth, Martina, 244
Drucker, Johanna, 257
Duggan, Mark, 271
dystopias: examples of works by authors other than Morris, 154, 162, 172;

Morris's *News from Nowhere* as a dystopia, 43, 161, 170; Morris's *The Story of the Glittering Plain* as a dystopia, 71–72. *See also* utopias and utopian literature

Early Poems of Geoffrey Chaucer (Milton), 179
The Early Poems of William Morris Illustrated by Francis Harrison (Blackie and Sons edition), 180, 182–83
The Earthly Paradise (Morris), 3, 44, 66, 187, 271
"*The Earthly Paradise:* The Greatest Hits" (from Pinkney's Morris blog), 270
"earthly paradox," 7
e-books, 7, 277, 280
Economic and Philosophic Manuscripts of 1844 (Marx), 164
education: "Education at Its Finest" at Kelmscott House and the Kelmscott Museum, 5, 49–62; and the importance of reading, 123; redesigning design education, 224–27; as seen in *News from Nowhere*, 122, 156–57. *See also* curriculum
Eisenman, Stephen, 215
Eliot, George, 275
Ellen (fictional character in *News from Nowhere*), 123–24, 125–26, 143, 169, 255, 256
Elletson, Helen, 5, 49–62
Ellis & White (publishers), 81
Emerson, Ralph Waldo, 14, 15, 152
Emery Walker House, 57
Empower Yolo, 230
Engels, Friedrich, 79, 84, 85, 164–65; in course syllabus for Radical Victorians, 90
English/literacy curriculum at Kelmscott House and Kelmscott House Museum, 52
English Radicalism, 83

environmental education curriculum at Kelmscott House and Kelmscott House Museum, 54–55
The Epistemology of Utopia (Silva), 163
Erewhon (Butler), 162–63
Eros and Civilization (Marcuse), 164, 166–67
Excel (Microsoft program), 258
"extraction capitalism," 136

Fabian Society, 55; Shaw's 1884 Fabian manifesto, 83
Facebook, 272
factory system, 16, 28, 29
family workshops at Kelmscott House and Kelmscott House Museum, 59–61
fantasy genre, 5, 42, 44, 47; Morris combining romance and utopian fiction, 70–72; teaching Morris through Tolkien's fantasies, 5, 65–72; theory of Utopian fantasy, 137–38, 141; *Time and the Tapestry: A William Morris Adventure* (Plotz), 41–47. *See also* dystopias; utopias and utopian literature
Faulkner, Peter, 208
Fauvism, 239
Federation of Artists, 100
Felluga, Dino, 259
feminist activism: and crafts as political statements, 227–32; Women's March of 2017, 220–21, 228
Field Columbian Museum, 33
fine arts, 124, 208, 235, 240–41, 242, 244; distinguished from craft, 243; at Hull-House, 27, 28; infusing and elevating crafts with fine arts, 236, 244; and relationships between past, present, and future, 242; Victorian fine arts movements, 207
Finkel, Jori, 232
Fitzpatrick, KellyAnn, 5, 65–72
Fontaine, Tess, 58
The Forest tapestry (Morris & Co.), 211

forged texts, 261
Four Futures: Visions of the World After Capitalism (Frase), 172
Fourierism, 255
Frankenstein (Shelley), 43
Frase, Peter, 172
Freedgood, Elaine, 135, 141, 142
Freud, Sigmund, 167
F. R. Leavis & Co., 188, 197
Frost, Samantha, 135
Fruitlands (utopian colony in Massachusetts), 152
Fry, Roger, 235
Frye, Northrop, 119–20
furnishings and furniture, 41, 49, 54, 210–11, 221, 222, 235–36, 236, 239, 241–44, 244; Green Dining Room (Morris), 214, 232; Morris and Co.'s as luxury items, 239–40; should be works of art, 208–9

Garden Cities of Tomorrow (Howard), 255
Gell, Alfred, 239
Georgia Institute of Technology, 275
Gere, C. M., 138–41
Germanic influences on Morris, 3
Gesamtkunstwerk [total work of art], 222, 241
Gilman, Charlotte, 19
Girls Garage, 226
The Giver (Lowry), 154
Glaspell, Susan, 15
"Goblin Market" (Rossetti), 277, 278
Golden, Amanda, 7, 275–80
"Golden Wings" (Morris), 141
Gold Hair (Browning), 261
Goldsmith, Alyssa, 230
Google, 176, 179, 258, 278; Google Documents, 277; Google Images, 180, 277
"Gothic Architecture" (Morris), 66
Government School of Design, 237
Grammar of Ornament (Jones), 237–38
Gramsci, Antonio, 150, 156

"A Great Angel Standing" (King's image in "The Defence of Guenevere"), 180
Great Exhibition (1851), 236–37, 240; Morris refusing to enter, 241
Green Dining Room (Morris), 214, 232
Greenfield, Lauren, 151
Grimm, Brothers, 52
Gropius, Walter, 221
Grundrisse (Marx), 164, 195
Guenevere. *See* "The Defence of Guenevere" (Morris)
Guest, William (fictional character in *News from Nowhere*), 42, 46, 103, 118–20, 122, 124, 125–26, 136–37, 138–40, 152, 155, 165–66, 255; questions about role of the narrator in *News from Nowhere*, 167–69
Guild Socialism movement, 4

Hannah, Matthew, 257
Hardie, Keir, 55
Hard Times (Dickens), 141, 154
Hardy, Thomas, 273
Harper, Julia Boorinakis, 230
Harper, William Rainey, 17
Harris, Emily, 226
Harrison, Francis, 180, 182–83
Hart, Imogen, 6, 207–16, 276
hats, knitted as political activism, 228–29
"The Haystack in the Floods" (Morris), 175–76, 252
Haywood, Ian, 84, 87
HCD. *See* "Human-Centered Design"
"Heart of the Hills" (utopian community), 15
Helsinger, Elizabeth, 4, 11–20
Hencroft works, 241
Her (film), 43
Herbert Spencer-Walt Whitman Center, 19
Hill, Mary, 34
Hill, Rosemary, 240
historical fiction of Morris, 69–70

history curriculum at Kelmscott House and Kelmscott House Museum, 50–51, 53–54
The Hobbit (Tolkien), 65, 67, 68–69, 70
Hobson, J. A., 79
Holst, Gustav, 55
Homer, questions on translations of, 190–93, 195
hope and change in *News from Nowhere*, 5, 115–27, 166
Horne, Herbert, 241
Housefield, James, 6, 219–32
The House of the Wolfings (Morris), 69–70
Howard, Ebenezer, 255
"How I Became a Socialist" (Morris), 117–18
Huang, Belinda, 230
Hughes, Linda K., 5, 79–94
Huish, Marcus, 240
Hull-House and the Hull-House Labor Museum, 5, 20, 25–35; Arts and Crafts focus of the Labor Museum, 32; Butler Art Gallery in, 28; Chicago Arts and Crafts Society based at, 14, 29; and the fostering of Arts and Crafts movement, 26–29; impact of the Pullman Strike on, 29. *See also* Addams, Jane
Hull-House Labor Museum: foundational mission of the Labor Museum, 34–35; opening of the Labor Museum, 29
"Human-Centered Design," 224–27
human nature in *News from Nowhere*, 154–55
Hunger Games (Collins), 43, 154
Huysman, Joris-Karl, 277
Hyndman, H. M., 103

iBooks Author (app), 277–78
Icelandic Sagas of Morris, 3, 50, 52, 68, 191. *See also The Earthly Paradise* (Morris); "Sigurd and the Dragon" (Morris); *Sigurd the Volsung* (Morris); *Völsunga Saga*
The Ideas in Things: Fugitive Meaning in the Victorian Novel (Freedgood), 135
Idylls of the King (Tennyson), 66
IKEA, 223
Iliad (Homer), 195
illusionism, 239
illustrated texts and the teaching of "The Defense of Guenevere," 175–83
"Imagine" (Lennon), 116
imprisonment, *News from Nowhere* condemning, 256
Industrial Art League, 14, 16, 18
Industrial Arts College, 14, 19
industrialism: in Chicago, 26–27, 32; communicative capitalism, 136; dehumanizing effects of the machine on workers, 28; extraction capitalism, 136; industrial capitalism, 31, 167, 195; Marcuse on, 117, 167; Morris's resistance to, 242; new industrialism, 13, 16–17
"The Influence of Building Materials on Architecture" (Morris), 140
"In Memory of the Paris Commune" (Crane cartoon), 101, 102, 109
In-Service Training for Teachers program at Kelmscott House and Kelmscott House Museum, 58–59
Instagram, 272
integrative learning, 4
interdisciplinary teaching, 4, 5, 86, 99, 149, 196, 241, 251
Internet Archive, 180, 182, 183
Iowa Digital Studio, 257
Ivanhoe (Scott), 66

Jameson, Fredric, 137–38, 163, 188, 266
Jane Addams Settlement house. *See* Hull-House
Jane Eyre (Bronte), 135
Jasmine wallpaper (Morris), 238

Jefferies, Richard, 162
jigsaw puzzles as a learning tool, 60
John Lane Bodley Head (publisher), 180
Jones, Ernest, 79
Jones, Owen, 237–38, 239
Jonsson, Fredrik Albritton, 150
Jørgensen, Marianne, 227–28
Journal of Political Economy, 16
Justice (magazine), 81–82
Juxta (a versioning program for textual variants), 258

The Kalevala (Finnish epic), 67
Kelley, Florence, 30
Kelmscott Church, 256
Kelmscott House and the Kelmscott Museum, 5; Coach House at, 55, 56, 57, 58; Socialist Choir at, 55; teaching Morris at, 5, 49–62
Kelmscott Manor: as central site in *News from Nowhere*, 118, 135, 138, 256; as Morris's home, 153, 213
Kelmscott Press, 66–67, 133, 134–35, 175, 261; and "The Defence of Guenevere," 176–83, 252, 254; Kelmscott Chaucer, 49, 51, 67, 138, 179, 231; and *News from Nowhere*, 138–41, 253; publishing Morris's translation of *Beowulf*, 68; slow care given to manuscripts, 231, 254; and works of Ruskin, 79, 223, 231
Kelmsgarth Press, 265
Kelvin, Norman, 178
Kennet chintz (Morris), 210, 213
Khan Academy website, 178
King, Jessie, 180–81, 182
"King Arthur's Tomb" (Morris), 115, 252
Kingsley, Charles, 85
Kipling, Rudyard, 275
Klem, Stephanie, 138–41, 142, 143, 144
Knights of Labor, 30
knitted hats as political activism, 228–29
Konkol, Margaret, 279–80

Kreisel, Deanna K., 6, 161–72
Kropotkin, Peter, 55

La Belle Iseult (painting by Morris), 66, 252
labor and the labor movement, 30, 55, 167, 220; attitude towards labor in *News from Nowhere*, 124–25, 170, 171; creative labor, 189, 194; labor rights, 56, 85; manual labor, 104, 109, 121, 228, 235, 240; naturalizing the dignity of labor at Hull-House, 5, 25–35; relation of art, and labor, 79–80, 82, 107, 207, 211, 225; Ruskin on, 238
Labor Party, 55
"The Lady of Shalott" (Tennyson), 277
Lancaster University, 269, 272
Lane, Charles, 152
Lang, Andrew, 68
language fluency of Morris, 67–69, 119, 191–92, 194–95
Lasi, Bianca, 62
Late Marxism: Adorno, or, the Persistence of the Dialectic (Jameson), 266
Latham, David, 5, 115–27, 179
Laurie, Margaret, 178
Leavis company, 188, 197
Le Guin, Ursula, 43
Leighton, Frederic, 240
Lennon, John, 116
"The Lesser Arts" (Morris in 1877), 211, 235
"The Lesser Arts of Life" (Morris in 1882), 208
Levitas, Ruth, 163–65, 166, 167
The Life and Death of Jason (Morris), 187
The Lifted Veil (Eliot), 275–76
literary canon of William Morris, 187–98
"The Literary Study of the Bible" (Moulton), 11
Lives of the Artists (Vasari), 243

"'Living in Heaven': Hope and Change in *News from Nowhere*" (Latham), 5, 115–27
locks on the river. *See* wooden locks in *News from Nowhere*
London, Jack, 19
Longfellow, Henry Wadsworth, 16
Looking Backward (Bellamy), 94, 162
The Lord of the Rings (Tolkien), 65, 66, 67; similarities to Morris's novels, 69–70, 71–72
Love Is Enough (Morris), 179
The Ludgate Monthly (periodical), 136–37
Lydgate, John, 14

MacCarthy, Fiona, 150, 187, 267, 270
machines: Morris's views on, 55, 125, 221, 223–24, 237, 241–42; Triggs's views on, 16
Mackail, John William, 220
Mackmurdo, Arthur, 241
Magnússon, Eiríkr, 68
Manifesto of Federation of Artists, 100
Maple-Durham lock on the river. *See* wooden locks in *News from Nowhere*
Marcuse, Herbert, 117, 164, 166–67, 171
Martinek, Jason D., 1–7
Marx, Karl, 79, 84, 85, 102, 153, 164–65, 195; in course syllabus for Radical Victorians, 90
Marxism and Marxist thought, 85, 121, 143, 163, 164–65, 166; psychoanalytic-Marxist analysis of utopia, 166–67
Match Girls Strike of 1888, 55
material objects in *News from Nowhere*. *See* thing theories, thing case studies
math curriculum at Kelmscott House and Kelmscott House Museum, 51, 57
matter theories and materialism in *News from Nowhere*, 134–35
Matthews, Rachael, 228
Mazzini, Giuseppe, 79

McAdoo, Laura (Trigg's first wife), 15, 19
McGann, Jerome, 177, 179–80, 257
McLeod, Mr., 62
medievalism, 221, 243; in Arts and Crafts movement, 66–67; defining, 66; happiness of medieval working man, 82; medieval age used as setting by Morris, 43, 103, 118, 121, 136, 162, 251; medieval craft techniques, 55; medieval guild model, 55, 108–9; medieval manuscripts, 178, 278; medieval romances, 181, 188; Morris's preference for craftsmanship of 14th century, 121–22, 221; teaching medievalism of Morris through Tolkien, 65–72
"The Medievalism of William Morris: Teaching through Tolkien" (Fitzpatrick), 5, 65–72
Medieval Revival in Britain, 66, 67
Meier, William H., 5, 79–94
Merton Abbey, 12–13, 214
Michael, Louise, 105
Microsoft programs, 258, 277
Miles, Rosie, 176, 180
Millais, John Everett, 240, 276
Miller, Elizabeth Carolyn, 1–7, 136, 137–38, 142–43, 180, 231, 276, 278
Milton, John, 12, 16, 179, 194, 271
Modern Language Association, 141–42
Mo from Boston, 273
More, Thomas, 149, 150, 162
Morris, Jane (wife), 214
Morris, Marshall, Faulkner & Co., 66, 214, 222, 236
Morris, William, 1, 67, 153, 193; alleged assault on a police officer, 1; and the American Settlement House movement, 5, 25–35; and the Arts and Crafts movement, 5, 26, 208, 222; Crane and Morris and the Paris Commune, 5, 99–110; death of, 214; "The Defense of Guenevere"

Index   293

taught through word and image, 6, 175–83; and digital design, 7, 275–80; *A Dream of John Ball* in a course on Victorian Radicalism, 5, 79–94; finding hope and change in *News from Nowhere*, 5, 115–27; focusing on Morris as a utopian, 6, 161–72; and the history of design as social engagement, 6, 219–32; the literary canon of, 6, 187–98; and medievalism, 5, 65–72; Morris's attempts to integrate art and craft, 6, 235–44; *News from Nowhere* in a course on "The Simple Life," 5, 149–57; *News from Nowhere* in a seminar on Victorian Materialities, 5–6, 133–44; place in art history, 6, 207–16; as a possible successor to Tennyson as Poet Laureate, 187; and Ruskin, 27–28, 83–84, 94, 121, 141, 153, 223–24, 239–40; and social media, 7, 258–59, 265–73; teaching Morris at Kelmscott House and Museum, 5, 49–62; *Time and the Tapestry: A William Morris Adventure* (Plotz), 5, 41–47; as a translator, 68, 69, 191–92, 191–93, 194–95, 194–98, 196; and Triggs basing his work on, 11–20; using the William Morris Archive to teach about, 5, 251–61; and utopian political theory, 163–67

Morris & Co., 12, 41, 52, 53, 220, 222–23, 236, 252; collaborative nature of, 214; contribution to the Arts and Crafts movement, 66–67; products, methods, and materials, 2, 49, 53–54, 65, 66, 210, 211

"Morris and the Literary Canon" (Weinroth), 6, 187–98

"Morris for Art Historians" (Hart), 6, 207–16

"Morris for Many Audiences: Teaching with the William Morris Archive" (Boos), 6, 251–61

"Morris Matters: Teaching *News from Nowhere* in a seminar on Victorian Materialities" (Bernstein), 5–6, 133–44

Moulton, Richard Green, 11–12, 15, 20

Muncie, Indiana library reading records, 45–46

Museum of Art at University of California, Davis, 230

"Nasty Women" project, 229–30

National Association for the Advancement of Art and Its Application to Industry, 238

National Curriculum of the United Kingdom, 49, 50, 53, 62

National Gallery, 242

National Library of Scotland, 258

"Naturalizing the Dignity of Labor: The Hull-House Labor Museum and William Morris's Influence on the American Settlement House Movement" (Browning), 5, 25–35

nature: in art at Kelmscott House and the Kelmscott Museum, 50, 56, 59, 61; treatment of in *News from Nowhere*, 141, 142, 143, 144; use of Morris in designs, 50, 236, 238, 239

"The Nature of Gothic" (Ruskin), 27, 79, 238; introduction by Morris, 79–80, 83; in *Stones of Venice*, 92, 121, 223, 243

NBC News, 229

neoliberalism, 2

Newman, Francis, 190–91, 192

new materialism, 6, 133, 134, 135, 142, 144

New Sculptors of the 1880s, 244

News from Nowhere (Morris), 5–6, 42, 46, 47, 53, 71, 72, 103, 179; in a course on "The Simple Life," 6, 149–57; finding hope and change in, 115–27; focusing on Morris as a utopian, 6, 161–72; illustrated version of, 255–56; imagining a

future that resembles the past, 106; introduction to, 54–55; map of the route traced in, 253, 258, 260; medieval setting for, 103, 118, 121, 136, 162; Pinkney's idea of a sequel to, 266–68; questions about the narrator, 167–69; in a seminar on Victorian Materialities, 5–6, 133–44; status of women in, 251. *See also* names of fictional characters in (i.e., Ellen, Guest, Old Hammond, etc.)
Nineteen Eighty-Four (Orwell), 43, 154
Nochlin, Linda, 100, 105
North American Victorian Studies Association, 259
Northern State Prison (NJ), 149
The Norton Anthology (Greenblatt and Abrams), 178, 182
"Notes on News" (Morris in *Commonweal*), 258–59, 271; tweeting items from, 258–59
Nowviskie, Bethany, 279, 280

"Object Biographies" (Dannehl), 135–36
O'Connor, Feargus, 79
Odyssey (Homer), questions on translations of, 190–93; Arnold on, 193, 194, 195–96; Morris's translation of, 191–92, 194–95, 196
The Old Curiosity Shop (Dickens), 141
Old Hammond (fictional character in *News from Nowhere*), 118, 122–23, 124–25, 154, 170, 171, 255–56
Oliver Twist (Dickens), 141
"Olympics 2012—William Morris-Style" (from Pinkney's Morris blog), 270
Omega Workshop, 235
Omeka (file management and indexing program), 258
O'Neill, Morna, 5, 99–110
"On Fairy Stories" (Tolkien), 69
"On the Structure and Evolution of the Decorative Pattern" (Crane), 104

"On Translating *Beowulf*" (Tolkien), 68
On Translating Homer (Arnold), 193, 194
"The Origin of Repressive Civilization" (Marcuse), 167
Origin of Species (Darwin), 190
ornaments. *See* decorative arts
Oryx and Crake (Atwood), 43
Oxford & Cambridge Magazine, 178

painting, 53, 107; as a craft, 236; and Morris, 2, 54, 66, 122, 236, 252; question of choosing painting or decorative arts, 208, 210, 236, 239, 241
Papanek, Victor, 224–25
Paris Commune and the Arts and Crafts movement, 5, 99–110
Parliamentary Select Committee of Arts and Manufactures, 237
Parsons, Lucy, 55
patterns: in art at Kelmscott House and the Kelmscott Museum, 49–50, 51, 53, 54, 56, 57, 58, 59, 60; and Crane, 104; and Morris, 2, 49–50, 58, 134, 142, 177, 213, 238; "Some Hints on Pattern-Designing" (Morris), 210–11, 243
Peasants' Revolt of 1381, 66, 79, 82
People's Industrial Arts College (Chicago), 14, 19
Periam, Amy, 62
Perugino, Pietro, 243
Pevsner, Nikolaus, 221–22, 223, 239
phalansteries, 255
"Phantasy and Utopia" (Marcuse), 167
Phoenix and the Carpet meets *News from Nowhere*, 41
The Picture of Dorian Gray (Wilde), 7, 280; illustrating using Morris designs, 276, 277–78
Pierazzo, Elena, 257
The Pilgrims of Hope (Morris), 102, 251
"Pilgrims Rest" (porch at the Red House), 66

Pilloton, Emily, 225–26
Pink M.24 Chaffee (Jørgensen and the Cast Off Knitters), 227–28
Pinkney, Tony, 7, 265–73; thinking of doing a sequel to *News from Nowhere*, 266–68
Pioneers of Modern Design: From William Morris to Walter Gropius (Pevsner), 221–22
Plato, 117, 149
Plotz, John, 5, 41–47, 267
"pocket of stasis" in *News from Nowhere*, 138
Poet Lore (magazine), 12–13, 14
poetry, 117, 177–78; Chartist poetry, 87, 89; as a craft, 236; in curriculum of Kelmscott House and the Kelmscott Museum, 61; of Eliot, 275–76; Imagist poetry, 267; of Milton, 12; Morris as a poet, 3, 6, 66, 67, 70, 180, 183, 187, 251, 252; of Pre-Raphaelites, 276; Triggs on, 15, 16. *See also* "The Defence of Guenevere" (Morris)
PoetryGenius (website), 276
The Poetry of Architecture (Ruskin), 140
political cartoon about William Morris (1885), 1
"political ecology," 134, 140, 144
political statements: crafts and handiworks as political statements, 227–32; design as a political statement, 220–21
"Porphyria's Lover" (Browning), 176
posthumanism, 133, 134
Pre-Raphaelism, 66, 236, 276; and Morris, 49, 65, 187, 252; Morris sharing qualities but not a Pre-Raphaelite, 207–8
Prettejohn, Elizabeth, 214–15
Principle of Hope (Bloch), 164, 165–66
printmaking curriculums at Kelmscott House and Kelmscott House Museum, 51, 54, 58–59

Prison Notebooks (Gramsci), 150
"Project H" (founded by Pilloton), 226
Pryor, Naomi Acuña, 230
"Public Archives, New Knowledge, and Moving Beyond the Digital Humanities/Digital Pedagogy Distinction" (Konkol), 279–80
Pugin, A. W. N., 223, 237
Pullman Strike of 1894, 30
Pussyhat project, 228–29

The Queen of Versailles (documentary), 6, 151, 157

Rand, Ayn, 154
"Rapunzel" (Morris's version of), 50, 52
Raul, Carmel, 61–62
reading: importance of for education, 123; at Kelmscott House and the Kelmscott Museum, 52; reading habits in Muncie, Indiana, 45–46; "strong metonymic reading," 135, 141, 142; and Tolkien, 52; verbal-visual reading, 179, 183
red bricks, 6, 133, 136, 138, 141; in Dickens' novels, 141; in *News from Nowhere*, 136, 139–40, 142, 143–44; Red House (designed by Morris), 133–34, 136, 140, 214; Ruskin on, 140–41
Red Fairy Book (Lang), 68
Red/Green/Blue Mars trilogy (Robinson), 43
Red House (designed by Morris), 66, 133–34, 136, 140, 214
"Red Virgin" of the Commune, 105
Republic (Plato), 149
Research Excellence Framework exercise, 269, 272
"Resistance in the Materials" (Nowviskie), 279
Revolution in Popular Literature (Haywood), 84
Robbins, Ariel, 230
Robinson, Kim Stanley, 43

Rockefeller, John D., 16, 17
The Roots of the Mountains (Morris), 69–70, 270
Ross, Kristin, 99, 100
Rossetti, Christina, 276, 277
Rossetti, Dante Gabriel, 53, 276
Rossetti Archive, 177
Royal Academy, 107, 237, 240
The Runaway Slave (Browning), 261
Rural Rides (Cobbett), 81
Ruskin, John, 17, 150, 153, 237; on art, design, and architecture, 121, 140–41, 224, 239–40; and the Arts and Crafts movement, 26, 29; on division of labor, 238; and Hull-House, 26, 27–29, 31; and the ideal medieval carver, 243; and Morris, 27–28, 83–84, 94, 121, 141, 153, 223–24, 239–40; and *Time and the Tapestry*, 42, 44. See also "The Nature of Gothic" (Ruskin)
Ryton Willows, meeting at, 1

St. Paul's Cathedral, 122
Sandburg, Carl, 11, 15
Sanders, Bernie, 228
Santich, Sinead, 230
Sargisson, Lucy, 153
Satt, Hilda, 25, 32, 34
Satt, Louis, 25
Scandinavian myths. *See* Icelandic Sagas of Morris
Schloss, Murray, 15
School Workshops at Kelmscott House and Kelmscott House Museum, 50–55, 57–58
science curriculums at Kelmscott House and Kelmscott House Museum, 57
Scott, Walter, 66
Scottish Labor Party, 55
Second Reform Bill (1867), 190
Sercombe, Parker H., 19
sex/gender system in *News from Nowhere*, 170–71
Shakespeare, William, 2, 11–12, 16

Shakespeare as a Dramatic Artist (Moulton), 15
"Shakespeare's Tempest" (Moulton), 11
Shaw, George Bernard, 55, 83
Shelley, Mary, 43
Shelley, Percy, 14, 266
She's Rogue workshops and retreats, 226
Shi, David E., 150
Shklovsky, Viktor, 152
Shmoop (digital publisher), 176
A Short Account of the Commune of Paris of 1871 (Bax, Dave, and Morris), 102–3
Shrem, Jan and Maria Manetti, 230
Sibyl (fictional character in *Picture of Dorian Gray*), 278
Siegel, David and Jacqueline, 151
"Sigurd and the Dragon" (Morris), 50, 52
Sigurd the Volsung (Morris), 3, 12, 251
Silva, Jorge Bastos da, 163
The Simple Life (MacCarthy), 150
The Simple Life (Shi), 150
"The Simple Life," course (Robertson), 6, 149–57
Sinclair, Upton, 19
The Sky of Our Manufacture: The London Fog in British Fiction from Dickens to Woolf (Taylor), 143
Sloboda, Stacey, 237, 239
Slow Print: Literary Radicalism and Late Victorian print Culture (Miller), 137–38, 231, 276, 278
Smith, Henry, 82
social conditions, Morris on, 1–2, 120; Morris's influence on the American Settlement movement, 25–35
Social Democratic Federation, 102–3; Morris designing membership card, 220
social engagement, the history of design, and William Morris, 6, 219–32
socialism and Morris, 1, 55, 56, 66, 153, 214; agrarian socialism, 43;

versus anarchism, 103; and Cobbett, 83; in course syllabus for Radical Victorians, 91–92; Guild Socialism movement, 4; and the Paris Commune, 102–3, 109; socialism in *A Dream of John Ball*, 83–84, 85, 94; socialism in *News from Nowhere*, 117, 119, 165; and Triggs, 16, 19, 20; utopian socialism, 164–65, 172
"Socialism from the Root Up" (Bax and Morris), 83
Socialist Choir, 55
Socialist League, 56, 106, 168, 272; Morris as a founding member of, 55
social media and William Morris, 7; personal experience on dealing with, 7, 265–73; use of Twitter to post for William Morris Archive, 258–59
social science fiction, 172
Society for Checking the Abuses of Public Advertising, 269
Society for the Protection of Ancient Buildings, 54, 122
"The Society of the Future" (Morris), 256
Socratic dialogue in *News from Nowhere*, 117
"Some Hints on Pattern-Designing" (Morris), 142, 210
Sonnets (Browning), 261
South Kensington Museum (now Victoria and Albert Museum), 214, 242–43
South Kensington School of Design, 238
Spencer-Whitman Center, 19
Spirited Away (animated film), 154
Springer, Marguerite (Maginness), 18–19
Springer, Warren, 18–19
stained glass, 66, 252; workshops at Kelmscott House and Museum, 49, 54, 60–61
"Stained Glass Sidcup" (from Pinkney's Morris blog), 269

Stanley, Henry Morton, 255–56
Stansky, Peter, 107
Starr, Ellen Gates, 5, 14, 25–26, 30; as arts-programming leader at Hull-House, 27–28, 33
Steedman, Carolyn, 136
Steichen, Edward, 15
Steichen, Lilian, 15
Stevens, Alzina, 30
Stevenson, Robert Louis, 275
Stewart, Susan, 136
Stickley, Gustave, 14, 17, 222
Stitch 'n' Bitch feminist fibre collectives/groups, 230
The Stones of Venice (Ruskin), 92, 121, 223, 243. *See also* "The Nature of Gothic" (Ruskin)
"Stories as a Mode of Thinking" (Moulton), 11
"Story Maps," 260
The Story of the Glittering Plain (Morris), 71, 179
"The Story of the Unknown Church" (Morris), 251
storytelling curriculum at Kelmscott House and Kelmscott House Museum, 50
A Strange Manuscript Found in a Copper Cylinder (DeMille), 162
Strawberry Thief (Morris), 238, 278
Suh, Krista, 228, 229
The Sundering Flood (Morris), 47, 71
"The Superseded" (Hardy), 273
Suvin, Darko, 152
swan tile (Morris), 210

"The Tables Turned, or Nupkins Awakened" (Morris), 251
tapestries, 66, 134, 141, 142, 222, 238, 244, 252; *Adoration* (Burne-Jones, Morris and Dearle), 214; *The Forest* tapestry (Morris & Co.), 211; Holy Grail tapestries, 66; in *News from Nowhere*, 141–42, 143–44
Taylor, Jesse Oak, 143

teacher training at Kelmscott House and Kelmscott House Museum, 58–59
"Teaching *Guenevere* Through Word and Image" (Bracken), 6, 175–83
teaching methods of William Morris, 1–2
"Teaching Morris in Chicago, c. 1900" (Helsinger), 4, 11–20
"Teaching Morris the Utopian" (Kreisel), 6, 161–72
"Teaching *News from Nowhere* in a Course on 'The Simple Life'" (Robertson), 6, 149–57
technology and art and the teaching of William Morris, 7, 275–80
TEI-coding, 257
Tennyson, Alfred, 66, 187, 277
textiles, 7, 236, 238; in curriculums at Kelmscott House and Museum, 50, 54, 57, 58, 60, 61; of Morris, 49, 210, 213, 236, 238, 252, 278; textile exhibits at Hull-House Labor Museum, 32, 33
The Textual Condition (McGann), 177, 179–80
"Theses for a William Morris Communism Network" (from Pinkney's Morris blog), 270
Year's Art (Huish, ed.), 240
thing theories: of Bill Brown, 133; "political ecology" of matter, 140; "strong metonymic reading," 141, 142; thing case studies in *News from Nowhere*, 133–34, 135–42, 143–44; thingness theories, 136; "thing power," 142
Thoreau, Henry David, 6, 152–53, 157
"'A Thoughtful Sequence': Nature as Tapestry in *News from Nowhere*" (Wells), 141–42
tiles as art, 209; swan tile (Morris), 210
Time and the Tapestry: A William Morris Adventure (Plotz), 5, 41, 42–43, 44, 45, 46–47
The Time Machine (Wells), 162–63

"Time Travelling with William Morris" (Plotz), 5, 41–47
Tolkien, J. R. R.: choosing to model writing after Morris, 67; early career of, 67; teaching medievalism of Morris through Tolkien, 5, 65–72; use of Morris's historical fiction, 69–70
To-Morrow: A Magazine for Rational Thinkers/A Monthly Handbook of the Changing Order, 14, 15, 19
total design, varieties of, 222–23
Toynbee Hall (settlement house in East London), 26
"Transcendental Wild Oats" (Alcott), 152
translations: domesticating approach to, 192, 195; of Homer, 190–93, 194–95, 196; of Old Norse or Old Icelandic, 67–69
Triggs, Oscar Lovell, 11–20; death of, 19; and Moulton, 15
Trump, Donald, 228, 229, 272
Trumpism, 2
Turner, Frederick Jackson, 34–35
Twitter: Pinkney's tweets, 265, 271; use of to post for William Morris Archive, 258–59
Tyler, Wat, 82
typography: Kelmscott Press use of, 179, 254; Morris's designs, 239, 276, 277, 278

university extension movement, 11, 20
University of California, Davis, 226, 228, 229, 230
University of Chicago, 4, 11; importance of Rockefeller to, 17; Laboratory Schools, 16; Trigg's work at, 13–14, 16
University of Iowa, 176. *See also* William Morris Archive
Utopia (More), 162
"Utopias and Utopianism" (from Pinkney's Morris blog), 273

utopias and utopian literature, 5–6, 43, 47, 219; cognitive estrangement and defamiliarization in, 152; design as a utopian statement, 219, 220–21, 224; *A Dream of John Ball* as revolutionary rupture or utopia, 79, 86; Jameson's theory on, 137–38; and Morris, 70–72, 162, 163–67, 270; *News from Nowhere,* finding hope and change in, 115–27; *News from Nowhere,* Morris as a utopian, 5, 161–72; *News from Nowhere* in a course on "The Simple Life," 6, 149–57; *News from Nowhere* in a seminar on Victorian Materialities, 5–6, 133–44; Paris Commune seen as a utopian community, 102; psychoanalytic-Marxist analysis of utopia, 166–67; seeing *Walden* as, 152–53; and social science fiction, 172; *The Story of the Glittering Plain* as utopian or dystopian, 71–72; titles for a course on British utopianism, 162–63; "utopian impulse," 6, 164, 165, 166, 171, 172; utopian political theory, 163–67. See also dystopias; *News from Nowhere* (Morris)

V&A. See Victoria and Albert Museum
Vane, James (fictional character in *Picture of Dorian Gray*), 278
Vasari, Georgio, 243
Veblen, Thostein, 16
Vibrant Matter: A Political Ecology of Things (Bennett), 134, 137
Victoria and Albert Museum, 214, 232; previously South Kensington Museum, 214, 242–43
Victorian Britain, curriculum on history of at Kelmscott House and Kelmscott House Museum, 50, 53
"Victorian Objects, Things and New Materialisms" seminar teaching *News from Nowhere,* 5–6, 133–44

Victorian Radicalism and the teaching of Morris's *A Dream of John Ball,* 5, 79–94
"Victorian Technology and Art" course and digital design with William Morris, 7, 275–80
Victorian Web (hypertext site), 176
Vieira, Fátima, 163
Vieth, Aaron, 135, 136–38, 140, 143–44
Vine wallpaper (Morris), 207, 210, 211–13
visual-text analysis of "The Defence of Guenevere," 6, 175–83
"'Vive La Commune!' The Imaginary of the Paris Commune and the Arts and Crafts Movement" (O'Neill), 5, 99–110
Völsunga Saga: The Story of the Völsungs and Niblungs, with Certain Songs from the Elder Edda (Morse and Magnússon translation of, 68, 69
Voyant (software program), 258

Walden (Thoreau), 6, 152–53
Walker, Emery, 47
"The Wall of Stone" (King's image in "The Defence of Guenevere"), 181
wallpaper, 41, 49, 104, 176, 208, 209, 239, 242; *Daisy* wallpaper (Morris), 238; *Jasmine* wallpaper (Morris), 238; *Strawberry Thief* (Morris), 278; using Morris's designs to decorate poetry, 277–78; *Vine* wallpaper (Morris), 207, 210, 211–13; wallpaper printing curriculum at Kelmscott House and Museum, 50, 51, 54, 57, 58, 60, 61; *Willow* (Morris), 238
Walt Whitman Archive, 257
Walworth, William, 82
Wardle, Thomas, 241
Wardour-Street English, 192, 197
Water Colour Society, 240
Waterhouse, John William, 276

The Water of the Wondrous Isles (Morris), 71, 251
Watkinson, Ray, 241
We (Zamyatin), 43
weather, importance of in *News from Nowhere*, 117, 120, 143
Webb, Beatrice, 55
Webb, Philip, 53, 66, 136, 140, 210, 214, 241, 256
Webb, Sidney, 55
Weinroth, Michelle, 6, 187–98
The Well at the World's End (Morris), 71, 270
Wells, H. G., 43, 162
Wells, Lindsey, 141–42, 144
Werkbund movement, 222–23
"What is an Illuminated Manuscript?" (Khan Academy website), 178
What Middletown Read (Felsenstein and Connolly), 45
WhatsApp, 272
"Whence This Great Multitude of Painters?" (Huish), 240
White, David, 81
Whitman, Walt, 13–14, 15, 16, 17, 19, 149
Whitman Archive, 257
Wilde, Oscar, 7, 192, 194–95, 196, 197, 276, 278
"William Morris, designer: Morris and the History of Design as Social Engagement" (Housefield), 6, 219–32
"William Morris and the Intersection of the Histories of Art and Design" (Codell), 6, 235–44
William Morris Archive, 6, 83, 178, 277; hosted by the University of Iowa, 176; Sample Assignment in class using, 261; teaching Morris using, 6, 251–61
"William Morris Fan Club," 273
William Morris in Oxford: The Campaigning Years 1879–1895 (Pinkney), 265–66, 272

"William Morris on Social Media: A Personal Experience, 2007–2017" (Pinkney), 7, 265–73
William Morris Society (Chicago), 14, 15
William Morris Society (United Kingdom), 20, 141; Arts and Crafts Hammersmith project, 57–58; family learning activities at, 59–61; having a blog, 273; headquarters of, 49, 50
William Morris the Blog: Digital Reflections 2007–2011 (Pinkney), 265, 269
"William Morris Unbound" as a title for Pinkney's idea of sequel to *News from Nowhere*, 266–68
Williams, Lilibet, 58
Williams, Raymond, 265
Willow (Morris), 238
"Willow Bough Bedding Sets" (from Pinkney's Morris blog), 269
Wilson, Kate, 45
"Wireless" (Kipling), 275
Wix website, 277–78
WMS. *See* William Morris Society
Wolf, Friedrich August, 191
women, status of in *News from Nowhere*, 170–71, 251
Women's March of 2017, 220–21, 228
Women's Trade Union League, 30
The Wood Beyond the World (Morris), 71
"The Woodcuts of Gothic Books" (Morris), 175
wooden locks in *News from Nowhere*, 136–38, 143–44
Woolman, John, 151–52, 157
Word (Microsoft program), 277
word-image relationships in "The Defence of Guenevere," 6, 175–83
Wordsworth, William, 150, 271
Work (painting by Brown), 53

"'Work and Fun' and 'Education at its Finest:' Teaching Morris at Kelmscott House" (Elletson), 5, 49–62
working-class, 119, 272; in Chicago, 26, 27, 28, 29, 30; and crafts, 107, 235, 236, 240; and Morris, 1, 220; in Paris, 105
workshop-based system of Triggs, 16–17, 18–19
Works of Geoffrey Chaucer (Kelmscott edition). *See* Kelmscott Press, Kelmscott Chaucer
World of Warcraft (on-line game), 65, 72

WOVEN (Written, Oral, Visual, Electronic, and Nonverbal) framework, 275
Wright, Frank Lloyd, 16, 29
Wright, Peter, 83, 94
Wuthering Heights (Bronte), 135
Wyatt, A. J., 68

Yellow Book, 277
Yellow Nineties Online (via NINES), 277
Yonan, Michael, 244
YouTube, 228; Pinkney's films posted on, 7, 265, 271–72

About the Contributors

Susan David Bernstein is research professor of English at Boston University. Her most recent publications include *Roomscape: Women Writers in the British Museum from George Eliot to Virginia Woolf* (2013) as well as articles on Victorian seriality, on transatlantic reading in the nineteenth century, and on conceptual art and the Brontës.

Florence Boos is a professor of English at the University of Iowa. She has published several books on Morris and the Pre-Raphaelites, most recently *History and Poetics in the Early Writings of William Morris* (2015) and an expanded version of an edition of Morris's *Socialist Diary* (2018). She is the general editor of the William Morris Archive and author of *Memoirs of Working-Class Women: The Hard Way Up* (2017).

Pam Bracken is a professor of English at Southern Nazarene University in Bethany, Oklahoma. Her area of specialization is nineteenth-century British literature, with a focus on visual narrative. She has published several articles on William Morris in both the *Journal of William Morris Studies* and the *Journal of Pre-Raphaelite Studies*. She is also the editor of an edition of Morris's only play, *The Tables Turned; or Nupkins Awakened*. Her research and writing interests include the graphic novel, literary theory, and film studies. She is currently a member of several professional organizations, including the Modern Language Association and the William Morris Society in the United States. She is the wife of a librarian and the mother of two daughters, Madeleine and Nell. She currently serves on the Executive Board of the Ralph Ellison Foundation.

Elizabeth Grennan Browning is a US historian specializing in environmental history and intellectual history. She is the Midwestern/Indiana Community History Fellow at Indiana University's Environmental Resilience Institute in Bloomington, and adjunct faculty in the Department of History. Browning's current research and public history work focus on histories of environmental health and environmental justice in the Midwest.

Julie Codell is art history and museum studies professor and former director of the School of Art at Arizona State University, and affiliate faculty there in English, women and gender studies, film/media studies (interim director 2010–2011) and Asian studies. She is blog editor for the International Art Market Studies Association. She wrote *The Victorian Artist* (2012); edited *Nineteenth-Century British Artists' Autograph Replicas: Auras, Aesthetics & Economics* (2020); *Transculturation in British Art* (2012; pbk. 2017); *Power and Resistance* (2012); *The Political Economy of Art* (2008); *Imperial Co-Histories* (2003); and co-edited with L. Hughes, *Replication in the Long 19th Century* (2018); with J. DelPlato, *Orientalism, Eroticism and Modern Visuality in Global Cultures* (2016; pbk. 2018); with L. Brake, *Encounters in the Victorian Press* (2004); and with D.S. Macleod, *Orientalism Transposed* (1998). She received fellowships from the National Endowment for the Humanities, American Institute of Indian Studies, Getty Foundation, Kress Foundation, Huntington Library, Harry Ransom Center, and Yale Center for British Art.

Helen Elletson has been curator of the William Morris Society's collection at Kelmscott House since 2000. She is also the manager and curator of Emery Walker's House, a riverside property with one of the best preserved Arts and Crafts interiors in Britain, situated just ten minutes' walk from Kelmscott House. Helen wrote *A History of Kelmscott House* in 2009 and *Highlights from the William Morris Society's Collection* in 2015, as well as publishing articles in magazines and books on the collections of both houses. Helen is responsible for the educational program of the William Morris Society and is also project lead of Arts and Crafts Hammersmith, a joint initiative between the William Morris Society and Emery Walker Trust that aims to develop innovative learning and outreach programs.

KellyAnn Fitzpatrick is an affiliated researcher at the Georgia Institute of Technology and an industry analyst at RedMonk. She holds a PhD in English from the University at Albany and a BA in English and medieval studies from the University of Notre Dame. Her book, *Neomedievalism, Popular Culture, and the Academy: From Tolkien to Game of Thrones* (2019), considers evolving forms of medievalism (the ways that post-medieval societies reimagine or appropriate the Middle Ages) in both consumer culture and academic discourse. Through its analysis of the labor processes involved in the production of online games and electronic texts, KellyAnn's work with medievalism overlaps with her interest and experience in technical communication, software development, and rhetoric and composition.

Amanda Golden is associate professor of English at the New York Institute of Technology. She previously held the Post-Doctoral Fellowship in Poetics at Emory University's Fox Center for Humanistic Inquiry and a Marion L. Brittain Postdoctoral fellowship at the Georgia Institute of Technology. She edited *This Business of Words: Reassessing Anne Sexton* (2016) and her book *Annotating Modernism: Marginalia and Pedagogy from Virginia Woolf to the Confessional Poets* is under contract. She is also the book review editor of *Woolf Studies Annual* and has published in *Modernism/modernity*, *The Ted Hughes Society Journal*, and *Woolf Studies Annual*.

Imogen Hart teaches in the History of Art Department at the University of California, Berkeley. She works on modern art and material culture in Britain, especially the objects and interiors associated with the Arts and Crafts movement. She is the author of *Arts and Crafts Objects* (2010) and co-editor, with Jason Edwards, of *Rethinking the Interior, c. 1867–1896: Aestheticism and Arts and Crafts* (2010). She has published chapters on William Morris in *William Morris and the Art of Everyday Life*, edited by Wendy Parkins (2010), and *The Cambridge Companion to the Pre-Raphaelites*, edited by Elizabeth Prettejohn (2012). Her current book project explores decorative art from William Morris to the Second World War.

Elizabeth Helsinger is the John Mathews Manly Distinguished Service Professor Emerita at the University of Chicago. Her books include *Ruskin and the Art of the Beholder*, *Poetry and the Pre-Raphaelite Arts: Dante Gabriel Rossetti and William Morris,* and *Poetry and the Thought of Song*. She is a co-editor of *Critical Inquiry*.

James Housefield is associate professor of design and affiliated faculty in art history at the University of California, Davis, where he teaches the Introduction to Design course. Housefield's research focuses on the variety of ways we design experiences. He is especially interested in the histories of exhibition design, and modern cultures of immersive experience like those treated in his monograph *Playing with Earth and Sky: Astronomy, Geography, and the Art of Marcel Duchamp* (2016). He continues to research the histories of design, modern art, and their intersections.

Linda K. Hughes, Addie Levy Professor of Literature at TCU, specializes in historical media studies (poetry, periodicals, serial fiction); gender and women's studies; and transnationality, including transatlanticism. She is the recipient of several teaching awards at TCU and a past vice president for programs of the William Morris Society in the United States. Her prior Morris-related scholarship includes *The Victorian Serial* (with Michael Lund, 1991), *The Cambridge Introduction to Victorian Poetry* (2010), and "Visible Sound and Auditory Scenes: Word, Image, and Music in Tennyson, D. G. Rossetti, and Morris" (*Media, Technology, and Literature in the Nineteenth Century*, eds. Colette Colligan and Margaret Linley, 2011). She is co-editor, with Julie Codell, of *Replication in the Long Nineteenth Century: Re-makings and Reproductions* (2018), which includes an essay on William Morris by Elizabeth Carolyn Miller.

Deanna K. Kreisel is associate professor of English at the University of Mississippi. She is the author of *Economic Woman: Demand, Gender, and Narrative Closure in Eliot and Hardy* (2012). She also has published articles on Victorian literature and culture in such journals as *PMLA*, *Representations*, *ELH*, *Novel*, *Victorian Studies*, *Mosaic*, and others. She is currently working on a new project on utopia and sustainability in Victorian culture.

David Latham teaches Victorian studies at York University and edits *The Journal of Pre-Raphaelite Studies*. He is also, with Lesley Higgins, the co-general editor of *The Collected Works of Walter Pater*, a ten-volume edition scheduled for publication by Oxford University Press. His books, chapters, and articles are on Victorian and Canadian literature. Three of his books, and more than thirty of his chapters and articles, are on Morris.

Jason D. Martinek is associate professor of history at New Jersey City University. He is the author of *Socialism and Print Culture in America, 1897–1920* (2016) and co-editor of *Transformations: The Journal of Inclusive Scholarship and Pedagogy*. He is past president of the William Morris Society in the United States. Currently, he is investigating William Morris's influence on John Collier, head of the Bureau of Indian Affairs under Franklin D. Roosevelt.

William Meier is associate professor of history at Texas Christian University, where he teaches courses on modern Britain, Ireland, and the British empire. He is the author of *Property Crime in London, 1850–Present* (2011) and co-editor (with Ian Campbell Ross) of a special issue of Éire-Ireland on

Irish crime since 1921 (2014). He specializes in the study of crime, punishment, and violence, and is currently writing a book on the history of terrorism in Britain and its empire.

Elizabeth Carolyn Miller is professor of English at the University of California, Davis, and the author of two monographs: *Slow Print: Literary Radicalism and Late Victorian Print Culture* (2013), which was named Best Book of the Year by the North American Victorian Studies Association and received honorable mention for the Modernist Studies Association Book Prize, and *Framed: The New Woman Criminal in British Culture at the Fin de Siècle* (2008). Currently she is working on a study of mining, capital, and ecological disaster titled *Extraction Ecologies and the Literature of the Long Exhaustion, 1830s–1930s*. She recently edited a special issue of *Victorian Studies* on "Climate Change and Victorian Studies" (2018) and a volume of George Bernard Shaw's political essays for Oxford World's Classics (forthcoming 2021).

Morna O'Neill is associate professor of art history in the Department of Art at Wake Forest University. She is the author of *Walter Crane: The Arts and Crafts, Painting, and Politics* (2011) and *Hugh Lane: The Art Market and the Art Museum, 1893–1915* (2018). She is co-founder and co-editor (with Anne Nellis Richter and Melinda McCurdy) of "Home Subjects," a digital humanities working group dedicated to the display of art in the private interior in Britain (http://www.homesubjects.org/).

Tony Pinkney is senior lecturer in the Department of English Literature and Creative Writing at Lancaster University, England. He has published books on T.S. Eliot, D.H. Lawrence, and Raymond Williams. Work on William Morris includes *William Morris and Oxford: The Campaigning Years, 1879–1895* (2007) and *William Morris: The Blog* (2011). He is now completing *William Morris and the Utopian Tradition: Collected Essays* (forthcoming 2021), and his blog on Morris and utopias continues at http://williammorrisunbound.blogspot.com/.

John Plotz is professor of Victorian literature at Brandeis University. He is the author of *Time and the Tapestry: A William Morris Adventure* (2014), as well as *The Crowd: British Literature and Public Politics* (2000), *Portable Property: Victorian Culture on the Move* (2008), and *Semi-Detached: The Aesthetics of Virtual Experience since Dickens* (2018). He and his partner, Lisa, live in Brookline with two children and three chickens.

Michael Robertson is professor of English at the College of New Jersey. His most recent book, *The Last Utopians: Four Late Nineteenth-Century Visionaries and Their Legacy* (2018), is a group biography of William Morris and three contemporaries. His current book project is a full-length biography of Morris.

Michelle Weinroth taught English literature at the University of Ottawa and Carleton University (Ottawa) for many years. Author, editor, and translator, her books include *Reclaiming William Morris: Englishness, Sublimity, and the Rhetoric of Dissent* (1996) and *To Build a Shadowy Isle of Bliss: William Morris's Radicalism and the Embodiment of Dreams* (2015). As a translator, she was twice shortlisted for the Governor General's Literary Award (1995 and 2008). Her publications on William Morris have appeared in *Victorian Studies*, *The Journal of William Morris Studies*, and *Socialist Studies*, inter alia.